Controversies in Local Economic Development

Efforts to promote the eco͟͟͟͟͟͟nt of individual localities engage the attention of academics, stud͟͟͟͟ ͟ofessionals. Many such analysts argue that competitive advantage can b͟ ͟͟stered within local economies, complementing the advent of a more globalized economy. Intensified efforts to build new economic foundations show no sign of abating, despite the apparent increase in the international mobility of businesses and employment. Where once local economic development comprised mainly efforts to redistribute employment among regions within a national economy, in recent decades a large diversification in the tools and strategies promoted to local economic development officials has taken place. Benchmarking regional competitiveness, building a learning economy, supporting enterprise clusters, incubating high-tech enterprise, creating an environment appealing to the creative class and promoting eco-industrial development are among the aspirations frequently now informing local economic plans.

Unpicking the arguments supporting different strategies for promoting local economic development, *Controversies in Local Economic Development* is an introductory guide to some of the major ideas and policy tools that have influenced academic debate and development practice. Taking the view that economic processes are mechanisms that promote desired outcomes only in particular contexts, the book asks questions of both academic debates and the prescriptions of policy experts.

Designed to encourage a search for evidence rather than offering a set of policy solutions, this work nevertheless offers more than a critique of existing ideas. In place of the slavish replication of perceived best practice derived from exemplar economies, policy makers are challenged to think critically about the lessons to be applied from local economic development experiences. As an original and worthy contribution to the academic debate in this field, this work will prove invaluable to postgraduates and economic development professionals alike.

Martin Perry is an associate professor in the Department of Management, Massey University (Wellington). His publications include two books published by Routledge, *Business Clusters: An International Perspective* (2005) and *Small Firms and Network Economies* (1999).

Regions and Cities

Series editors: Ron Martin, University of Cambridge, UK; Gernot Grabher, University of Bonn, Germany; Maryann Feldman, University of Georgia, USA; Gillian Bristow, University of Cardiff, UK.

Regions and Cities is an international, interdisciplinary series that provides authoritative analyses of the new significance of regions and cities for economic, social and cultural development, and public policy experimentation. The series seeks to combine theoretical and empirical insights with constructive policy debate and critically engages with formative processes and policies in regional and urban studies.

1. Beyond Green Belts
Managing urban growth in the 21st century
Edited by John Herrington

2. Retreat from the Regions
Corporate change and the closure of factories
Stephen Fothergill and Nigel Guy

3. Regional Development in the 1990s
The British Isles in transition
Edited by Ron Martin and Peter Townroe

4. Spatial Policy in a Divided Nation (April 1993)
Edited by Richard T. Harrison and Mark Hart

5. Sustainable Cities
Graham Haughton and Colin Hunter

6. An Enlarged Europe
Regions in competition?
Edited by Louis Albrechts, Sally Hardy, Mark Hart and Anastasios Katos

7. The Regional Imperative
Regional planning and governance in Britain, Europe and the United States
Urlan A. Wannop

8. The Determinants of Small Firm Growth
An inter-regional study in the United Kingdom 1986–90
Richard Barkham, Graham Gudgin, Mark Hart and Eric Hanvey

9. The Regional Dimension of Transformation in Central Europe
Gorzelak Grzegorz

10. Union Retreat and the Regions
The shrinking landscape of organised labour
Ron Martin, Peter Sunley and Jane Wills

11. Regional Development Strategies
A European perspective
Edited by Jeremy Alden and Philip Boland

12. British Regionalism and Devolution
The challenges of state reform and European integration
Edited by Jonathan Bradbury and John Mawson

13. Innovation Networks and Learning Regions?
James Simme

14. Regional Policy in Europe
S. S. Artobolevskiy

15. New Institutional Spaces
TECs and the remaking of economic governance
Edited by Martin Jones and Jamie Peck

16. The Coherence of EU Regional Policy
Contrasting perspectives on the structural funds
Edited by John Bachtler and Ivan Turok

17. Multinationals and European Integration
Trade, investment and regional development
Edited by Nicholas A. Phelps

18. Unemployment and Social Exclusion
Landscapes of labour inequality and social exclusion
Edited by Sally Hardy, Paul Lawless and Ron Martin

19. Metropolitan Planning in Britain
A comparative study
Edited by Peter Roberts, Kevin Thomas and Gwyndaf Williams

20. Social Exclusion in European Cities
Processes, experiences and responses
Edited by Judith Allen, Goran Cars and Ali Madanipour

21. Regional Development Agencies in Europe
Edited by Charlotte Damborg, Mike Danson and Henrik Halkier

22. Community Economic Development
Edited by Graham Haughton

23. Foreign Direct Investment and the Global Economy
Corporate and institutional dynamics of global-localisation
Edited by Jeremy Alden and Nicholas F. Phelps

24. Restructuring Industry and Territory
The experience of Europe's regions
Edited by Anna Giunta, Arnoud Lagendijk and Andy Pike

25. Out of the Ashes?
The social impact of industrial contraction and regeneration on Britain's mining communities
Chas Critcher, Bella Dicks, David Parry and David Waddington

26. Regional Innovation Strategies
The challenge for less-favoured regions
Edited by Kevin Morgan and Claire Nauwelaers

27. Geographies of Labour Market Inequality
Edited by Ron Martin and Philip S. Morrison

28. Regions, Spatial Strategies and Sustainable Development
David Counsell and Graham Haughton

29. Clusters and Regional Development
Critical reflections and explorations
Edited by Asheim Bjorn, Philip Cooke and Ron Martin

30. Regional Competitiveness
Edited by Ron Martin, Michael Kitson and Peter Tyler

31. Regional Development in the Knowledge Economy
Edited by Philip Cooke and Andrea Piccaluga

32. The Rise of the English Regions?
Edited by Irene Hardill, Paul Benneworth, Mark Baker and Leslie Budd

33. Geographies of the New Economy
Critical reflections
Edited by Peter W. Daniels, Andrew Leyshon, Michael J. Bradshaw and Jonathan Beaverstock

34. European Cohesion Policy
Willem Molle

35. Creative Regions
Technology, culture and knowledge entrepreneurship
Edited by Philip Cooke and Dafna Schwartz

36. Devolution, Regionalism and Regional Development
The UK experience
Edited by Jonathan Bradbury

37. Intelligent Cities and Globalisation of Innovation Networks
Nicos Komninos

38. Controversies in Local Economic Development
Martin Perry

Controversies in Local Economic Development
Stories, strategies, solutions

Martin Perry

LONDON AND NEW YORK

First published 2010
by Routledge
2 Park Square, Milton Park, Abingdon, Oxon OX14 4RN

Simultaneously published in the USA and Canada
by Routledge
711 Third Avenue, New York, NY 10017

Routledge is an imprint of the Taylor & Francis Group, an Informa business

First issued in paperback 2012

© 2010 Martin Perry

Typeset in Times New Roman by Exeter Premedia Services

All rights reserved. No part of this book may be reprinted or reproduced or utilised in any form or by any electronic, mechanical, or other means, now known or hereafter invented, including photocopying and recording, or in any information storage or retrieval system, without permission in writing from the publishers.

British Library Cataloguing in Publication Data
A catalogue record for this book is available from the British Library

Library of Congress Cataloging in Publication Data
A catalogue record for this book has been requested

ISBN13: 978-0-415-48968-3 (hbk)
ISBN13: 978-0-415-53978-4 (pbk)
ISBN13: 978-0-203-84949-1 (ebk)

Contents

List of illustrations   ix
Preface   xi

1 Controversies in local economic development   1
    Participants in local economic controversy 3
    Can controversies be resolved? 7
    The controversies 15

2 Regional competitiveness and local economic development   18
    The nature of regional competitiveness 20
    Regional economic performance 26
    Regional absolute advantage 30
    Regional environments for competitive enterprise 32
    Benchmarking competitiveness 36
    Regional strategies 39
    Reflecting on regional competitiveness 45
    Conclusion 49

3 Regional policy and inward investment   51
    Regional policy 53
    Local economic policy 69
    How to revive regional policy 75
    Conclusion 77

4 Learning regions   79
    The learning region 82
    Macro context for learning regions 84
    Micro context for learning regions 85
    Learning region varieties 87
    Evaluating the learning region 94
    Four areas where evidence exists 99
    Conclusion 106

5	**Enterprise clusters and regional specialization**	108
	Industrial location trends 109	
	Counting clusters 112	
	Agglomeration economies 115	
	Agglomeration without agglomeration economies 124	
	Theory informed practice 127	
	Conclusion 132	
6	**Urban success and the creative class**	134
	The creative class and human capital theories of urban economic growth 136	
	Critical reflections on the creative class 140	
	Finding space for the creative class 147	
	Conclusion 155	
7	**Technology incubators: hothouse accelerators or life support shelters?**	158
	Innovation and high growth enterprise 160	
	Sector characteristics and new enterprise survival 164	
	Implications for incubators 166	
	Public knowledge and private enterprise 168	
	Evaluating technology incubators 172	
	Inside technology incubators 176	
	Conclusion 183	
8	**Local economic development and ecological modernization**	185
	Incremental 'win-wins' 187	
	Evidence of a business case 189	
	What influences the business case? 192	
	Eco-effective development 197	
	Discussion 208	
	Conclusion 212	
9	**Making progress in local economic development**	214
	Learning from regional development 217	

References	220
Index	251

List of illustrations

Tables

2.1	Frameworks for exploring regional competitiveness	25
2.2	Employment in the top 9 of 41 'narrow' industry clusters in the Harvard Cluster Map, 2000	36
4.1	Learning region variations	87
6.1	Creative class occupations	138
8.1	Evaluation frameworks for green initiatives	209

Boxes

1.1	Not much known about economic growth	4
1.2	Market failures for welfare economics	10
2.1	Components of regional competitiveness	26
2.2	Regions within regions	29
2.3	Studied trust	30
2.4	Nordic telecommunications: more than a diamond	34
2.5	Hard time for hard networks	37
2.6	Tests for benchmarks	38
2.7	High tech illusions	41
2.8	People before jobs or jobs before people?	42
2.9	A valley too far	45
3.1	Development Report Card for regional economic climates	55
3.2	A principal–agent critique of devolved regional policy	58
3.3	Work to the workers	59
3.4	UK Regional selective assistance	60
3.5	Judgements about job creation	61
3.6	The branch plant economy syndrome	64
3.7	The new branch plant economy	66
3.8	Local economies as leaky buckets	68
3.9	Selecting for high growth	72
4.1	Endogenous growth theory	80
4.2	From knowledge to learning economy	84

4.3	No sharing of shared trust	86
4.4	Trust and distrust	89
4.5	Silicon Valley stories	92
4.6	Evidence for spillovers	96
4.7	The Homebrew Computer Club	101
5.1	Inflexible flexibility	111
5.2	Implementing cluster templates	113
5.3	Marshall's cluster realism	115
5.4	Inner city incubators	117
5.5	Specialized versus diversified cities and questions of evidence	118
5.6	Sinos Valley transitions	120
5.7	Cluster idealism	122
5.8	Conflicts in a timber cluster	123
6.1	Bohemian index	138
6.2	Gay index	139
6.3	Measuring economic success	139
6.4	The Las Vegas critique	141
6.5	Indicators of performance in the USA	144
6.6	Creative doubt over the BBC's look north	146
6.7	Bohemia and business in Montréal	150
7.1	A theory of learning	161
7.2	Spinning the wheel	163
7.3	Entry points to fragmented industries	165
7.4	Open science	171
7.5	The long road from university to market	172
7.6	Limitations of quasi experiments	173
7.7	Stage models of enterprise formation	174
7.8	Network building tools	181
8.1	The N curve dilemma	186
8.2	Escalating environmental demands on dairy farms	188
8.3	Co-operative Bank sustainability downside	190
8.4	What is required for a first mover advantage?	192
8.5	Ecological modernization	193
8.6	Controlling sulphur dioxide emissions	195
8.7	Eco-localism	198
8.8	Product labelling	200
8.9	Red sheds and Mäori	201
8.10	Kalundborg, Denmark as prototype industrial ecosystem	205

Preface

This book reviews a selection of controversial issues in the field of local economic development. The discussion is premised on a view that too much debate in local economic development is driven by theories and economic modelling rather than by giving attention to what existing evidence supports. One reason for this is that the search for explanation and generalizations leads to the simplification of complex processes. This can be encouraged by the market for ideas about how to promote economic development. There is a natural desire to prefer simplified stories, to demand guidance on 'best practice' and to seek to emulate the experiences of the most successful regional economies. The underlying perspective of this book is that local economic development experiences of the form generating sudden jumps in a locality's prosperity are governed by regularities. Research can provide explanations and suggest strategies for policy makers to follow but this frequently depends on recognizing that there are both mechanisms and contexts to be considered. There is nothing particularly novel in this view. Indeed the chapter on cluster promotion includes the suggestion that Alfred Marshall writing about local industrial districts in the early part of the twentieth century had such an understanding. Nonetheless the subtleties of mechanism and context seem frequently to be overlooked possibly because revealing the connections can sometimes be easier if places are observed over time whereas much evaluation is based on judgements made at one point in time. Some have also commented on the tendency to assume that past experiences have little to inform the present day. The world and the nature of economic processes certainly evolve but the perspective of this book is that the rate and extent of change can sometimes be less than imagined.

My own awareness of theory about and the practice of local economic development dates back to the late 1970s. At the time I was studying urban and regional planning in Scotland. A shift in thinking took place during the time I was completing these studies. In the 'old days' it had seemed a good idea to assist businesses to shift to locations most in need of jobs. In the context of it becoming harder to find mobile investment and as questions were asked about the quality of the employment transferred to the regions, the new approach was to encourage development from within principally by promoting new enterprise. I got to see many projects inspired by this shift in thinking as a contributor to the Local Economic

Development Information Service (LEDIS), an initiative of the former Glasgow-based Planning Exchange. As a contributor, my role was to provide case studies of local projects as an aid to the sharing of experience among practitioners. The first project that I reported on involved the conversion of a derelict water mill in Devon, England into a working tourist attraction and museum to be run as a community business. Over the next 25 years I reported on projects from the United Kingdom, Australia, India, Indonesia, Japan, Malaysia, New Zealand and Singapore that revealed increasing ambition as well as a decline in novelty and originality in the projects to be found.

The increasing uniformity of projects from around the world may have contributed to the demise of LEDIS after 25 years of gathering case studies. Interestingly, and as forms the subject of one of the book's controversies, old style regional policy never fully disappeared in the United Kingdom. Fresh ideas have developed to build a case for local economic development, partly justified by reference to productivity. Nonetheless, some researchers have continued to argue that the most effective way of reducing disparities in unemployment remains the same as it always was: attracting inward investment, although from a wider range of projects than may have been considered appropriate in the past. This book is sympathetic to this assessment, recognizing that many of the ambitious agendas for local economic development are strong on theory but less well supported by empirical demonstration of the process purported to operate.

The writing of this book was assisted by the award of a Massey University Research Fellowship that gave me a semester away from teaching commitments. Some of the material for the book was gathered during a short period of sabbatical leave and I would also like to acknowledge the support of Massey University for this leave and Professor Richard Harrison, Department of Management, Queen's University Belfast for agreeing to host me during this leave. I would like to thank two members of that department – Mike Crone and Maura McAdam – for guidance on literature that started my review of two topics. I remain responsible for the interpretation made of their recommendations.

Martin Perry
Department of Management
Massey University (Wellington)
New Zealand

1 Controversies in local economic development

A story is frequently repeated in management text books of how Honda built its business in the USA. It draws on an account by Mintzberg (1987) who describes how Honda executives arriving in Los Angeles from Japan in 1959 to establish their North American subsidiary had intended to sell 250cc and 350cc motorcycles. In Japan a 50cc machine known as the 'supercub' was their marquee brand. Influenced by the marketing perception that the USA would demand big, high performance machines the company set out to sell their bigger models and did not include the supercub in their original plans. Sales of their big bikes proved less than anticipated and were not helped by high rates of mechanical failure. The company that in 2006 was the third largest manufacturer of passenger cars in the USA looked at one stage as though it would fail to stay in business. Honda, so the story goes, succeeded because of the unanticipated and unplanned for popularity of its supercub machine. As frequently presented to students of management, this shows how chance events rather than deliberate strategy can determine business success (Kay 2004). The supercub, we are told, captured buyer attention after being seen in use by Honda staff for travel around their sites in Los Angeles. A representative of Sears Roebuck was among those spotting the supercub who contacted Honda asking about their availability. The buyer gave Honda the idea of selling the bike through general retailers rather than specialist motorcycle dealers. Mintzberg (1987) says that they had been reluctant to sell the supercub for fear such a 'toy' machine would damage their broader appeal to serious bikers (although it should be noted that Pascale (1984) states that the initial stock taken to the USA included the 50cc bike). With flagging sales, the supercub was added to the marketing mix and by 1964 nearly one in two motorcycles sold in the USA was a Honda.

This entertaining story has been deconstructed by Mair (1999), who reflects on six other interpretations of the sources of Honda's successful entry to the American market. Broadly these alternative interpretations divide into analytical and behavioural theories. The analytical interpretation includes the analysis made by the Boston Consulting Group (1975) for the British government who wanted guidance on how to support the British motorcycle industry. In essence the account offered an explanation in which Japanese manufacturers such as Honda planned orchestrated attacks on Western markets. Having established large economies of scale in their home market, business growth was then based on exploiting its cost advantage globally. This account was subsequently embellished by the idea that companies such as Honda put themselves into a 'winner's competitive cycle': a virtuous circle of increased volume, decreased cost, increased profitability and financial power followed by reinvestment to fuel growth (Abbeglen and Stalk 1985).

The behavioural interpretation of Honda's successful entry to the USA includes Mintzberg's account which drew on an earlier study by Pascale (1984). Pascale's account sought to criticize the analytical interpretation offered by the Boston Consulting Group by stressing that rather than careful planning Honda's approach was typical of a Japanese preference to allow strategy to evolve through good bottom up communications and an avoidance of rigid advance planning. Another behavioural account shifts the focus to the idiosyncrasies of Soichiro Honda, whose technical skills and behaviour combined brilliantly with his risk-taking but more business-minded partner Takeo Fujisawa. With the leadership of mavericks who stood apart from the keiretsu capitalism more typical of Japanese business, organizational improvisations were needed that ultimately produced a highly successful company.

Reflecting on the competing explanations, Mair (1999) notes three general shortcomings. First, how any individual account tends to include potentially important analytical omissions or inappropriate treatments of empirical evidence. This may include a failure to recognize how things changed over time, incomplete coverage of relevant activities and not linking actions to outcomes. Second, with the focus on explaining success there is a tendency to overlook strategic errors. In Honda's case this included the costly and unsuccessful attempt to make a 'supercar' for the North American market to compete with models by companies such as Ferrari and Porsche. The supercub sold in large numbers up to 1966 but it was generally overlooked that sales then slumped, creating a huge excess stock and a cashflow crisis. Third, there is a tendency for researchers to opt for a specific interpretation and to justify this by the contrast with some other categorical interpretation. In reality it is more appropriate to envisage a need to synthesize multiple perspectives rather than to attempt to reduce complexity to a single line of enquiry.

Mair's (1999: 39) final reflection on the case is that more sophisticated reflection on Honda's experience is needed to understand the sources of their success in the USA. Instead of searching for a single line of explanation the possibility of success based on the reconciliation of apparently contradictory conceptual alternatives needs consideration. So, for example, rather than trying to establish whether the company's success was more to do with its capacity for learning or its capacity for original design, or whether it was more about its production or marketing skills, the company may have combined skills and resources in novel ways. This might sound commonplace but there is a strong tendency for academics and consultants to interpret stories in the light of their preconceptions and predilections. This is possible because each perspective is capable of illuminating some aspect of a multifaceted story. As Kay (2004) points out successful business strategy is a mix of luck and judgement, opportunism and design and so even with hindsight it is probably never going to be possible to disentangle the relative contributions of each.

The review of attempts to interpret Honda's business success is informative when approaching debates in local economic development. Much local economic development activity is similarly based on attempting to apply the lessons of successful local economies in much the same way that lessons for strategic management have been searched for from Honda. A frequent comment on local economic development is that the focus on high profile exemplar economies such as Silicon Valley encourages a 'one-size-fits-all' approach (Beer *et al.* 2003; Pike *et al.* 2006: 263). The same shortcomings in strategic research identified by Mair (1999) may apply equally to studies purporting to explain and draw lessons from the experiences of places such as Silicon Valley, Route 128, the Third Italy, Baden Württemberg, Motorsport Valley and numerous other influential business clusters. While different in nature and scale, researchers have a tendency to seek to reduce complex processes of regional transformation into a model that fits a preferred theoretical framework. The influence of high profile academics, business 'gurus' and consultants is frequently identified as the source of the tendency to favour 'enthusiastic borrowing' over the local customization of development strategies (Lovering 1999, 2003; Benneworth *et al.* 2003; Martin and Sunley 2003). In this regard it is worth reflecting on different kinds of evidence that academic researchers, policy consultants and economic development professionals variously supply and demand.

Participants in local economic controversy

In the context of the understanding of how to manage organizations, Thomas (2003) draws on Thorngate (1976) to suggest that the various contributors to knowledge have different goals and priorities. This framework seems equally relevant to an assessment of the state of knowledge about local economic development. A desirable quality about the knowledge possessed is that it has a degree of generality, simplicity and accuracy. A general theory encompasses the behaviour of all types of locality or business activity addressed by the theory. For example, a general theory of business clusters would apply to all instances of clustering. A simple theory is based on a small number of components to explain the focal issue. A theory that labour costs shape the attractiveness of a locality to business would be an example of a simple theory. An accurate theory predicts outcomes perfectly. So, for example, if it were known how business agglomerations strengthened business competitiveness it might then be possible to predict the level of business advantage obtained from an enterprise cluster of a certain scale or composition. It would appear therefore that the ideal is that the theories drawn on to inform local economic development are accurate, easy to comprehend and of wide applicability.

The observation made by Thorngate (1976: 126) is that social science theories are typically unable to possess all three attributes at the same time. As a consequence of the complexity of the real world, it may be possible to build theories and explanations that have two of the attributes, but it is generally not possible to include all three qualities simultaneously. This implies that if a theory is accurate and applicable to a wide range of cases it is unlikely to be a simple idea. Alternatively, if the idea is simple it will need to sacrifice its accuracy or its generality. In Thorngate's original presentation the significance of the framework is to discourage the futile search for 'perfect' theories while still claiming the importance of continuing the search for explanation: social phenomena, he argues, are 'sufficiently predictable to intrigue us with their transient patterns and sufficiently irregular to provide us with constant and joyous surprise' (136). This may be seen as still a good judgement on the nature of the understanding of economic development processes (Box 1.1). It can then be asked how decisions are made about which two of the three attributes are given priority. Thomas (2003) suggests that the contributors and users of management knowledge theories tend to have different priorities in what they seek from ideas based on a distinction between scientists, gurus and managers. Substituting local economic development professionals for managers, this tripartite division seems relevant to understanding the influence attained by policy gurus in the market for ideas about local economic development, although immediately it suggests that each party has reasons to devalue the contributions of others. When faced with the need to sacrifice one of the three characteristics of a good theory, the priority of a policy guru is to focus on simple ideas that are easy to communicate and that have general applicability. The economic development professional wants ideas that can be applied to their immediate situation and that appear to give certainty; this suggests a preference for simple but accurate ideas. Scientists prioritize the search for accurate and general ideas and are least concerned with simplicity.

Box 1.1 **Not much known about economic growth**

Examining the efforts to explain variation in national economic growth rates, different studies suggest that doing any of the following will increase per capita growth by one per cent:

- Increasing the average age of schooling in the labour force by 1.2 years.
- Increasing the ratio to GDP of investment in transport and communication by 1.7 per cent.
- A fall in inflation of 26 per cent.
- A reduction in the ratio of government budget deficit to GDP of 4.3 per cent.

It is also known that these results are not robust; the size and the significance of the relationships vary between studies. One of the reasons for this variability is that individual variables are linked to many other components of an economy. An issue such as participation in schooling may be connected to other aspects of an economy and school participation will have no effect on economic performance unless these other features are aligned appropriately. Interaction affects may also complicate relationships. If budget deficits fund transport and communication infrastructure the impact on growth might be less than where funding goes elsewhere. Initial conditions and country circumstances may also affect outcomes. At the same time, many of the variables judged insignificant in cross country studies might have a large effect in certain countries at certain times. While it can be argued that saying everything is important has little practical value this may be a more accurate summary of the development process than focusing on a few components as the levers to development success.

Source: Kenny and Williams (2001)

This framework depicts a situation where there is a lack of fit between the knowledge and ideas presented by scientists and gurus and that which is sought by local economic development professionals. Practitioners must expect to apply the ideas of gurus with caution or they must work to customize the more complex but possibly more accurate ideas of scientists so that they can be applied to their locality, or they must do both these tasks. In practice there is much social pressure that tends to suppress the extent to which suppliers of knowledge admit to the limitations of their ideas, and that discourages practitioners from recognizing the need to customize 'off-the-shelf' theories to fit their particular circumstances. Beer (2009: 85), for example, characterizes economic development professionals as being under considerable pressure to achieve growth targets and of frequently lacking the time and the background to consider alternative approaches to the practice of developing locally. His analysis indicates that the ideas most likely to be accepted by economic development professionals and translated into practice are those that secure the support of high profile institutions and governments; that present themselves as novel and having universal applicability; and that do not overly challenge public expenditure or imply close involvement in economic development.

As is given more consideration in Chapter 5, the case of Michael Porter and business clusters is a well known example of a simple and general idea being embraced by the policy community. This influence grew from Porter's (1990) study of the sources of national competitive advantage. From this original academic investigation the argument that competitive advantage developed from characteristics encompassing entire industries in their 'home region' evolved into a universal policy prescription that offered the promise of sustained growth to any locality or region. Part of the appeal was that Porter-inspired cluster development provided policy professionals with a rationalization for local action in the context of a widespread anxiety about the drift of much economic and business activity into a global sphere of operation (Peters and Hood 2000). Equally significant may have been the ability to combine cluster promotion with any position along the intervention spectrum, from simply recognizing the presence of a cluster to the micro management of business relations among cluster participants. Direct 'missionary' work by Porter and the associated Monitor Consultancy has also been credited as a reason for the diffusion of cluster strategies in many European countries (Benneworth *et al.* 2003). Others have interpreted cluster advocacy has an example of the techniques of brand management intruding into intellectual discourse (Martin and Sunley 2003: 29). Just as commercial organizations use a brand image to seek to differentiate an otherwise 'ordinary' product, the cluster label has been attached to a set of ideas that derived from standard business agglomeration theory and that had been in existence for decades. Tired academic arguments gained a new lease of life through the 'cluster brand' and skilful linkage to an image of high productivity, knowledge rich, decentralized, entrepreneurial and socially progressive local economies being within the reach of policy makers wherever located. As a brand, cluster has five essential attributes: (i) accordance with strongly held aspirations, in this case innovation and competitiveness; (ii) expressed in language that is flexible enough to permit a wide range of interpretations; (iii) backed by authority, in this case Michael Porter's expert knowledge of competition and business strategy; (iv) capable of continual and consistent renewal to keep pace with changing environments, as achieved with cluster applications to the dot.com and knowledge economies; (v) permit practical action, in this case the replication of cluster successes.

Undoubtedly, clever marketing has been behind the influence attained by the cluster idea, although the full account of the campaign has yet to be written. As well as the influence of Michael Porter, the supporting role of 'new economic geography' also needs to be included in the credits. While perhaps not intended by most proponents, this linked cluster promotion to the esoteric and rigorous world of econometrics. The status imparted by quantitative forms of analysis has also been noted as an influence on the more recent popularity of Richard Florida's ideas about 'creative cities' (see Chapter 6). Florida uses an analysis of growth rates for cities in the USA to argue that places with high concentrations of workers in a group of occupations distinguished by their exercise of creativity grow at faster rates than comparable places with predominantly non-creative workforces. Academics have generally been sceptical that this observation should be converted into a policy prescription that city resources should be channelled into making places attractive to creative talent. Nonetheless the creative city thesis has gained worldwide influence partly through the way arguments and evidence of effectiveness can be demonstrated in league tables (Peck 2005). Others as well have noted a break from conventional academic practice in the willingness of Florida to propagate his ideas to wide audiences through the repeated presentation of a well rehearsed message (Beer 2009: 70).

The conversion of academics into policy gurus may be a new phenomenon but it would be wrong to view local economic development as having been captured by simple but prestigious ideas as this tends to suggest the blame for unsatisfactory outcomes attaches to the policy community alone. The social pressure to produce useful knowledge affects the scientific community more broadly than just in the rise of academic superstars. It has long been seen that social science researchers faced with a demand to know and apply the results of their investigations are frequently inclined to simplify what they have or have not discovered. Some observers see powerful disincentives to acknowledge the uncomfortable fact that most of the products of the social sciences are controversial (Thomas 2003: 15). Reflecting on his experience of social science research, Shipman (1997: 118) notes how the pressure to produce research findings leads many university-based researchers to rush out findings, noting how anything in print can add to an author's reputation and that shoddy work is frequently the result. This pressure can also lead to results being presented with more certainty and clarity than findings frequently merit, with academic conventions being to stress the case for and under play the opposition (Shipman 1997: 136). Moreover, the nature of academic publishing is that much of the information required by someone from outside specialized subject areas is missing as scientific publications are peer reviewed by people who are familiar with conventions and do not require the complete explanation that an outsider needs to evaluate the significance of the evidence.

Discussing the work of economic geographers, Markusen (1999) argues that academic research would benefit from further pressure to integrate with the policy community. A lack of integration between the academic and policy communities allows poorly specified ideas to be propagated because the standards academics demand of each other are too low. Practitioners, it is argued, set high standards of explanation and evidence because of their accountability for action that results from their recommendations. The need to adapt ideas for application can also lead policy makers to scrutinize ideas more critically than those whose responsibility does not extend beyond publication in journals. Some may suggest that there is a value in role specialization, allocating one community the job of generating ideas and another community the responsibility for applying them (McCann 2007: 1218). For Markusen (1999), separation of these two roles has resulted in academic research delivering theories and concepts that are too under developed for practical application. Much contemporary economic geography is characterized as propagating 'fuzzy concepts', defined as entities, phenomena or processes that possess two or more alternative meanings. Reliable identification or application by different readers or researchers is difficult when dealing with fuzzy concepts. New concepts still under development may inevitably have a degree of fuzziness. They can be deliberately vague so as to appeal to a range of different audiences. For Markusen, of more significance is that a lack of desire to guide action has allowed standards for admissible evidence to drop too low. A tolerance of under researched fuzzy concepts commences a downward spiral of declining precision and an absence of evidential confirmation. The outcome is increasing distance between the academic and policy communities. Markusen traces this situation to the unwillingness of most academics to be explicit about the values and priorities guiding recommended courses of action if they are to address policy. On the other hand, declarations of political preference can be seen to compromise the claims to be conducting 'scientific' investigation. Rather than deal with this potential conflict, many social scientists shy away from close engagement with the policy community and instead stay within their community and its less exacting evidential standards.

Can controversies be resolved?

In posing the question of whether controversies can be resolved, Thomas (2003) points out that this depends partly on the source of the controversy. Individual controversies can arise through differences at multiple levels but with respect to the chances of resolution it is helpful to distinguish controversies of facts, values and frameworks. A controversy that arises from the interpretation of factual evidence is in principle resolvable as long as there is agreement over which facts are relevant. Some examples relevant to local economic development where a shortage of facts continues to prevent agreement can be given.

- Do enterprises grow more when they are located where other parts of their industry are concentrated compared with what would happen if the same enterprises were dispersed across different locations? This issue is currently a controversy that in theory could be resolved if appropriate data could be assembled for analysis and there was agreement over the comparability of the samples and performance measures utilized, including the timescale over which performance differences are to be counted.
- Are research findings produced in a specific university taken up by enterprises located near to the university before they are taken up by enterprises remote from the university? With agreement over what constitutes a research finding and over geographical boundaries to distinguish proximate from remote enterprises, evidence could be assembled to answer this controversy, although this might require studies of multiple universities generating different types of research finding.

It is less clear that value controversies are open to resolution. Thomas (2003: 17) illustrates this by the unlikelihood that someone who believes that it is always wrong to kill another human being would accept that capital punishment can be justified. Applied to local economic development, a difference of value exists between those who see the possibility of some form of ecological modernization resolving environmental problems as compared with those who advocate a more immediate need to change the nature of economic activity. A difference of value may also be seen between those who believe that it is more effective to promote the movement of labour to where employment is most in demand and those who advocate the movement of business to where jobs are most needed. While this issue is amenable to some factual evidence about the cost effectiveness of alternative strategies, assuming representative programmes are investigated, the debate is connected to deeper differences over the causes of regional economic inequalities and the priority to be given to different social groups. Those who favour strategies of moving business do so partly from the belief that market failures do not explain economic malaise such that correcting market imperfections will allow economies to revive. Those who favour taking work to the workers may also value addressing the employment needs of those who are unable or least unwilling to move to where chances of employment may be greater rather than relying on economic growth to eventually catch them up.

The third type of controversy arises from differences in the framework of concepts within which matters of fact and value are discussed. Thomas (2003: 18) suggests that the classic example of this is the division between theologians and scientists on the origins of the Universe: ultimately this divide attests to the willingness to form judgements on the basis of observational data as compared with giving status to scriptures handed down from previous generations. It may seem that this source of controversy has little representation within the world of local economic development except that some commentators have attempted to apply unconventional philosophical frameworks to economic development. Rowe (2009a: 5), for example, argues that existing concepts and theories are not able to account for the complexity associated with 'the chaos of markets, global forces and multiple actors'. He suggests the possibility of developing original insights based on Deleuzian philosophy which seeks to encourage a more open-ended process of investigation in place of framing discussions within currently accepted ideas and theories. An aspect of this being to avoid so-called 'arborescent' ways of thinking that assume hierarchical relationships between components of an economic system and instead employ 'rhizomial' ways of thinking based on the assumption of non-hierarchical networks akin to the organization of the Internet (Rowe 2009b: 347). A more prosaic case of different frameworks may be seen in the claim that more attention needs to be given to what makes people happy, as this ultimately identifies the issues that should absorb attention (Oswald 1997). It implies different frameworks for discussing economic issues as present theories tend to assume that increasing consumption, or at least the opportunity to consume, is a sufficient basis for selecting between development alternatives.

As Thomas (2003) admits, the boundaries between these sources of controversy are in themselves controversial. The type of factual evidence that is accepted as a significant contribution to resolving a controversy varies according to the preferences that researchers have for engaging in different types of research. Relevant to local economic development, McCann (2007) discusses this in terms of the difference between the 'regional science' and 'regional studies' traditions. The former is identified as based on mathematical and empirical approaches while the latter are primarily associated with qualitative forms of evidence. McCann is concerned that the relationship between these two modes of enquiry has been lost and that too much discussion of local economic development issues is conducted on the basis of hybrid ideas that draw on a mixture of regional science and regional studies. This is problematic as the role of regional studies should be limited to drawing the attention of regional scientists to issues that need the scrutiny of econometric methods before they are presented to policy makers (McCann 2007: 1218). The main argument for this is that regional science is based on a standardized value framework such that findings of individual studies can be compared with each other and policy makers are presented with evidence that can be evaluated impartially. In broad terms this refers to regional scientists' affinity to welfare economics.

Welfare economics is based on the notion that individuals, through market mechanisms, should be relied upon to make most social decisions. The methods of analysis used by welfare economists recognize instances where markets cannot be relied upon to distribute resources efficiently. To use economists' language, there are times when markets cannot aggregate individual utility-maximizing behaviour (meaning decisions to purchase or not purchase some good or service) so as to optimize overall social welfare. When this occurs, markets are said to fail and there is a justification for government actions to supplement or replace markets. Welfare economists recognize many sources of market failure but there are a number of archetypal situations that are used to justify a need for public policy (Box 1.2).

Box 1.2 **Market failures for welfare economics**

Natural monopoly: in industries with large capital requirements and large economies of scale, such as railway networks and power generation, it can be difficult for new businesses to compete with established ones. Where one or a few firms dominate an industry, the lack of competition can reduce the ability of individuals to make welfare maximizing decisions.

Imperfect information: to maximize welfare, individual decisions must be made on the basis of adequate information but there are instances where either producers have no incentive to reveal information about their product or service, or consumers do not have the expertise to evaluate the information given, and instances where both failures arise.

Externalities: these arise in relation to those costs of production that are not paid for by the producer and in relation to those benefits that are not paid for by buyers of the producer's output. Externalities are an incentive to over produce some things, where costs are avoided, and under produce things where benefits are not fully remunerated.

Common property goods: resources that are open for anyone to draw upon risk being used unsustainably where individual decision makers maximize their current use of the resource without regard to its long term future. This context is known as the tragedy of the commons.

Destructive competition: competition between enterprises that causes negative side effects for employees and society may be seen as a market failure where inadequate wages and workplace investment produce living and working conditions with high social costs.

For commentators such as McCann, welfare economics is appreciated for its ability to inform the selection of an appropriate response on the basis of a neutral and dispassionate justification for intervention. Policy makers are recommended to act because a market is failing and society will work more efficiently if corrective action is taken. This does not mean that welfare economics reduces public policy to a technical process. It is frequently difficult, if not impossible, to convert real world situations into the data needed by welfare economists to run their forms of analysis and even where they can it should not be imagined that regional scientists necessarily believe that policy makers are 'won over' simply by evidence of a market failure. Neither should it be overlooked that there is much internal debate among welfare economists about the recognition of market failures and what, if anything, should be the response. Nonetheless, the market offers a benchmark and a rationalizing logic justifying policy intervention. In contrast, those working in the regional studies tradition may justify their policy recommendations on the basis of normative values such as their position on human rights, equity and local democracy. According to McCann (2007: 1214), regional scientists may sympathize with these concerns on a personal level but they do not allow their political preferences to transfer into their regional analysis.

From the perspective of those working in McCann's regional studies tradition, the notion of their contributions being subsidiary to those of the regional scientist is deeply disconcerting. Equally they would challenge the suggestion that their work is tainted by personal values whereas welfare economics is value free. For their part, the issue is less between the use of personal judgemental values or welfare economics than between the willingness to engage in shallow rather than deep forms of policy analysis (Peck 1999; Henry *et al.* 2001). Shallow policy research involves evaluating the impact of policy interventions and can be completed using standardized impact assessment methodologies. The aims and objectives of the policy research are proscribed by the agency seeking the evaluation, leaving little scope for exploration of the issue outside the agency's narrow interests. Researchers tend to accept markets as they exist and do not question how a market has come about and how it might be constituted differently. Deep policy analysis, on the other hand, is not restricted to the parameters and exclusions set by a policy agency and recognizes that the policy process itself is a worthy target of investigation, as well as policy outcomes. There is a preference to see markets as socially constructed phenomena created by actors whose perceptions and resources are a product of particular circumstances. Economic geographers, for example, devote more of their effort to understanding how the environment has constructed a market than to analysing whether the market is failing and how it should be corrected according to welfare maximizing criteria. Whereas deep policy analysis potentially offers the greater insight, much of the demand for policy research is concerned only to obtain a shallow analysis. Supporters of regional studies tend see themselves as conducting deep analysis and disparage economists and others aligned to regional science for their willingness to provide shallow policy guidance. Economic geographers are, for example, frequently preoccupied with demonstrating the local embeddedness and path dependency of economic and social phenomena. Compared with economists they are also more likely to wish to collect their own data and to do this locally. Deep policy analysis may generate unique insights into the 'real' nature of social and economic processes. It can also be viewed as knowledge that is more relevant to policy implementation issues and programme outcomes than to the 'front end' of the policy process where policy is first conceived and designed.

A further distinction between regional science and regional studies can be the understanding of what is needed to make a claim of causation. Research of the type favoured by regional scientists tends to follow a successionist logic whereas that conducted in regional studies is more likely to adopt a generative logic (Pawson and Tilley 1997; Robson 2002). Successionists believe that causation is unobservable and that it is possible only to draw inferences on the basis of observational data. The key is to design a form of scientific enquiry that as far as possible controls for issues other than those that the investigation seeks to explore. According to successionists, some form of randomized allocation of subjects to experimental and control groups is the ideal way of making observations. The assumption is that any difference in behavioural outcomes between the two groups is accounted for in terms of the action of the treatment, which in regional science might be participation in a public policy programme or location in a specific place of interest. Causation is not observed but rather it is taken to exist if statistical analysis shows that the differences between the control and treatment groups are more than could be explained simply by chance. A generative view of causation seeks to establish a connection between action and outcomes in a way that gives a fuller explanation of how the two are linked. To this extent it seeks to dig deeper into the process that causes change. A generative explanation makes reference to some underlying mechanism which generates the connection and how the workings of such mechanisms are contingent and conditional on particular contexts that allow the mechanisms to operate. Or as Mackie (1980) suggests, a cause is any factor or condition that is in itself insufficient but that is necessary as part of the conjuncture of several factors or conditions.

The contrast in the form explanation needed to substantiate a causal relationship has been discussed by Storper and Scott (2009: 154) in the context of a review of the evidence relating to the role of environmental amenities in influencing location choices. They suggest that regional scientists are content to draw conclusions on the basis of 'revealed preferences': if people are concentrating in a place with attributes y it follows that those people must have a preference for y as revealed by their choice of location. Essentially this is the evidential base on which those who are arguing that amenity-rich localities are increasingly favoured for economic growth. The problem is that no matter how strong the statistical association there is no demonstration that actual preferences coincide with the revealed preferences. As Storper and Scott (2009) explain, at least two additional types of evidence are required. There must be some assurance that location selections have responded to the influences thought to be responded to. Second, it is necessary to scrutinize the conditions under which particular opportunities (such as location in an amenity-rich locality) and constraints (for example changes in employment in older cities) make it possible for an individual to engage in a course of action. So, for example, even if individuals have a preference for sunny climates they may not be able to make it a permanent part of their lives if there is not the opportunity to work in the preferred locality.

The outcome of successionist forms of enquiry tends to be the presentation of findings in the form of universal laws in the sense of them not being conditional on particular times or places. It tends to encourage what others have called 'ontological universalism' (Kenny and Williams 2001: 3). This idea has two closely connected aspects. First, the 'components' of economies are in some way the same, such that economies and economic processes are comparable across time and space. Second, these components of the economy interact with one another in the same kind of ways and so it is possible to compile evidence from different contexts. As McCann (2007) claims, the basic requirement for generalization in regional science are a large number of observations, based on standardized definitions and the ability to reduce regional phenomena to a parsimonious number of relationships.

The generative enquiry is consistent with the perception that events rarely have a single cause but are rather the result of a conjuncture of several factors or conditions (Kenny and Williams 2001: 13). Such complexity is especially likely to arise when the issues of interest are part of the social rather than natural world. When seeking to understand processes involving events in the social world there are many more things that can interfere with a supposed causal connection than when process can be studied in isolation from the particular context in which it occurs. Kenny and Williams (2001) suggest that this has been recognized by the concept of 'circular causation' as explained by Myrdal (1957), although this does not resolve how to progress investigations and gather data as much as indicate the challenges in explaining causal connections. With a process of circular causation a change in one factor affects a number of other factors and these changes in turn feed back on the item that was changed initially. This depicts the process of economic change as interlocking, circular and cumulative. The implications are then that it is wrong to look for a single cause as economic change involves circular connections and the variables to be considered and the potential connections between them are too many to be simplified within a single universal law. Kenny and Williams also draw on ideas that virtuous and vicious cycles influence economic development processes and that economic development can be affected by threshold effects. A threshold is the idea that there may be certain critical resource levels above which economic development can gain momentum, or below which decline can accelerate. Interventions may then have different outcomes according to how close the starting point is to the threshold beyond which progress can be rapid or below which intervention will prove ineffective.

Recognizing that economic development is a complex process may not deter regional scientists and their conviction that ultimately economic development patterns rely on core processes which it should be possible to isolate and demonstrate in an economic model. The challenge is harder when it comes to recognizing that economic activity involves industries and enterprises that are highly variable in character and when the concern is with trying to promote change among particular communities of enterprise. Take an example such as the interest that arose from evidence that accumulated in the 1980s of the greater use of 'obligational contracting' (or what today might be called supply-chain partnering) among businesses in Japan than in other economies. A simple interpretation of this evidence when combined with high rates of economic growth was that the style of contracting was a contributory cause of economic success and it was therefore advocated that Western business should modify its contracting practices. Local economic development policies were devised to support this conclusion (Perry 2007a).

Close investigation of the origins and operation of contracting in Japan revealed that it was wrong to think universal rules could exist about the superiority of one form of contracting over another (Sako 1992). Rather than it being possible to explain the Japanese preference for one form of contracting as a product of transaction cost savings it was more appropriate to envisage a two-way relationship in which organizational structures partly determine transaction costs and transaction costs encourage certain organizational forms. Detailed comparative investigation revealed that universal rules about when transaction costs were minimized were difficult to sustain and that the context in which transactions took place had an important bearing on the effectiveness of one form of contracting over another. For Sako (1992), the full understanding of organizational differences required reference to five influences: economic and technological variables; legal environments; financial market structures; employment relations; the environment for small-firm entrepreneurship. In any one of these areas, a range of issues had encouraged obligational contracting in Japan. The complexity can be illustrated through a summary of the influential components of the economic and technological conditions in Japan that were then associated with the form of contracting that enterprises tended to follow.

- Industrial sectors vary in their suitability for obligational contracting. Japan had more of those sectors suited to obligational relations than might be found in other economies.
- The use of external suppliers typically required the buyer to invest in assets specific to the transaction. This gave the buyer an incentive to cultivate a long term association so as to avoid suppliers exploiting their sunk investment.
- Subcontracted inputs included some that relied on customized design input existing in the supplier firm.
- Buyer competitive strategies included product differentiation and diversification and accelerated product cycles.
- Transactions were conducted in the context of comparative market stability, both in respect of final sales and the buyer's preparedness to even out market swings for their suppliers (the latter willingness being influenced by the buyer's asset specificity and product cycle strategy).
- Market growth made trust relatively inexpensive to acquire as growth generates business confidence and a sense of shared success between the buyer and supplier.

The interest that was once given to business practices in Japan was encouraged by a belief that there was a distinct Japanese approach to industry organization. Such a perception again could have been lessened if greater notice had been taken of the variability within the Japanese economy (Edgington 1997). Practices that were actually only strongly developed in the case of a few sectors too frequently were assumed to be an aspect of national cultural differences. This goes back to the case of Honda given at the start of the chapter where different initial starting points for investigation led to different interpretations of the sources of success. No interpretation may be entirely wrong but it may not always be recognized how only part of the story was being illuminated. Relaxing the assumption that national distinctiveness permeated all industrial activity in Japan, it was possible to discern explanations for industrial practices that were unconnected to any cultural proclivities for trust or long term obligational relationships. Examining industries such as ceramics, textiles, machine tools and office equipment it was discovered that 'structured relationships' were more of a feature of the auto assembly industry than other sectors (Edgington 1997). This then led to an explanation of the development of interfirm cooperation according to industry-specific factors: the use of components, mechanical requirements and design standards, and the length of product cycles. For instance, it was found that the office equipment industry relied largely on 'off-the-shelf' electrical parts which were available nationwide while in ceramic tiles and textiles, short production runs mitigated against the use of custom-designed parts and thus reduced the impetus to build formal relationships with suppliers (Edgington 1997).

The awareness among adherents to regional studies that economic processes are rarely reducible to simple, universal laws makes it unlikely a harmonious relationship with regional scientists will come to pass. For their part, regional scientists are unlikely to give up their preferences for testing ideas through economic models and mathematical equations (see Overman 2004). This review of selected controversies in local economic development is written from the perspective of regional studies and the preference to seek generative forms of explanation. The aim is to assist those willing to work within these frameworks and values to arrive at some personal resolution of the controversy that can be applied in developing further insight into the area of concern.

The controversies

The following chapters are organized around seven controversies in local economic development. The selected topics encompass issues of importance to the practice of local economic development in that they inform archetypal strategies that have to some degree influenced policy initiatives. As well, to be included they must be live issues still open to new evidence, new theories and new arguments. A further requirement is that the topic must have been researched through the collection of evidence rather than simply being a controversy between speculative claims or competing lines of advocacy not supported with some form of research evidence. Depending on the nature of the debate that has occurred, the reviews draw on evidence and arguments that may have been developed in regional studies or regional science but it is probable that most attention is given to the contributions from those most aligned to the regional studies tradition. The attempt at resolution is based on a search for levels of explanation that are more generative than successionist in character, it being an understanding that economic development experiences and processes are generally not well understood through universal laws that are not anchored to specific contexts. Industry characteristics, enterprise type and geographical environments are typically important contexts shaping local economic development. The seven selected controversies are briefly outlined below.

The next two chapters are included to give an introduction to the idea of local economic development as well as to identify areas of difference. Chapter 2 explores how the concept of territorial competitiveness can be applied to local economic development. At the broadest level this explores whether there is some way for economic development agencies to augment the competitive strength of the enterprises located within territory. Chapter 3 compares regional policy with local economic development policy as approaches to reducing spatial differences in unemployment. This issue is controversial as while both forms of policy co-exist there has been a widespread tendency to assume that regional policy has become ineffective. The case for local economic policy is that many of the barriers to economic development have local origins connected with the effectiveness of institutions and markets.

The idea that knowledge and learning are potentially localized processes is the subject of Chapter 4. This has been an influential argument based on the claim that knowledge is more likely to be shared with immediate neighbours than diffusing more widely, in technical terms that knowledge is shared through spillovers rather than deliberate decisions to acquire or share knowledge. This claim is given attention as it leads to strong policy recommendations about the benefits to be obtained from strengthening capacities to generate and share knowledge as well as being part of the justification for supporting enterprise clusters. Chapter 5 takes up the case for including the promotion of business clusters with local economic policy noting that some have seen this as one of the widespread policy initiatives of recent decades.

An aspect of regional policy was the view that it was more effective to bring work to the workers than to encourage migration to where employment was most plentiful. Chapter 6 examines a reversal of this policy assumption in the form of the argument that creating environments attractive to creative-class workers has been a viable alternative approach to promoting local economic development. Like the promotion of enterprise clusters, this has been viewed as another case of 'guru-led' policy but as the chapter discusses there are aspects of the creative class thesis that have gained academic support.

The contribution of technology incubators to increasing the rate at which scientific discoveries are converted into commercial enterprises is examined in Chapter 7. This discussion necessarily encompasses a larger debate about the relationship of publicly funded research to private enterprise as well as the evidence about the contribution of innovation to the generation of high growth enterprise.

The final controversy deals with the question of whether promoting good environmental practices can be a basis for stimulating local economic development. In some accounts local economic agencies have it in their power to start a virtuous circle in which building a more self contained local economy brings reduced environmental impacts alongside increased opportunities for local enterprises. Others dismiss this possibility as unrealistic in terms of the challenge this would present to maintaining existing standards of living and as being too simplistic in assuming that local business necessarily has less environmental impact than other forms of enterprise. The possibility of shifting to a more benign form of economy is discussed in terms of the case for forms of industrial organization based on industrial ecology.

A final chapter reflects on the controversies and offers some suggestions as to how future research might be progressed. The focus is on local economic development. In Chapter 3 this takes on a specific meaning to provide a contrast with regional policy. Elsewhere in the book local economic development is used loosely to refer to ideas about and policies to promote economic development within subnational territorial units that may include regions but which is separate from national economic and industrial policy.

2 Regional competitiveness and local economic development

Over any period of time some places enjoy higher levels of economic growth than others. An interpretation is that these differences in economic success reflect how some places are more competitive than others. This may merely be taken to imply that that some regions have a disproportionate share of successful enterprises and that business success helps to maintain the supply of resources needed for business expansion such as labour and business service infrastructure. Contrary to this restricted interpretation the idea has grown that regional economies are more than an aggregation of individual enterprises; this implies that qualities of the region as a whole augment the resources of its component firms in a unique or at least distinctive way. In this sense it is possible to envisage that places compete with each other at the same time that individual enterprises are competing with one another. This extension of the application of competitiveness to places remains controversial but it has been used to strengthen the case for and the scope of local economic development action. Competitiveness is understandably a much sought after attribute but it remains an elusive concept, especially when applied to groups of people and organizations defined in territorial terms (Begg 2002).

From the perspective of a prominent economist, interpreting the relative performance of economies as an indicator of their competitiveness is ill-informed and action derived from it a potential danger to the issues of concern (Krugman 1994). Writing from the perspective of the world's largest economy, Krugman is concerned that appeals to competiveness assume that economies are locked in a struggle over finite markets. Increased susceptibility to the demands of protectionists is the danger when one place's gain is seen to be another place's loss. Krugman argues that competition affects places differently from how it affects individual businesses. Companies may compete over a finite market and this makes one firm's expansion another firm's loss. Territorial economies comprise a diversity of activity and are more interdependent than are individual businesses. A loss to one sector can be offset by opportunities created for other enterprises and the economy as a whole can be strengthened when exposed to competition. Consequently places do not go out of business in the same way that a company can. Moreover, whatever the impression of a globalized world economy and national economies going 'head to head', most economic activity is unaffected by the relative economic success of other territories as it is orientated to local markets.

The perspectives of an international trade economist have been challenged from observations of regional economic success. Just as companies differ from countries, so regions and smaller territorial units differ from national economies and have their own form of competitiveness (Cellini and Soci 2002). Consistent with this, it is argued that the competitiveness of local economies can be based on an absolute advantage rather than just a comparative advantage in a particular area of business specialization (Camagni 2002). The idea of comparative advantage is important in international trade theory as it explains why every economy can gain from being open to the exports of other economies (Armstrong and Taylor 2000: 123). An assumption permitting the existence of comparative advantage is that an economy always retains its capacity to participate in some branch of economic activity. This may not be the case for a smaller territorial unit, as they are highly vulnerable to losing people and productive capacity to those localities with a more successful enterprise population. In a worst case scenario, weakness in a local economy arising from the poor performance of its businesses or its disadvantageous geographical circumstances can result in mass unemployment that triggers emigration and perhaps even total abandonment of settlements (Camagni 2002: 2404). In this sense localities are in a competitive relationship with other places, as there is no guarantee that a weakening of existing economic activity will be offset by the redeployment of resources to new opportunities. This possibility is not under dispute, as Krugman (1993: 242) has explained that a region whose established industries are faring badly may simply shed people rather than attract new industries. The debate is over the precise nature of regional competitiveness and the source of territorial advantage that local economic development policy is best advised to focus upon.

A viewpoint is that almost every place has some competitive advantage that it can exploit: the challenge is merely to identify it and to use it to grow the economy (Luger 2009: 114). Encouragingly this same perspective holds that in today's world the capacity for policy interventions to stimulate competitive advantage has grown. Two assumptions lie behind this claim. First, many of the value-adding functions supporting the production of goods and services such as R&D, design, logistics management and financing can be physically remote from the place of production to which they relate. Second, high value-adding activities are willing to go where their knowledge and service workers wish to live. Some aspects of residential preference remain intractable to policy initiatives, such as the weather or availability of natural amenities, but there is still much that can be done: 'build golf courses and other recreation, develop and market attractive science parks, move and/or expand colleges and universities and research facilities, work with airlines to expand air services, and so on' (Luger 2009: 116).

A different agenda assumes the opposite about the location flexibility of contemporary enterprise while being equally optimistic that regions can augment the competitive advantage possessed by individual enterprises. 'New regionalism' has been built upon the possibility of localities acquiring three sources of absolute advantage: a local business culture that promotes collaboration among firms as much as competition; specialization in a related set of activities rather than being a concentration of unconnected enterprises; and soft or intangible location assets arising from shared values, trust and collective learning processes (Turok 2004: 1078). The basic proposition is that contrary to the expectation of footloose globalization the capacity for regions to be competitive has actually increased as enterprise advantage is now frequently dependent on localized 'untraded interdependencies' such as flows of tacit knowledge, technological spillovers, trust-based business relationships and shared values (Storper 1995a; Camagni 2002).

Such optimism about the ability to manipulate territorial performance is backed up by various proposals for measuring a region's level of competitiveness. If accepted as offering valid insight, such measurement opens the prospect of managing regional competitiveness by demonstrating the outcomes of policy measures and guiding where future public investment is needed. Other researchers are less certain about the competitiveness agenda and suggest that basic questions still need to be asked about the concept of regional competitiveness. What precisely does competitiveness mean when applied to a region or other small territory; how can it be measured; and how do levels of regional competitiveness relate to living standards and regional prosperity (Gardiner *et al.* 2004; Kitson *et al.* 2004)? Such questioning may yet reveal insight that sustains efforts to promote regional competitiveness of some form. A further perspective presented as 'post New Regionalism' sees that it is first important to reflect on how and by whom the interest in competitiveness has been promoted (Lovering 2003). This perspective turns attention to the 'regional service class' of economic development professionals, policy makers and practitioners and asks what influences shape their regional policy agendas (Lovering 1999, 2003).

This chapter approaches this range of views on regional competitiveness first by commenting on alternative definitions and explaining ways that regional competitiveness is constrained by national influences. Five ways that regional competitiveness has been investigated are then outlined and issues raised by each area of enquiry are identified. The final part of the chapter offers a way of integrating these partly interconnected frameworks for exploring regional competitiveness and considers the suggestion that every locality has some potential source of competitive advantage that can be the basis of local economic development.

The nature of regional competitiveness

Competitiveness is not a formal economic concept with broad agreement over its meaning and measurement (Wren 2001: 848). Rather it is an idea that has gained attention through the policy making process and remains an ill-defined term that is potentially open to misuse. Competition between firms is a selection mechanism that redistributes resources between enterprises and provides an incentive for improving the efficiency and effectiveness of business operations (Turok 2004). Competition between regions does not redistribute resources as directly as this: public expenditure cushions economic shocks to a regional economy; 'new entrants' do not substitute for long established regions; and regional managers are not rewarded according to their locality's economic performance, partly as their control over economic agents is limited. One interpretation is that regional competitiveness refers to the presence of conditions that enable firms in a region to compete in their chosen markets and to generate value within their home region (Begg 1999). This offers a static interpretation that discounts how regions can vary in their capacity for encouraging new enterprise and industries. An alternative conception highlights the importance of export activity, but this can overlook the importance of internal market activity. A vague but encompassing perspective interprets regional competitiveness as the underlying drivers and dynamics shaping a locality's prosperity, including the possibility of attracting or developing new sectors. This can be distinguished from more superficial forms of regional competitiveness, such as that associated with capturing major sporting events or the investment of a multinational corporation. Competitiveness of this sort affects particular targets and short term campaigns although it may be linked to larger strategies and ambitions.

In the interests of increasing conceptual clarity it is sometimes suggested that competitiveness is best understood as productivity. In conditions of full employment, changes in productivity control the rate at which national living standards grow, which is the outcome that motivates interest in national and regional competitiveness (Krugman 1996; Porter and Ketels 2003). Applied to regions, this interpretation overlooks that employment conditions typically vary between labour markets and that labour mobility can affect regional prosperity. Consequently, Turok (2004: 1070) indicates that the notion of competitiveness as the underlying driving force of a regional economy needs to encompass three components:

- Trade: the ability of local firms to sell their products in contested external markets.
- Productivity: the value of the products traded and the efficiency with which they are produced.
- Employment rate: the utilization of local human, capital and natural resources.

The need to consider multiple processes reflects the dangers of seeking to maximize any single source of competitiveness. Export capacity alone is an insufficient basis for judging competitiveness as the value of the income obtained relative to the price of locally produced and imported goods and services affects living standards. The productivity of export activity has also to be considered but high value-adding industry tends to be highly capital intensive with relatively low levels of direct employment. Consequently while the productivity of a region's industry is important it is not appropriate to focus on it alone. A region's productivity can increase significantly if businesses cut out their least efficient operations and reduce the size of their workforce. Such changes may cause a one-off increase in productivity without any benefit for the region's overall output or long term ability to expand exports and at the expense of a rise in unemployment (Gardiner et al. 2004: 1049).

22   Regional competitiveness

Regions are in a competitive relationship with each other in the sense that some regions grow faster than others and that some of this growth redistributes regional shares of the national and perhaps world economy. Nonetheless it is evident that not all the differences in regional performance can be ascribed to inter-regional rivalry.

- Direct face-to-face competition between regions is restricted to those that share similar economic specializations and markets (Boschma 2004a: 1005). For example, in north Europe direct competition goes on between neighbouring regions with large port-based economies that serve overlapping hinterlands. More typically the basis of individual regional economies is sufficiently distinct that they may face no directly competing region. In these cases regions may compete for the attraction of additional resources in the form of labour, inward investment and government budgets although even this will depend on them sharing the same resource pool as other regions.
- Regions exist within integrated national economies and this limits the scope for inter-regional competition. A simple economic framework for examining a region's competitiveness relative to other regions focuses on the interaction of a region's product market and its labour market (Armstrong and Taylor 1993: 138). Regions with the fastest growing industries and enterprises must draw in additional labour and other resources to fuel their expansion above that satisfied by increased productivity. The price of labour and other inputs to production can be expected to increase in response to demand. Slower growing regions are not isolated from this cost inflation as labour and other business costs tend to be transmitted across regions rather than being fixed by local demand and supply conditions. For example, employers are obliged to narrow the gap between their pay rates and what their workers may earn elsewhere, even where this is not enforced through national wage setting, because people may move to where wages are higher. In this way regions are not free to compete as they must accept market conditions that limit their capacity to attract business away from the fastest growing regions. In the long term, the inability of weaker regions to adjust can encourage outflows of people that further weaken the capacity for regional revival. The traditional response to these problems has been some form of regional policy using regulatory controls and financial subsidies to redistribute industrial activity (see Chapter 3). Even with such intervention the relative levels of regional economic prosperity tend to be remarkably persistent over time, as in the long established north–south divide in the United Kingdom (Adams et al. 2003; Moore and Begg 2004). Periodic shifts in the position of regions relative to each other might be seen as a necessary indicator of a competitive relationship: if one group always stays on top it suggests some form of 'market dominance' exists rather than competition.
- Business ownership linkages and trade relations reinforce economic processes and the openness of regional economies. Rather than being a discrete container of enterprises pursuing independently determined business strategies,

regional populations exist within various networks of control by, responsibility for and obligation to entities external to the region. In this way regions have been conceived as 'spaces of flows' constituted by a multiplicity of network connections that establish dependencies upon a wide diversity of other places and outside agencies (Doel and Hubbard 2002). This relational perspective sees that patterns of regional development are more affected by the power and control of corporate headquarters and other external entities than they are by autonomous decision making within regions (Cumbers *et al.* 2003). It has long been recognized, for example, that there are distinctive patterns to the distribution of jobs within multi-site organizations that influence the capacity for future economic growth (Massey 1984). More recently this has been discussed in terms of the way that some regions hold dominant political and economic positions that shape their own development and that of the subordinate regions under their influence (Massey 2004). Spatial divisions of labour are one result, with some regions capturing most of the higher order managerial and professional functions within both the public and private sectors. These better remunerated jobs contribute to some regions having a higher GDP per employee than others. This can be taken to indicate that they are more productive and by implication more competitive than other regions, whereas it really shows how different types of job tend to concentrate in different types of region (Fothergill 2005: 664).

- When enterprise managers are asked about the aspects of a region affecting their competitive performance they most usually identify national economic conditions and regulations as the primary influences (for example see Armstrong and Taylor 1993: 138). The national factors of concern include national tax rates, national growth, exchange rates, the cost of credit and labour market regulation. Moreover the non national influences tend to be local issues such as labour market conditions and the state of transport infrastructure rather than region-wide issues. The responses of managers to factors affecting their business performance can be expected to be influenced by their political agenda (Healey 1991). Neither are they necessarily based on deep insight into the ultimate sources of their business performance. Nonetheless it cannot be denied that national economic conditions are a strong determinant of regional economic prosperity and that there are reasons to doubt that regional levels of organization have much significance to business entities: local enterprises are too small and most multinational organizations too large to have an interest in regionally specific processes (Lovering 2003: 53). Similarly, it has been noted that the extent to which regional boundaries have significance for business competitiveness will vary according to a region's particular industrial structure and context, the balance of locally orientated versus nationally and internationally orientated enterprises and the extent to which the regional economy comprises homogenous enterprises that are interconnected through their business operations (Bristow 2005: 293).
- Like firms, a region's performance can be influenced by unforeseen events and unanticipated outcomes of investment decisions (Boschma 2004a: 1005).

There is rarely perfect foresight as to where sources of future demand will come from. Firms that become winners are frequently those that fortuitously have the required resources to meet demand as it emerges rather than being enterprises that consciously identified market changes in advance of their emergence. By extension, changes in regional performance may simply reflect the distribution of 'lucky' enterprises. Randomness in regional performance questions whether it is appropriate to ascribe outcomes to a region when it did not do anything to determine the outcomes.

- Regional level competitiveness can disguise significant variations in the performance of different branches of the regional economy and the standard of living enjoyed by individual sections of the region's population. Where high productivity activity exists alongside low productivity activities it is hard to sustain claims for a distinct regional experience that is more than the sum of its parts. As well, the diversity of sub populations within regions questions the ability for economic development policy to change the fortunes of the region as a whole. Rather than addressing collective territorial economic performance, policy initiatives target a particular aspect of a particular subset of activities within a region (Bristow 2005: 3000).

Given these many constraints on the ability for regions to compete it is understandable that some have questioned whether there is any validity in the concept. Bristow (2005: 300), for example, considers that emphasis on regional competitiveness exaggerates the importance of the region to firm competitiveness and the importance of firm competitiveness to regional prosperity. Nonetheless the urge among economic policy makers to intervene in the interests of promoting regional competitiveness is strong and in this context it is important to examine the basis on which regional competitiveness is being conceptualized, and the resulting policy strategies.

Discussions of regional competitiveness among those seeking to maintain its importance tend to be directed at one or more of the following themes (Table 2.1).

- Explaining regional performance – identification and implications of the fundamental determinants of a region's economic performance.
- Regional absolute advantage – the mechanisms allowing a region to acquire an absolute advantage in a branch of economic activity.
- Aligning business and regional competitiveness – identification of how regional environments can be made to fit competitive business structures and strategies.
- Benchmarking regional competitiveness – the measurement of regional competitiveness in terms of the comparative strengths and weaknesses of regions relative to each other.
- Regional strategies – strategies to be pursued by regional development agencies to enhance economic well being and future development opportunities.

Table 2.1 Frameworks for exploring regional competitiveness

Framework	Key issues considered	Main contribution	Unresolved issues
Explaining regional performance	Identification of the underlying causes of differences in regional economic performance.	Economic governance varies between high performing regions; regional characteristics driving economic performance are embedded and slow to change.	Openness of regional economies and integration with other regions questions the survival of regional differences.
Regional absolute advantage	Components of regional economic governance allowing a region to sustain high performance in a regionally specialized industry.	Theoretical model of how 'soft' externalities can enhance business performance and encourage industry clusters.	Absence of real examples that show the model works; has not kept up with the evolution of industrial districts; does not recognize industry differences as there is 'one best way'.
Aligning business and regional competitiveness	Regional characteristics matching the characteristics of competitive industries.	Method for analysing and promoting regionally based industry clusters.	May wrongly attribute causal properties to the outcomes of competitive success; national cluster templates exaggerate the scope for regional clusters.
Benchmarking regional competitiveness	Determining the relative strengths and weaknesses of regions.	Application of survey instruments for performance benchmarking and the development of more complex process and policy benchmarking.	Risk of league tables distorting public policy; ability of policy and process benchmarking to improve on superficial forms of benchmarking not yet proven.
Regional strategies	Methods for strengthening regional economic performance by increasing the attachment of existing enterprises and strengthening regional marketing to new investors.	Typology of strategic options and evaluation of effectiveness of alternative policy options.	Promotes idea that regional policy makers have choices but in practice policy making tends to eschew local distinctiveness in favour of copying the strategies recommended by policy gurus.

These areas of interest are not distinguished by tight boundaries, partly as there are a number of dominate perspectives, broadly referred to as 'new regionalism', that tend to influence debate in whichever context it occurs. The themes are nonetheless useful to separate as they partly identify a hierarchy of questions that can be asked of regional competitiveness and because it can assist in evaluating any specific area of concern. On this basis the remainder of the chapter gives a brief commentary of each area of investigation and then considers the implications for local economic development policy.

Regional economic performance

The immediate reasons for a region's economic performance are broadly identifiable in terms of its industry and enterprise composition, the quality and capacity of its infrastructure characteristics, workforce characteristics and ability to support growth (Box 2.1). As discussed above, such immediate regional characteristics are partly determined from outside the individual region and the networks within which regional actors operate. This being so, to sustain the importance of regional competitiveness some researchers have recognized a need to establish that the allocation of regional roles is governed by some more fundamental processes. This leads to a more searching question about the ultimate determinants of a region's current characteristics affecting its economic performance. Answers to this question can help determine whether and if so how region competitiveness can be conceptualized and shown to be a meaningful unit affecting the performance of firms in some distinctive way (Boschma 2004a: 1003). One attempt to distinguish region competitiveness on this basis makes use of ideas developed in evolutionary economics.

Box 2.1 **Components of regional competitiveness**

Gardiner *et al.* (2004) propose a 'pyramidal' model of regional competitiveness that distinguishes revealed competitiveness from the sources of competitiveness. The revealed competitiveness is a region's labour productivity and employment rate, which are taken as the direct determinants of gross regional product which, in turn, is taken to be the aspect of regional performance determining the quality and standard of living of a region's population (the targeted outcome of being a competitive region). Five sources of competitiveness are identified: research and technological development; SME development; foreign direct investment; infrastructure and human capital; and institutions and social capital. These five sources of competitiveness are themselves the product of: economic structure; innovative activity; regional accessibility; skills of the workforce; environment; decision centres; and social structure and regional culture.

Applying their model to European regions, there are large variations in regional productivity and a strong positive relationship between productivity growth and growth in per capita GDP. Over time there is little convergence in per capita GDP. Two types of region are identified: those with growth in employment and productivity and those with growth in productivity and falls in employment. Regional productivity variations are highest in high income countries. It is suggested that differences in industrial structure and specialization partly explain the variation in productivity, but that other unknown influences are important too.

It remains open to investigation whether the revealed preferences are a product of the components identified in the pyramid model. In the United Kingdom, it has been argued that most regional differences in productivity are the result of differences in industrial structure and the spatial division of labour that means the same activity can give rise to quite different types of operation according to where it places its 'high level' jobs (Fothergill 2005). The evidence for this is that productivity can vary sharply between places that are located close to each other. In high income economies with mobile resources and well developed infrastructure the obvious explanation for sharp changes in productivity over short distances is a change in the locality's economic specialization. This can also explain the persistence of regional differences in productivity as economic specializations tend to persist.

As explained by Boschma (2004a), evolutionary economics provides an interpretation of how uncertainty affects business behaviour. In the face of the inability to know how markets will develop, enterprises tend to operate on the basis of their existing practices or routines combined with experimentation along a number of 'natural trajectories' (Nelson and Winter 1982: 258). Routines are envisaged as playing the role that genes play in biological evolutionary theory: they are a persistent feature of the organism and determine its possible behaviour (although environment affects behaviour too); are inherited (for example in the characteristics of a subsidiary company or new branch plant); and are the basis for selection (some routines may be better in certain conditions than others) (Nelson and Winter 1982: 14). A broad outcome expected is that firms stay within established ways of working and adapt them incrementally in the light of their own experience and by observing and learning from the actions of other firms. Rather than enterprises seeking to predict the future, market processes select those enterprises with the 'fittest' routines to expand at the expense of less efficient firms with 'unfit' routines. Business development proceeds along narrowly defined trajectories within which organizations search for new knowledge that builds on their existing knowledge base and network of information sources. Business communities are, therefore, seen to develop according to how historical experience has shaped current routines and how well these routines fit current markets. In this way routines are envisaged to be a kind of 'organizational memory' that is embedded in the skills of employees, its working practices and fixed capital.

Boschma (2004a) argues that the incremental learning process of individual enterprises has a parallel imprint on regions. Just as enterprises carry the legacy of past investment and experience so can regions. Indeed history may be especially significant for regions as they continue to exist whatever their economic fortunes, whereas individual enterprises can be liquidated and their memory erased. This is argued to make it meaningful to discuss regional competitiveness in the sense that 'actors and organizations are embedded in a territorial context that determines largely their behaviour and level of performance' (Boschma 2004a: 1005).

The evolutionary view of regional competitiveness assumes that enterprises adapt their routines mainly through the influence of locally obtained knowledge and by copying neighbouring enterprises. If enterprises draw on a wide range of knowledge sources it lessens the possibility of a distinctive regional experience. The assumption that learning is a highly localized process is controversial, being mainly based on indirect indicators and theoretical assumptions (see Chapter 4). While acknowledging this debate, Boschma endorses the view that firms in the vicinity of knowledge sources are the most likely to benefit from the knowledge that is given out. It is imagined, for example, that knowledge can be absorbed locally by informal connections rather than requiring specific transactions. It is also explained by receptivity: local firms are more receptive to knowledge arising within each other than are firms that do not share a similar history. Further reinforcing the localization of learning it is assumed that a specific institutional environment will arise that helps to coordinate the actions within and between individual enterprises. This will partly take the form of specialized services to business such as research institutions, education and training facilities and finance companies. It is also envisaged as taking the form of a common culture and shared expectations that helps to regulate and facilitate cooperation and interaction among regional actors.

It is recognized that countervailing forces work against the smooth evolution of separate regional experiences. Too much intra-regional connection and receptivity risks locking a region into a pattern of working that becomes inefficient, while extra-regional connections can reduce regional distinctiveness. Connections to entities outside the region give access to a variety of knowledge sources and the possibility of acquiring novel insights, but this also erodes regional distinctiveness if regions copy from each other. It is assumed that these challenges do not overwhelm regional differences but rather become a source of diversity as individual regions balance internal integration with the need for external connection. Different regional trajectories are expected with respect to the types of organization participating in the regional economy, how knowledge is transmitted and diffused through the area, which institutions arise, how they evolve and how they affect business development (Boschma 2004a: 1008).

Drawing on Evangelista *et al.* (2002), the case of Italy is referred to as an illustration of the way distinctive regional environments can be produced within the same national space, each of which has a continued legacy in shaping future development capacities and opportunities.

- The north of Italy is mainly characterized as a science-based system focused on large firms with a high amount of research and development effort and strong capability to innovate.
- Central Italy or the so-called 'Third Italy' is characterized by strong learning systems at the level of industrial districts. These districts are seen to be based upon informal and loosely structured relationships between mainly small and medium sized organizations that collectively provide a strongly basis for learning.

- The south of Italy is characterized as backward and vulnerable with poor internal capacity to grow and a high dependency on external knowledge. The weak integration of economic actors within this part of Italy is ascribed to an institutional environment lacking in social capital.

The Italian example is open to question (Box 2.2) but it at least shows how an evolutionary perspective on regional competitiveness does not lead to the identification of a superior or optimal model. The north and centre of Italy provide high levels of innovative performance relative to the south but based on different competitive environments, each of which has a particular mix of strong and weak components. Applying evolutionary economics to regional competitiveness, therefore, questions whether there are ready-made blueprints that can be applied to strengthen regional economic performance. Regional policies are not expected to be effective if local strategies deviate from the regional context to which they are applied, and this leads to a recommendation for 'bottom-up' policy that addresses weaknesses and gaps in the region's institutional environment.

Box 2.2 **Regions within regions**

New regionalism and accounts of regional competitiveness based on absolute advantage are influenced by interpretations of Italy's industrial districts. An archetypal industrial district comprising many small scale enterprises that compete and collaborate while drawing on collective industry resources is envisaged. In practice, this is based on an idealized interpretation of some districts at one point in time. Over time the small scale flexible capitalism that once characterized some districts has been challenged by the search for market growth in the context of competition from low cost countries and changing local contexts, including the increasing use of immigrant labour in place of an indigenous workforce. Efforts to strengthen innovation have been one response, but loss of competitiveness and restructuring through mergers and acquisition has been another and this has resulted in vertically integrated large enterprises.

Source: Perry (1999); Eraydin (2001); Hadjimichalis (2006)

Evolutionary perspectives have become influential as a basis for discussing how regions change and provide different contexts for business development (see Sunley 2000). The extension of ideas developed originally to understand how enterprises cope with uncertainty to an interpretation of regional competitiveness is nonetheless problematic. People and enterprises migrate and local businesses are frequently absorbed into national and international organizations with the consequence that regional distinctiveness is weakened. As in the case of the Third Italy the assumption that localized experiences have a long history may not be justified (Box 2.3). Moreover, while it is possible to identify some broad differences across Italy most countries comprise regions that seem to lack any particular distinctiveness and are consequently hard to categorize (see Crouch *et al.* 2001). Even where regions become associated with a particular specialization this may just produce a clustering of like enterprises rather than having any larger regional significance (see Chapter 5). Finally, there is also difficulty in defining boundaries to the reach of regional institutions and business cultures and no certainty that they overlap with the boundaries of policy-making regional bodies.

Box 2.3 **Studied trust**

Studied trust refers to cases where current trustful environments arise in localities without any tradition of high trust relations between business owners. Instead of embedded culture, studied trust relies on sufficient members of the contemporary business population having a motive for wanting to trust each other. Some historical association might be identified to explain present behaviour but this reflects the present day interest in trust rather than any real impact of the past. Studied trust arises where there is a functional need for trust and it is consistent with making provisions for a time when trust may become less necessary. It is not a breach of studied trust to make provision for the possibility that trust might be broken. This may involve arranging for 'shadow' suppliers in the event of one relationship breaking down.

Source: Sabel (1992)

Regional absolute advantage

Explanations of how regions obtain an absolute advantage share much underlying theory with the evolutionary perspective. They differ in suggesting that a specific set of organizing principles will produce higher economic performance. This claim is potentially important except that there is no known way of replicating the regional characteristics believed to give an absolute advantage. Nonetheless it merits explanation as the model has been given credence by regional economists and it draws on ideas that are widely accepted (Kitson *et al.* 2004).

In trade theory, to have an absolute advantage means to be better at something than any other entity to a degree that limits anyone else's participation in the activity. It can be compared with comparative advantage, which refers to the relative efficiency with which different activities are performed. In this case places differ by a matter of degree and specializations are explained by what is best performed in any individual locality. International trade theory is built on the idea of comparative advantage partly as it deals with a context where countries with varying levels of economic wealth continue to participate in international trade. There is a case for arguing that regions need a different basis for economic development than a country. In the wake of an economic shock, regions may stagnate and gradually lose productive resources rather than retain a capacity to shift to their 'next best' activities. Camagni (2002) argues that regions have potential to acquire an absolute advantage by developing superior technological, social, infrastructural or institutional assets that are external to individual firms but which benefit them nonetheless. Hence competitiveness is a regional process as it depends on collectively utilized assets rather than just arising from a concentration of individually productive and innovative enterprises. Given difficulty in replicating collective resources, lower input costs in another location (such as lower wage and property costs) are not a threat to the survival of the enterprises or an inducement to relocate.

Linked to this larger paradigm Camagni (2002: 2405) identifies three dimensions to a region that affects the ability of enterprises to operate competitively:

- The concentration of local technological externalities: with the assumption that proximity influences the ability to access and utilize technological expertise, regions benefit from the local presence of agencies variously engaged in supporting technological development.
- The density and quality of economic and social relations: high reliance on external assets that cannot be accessed through market transactions makes inter-personal, informal exchanges important to the transfer of information and learning. Attributes facilitating a high density of productive interaction include shared values, a strong sense of belonging, trust, common professional background and economic specialization.
- Local governance: management and administrative processes can vary in the extent to which they bring together representatives of private and public sector bodies and encourage a collective approach to problem solving and coordinated investment in regional infrastructure and productive assets. Industrial organization is a part of this dimension in terms of the extent of value-chain integration.

These dimensions are consistent with the wider tendency to explain regional growth and development as an outcome of 'soft' externalities as compared with physical infrastructure and natural endowments such as mineral resources. A key proposition is that enterprises that rely on learning things for themselves or through purposely constructed relationships are at a significant disadvantage to those whose learning comes through informal, unplanned and direct exchanges with other enterprises and agencies. Learning processes developing outside the individual firm but inside a local labour market operate through labour mobility, a high density of customer–supplier relationships and professional networks. They are seen to be of peculiar value in combining the insight of multiple parties, sharing knowledge and allowing for tacit learning processes to occur (Camagni 2002). Getting to a position where these external mechanisms uplift enterprise performance requires a concentration of inter-connected enterprise, a willingness among entrepreneurs to cooperate with each other (that does not lessen competitive rivalry) and public agency investment in appropriate collective resources. On this basis, localities are argued to possess competitive advantages in the sense that they can foster the development of externalities among co-located enterprises.

This account is presented as a larger interest in innovative milieu promoted by the GREMI research group of mainly European scholars chaired by Camagni. The mission of GREMI has been to identify the attributes of already innovative environments with its findings stressing the importance of collective learning processes (see Camagni 1991). Camagni (2002) does not give specific examples of regions with the attributes that are claimed to generate an absolute advantage. Similarly, the attainment of the model attributes is said to be assisted by 'imaginative and proactive public administration' but the nature of this intervention is not explained (Camagni 2002: 2405). The argument is focused on the attributes possessed by a high performing region and gives little or no guidance as to what actions are needed when in the process of building an absolute advantage. This neglect may reflect uncertainty that absolute advantage can be designed for as compared with it being the outcome of fortuitous circumstances. Processes are depicted as operating spontaneously as advantages build upon each other and it is acknowledged that this depends upon conditions that are rare (Camagni 2002: 2407). One conclusion, therefore, is that this version of regional competitiveness may help understand some places associated with new areas of technology but that it has no wider significance.

Regional environments for competitive enterprise

A third approach to regional competitiveness starts from an understanding of what drives the competitive advantage of individual enterprises and then considers how regional environments can be configured to support enterprise competitiveness. The most influential set of ideas in this area is linked to Michael Porter and his explanation of how the competitiveness of firms is linked to the organization of industries and the characteristics of nations. Porter (1990) argues that competition is ultimately between firms but that countries have competitive advantage in specific industries and industry segments. This is a product of the way that national characteristics influence entire industries or segments of industries rather than being captured exclusively by individual enterprises. Consequently, his theory of what determines competitive advantage makes industry the prime unit of analysis. Nations, he argues, succeed not in isolated industries but in clusters of industries connected through vertical and horizontal relationships (Porter 1990: 73). Nonetheless, there is overlap with regional development because industry clusters can be concentrated in a region, and he suggests that such geographical concentration strengthens industry competitiveness. Thus he has argued more recently that a nation's most competitive industries are likely to exist in geographical clusters (Porter 2000).

In Porter's diamond model, local conditions shape industry competitiveness mainly through four attributes:

- Factor conditions, such as a specialized labour pool, specialized infrastructure, and sometimes selective disadvantages that drive innovation to overcome these adversities.
- Home demand, or demanding local customers who push companies to innovate, especially if their tastes or needs anticipate global or local demand.
- Related and supporting industries, internationally competitive local supplier industries who create business infrastructure and spur innovation and spin-off industries.

- Industry strategy, structure, and rivalry, intense local rivalry among local industries that is more motivating than foreign competition, and a local 'culture' which influences attitudes within individual industries to innovation and competition.

This model relies on enterprises having a 'home base'; a location in which their essential competitive advantages are created and sustained, including the most productive jobs and core technologies (Porter 1990: 19). Home-base activities are expected to stimulate other linked domestic industries and help to define the geographical region on which competitive advantage is built. This claim is relatively unproblematic in the sense that even large multinational corporations tend to retain a home country affiliation in which key decision making, research and development and production facilities are concentrated (Dicken 2007). International companies frequently operate with a home-country bias when allocating investment and rationalizing existing facilities (Birkinshaw and Ridderstråle 1999). The claim has proved more problematic for high income resource-based economies such as Australia, Canada and New Zealand (Yetton *et al.* 1992; Dunning 1993). Prominent exporters from these countries frequently pursue strategies of offshore production and value adding so as to process commodities close to their end buyers. Home-country attributes may play a lesser role in the competitiveness of these exporters than the success of their overseas subsidiaries. This complication is reconcilable with Porter's original model by extending it to a 'double diamond' or 'multiple diamond' to include the influence of overseas operations. Two more fundamental criticisms are a greater challenge to Porter's ideas.

First, the diamond model offers an ex ante explanation of the sources of industry advantage but it lacks the ability to isolate characteristics that predict the creative forces which lie behind the formation of successful, integrated regional economies. This point has been raised as a weakness in Porter's interpretations of cluster advantage, including by one of his former collaborators, Michael Enright (Glasmeier 2000: 567). A similar conclusion was reached and made more simply in a study that compared a sample of 'new Silicon Valleys' with the original Valley (Bresnahan *et al.* 2001). The idea of this study was to see whether replication of similar industry conditions enabled late comers to catch up with the California's Silicon Valley. It was found that a large gap in performance tended to persist, indicating that competitiveness is affected by first-mover advantages as well as home-base conditions. As well, the study highlighted how many of the advantages thought to accrue to an industry cluster are not able to exist at the outset of a concentration. There are not, for example, other firms around in sufficient numbers to gain mutual advantage from. This implies that the factors identified in the diamond model should be seen more as the outcome of a competitive industry in a region rather than being the factors that explain why the industry was successful. A case study of Finland's success in telecommunications illustrates this point (Box 2.4).

Box 2.4 Nordic telecommunications: more than a diamond

Porter's diamond model has been seen to fit Finland's and Nokia's success in telecommunications (Table B2.1). Such rationalization does not explain how these mutually reinforcing attributes came about. Looking at the larger Nordic participation in telecommunications, a particular technological and regional context needs to be acknowledged.

Table B2.1 Porter's diamond and Nokia

Factor conditions	Liberalization of the capital market and the Telecommunications Services Act 1987 promotes venture capital and foreign investment and facilitates private sector access to the mobile communications.
Demand conditions	By the end of the 1990s a fifth of Finish households use mobile telephones. A strong home market enables product and service experimentation.
Related industries	Presence of supporting industries specialized in telecommunications development allows Nokia to build 300 business partnerships in Finland.
Industry conditions	The least developed component of the diamond: mobile phone production starts in Finland in the 1970s with four competitors; by the early 1980s, this had reduced to Nokia and Ericsson, the Swedish telecommunications conglomerate.

Source: Maskell *et al.* (1998); Paija (2001)

Telecommunications drew on electro-mechanical technology rather than being an entirely new industry. Nokia's expertise came from acquisitions of a television company (Salora, established 1928), the Finnish Cable Works (Suomen Kaapelitehdas, founded 1917) and the State Electric Works (Valtion Sähköpaja, established 1925). The ability to use 'off-the-shelf' components further assisted the shift to telecommunications. As components got progressively cheaper and more plentiful Nokia added new models and features to grow demand. The first mobile phone systems fitted Nordic conditions in being most effective when serving comparatively small numbers of subscribers over large geographical distances. Cross-border cooperation in industry development gave a Nordic producer further advantage. Cooperation required the setting of standards for technology still at an early stage of development. The launch of the Nordic Mobile Telephone (NMT) system in 1981 increased the size of the market for equipment suppliers and gave a platform that Nordic firms were able to exploit when the GSM standard was introduced in 1992. The particular effectiveness of public–private 'development pairs' was another Nordic advantage as it facilitated the integration of equipment manufacturers and network operators. Being small countries, personal connections between individuals on 'different sides of the table' assisted collaboration that would not easily arise in 'normal' market economies.

Second, the diamond model was first developed to explain national competitiveness and subsequently the ideas have been applied to regional industry clusters. In making this transition it becomes necessary to determine how much of the national industry needs to be present in a region for it to be claimed to be a cluster in its own right as compared with being part of a larger constellation of resources (Martin and Sunley 2003). The Harvard cluster-mapping project has been developed to provide further guidance to economic development agencies on the existing and potential clusters in their territory (Porter 2003). This project is based on identifying 'cluster templates' (see Chapter 5). These templates aim to identify which 'traded' industries tend to share a location because of mutual advantages to the co-locating activities. Regional agencies might use the templates to help identify which clusters are strongly represented in their territory and prioritize their development on the grounds that the region is an important home-base for the cluster. Alternatively, where only a fragment of a cluster is represented in a region there is guidance on what industries might be encouraged to locate in the locality based on their ties to the part of the cluster that is already present. Supplemented by local investigations to support the conjectures of cluster maps, these are potentially powerful economic development tools although their effectiveness has yet to be proven.

A key assumption of the Harvard cluster mapping is that co-location reflects functional ties or at least some common dependencies between industries. In this respect it is important to recognize how the Harvard approach to mapping clusters relies on attributes that are more likely to be a feature of a geographically and economically large country such as the USA, where the methodology was devised (Porter 2003). The key requirement is for a sufficient diversity of economic activity in a large number of distinct locations. If too many locations have no or little representation in an industry, all other locations will be registered as having high concentrations. Location correlations might then simply indicate a tendency for activity to favour a few locations rather than industry interdependencies. Even in the USA this problem arises. Industries with a major presence in large employment states like California and New York can register a high location correlation without any common interests actually existing between them. Within large states, correlated industries may be separated geographically and have few mutual externalities. The researchers are aware of this problem and report that judgemental adjustments are made to the statistical results to try and minimize spurious location correlations. Nonetheless the tendency to capture shared location preferences rather than interdependencies is suggested by the nature of the character of the nine largest industry clusters (Table 2.2). These clusters encompass activities for which proximity to a large population, transport infrastructure and resource availability are potential influences on location rather than intra-cluster linkages. The tendency for most traded industries to belong to multiple broad clusters provides another source of doubt about the extent to which the Harvard method succeeds in separating linked activity. Activity that is simultaneously associated with many other activities suggests the operation of urbanization economies rather than localization economies, or that the level of analysis does not identify sufficient detail to separate clusters.

Table 2.2 Employment in the top 9 of 41 'narrow' industry clusters in the Harvard Cluster Map, 2000

Cluster	Employment 2000	Share (%) of all traded cluster employment
Business services	4,667,320	13.3
Financial services	3,242,151	9.2
Hospitality and tourism	2,565,077	7.3
Education and knowledge creation	2,246,974	6.4
Distribution services	1,962,523	5.6
Heavy construction services	1,883,271	5.3
Transport and logistics	1,644,641	4.7
Metal manufacturing	1,412,368	4.0
Processed food	1,388,073	3.9
All traded clusters	35,028,441	59.7

Source: Porter (2003)

Benchmarking competitiveness

From the perspective that competitiveness is about the relative performance of different entities, benchmarking the strengths and weaknesses of regions has become a popular aspect of regional economic policy (Huggins 2003, 2009). The basic rationale is that it is meaningful for a region to compare itself with others in order to assess the suitability of its strategy and whether or not current policy is addressing the right problems and agencies. Huggins (2009: 4) suggests that benchmarking can be used in three ways: designing and monitoring regional economic development and its progress; facilitating the exchange and gathering of knowledge on regional practices and policies; promoting the image and attractiveness of regional economies. Most takes the form of performance benchmarking where the key decisions are the selection of indicators to compare and the choice of regions to benchmark against.

The indicators encompassed by regional performance benchmarking are typically influenced by the perceived desirability of increasing participation in the knowledge economy (Malecki 2007). This emphasizes indicators such as research and development expenditure, patent applications, specialization in high technology industries, size of the scientific workforce, presence of research institutions and new technology incubators. The choice of regions against which to benchmark may target those judged to be at a similar level of development, a set of regions with whom there is agreement to improve cooperation and linkage, regions sharing some common characteristic or regions that it is an aspiration to emulate because of their perceived success.

Performance benchmarking can be seen as a form of regional stocktaking that can identify comparative strengths and weaknesses at one point in time. Advocates of benchmarking believe that its purpose should be greater than this if insight is to be gained into how to change a region's status. In this context Huggins (2009) sees the need for process and policy making benchmarking. Process benchmarking is intended to give insight into how a region operates. For example, a performance benchmarking study might record the rate of research commercialization while a process benchmark will aim to explain why the rate is not higher or lower.

Policy benchmarking aims to help regional authorities identify policies and strategies that may usefully inform their future policy selection. This ideally enables policy selection informed by an understanding of administrative requirements and evidence of effectiveness rather than copying on the basis of superficial evidence and the perceived prestige of policy, as some allege tends to occur at present (Lovering 2003). Huggins (2009) identifies some attempts at process and policy benchmarking but recognizes that these forms of benchmarking are relatively rare and that the methodologies are underdeveloped. Policy making certainly stands to benefit from improved understanding of what works (Box 2.5) but the challenges in developing evidence-based policy are considerable and beyond the scope of benchmarking studies to resolve (Pawson 2006).

Box 2.5 Hard time for hard networks

During the 1990s, the Danish Technological Institute (DTI) promoted its 'hard networks' programme to economic development agencies in Australia (Bureau of Industry Economics, 1995), the United Kingdom (Chaston 1996) and other European countries (OECD 1995). The scheme was based on using business consultants employed as independent network brokers to identify business network opportunities, recruit members and facilitate their activity. The idea was that this would allow collections of small enterprises that combined expertise to compete with large enterprises. Evidence of the programme being taken up in other countries, the apparent fit with the small business dominance of the New Zealand economy plus a small scale trial convinced Trade New Zealand to bring the programme to New Zealand.

New Zealand's hard network programme ran from 1994 to 1999. Efforts to trace impacts of the scheme in 2000 failed to reveal any surviving networks. The assumption behind the programme was that small firms would wish to join a network because it would be easier and less risky than entering export markets alone. The motivations of people in business and the difficulty of maintaining agreement over inputs and returns from a venture on which individual participants have differing degrees of dependence were overlooked. The scheme relied on the ability and energy of brokers to build networks. New Zealand's programme relied on part time brokers with a main occupation as an accountant, management consultant or other professional. Broker interest in the scheme tended to lapse quickly as the extent of the challenge became recognized and the option of falling back on their other activities existed.

Closer investigation of the Danish experience with its own hard network programme might have forewarned of the likely failure in New Zealand. In Denmark, networks received an average public subsidy of over US$260,000 (Henriksen 1995; OECD 1995: 90), whereas in New Zealand the maximum subsidy available was about a tenth of this amount. In Denmark, once public subsidies were withdrawn networks rapidly ceased to function (Huggins 1996; Amphion Report 1996). An evaluation linked to the DTI programme concluded that attempting to accelerate cooperation among businesses that have little prior familiarity with each other was likely to be fraught with 'serious problems' (Henriksen 1995: 259). Getting small firms to cooperate is highly problematic wherever you are.

Source: Perry (2007a)

An evolutionary interpretation of regional competitiveness is at odds with the use of regional benchmarking (Boschma 2004a: 1010). The value of benchmarking is circumscribed by the variability of regional environments and the absence of any optimum model of regional development. Variability means that there is limited scope to transfer learning across regions as each region tends to have a specific context to its development experiences. Imitation of exemplar regions is not viable as development experiences are viewed as having deep roots rather than emerging from immediate sources of influence alone. Even attempting the transfer of one part of another region's innovation system is unlikely to succeed because competencies and institutional environments must be shared as well as organizational structures (Boschma 2004a: 1011). These types of doubt over benchmarking rely on an extreme view of the uniqueness of regional economic environments and overlook the possibility of some customization of development efforts. There is more in the criticism that benchmarking risks the replication of policy targets given that this is something that has occurred, particularly with the promotion of business clusters (Hospers 2006).

Optimism exists that benchmarking can be developed into a tool that will be used to inform regional policy development (Huggins 2009). It has been claimed that regional benchmarking has produced increasingly sophisticated policy making and that it is giving increased understanding of the way that regions develop (Malecki 2007). Such claims overlook the fact that most benchmarking is limited to the performance variety and at best results in the measurement of points of difference (Arrowsmith *et al.* 2004). Rather than verification of the accuracy, the main evidence for effectiveness seems to be the increasing frequency of studies and the supposition rather than actual demonstration that they improve policy making. Critical commentaries on regional benchmarking are mindful that a policy tool leading to various forms of league table can have unintended as well as intended outcomes (Bristow 2005; Hospers 2006; Boland 2007; Greene *et al.* 2007). Where individual indicators are combined into composite scores there may be a loss of insight compared with using original data (Box 2.6). Attention may be drawn to changing the standing in a league table to the detriment of addressing economic development opportunities that do not have potential to shift the region's position. It is an ideal that policy making responds objectively to what the evidence shows and that evidence is not interpreted to suit preconceived agendas. The policy making environment needs to change as well as the forms of benchmarking exercise undertaken if this aid to strengthening regional competitiveness is to reach the potential looked for by supporters.

Box 2.6 Tests for benchmarks

A number of guidelines can be employed to test whether regional competitiveness scores are more than an exercise in bogus quantification:

- Is there agreement over the construction of the index score and objective criteria to determine which factors contribute to regional competitiveness

and how the influence of the individual factors on the final score should be weighted?
- Does the index score report something more than what was already known from the information gathered to construct the index?
- Does the index result increase the understanding of the relative status of a locality compared with qualitative descriptions such as the 'region is distinguished by the availability of skilled workers and depth of industry expertise'?
- Would an index score reporting an unexpected status for a locality lead to a changed perception of the region or to questions over the accuracy of the index construction?

Regional strategies

Regional competition exists in the form of marketing campaigns and efforts to enhance the attributes of regions that are thought likely to help retain and attract business investments and skilled workers. One perspective on this activity views it as an effort to promote distinctiveness to increase local prosperity (Turok 2009). This idea draws on discussions of business competitiveness that conventionally distinguish cost and differentiation strategies as the basic approaches to building enterprise advantages. In a similar way it has been suggested that regions can choose between a low and high road to regional competitiveness (Malecki 2004).

The low road is equated with competition on the basis of low wages, the absence of labour regulation, lax environmental controls and low taxes, and in Malecki's account is associated with southern states in the USA. The high road is equated with efforts to encourage entrepreneurship and technology-based economic development, and among the localities considered to have pioneered this approach are industrial districts in Italy and Denmark and 'new economy' clusters in various parts of the USA and Europe, some of which he considers to have been 'policy led'. While these places vary greatly in the nature and scale of their economic success, imitation of high road development is considered more difficult than following the low road. Distinctiveness as discussed by Turok (2009) is consistent with the high road as it is viewed as a way localities build their economy around activities and resources that are not open to easy imitation. Moreover, as differentiation can be built on any range of attributes, indigenous capabilities and relationships are a viable starting point.

Four broad sources of differentiation are identified that vary according to the extent to which they encompass tangible or intangible attributes and the extent to which attributes are amenable to policy influence within the investment horizon of development agencies. The schema aims to encompass the components that are included in competitive strategies or are potentially under the influence of policy intervention. It does not purport to include all sources of difference between places, and while the framework was developed for assessing urban competitiveness it seems to be a good starting point for commenting on place competitiveness more broadly.

- Tangible and slow to change: the industries and major enterprises found in a locality are manifest features of the economy that typically change slowly. Localities tend to have particular mixes of activity, including some with a long attachment as well as representation of newer industries. Industries vary in their requirements for local supporting industries, their reliance on local resources and the types of employment provided.
- Intangible and slow to change: labour force characteristics are considered intangible because skills encompass tacit understandings, experience and soft behaviours as well as objective characteristics such as qualifications and occupational categories. These intangible aspects are seen to underpin the requirements for effectiveness in occupations which are of growing importance to business competitiveness because they draw on creativity and design awareness.
- Tangible and amenable to change: the built environment and amenities encompassing functional infrastructure, public spaces and consumption activities generate distinctiveness through their quality, aesthetic appearance and user populations. Environmental impact, design features, capacity and availability to users are among the ways of distinguishing the built environment.
- Intangible and amenable to change: image and reputation affect the willingness to reside, work, study and utilize the services of any locality. Subjective considerations are formed from the historic associations of places, the perceptions of dominant institutions, physical environmental features and reactions to current events and media coverage. This can lead to assessments of the attractiveness of places deviating from what actual objective conditions suggest are merited (Ashworth and Voogd 1988). Place promotion strategies aim to close this gap and enhance reputations to at least ensure that objective conditions are recognized appropriately.

Different issues are raised over the effectiveness of intervention in each of the four areas. Action designed to influence the industry and enterprise composition of the economy is generally advised to focus on tradeable sectors that do not rely exclusively on local markets. This once encouraged a manufacturing bias but in high income economies manufacturing has ceased to be the engine of employment growth that it once was. A government office, a call centre, a tourist attraction, a bank or a university are now all potential drivers of local economic development (Fothergill 2005). Promotion strategies are frequently inclined to emphasize new, technology-based activity over older sectors despite reasons to question the benefits to local economies of pursuing high tech industries (Box 2.7). More broadly, regional strategies need to balance the considerations pointing to the building of a more specialized economy versus the encouragement of a diversified economic base. This topic is given further consideration in Chapter 5, with the key point being that most evidence points to economic advantage residing more with diversified than specialized economies in terms of their ability to sustain employment and income growth. The lesson of history is that specialized economies can find it hard to adapt to changes in technologies and markets and that regions can experience extended periods of slow decline as a consequence. Nonetheless, promotion strategies are frequently advised to focus on specialized sectors or broader clusters of related activity rather than on promoting diversification.

Box 2.7 **High tech illusions**

The gains to a regional economy from high technology industry tend to be overestimated and the costs may be considerable although they are partly indirect and hidden. High technology is valuable in leading to a re-structured economy that is based more on processing information than was industry of old. This impact emerges outside the high tech sector itself, which is directly of employment significance only when looking at rates of employment change rather than absolute impacts. The proportional growth in high technology employment can be high because it starts from a small base. High technology industries are imagined to employ only highly qualified and well remunerated employees, but in practice can rely on large amounts of factory work that is susceptible to relocation to cheap-labour countries. The products of high tech industry risk facilitating jobless growth in other sectors. Many high tech firms fail, most survive with marginal viability and few achieve instant success. Environmental impacts and working conditions can be poor. Policy interventions often fail to work because of misplaced assumptions that high technology is a single industry with uniform requirements. Government incentives for high technology are frequently no more than subsidies that shelter industry from competition.

Source: Macdonald (1987)

Partly through the impact of demographic changes and a period of high employment growth prior to the world financial crisis of 2008, there has been increasing attention on the attraction and retention of skilled workers as a basis for building regional advantage. Some regional analysts go as far as suggesting that it is now more meaningful to evaluate regional economies through their occupational structure than their industry structure, as has been the traditional priority (Box 2.8). As well as to overcome recruitment constraints, shifting attention to occupational groups and people with particular qualifications provides a way of strengthening many activities that share common skill needs. This may bring bigger benefits than investing equivalent effort in attracting individual employers to the region. The possibility of success is encouraged by the perception that skilled and creative professionals are increasingly motivated to move to where their employment and lifestyle aspirations are most satisfied. One influential thesis is that key professionals are distinguished by their need to exercise creativity at work and a strong preference to live in places which give access to other creative people and activities (see Chapter 6). As people are more likely to move to where jobs are already available, prioritizing labour mobility over the attraction of enterprises has limits. In the extreme it may even damage place reputations if highly qualified workers are brought to places without work available for them (Turok and Bailey 2004). A factor that can also be overlooked is that much employment is now in multi location organizations that rely on an internal workforce as well as externally recruited employees.

Box 2.8 People before jobs or jobs before people?

Markusen (2004) argues that it is now more effective for development agencies to target their promotional efforts on occupations rather than employers.

- Economic activity has become more footloose and consequently local economic development must rely on unique skill sets and talents to encourage enterprises to stay in their territory; but labour is highly mobile and so development agencies need to focus on protecting their region's key resource.
- It may be hard for employers to discern workforce qualities; public agencies working with occupational groups can signal attributes valued by new and existing employers.
- Individuals now have more commitment to their occupation than their employer. To retain its labour pool regions must offer occupational groups access to training and information networks that facilitate career building and mobility between employers.
- Industries are increasingly based on generic skill sets so that one occupational group is employed across many sectors.
- New firm formation varies more strongly between occupational groups than industry groups and so enterprise start up initiatives should target selected occupations.
- Individuals can work remotely from their employer and workers are more committed to their locality than firms are.
- Employment outcomes for minority groups and groups experiencing high underemployment are best addressed through occupational initiatives.

Against these possibilities there are grounds to argue that industries and enterprises should continue to be the main focus of economic development agency work.

- Long distance migration of people of working age is governed by the availability of employment opportunities if not being a direct response to a job offer or a request by their employer to relocate.
- The regional economic multiplier of a single job is considerably less than the multiplier of a single employer.
- The increased externalization of business services means that shared occupational groups tend to concentrate in specialized businesses that supply many sectors rather than occupations dispersing across all industries.
- Industries continue to develop their own work patterns, social conventions, areas of expertise and industry-specific networks; this reduces the ability and interest of many workers to shift between industries.
- Many people of working age are unable or unwilling to relocate and their participation in the workforce depends on bringing employment to them.
- Occupational groups frequently have no local collective organization or entity; large employers can provide locations with identity, sponsorship of community initiatives, national and international connections and support for economic development.

- Offsite home-based work remains a small share of the labour market and mainly involves people within commuting distance of a central office to facilitate interaction with co-workers and managers.
- Outside unusual industry-specialized labour markets such as Silicon Valley, job tenure has changed little and most employers continue to rely on low levels of labour turnover for the effectiveness of their business.

The built environment has significance to economic development in at least three ways. It provides infrastructure to facilitate economic activity in the form of transport facilities, waste management, work space, health facilities and other necessary resources; it can be associated with iconic buildings and spaces that are designed to increase the appeal and awareness of a place; directly, investment in the built environment is a source of employment and the way that changes in the built environment are managed can affect the survival of economic activities in locations that are redeveloped. Good quality infrastructure facilitating physical and electronic communication is generally recognized as a feature of the most successful economies (Boddy and Parkinson 2004: 426). One of the challenges for urban economies has been in finding sufficient space to accommodate remaining manufacturing workers. Declining employment densities imply a need for larger and larger areas of factory space to keep the same number of people employed (Fothergill et al. 1987). Flagship urban developments tend to get most attention as an aspect of the built environment that can give distinctiveness to a place. They can be seen as symbolic of larger urban achievements and intentions, be used to accommodate cultural resources and events and to provide places of consumption that will draw visitors from a wide area (Imrie and Thomas 1999). Depending on where these developments are located and the extent to which they draw resources away from addressing the concerns of local populations, flagship projects have frequently been sources of controversy (Foster 1999). Encouraging the renewal of rundown neighbourhoods requires management of the consequences of gentrification in terms of the displacement of economic activities dependent on the unimproved environment and the risks of property speculation, encouraging over development based on unrealistic expectations of continued rises in property values (Curran 2007).

Attention to reputation and image building is associated with the development of place branding and events promotion such as the hosting of festivals and major sporting competitions. It is generally accepted that human decision making is based on judgement heuristics and biases that include a tendency to be influenced by the ease of recalling events or messages irrespective of their accuracy (Tversky and Kahneman 1973, 1974). In this context and encouraged by media representations, stereotypical images tend to persist over many social issues including the perception of places. An additional argument for place promotion is that the qualities of a locality are hard to identify prior to a decision to make some form of commitment to going or investing there. A brand and associated marketing imagery and slogans can help to distil the essence of a place and reduce the barrier to generating interest in the locality (Anholt 2007). The division of places among communities with different experiences and expectations and the lack of control over what individual communities say and do are among the difficulties in transferring branding and advertising techniques to places. Identifying a truly shared vision is a problem for cities that is even greater for a larger region with more potential for inconsistent agendas (Wilkinson 1992). In practice, place promotion tends to have a selective focus that might variously target inward investors, tourism or a segment of the local population. The ability to change perceptions is increased where place promotion extends to the sponsorship of events and investment in real assets that can influence the image of a place, at least among some people (Strom 2002). Individual sporting or cultural events may have only a short lived impact on what people think of a place but events that become a regular fixture can play a role in changing a locality's image as well as bringing direct economic benefits (Smith and Fox 2007). Place promotion has some impact when it affects observable reality. It is criticized for trying to disguise real conditions that deter local commitment to the locality and discourage new activity, but advertising strategies are generally focused on promoting awareness of positive attributes, believing that this can start to change how people think about a place.

A reflection on these four areas of activity is that distinctiveness can be pursued in many different ways. In contrast a frequent evaluation is that there is a strong tendency for places to follow similar strategies (Hospers 2006). The tendency to policy replication has led to questioning of who actually develops regional strategies, for whom and with what outcomes (Lovering 1999, 2003). Recent decades have seen the growth of economic development professionals, policy makers and practitioners engaged in setting and implementing new regional policy agendas. Collectively, this new set of policy makers has been referred to as the 'regional service class' (Lovering 1999, 2003). Previously, regional policy had largely been under the control of central government officials with comparatively little local participation beyond the staffing of decentralized offices of national agencies. As a relatively new grouping they lack experience, confidence and resources to develop original responses to their individual situations. Lovering (2003) suggests that this has made the regional service class particularly susceptible to the advocacy of policy gurus (see Chapter 1). In the absence of economic entities for which regions are a significant scale of operation, regional policy makers tend to operate in a vacuum rather than interacting with an engaged constituency of business interests. Without local input policy makers have sought legitimacy for their actions by engaging the guidance of international policy gurus and following strategies that promise to emulate the experience of other places (Lovering 2003: 55). Among these policy gurus particular influence has been attained by Michael Porter, whose ideas have been taken up around the world and applied to widely different types of regional economy. As others point out, this diffusion gives a misleading impression of the extent to which effective policy can be based on a strategy of emulating regional success stories (Box 2.9).

Box 2.9 **A valley too far**

Local economic policy ideas are frequently based on the enthusiastic borrowing of perceived best practice rather than detailed understanding of what works when. The aspiration to imitate Silicon Valley is a pronounced case of policy imitation. In the United Kingdom, there is Motorsport Valley; in France, the Paris Optics Valley and the Mechanic Valley in Midi Pyrénées; in Belgium, Flanders Multimedia Valley and DSP Valley (microelectronics); in Germany, Materials Valley in the Rhein-Main area; in Sweden, Strängäs Biotech Valley and Dalarna Crystal Valley; in Denmark, Medicon Valley; in Poland, Plastics valley; in Lithuania, Sunrise Valley (lasers); in Japan, Sweet Valley (software).

Rose (1993) identified seven contingencies affecting the likely success of transferring policy experience between countries:

- The policy does not address a problem unique to the location where it developed.
- Sufficient resources exist (financial, human and regulatory) to replicate the policy design.
- The programme does not depend on institutions unique to one locality.
- The policy initiative is not as complex as when it works through the coordination of many separate elements.
- The scale of change envisaged is minor.
- There is some interdependency between the original location and the place where it is attempted to replicate the programme.
- The policy is consistent with the values of policy makers.

Hospers (2006) reclassifies these preconditions into necessary, structure-based and culture-based contingencies and argues that, when applied to regional policy initiatives, such as the efforts to replicate Silicon Valley, structure and culture-based contingencies are missing. Regional success is largely the result of a complex interplay of factors that are hard to isolate or even to identify. The policy intervention is part of a larger regional experience that defies the identification of a simple cause-and-effect structure. Regional policy impacts are diffuse and hard to measure. Copying experiences may require policy officials to change their way of thinking as policy experiences can be linked to the culture and political ideology of specific locations. Rather than replication, the starting point for effective local economic policy is to be found in the existing structure and culture of the regional economy. Experiences in other places should be treated as sources of inspiration rather than recipes that can be copied.

Reflecting on regional competitiveness

The possibility of regional competitiveness is based on a range of abstract theories and interpretations of specific regional economies rather than being a single, coherent idea. Kitson *et al.* (2004: 996), for example, identify six separate bodies of theory that are variously being drawn upon to explain how 'soft' externalities shape regional outcomes, with each theory having its own assumptions and limitations. The diversity of theories is even greater than this when account is taken of the divisions within each area of enquiry. It draws attention to many phenomena including business networks, technology spillovers, learning processes, business clusters, shared labour markets and local culture. The relationship between these components and how they interact to shape the development of a regional economy remains poorly understood (Lovering 2001). The wide ranging agenda is reflected in the diversity of issues and contexts under study rather than the accumulation of empirical evidence that addresses a specific model of regional development. In practice, there is surprisingly little systematic empirical research to substantiate many of the claims being made (Turok 2004: 1079). The optimal spatial scale at which territorial competitive advantage is realized provides one illustration of the gap in understanding (Kitson *et al.* 2004: 997). There is no reason to assume that the sources of competitive advantage being talked of are all optimized at the same geographical scale or that their influence coincides with or can be contained within administrative boundaries.

A general message from interest in promoting regional competitiveness is that local environments affect business performance. This is a product of arguments that business specializations, institutional effectiveness and managerial cultures can be specific to individual localities. At this level, in Europe there has been an impact in encouraging the devolution of responsibility for economic development from central government to local agencies. This is accompanied by a tendency to see the strengthening of local institutions as a way of enhancing regional performance. In the United Kingdom, for example, it has been suggested that evidence of local variation in school student attainment, differences in the activities affected by skill shortages, the absence of industry clusters and variations in expenditure on research and development are indicative of the opportunities for strengthening regional performance (HM Treasury *et al.* 2003). Thus the lack of regional consistency in the occupations faced with skill shortages is taken as an indication that particular types of skill training are under-supplied in some localities, possibly because labour market information flows are being impeded. Similarly, areas with a high proportion of school leavers below national attainment levels are judged to have local failings in their school to work transition. Differences in the rates of new firm formation are ascribed partly to localized barriers to competition. Business managers' access to information is judged to be affected by the extent of local competition: local rivalry means that owners of firms are better able to assess the performance of their own managers and use this information to improve their productivity. From the perspective that many of the barriers to enterprise competitiveness have local origins, regional agencies have a role to play in encouraging economic growth.

The increased awareness of localized conditions affecting economic conditions is a potential benefit of the focus on regional competitiveness, but it is important that national industry policy continues alongside local initiatives. Demand for the outputs of local industry is still required even when local intervention succeeds in strengthening local institutions. Porter's diamond model goes some way to recognize this as it includes demand as one of the factors promoting a competitive industry cluster, but the importance of demand is larger than being one of the factors assisting productivity. Without demand regions risk an outflow of skilled workers, loss of financial capacity to support infrastructure investment, the development of unfavourable social conditions and less favourable conditions for entrepreneurial activity. Once the contribution of demand is recognized, emphasis shifts to the importance of national economic conditions and traditional regional policies (see Chapter 3).

Further doubts arise from the contradictions and uncertainties that are revealed when any individual theme associated with regional competitiveness is examined. Later chapters examine this in the case of learning economies (Chapter 4) and business clusters (Chapter 5). The emphasis given to the role of trust in facilitating qualitatively different forms of business relationship is a case in point. In essence, it is argued that proximity helps to build trust between businesses and that relations built upon trust are superior to relationships without trust. This is a problematic argument because there is little agreement as to what organizational arrangement makes most use of trust. Some research associates trust in small firm activity and see it as less relevant to large business organizations (Malecki and Tootle 1996). In contrast, the growth of big business has been taken as an indicator of higher levels of trust in a society. Only in societies with a prevalence of trust have large corporations with professional management emerged out of pre-existing small scale family enterprise that otherwise remains stymied by the mistrust of non kin (Fukuyama 1995). Similarly, it tends to be assumed that personalized forms of trust between businesses are more effective than other ways of securing trust (see, for example, Lever-Tracy 1992; Malecki and Tootle 1996). The assumption is that this form of trust will encourage mutual learning and the sharing of expertise in ways that promote improvement and innovation. Obviously, this requires that there is scope for such learning to take place: if a buyer's technology is far superior to that of the supplier there may not be much scope or interest in the mutual sharing of information. The advantage of building business around reciprocal relations depends on there being a broad stability in the business environment such that there is little risk attached to entering comparatively exclusive forms of relationship. The danger of exclusivity is that the strong commitments to one set of partners forecloses or at least makes harder the option of breaking those links and forming others in response to superior or more appropriate alternatives arising.

Some assumption about the level of and influences on the mobility of enterprises and people is needed to make informed decisions about the relative effort to be invested in the different ways of building distinctiveness. The possibility of building regional competitiveness has gained interest in the context of growing concerns about the impact of globalization on regional economies. A critique is that these concerns are being exploited by simultaneously exaggerating the extent of business mobility and the ease of reducing the inclination to operate with little involvement in any particular locality (Lovering 2003). This allows a theory of regional competitiveness that is based upon exploiting indigenous strengths and creating environments where innovative business can be encouraged to start up and grow to be contrasted with an alternative, less desirable, strategy of attracting mobile investment and the transfer of jobs from other places (Malecki 2004;

Turok 2004). In a world of global competition building regional development strategies around the attraction and retention of mobile investment is viewed as risking a 'race to the bottom' (Kotler *et al.* 1993). Enriching amenities and attracting skilled professionals are being presented as an antidote to footloose globalization. It is doubtful that regions are faced with such a stark choice of strategy or opportunity to deflect location decisions.

The idea has grown that the relative appeal of a locality's amenities now exerts a strong influence over the location decisions of individuals and firms (Glaeser *et al.* 2001; Clark *et al.* 2002; Glaeser 2005). This is a way places could be thought to compete, particularly where the sensitivity is to the forms of amenity that can be most easily manipulated such as parks, museums, waterfront consumer spaces and renovated historic areas. Indeed this is principally how some commentators envisage that regions do compete (Luger 2009). Evidence supporting this needs to show an association between present-day amenity and location decisions and explain why amenities such as weather have become more influential than in the past (Storper and Scott 2009). The location of new industries within some countries appears to confirm the influence of amenity because 'rustbelt' cities tend to have harsher climates than those in the growing 'sunbelt' cities. This may simply represent coincidence rather than the impact of location preferences. For example, Silicon Valley's commitment to the technology supporting personal computers is generally seen to have been the major influence on it, outpacing its initial competitor region in the north eastern USA whose companies were involved with mainframe computing (Saxenian 1994). New industrial areas have more complex origins than simply responding to climate, and location shifts are far from uniformly in favour of sunny places. In Europe, for example, the 'winterless' south of Italy is generally identified as economically backward compared with the less Mediterranean north (see above) and extremely harsh winters have not held back Nordic economic success (Maskell *et al.* 1998). The direction of causality complicates demonstration of how man-made amenities affect location decisions. As discussed in Chapter 6, it is hard to envisage that significant numbers of people relocate simply through amenity considerations, but it is evident that successful economies have an opportunity to enhance their environments in ways appreciated by existing residents.

The computer industry in the USA from 1977 to 1992, a time when it was expanding through the growing demand for personal computers, gives one perspective on the extent of location flexibility and commitment. Among the eight cities with the largest concentrations of computer employment in 1977, four remain in the top eight in 1992 (Beardsell and Henderson 1999). There are 13 big losers and 13 big gainers, measured by either at least a 50 per cent drop or gain on their 1977 employment. Seven cities entered and fell out of the top frame within the period examined ('flash-in-the-pans'). Employment changes are not the result of single large plant openings or closures: big employment gainers, for example, show much variation in their average plant size. Of the three location attributes linked to the chances of gaining employment, having a workforce with a high proportion of college educated workers is open to some manipulation by regional development agencies. The other two influences identified are less open to change: the size of the metropolitan economy (large economies experience most growth) and relative proximity to San Jose (Silicon Valley). Employment in associated electronic components, state taxes and diversity of the metropolitan economy were found to have no consistent relationship with the gain or loss of computer industry employment. The implication is that location shares of an industry can move up and down but that some geographical associations remain strong. Chapter 5 discusses some of the reasons for this attachment to place, including the importance of spinoff enterprises in industry growth.

Conclusion

Over any period of time the different regions of a national economy are likely to experience different levels of economic prosperity. A traditional interpretation ascribes these differences to industry structure and location characteristics. The structural component refers to the particular mix of economic activities found in a region and recognizes that some regions inherit a less favourable economic structure than others in terms of its likelihood of generating future growth. Location characteristics recognize that the economic performance of locations can be affected by endemic features that on balance advantage or disadvantage the region's economy. The general conclusion for a long period of time was that most of the difference in performance could be explained by structural factors. The evidence for this was that industry performance tends to be similar across regions and what differs more strongly is the distribution of the most strongly growing regions. This was not to suggest that there was no such thing as location disadvantage, but that this affected some types of activity more than others. There was also a view that some aspects of location disadvantage could be reduced by concentrating economic activity in the most favourable parts of a region. As well, there was seen to be scope to reduce location disadvantage by improvements in infrastructure that were relatively easy to make provided financial resources were available.

Contemporary discussions of regional competitiveness tend to reject the significance of structural explanations although, as discussed in the next chapter, it is important to recognize that not all regional economists agree that this is based on accurate reading of the evidence. The implications of this new perspective of regional differences vary according to whether the stress is placed on 'competition' or 'competitiveness'. Competition can be interpreted as a race between winners and losers: a zero-sum game in which a predetermined quantity of demand is allocated among competing entities. Envisaged in this way, regional competition is a problematic concept as there are many ways in which localities are not actually in competition with each other, and it can encourage misplaced efforts to protect industries and to manipulate rankings in a performance league table. Stress on competitiveness can be viewed as raising issues that are more than about one region capturing market share from another. Rather, it can focus attention on understanding the underlying drivers of regional economic performance and optimistically lead to understanding that helps promote efficiency and innovativeness across all regions. Discussions of regional competitiveness on this basis have tended to be guided by the perceived importance of localized networks, the geographical clustering of economic activities and other 'soft' externalities. The background assumption encouraging attention on such factors is of a widespread tendency for vertical disintegration within industries. This can overstate the actual change in industry structure and overlook how the consolidation of ownership and control tends to remain the most dominate trend. In practice much of the interest in competitiveness tends to come from the urge to replicate successful regional economies. Such an exercise is viewed as futile by those who interpret regional competitiveness as a search for the basis on which enterprises in an economy have acquired their ability to compete. The main point of agreement is the need for much more investigation and conceptual clarity to inform the analysis of regional competitive advantage.

3 Regional policy and inward investment

Broadly speaking there are two ways of addressing spatial differences in economic prosperity. Local economic development emphasizes a bottom-up approach and support for development from within by strengthening local institutions and business support services. Regional economic development is more of a top down approach that relies on central government discrimination in favour of some localities through its control of incentives, the location of major new investment projects and other resources for business growth. A general shift has occurred in Europe and elsewhere in favour of local economic development and away from regional policy of the form that discriminates between localities for the purpose of promoting growth in those areas that are most in need of additional employment. The philosophy underlying local economic development is that the gap between more and less prosperous areas will narrow if the right conditions for economic development prevail in all places and simultaneously this will uplift national economic performance. Regional policy has tended to be informed by the perception that spatially concentrated economic shocks can trigger a spiral of cumulative decline. Rather than relying on competitive processes to revive a region in decline, a real redistribution of resources is needed including an influx of inward investment, some of which may need to be diverted from its first choice location.

The distinction is not clear cut. Local economic development strategies have tended to diversify to include efforts to capture inward investment alongside support for new and already established local enterprises (Dicken and Tickell 1992; Wood 1996; Turok 2004). The administration of regional policy can be devolved to local agencies and this can blur the distinctions between national, regional and local economic policy (Wren 2001). It has been alleged, for example, that the UK government's approach to regional policy signalled in policy documents released during 2001 to 2003 is characterized most accurately as a locally administered national economic policy. With little discrimination in favour of the regions with the greatest problems, these policy documents are accused of simply envisaging a national industrial policy implemented in the regions (Fothergill 2005: 666). As discussed here, the regional and local policy approaches are separated according to their relative commitment to four issues:

- The extent to which there is equality in the capacity of localities to promote economic development in terms of the extent of business support that can

be offered and the establishment of development agencies. Regional policy includes positive discrimination in favour of weaker regions and constraints on the ability to support economic development in the most prosperous regions; local economic policy gives all localities access to a similar package of economic development tools.
- The relative emphasis on supply side versus demand side policy intervention. Local economic policy tends to be overwhelmingly focused on supply side initiatives addressing issues such as enterprise training, labour skills, innovation, productivity and investment. Regional policy gives most attention to demand through its primary focus on bringing additional investment to distressed economies that will help raise the demand for the area's goods and services. This is reflected in a willingness to use public money to alter location decisions and to encourage the relocation of existing activity from more to less prosperous regions.
- The extent to which underlying issues can be viewed as reflections of market failure. Local economic policy tends to assume that there are market failures inhibiting economic development such as inadequate incentives to innovate, information inequalities and barriers to matching job seekers with employment openings. A rationale for regional policy intervention is that regions whose established industries are faring badly may simply shed people and services to regions that accommodate expanding sectors of the economy. In this sense regional economic decline is an outcome of market processes rather than a sign that market imperfections are impeding adjustment. Nonetheless there are grounds for intervention when the negative externalities created by economic concentration are taken into account; these externalities need to be corrected as well as those affecting adjustment within declining regions.
- The breadth of the policy objectives. Regional policy has an overriding objective of reducing differences in regional rates of unemployment. Local economic policy can be directed to multiple policy objectives or policy targets such as 'regeneration' or 'social inclusion' which are composite concepts encompassing a range of potential outcomes.

Advocacy of local economic policy tends to assume that past regional policy intervention largely failed to meet its objectives and that its experiences have little ongoing significance. Indeed it is not unusual for the purpose of regional policy to be derided by those who advocate local economic policy. The central issue for this chapter is whether local economic development policy takes sufficient note of the experiences and impacts of regional policy. The review recognizes that some researchers and policy advocates have continued to argue the case for discriminatory regional policy partly on the grounds that much of the alternative policy agenda for local economic development is 'guru-led' rather than being informed by evidence of potential effectiveness (Adams et al. 2003). This has been viewed as a case of 'asymmetric evaluation': regional policy intervention has been subject to intensive evaluation using generally agreed evaluation methods whereas many of the tools of local economic policy are being judged on the basis of claims about how they might work in theory (Armstrong cited in Adams et al. 2003: 43; Fothergill 2005). The capacity for unequal comparison is increased by the tight focus of regional policy and the consistency with which some approaches have been applied, whereas equivalent evaluative evidence does not exist for alternative policy approaches (National Audit Office 2003). Indeed, local economic policy has been accused of being more of a 'flavour of the month' activity encompassing diverse objectives (Armstrong 2001). These perspectives are examined in three stages. First, evidence reviewing the effectiveness of targeting inward investment is examined with particular attention to the argument that this tends merely to subsidize the opening of branch plants in locations to which parent companies have no long term commitment. Second, the chapter considers how far the promotion of small firms represents a viable alternative to regional policy, this being a component of local economic policy for which evaluative evidence exists. Third, consideration is given as to how regional policy may need to be adapted to meet the changing structure of national economies and the increasing globalization of economic activity.

Regional policy

Efforts to redistribute existing economic activity and influence the location of new investment have been the hallmarks of regional policy that seeks to reduce spatial disparities in employment opportunities. There are four main arguments for using regional policy to reduce persistent geographical unevenness in the incidence of high unemployment (Taylor and Wren 1997):

- Reducing unemployment in areas of high unemployment has direct economic and social benefits. Reduced unemployment can increase national output, save transfer payments and raise taxation revenue.
- Reducing spatial unemployment disparities will reduce inflationary pressure in the economy as a whole. Where economic growth is geographically concentrated, inflationary pressure arising from a tight labour market, increased housing cost and other supply constraints emerges more quickly than it would if economic activity were evenly dispersed across the national economy.
- Unbalanced regional growth leads to the persistence and intensification of regional problems through the process of cumulative causation. Labour migration tends to follow the distribution of employment opportunities but mainly takes the most employable workers away from depressed regions. The net outcome can be to lessen the ability of declining regions to recover.
- Reducing unemployment in areas of high unemployment is politically necessary. Disparities in economic opportunities lead to expectations of government action and unless addressed the perceived unfairness can become a barrier to social cohesion.

Implicit in these arguments is evidence that regional disparities in economic wellbeing are persistent. For many industrial economies prior to the outbreak of the international financial crisis in 2008 it may have appeared that a period of high employment had rendered any regional problem historic. Greater equality at the level of regions can disguise the persistence of high unemployment within local labour markets and the regional unevenness in the distribution of these more localized concentrations of high unemployment (Taylor and Wren 1997; Adams et al. 2003). Persistent high unemployment tends to be disguised as individuals withdraw from the labour force (Green 1997). Another underlying assumption is that economic well being as measured by traditional indicators such as relative levels of employment, and income is what matters to most people. An alternative possibility is that, while one region may not match the economic prosperity of another, the population may be happier with their overall standard of living (Oswald 1997). This recognizes that a sense of community, absence of congestion and housing characteristics may be traded off against secure, well paid employment. A problem with this claim is that health is an important contributor to personal happiness and economic standards of living are correlated with self reported health levels and rates of mortality (Adams et al. 2003). It is also the case that employment is one of the other main influences on individual happiness.

Despite strong arguments for regional policy it has been falling out of use. One criticism is that it encourages a bidding war between localities looking for investment. Over any period of time there are a finite number of projects looking for a new location and this means that there are winners and losers in terms of the share of this investment captured by individual regions. To secure new investment, regional agencies may go 'head-to-head' with competing assistance packages and offers of assurance that the investor's requirements will be satisfied, perhaps even being prepared to adjust existing regional plans and regulations. This image associates the pursuit of inward investment with the low road to regional competitiveness (Malecki 2004). In a world of global competition, building regional development strategies around the attraction and retention of mobile investment is viewed as risking a 'race to the bottom' (Kotler et al. 1993). Where territories compete for a relatively small number of large investment projects, economic theory can be used to show that there is no incentive for promotion agencies to coordinate their negotiations or unify their offerings to would-be investors (Thomas 2003). The spectre is encouraged of a downward spiral in which larger and larger subsidies are offered to attract projects that offer fewer public benefits (Leitner and Garner 1993). Against this negative assessment the possibility exists of managing inter agency competition, of incoming firms acting as a catalyst for change by offering new markets for local suppliers, introducing new business methods, diversifying the economy and sending a positive signal to other would-be investors. This section considers four aspects of this debate: (i) agency rivalry and investor bargaining; (ii) regional policy effectiveness; (iii) changing evaluations of the branch plant; (iv) other regional policy experience.

Agency rivalry and investor bargaining

The image of regional promotion agencies locked in destructive competition with each other has some justification in past practice in the USA (Malecki 2004: 1104).

During the 1970s and 1980s state rivalry over the pursuit of inward investment was likened to a 'second world war between the states' (Business Week 1976; Ryans and Shanklin 1986). This rivalry was most visible in the annual rankings conducted by an accounting firm that focused on an interpretation of a positive environment for business investment in terms of costs, taxes and labour regulation. This form of measurement was criticized by the Corporation for Enterprise Development (1986) who advocated an alternative, more balanced, Development Report Card that has subsequently become the dominant basis for comparing state economic development (Box 3.1). This report card acknowledges that investors are not motivated solely by cost minimization or freedom from regulatory obligations and so permits a more balanced evaluation of alternative locations than where a few indicators are scrutinized. Nonetheless it is evident that cases involving large, high profile investments can attract an intense degree of competition between regional agencies, who respond with assistance that may include offers to fast track administrative processes at the expense of normal public and political scrutiny of their environmental impacts. Such a claim was made in a study of three cases of East Asian investment in the United Kingdom, but this case study also indicates that it is not a simple matter of footloose foreign investors holding regional agencies to ransom (Phelps and Tewdwr-Jones 2001).

Box 3.1 **Development Report Card for regional economic climates**

The US Corporation for Enterprise Development (CFED) devised the Development Report Card for the States (DRC) to counteract the influence of the Grant Thornton index, which in the mid-1980s was the only annual publication comparing state economies. From the perspective of CFED the Grant Thornton index identified 'good business climates' on the assumption that business only wished and needed to know which locations offered the lowest production costs. This was consistent with a traditional economic development formula of attracting footloose facilities with business incentives. The DRC wished to counteract this 'limited and limiting view' of state economies with a more expansive approach to development that identified and supported the 'real' strengths of state and regional economies: a skilled workforce and a high quality of life; technology development and transfer; entrepreneurs and existing businesses; a world class infrastructure and quality public services. These, along with a stable, adequate, but not excessive tax base, and predictable, professional regulation were judged to be the linchpins of a dynamic, globally competitive economy.

The structure of the DRC follows a simple line of reasoning:

> In order to succeed at obtaining a better life, people need money. Income is the most common source of money. Is income sufficient, growing and keeping up with the cost of living? Most people earn income by working. Are there enough secure, well paying jobs to go around? Do people have the skills to qualify for them? Jobs are created and offered by businesses. Are businesses growing, keeping pace with global conditions and doing things to ensure their success? Neither businesses nor people operate in a vacuum. Do they have the resources and amenities that they need and want? What contributes to the quality of life?

56   *Regional policy and inward investment*

The DRC is divided into three indexes:

- Performance: how well the economy is doing in terms of employment, income, the distribution of each within the population, stewardship of finite natural resources and social conditions.
- Business Vitality: the competitiveness of existing businesses as revealed by the strength of the traded sector, business closure rates and capital investment.
- Development Capacity: assessment of the investment in resources that support continued community and business prosperity, this includes education attainment, physical infrastructure, technical knowledge and technological resources, financial, amenity and natural resources.

Source: Malecki 2004; Corporation for Enterprise Development 2009

The case study examined the bidding by UK regional agencies for three large manufacturing projects originating from three Korean conglomerates: Hyundai, LG and Samsung. The final investment projects received total assistance packages that were valued at from around £48 million to £247 million (US$80 million to US$400 million). There was no evidence of these investors encouraging or exploiting competition among regional agencies. In the context of the United Kingdom the capacity to do this is controlled by a cap on the level of investment assistance that can be awarded by regional agencies and the equivalent bodies in Scotland and Wales as well as agreement that regional agencies should cooperate over prospective inward investment projects (Raines 2000). The extent to which major inward investment projects induce a bidding war can also be constrained by the exacting location and site requirements preferred by global corporations when seeking to establish strategic investments in high income economies. In the case of the three Asian projects, for example, the criteria set by Samsung included 'a high profile site on greenfield land with excellent road transport links, minimum land ownership constraints and high-quality environmental setting standards' (Phelps and Tewdwr-Jones 2001: 1260). When combined with a projected direct workforce of up 5,000, and presumably the investor's requirements for certainty over the capacity to make the investment realizable over a preferred timescale, there are potentially few realistic locations to consider. Indeed, the concern raised by the researchers was the extent to which national agencies coordinated processes to ensure sites preferred by major investors were available, circumventing local authority control over land use planning. This criticism is encouraged by the tendency to favour the decentralization of power and operational decision making in respect of environmental regulation and economic development. Such decentralization has in fact been an aspect of UK policy reform since the 1980s, as it has been across the European Union, where the argument has also been that regional policy should be bottom-up rather than under the control of central government (Raines 2000). The effective management of inward investment can mean going against this trend, but criticism of this can be misplaced (Fothergill 2005).

In the United Kingdom there has been a growing emphasis on regional and local partnerships to manage the attraction of inward investment. This devolution of responsibility arises from a particular understanding of the sources of regional economic problems (McVittie and Swales 2007). With the view that regional economic disparities stem from many individually small scale coordination and market failures, there is a case for arguing that local insight is likely to result in more effective policy intervention than relying on a central government agency (HM Treasury et al. 2003). This is consistent with the advocacy of the new regionalist literature (see Chapter 2) that subnational institutional capacity or 'thickness' underpins the attractiveness of places to investors (Turok 2004). This agenda has encouraged a belief that locations with broad-ranging and strong institutions for business match the preference of modern industry to operate within networks of mutual support that enable external relations to be localized. Of course, local expertise and knowledge can be brought to bear on policy development by decentralizing responsibility to regional offices of the national agency. A further argument for local agencies is that this can help demonstrate broad-based support for incoming investment and help to coordinate the provision of infrastructure to support new industrial investment (Fuller et al. 2003). A shortcoming of such arguments is that investors need assurance of the long term policy environment as well as the immediate situation; they may have more confidence in a national agency's ability to provide credible assurances of future tax, subsidy and support regimes than a local agency. Multiple, separate agencies may allow for local experimentation and the transfer of best practice but the scope for this will depend on the extent to which uniform approaches are appropriate, and meaningful comparisons of regional agency performance can be made (McVittie and Swales 2007: 271).

A test of the advantages being gained from decentralizing the management of inward investment through regional partnerships has been made in the United Kingdom (Fuller et al. 2003). The study revealed that inward investors were making little use of the services on offer. This finding led the researchers to speculate that subnational bodies have little capacity to influence regional and local economic development, as the support they can offer is not a critical part of an inward investor's decision (Fuller et al. 2003: 2048). A similar conclusion is made in a study of foreign direct investment into the United Kingdom, which found that initiatives undertaken by regional agencies had little influence over investment decisions whereas national incentives were of some influence (Phelps et al. 2003: 37). On this basis criticism of the centralized management of inward investment may be based on an unrealistic perception of the attention paid to regional institutions by incoming investors. As suggested by Lovering (2003: 53) most local enterprises are too small and most multinationals are too big to be influenced by regional administrative processes as compared with national regulation and site-related issues.

As well as the evidence that regional administration (as distinct from local and national tiers) does not appear to have much impact on investors, the theory of fiscal federalism can be marshalled in support of the national management of regional incentives (Armstrong and de Kervenoael 2000). A nationally directed regional policy has advantages in being able to respond to investment benefits that arise for the national economy. Particularly where large projects are involved, it is unlikely that all the spin off from a new investment will be retained within the immediate locality of the investment. A devolved regional policy might lead to an under provision of support where levels of assistance are tied to the benefit retained within the jurisdiction of the local agency. A second argument for national control is that it provides operational efficiencies. A single agency avoids competitive bidding for projects, accumulates expertise in negotiating with investors, has larger resources to proactively solicit investment and can integrate regional assistance with other forms of support that might be available. A further argument may be to guard against the risk that devolution would result in the most advantaged regions, capturing a disproportionate share of inward investment. National control of the funding of regional policy while local agencies retain administrative responsibilities can minimize this risk but not achieve the other operational efficiencies (Armstrong 2001: 251). Others have used a principal–agent framework to question the case for devolving regional policy responsibility (Box 3.2).

Box 3.2 **A principal–agent critique of devolved regional policy**

A principal–agent perspective focuses on the possibility that those charged with carrying out a task (the agent) may exploit a principal's lack of understanding or inability to monitor their actions. These risks are highlighted to question the wisdom of delegating responsibility to an agent. In relation to giving responsibility for regional policy to locally managed regional development agencies (RDAs) the potential risks arise from the inability to fully specify their role or control them with precise service contracts.

- RDAs may tend to 'bury' bad news and showcase the good, as suggested in the claim that local economic development generates job announcements rather than real jobs.
- RDAs tend to be given multiple policy targets without clear guidance on the allowable trade offs, an imperative to tackle any single outcome or ability to judge when individual targets have been satisfied.
- The ability of RDAs to achieve their objectives is affected by other agencies linked to individual sectors, making it hard to judge the performance of any one entity.
- Competition between RDAs over the attraction of inward investment, position in benchmarking surveys and other matters can discourage transparency.

Source: McVittie and Swales (2007)

Regional policy effectiveness – the case of regional selective assistance

The starting point for regional policy is to identify specific localities requiring assistance with this, typically tied to above average unemployment rates. Once areas that have been designated policy instruments are broadly of two types: (i) financial incentives to firms located in or moving to the designated priority development areas; (ii) controls on the expansion of enterprises outside the priority areas. In addition, regional policy may address infrastructure weaknesses in the priority areas by, among other initiatives, the provision of prepared sites and buildings to ease the process of inward investment (Slowe 1981; Fothergill *et al.* 1987). An underlying rationale was that moving work to where unemployment was concentrated was likely to be a more effective way of addressing regional inequalities than a strategy of encouraging migration to places of employment growth (Box 3.3). Cost barriers to industrial movement were recognized as significant impediments to the policy choice. Consequently, assistance that helped improve the investment environment by enhancing infrastructure and offsetting set up costs was emphasized (McCrone 1969). From the 1940s to the beginning of the 1980s, regional policy in the United Kingdom brought hundreds of thousands of jobs to the assisted areas that would not otherwise have been located there (see Armstrong and Taylor 1985 for reviews of this evidence). The subsequent questioning of regional policy has arisen because of uncertainty that the gains contributed to a region's long term development, doubt that the policy could continue in a context of widespread deindustrialization and greater perceived complexity to the distribution of economic problems than addressed by regional policy (Segal 1979; Armstrong and Taylor 1985; Fothergill and Guy 1990).

Box 3.3 **Work to the workers**

Regional policy has traditionally been based on the view that full employment and increased national economic activity is more likely to be achieved by bringing work to the workers than the migration of workers to the work. The main argument for taking work to the workers is that it is hard to maximize labour participation in the paid workforce by relying on labour mobility (McCrone 1969). Not everyone who is prepared to join the workforce is prepared to migrate, such as those near or at the usual age of retirement, and those that are tend to do so only in response to marked differences in the availability of job opportunities. Out migration can make it harder to employ those who remain in the depressed region as the local market shrinks and becomes too small for many types of activity. With surplus labour there is reduced pressure to move labour out of low productivity activity. In contrast, full utilization of a country's labour reserves can give a substantial addition to a country's national production capacity. Ireland illustrates these arguments as a country that experienced out migration over many decades without eliminating unemployment. In contrast a decade of inward investment resulted in increased labour force participation and inward migration.

In the United Kingdom regional policy was largely dismantled after the 1980s, with the main exception that some form of regional selective assistance has survived as a financial incentive seeking to influence the location of investment (Armstrong 2001). Requirements for new investment to be licensed have disappeared, although they were important while they existed in forcing businesses to contemplate alternative locations (Twomey and Taylor 1985). Regional selective assistance can be compared with the provision of automatic assistance to qualifying projects or assistance that targets specific investment outcomes such as employment. It has existed in some form since 1972 and outlasted other aspects of regional policy, although its significance has reduced (Box 3.4).

Box 3.4 UK Regional selective assistance

Regional selective assistance was introduced in 1972. Initially, guidelines differentiated the form and extent of assistance according to whether projects created additional jobs or maintained existing ones. The priority was manufacturing industry creating additional employment, although services not primarily serving a local market were also eligible. From 1979 a 'proof of need' condition was introduced and allocation in the form of loans was reduced to cut down on administration costs. After 1984 it was no longer payable for relocation projects where there was no net increase in employment in the United Kingdom, leaving it mainly as a project grant toward the cost of new fixed investment above a defined cost threshold, the majority of which continues to be funded by the applicant. A 'claw back' clause has been added under which money can be claimed back if job targets are not met. Other precautions added are a prior commitment clause that requires application for assistance before any commitment to proceed with the investment has been made, and that the employment generated is of high quality and ongoing.

Source: Wren (2005)

A general claim made about investment incentives is that even where they do not determine an investment outcome they are valuable in bringing investors into a relationship with public officials (Hughes 1993). Discretionary assistance in particular has a number of potential advantages arising from its requirement for engagement between grant administrators and potential recipients (Wren 2005). Government agencies have the opportunity to scrutinise projects and fix the terms of the assistance according to an understanding of the likely project outcomes. Selective assistance can be tied directly to job creation and the quality of employment provided (Swales 1997). At the same time, the investor's commitment to the project can be tested, and unrealistic or unlikely-to-be-completed components identified and excluded from influencing the assistance decision. The discretionary approach can also help to equalize the bargaining power of government officials and investors where the government agency can withhold assistance.

The value of discretion relies on there being insight into the characteristics of inward investment that will bring most long term benefit to a region. One influence that should give confidence is that the probability of branches closing has generally been found to reduce the longer the branch plant has been established (see studies cited in Fothergill and Guy 1990). Various studies have shown that closure rates peak at around five years after establishment. To the extent that early closures reflect uncertainties that exist at the time of opening, there should be some capacity for discretionary assistance to target well founded projects. The recent growth of foreign investment in parts of Eastern Europe has been an opportunity to identify some of the influences that determine the likelihood of branch plants being established with competencies that give capacity for long term growth (Fuchs and Winter 2008). Two aspects of the sales market have been found to be positive for the changes of sustained growth:

- Having a diverse product customer base rather than being established to serve a single customer or serving several customers with the identical product. Where the branch has a diverse market there is less vulnerability to changes in an individual client or product demand, the development of local management competencies and an enlarged network of business relationships.
- The knowledge intensity of the production process and the end product affect the likelihood of the subsidiary being delegated some research and development capacity to support its operation. Increased knowledge intensity increases the competencies possessed by the branch and this brings the possibility of sustained support from the parent organization.

These types of attribute appear unambiguous and within the capacity of investment promotion agencies to target, although their ability to exercise discretion will still depend on the level of investment interest. The same investigation also noted that years established matters, as the longer a subsidiary has existed the more probable it is that the plant has had to solve problems and deepen its expertise and in so doing gain support from its head office (Fuchs 2005). Of course, older established branches are not assured of upgrading but there is much research to indicate that their fate is affected by local management's effort to retain parent company support rather than branches simply operating at the behest of distant controllers (Birkenshaw and Ridderstråle 1999).

Offsetting the possible advantages of discretionary assistance, it can be comparatively costly to administer and is not guaranteed to produce more efficient outcomes than automatic assistance. Administrators may underestimate the level of assistance needed for the project to proceed or they may offer more assistance than was actually needed to secure the investment. There is no consensus over the precise achievement of regional selective assistance as assumptions need to be made about the immediate and longer term impacts of subsidizing investment (Box 3.5). A number of conclusions nonetheless attract broad agreement in the UK context (Armstrong 2001; Adams *et al.* 2003).

Box 3.5 **Judgements about job creation**

Estimates of the employment creation results of incentives can vary according to the assumptions made and methods of calculation. Adjustments are needed to separate additional jobs from those that would have been created without the assistance, and to take note of displacement effects where assisted jobs result in employment in non assisted activity being lost. As well as the direct employment created there may be a case for measuring multiplier and linkage effects. Further adjustment can recognize that jobs may arise in different time periods and have different lifetimes, suggesting a need to standardize impacts by applying discount rates to the value of future jobs. Some evaluations may attempt to measure the impact of incentives on wage costs and the impact of changes in labour costs on employment, which in turn necessitates judgements about the extent of labour market flexibility. Choice of evaluation method can add further opportunities for variable results. A questionnaire approach is frequently employed in which grant recipients are asked about the employment consequences of grant assistance. This approach is especially favoured where the scale of programmes is comparatively modest, but it results in questions about strategic bias in the data obtained (recipients looking at the possibility of making future grant applications exaggerate job outcomes, believing that this will increase the likelihood of schemes surviving). Some researchers believe adjustment is needed to counteract strategic bias.

- Evaluation indicates that the level of assistance has frequently not matched the support needed to secure the investment, but that the extent of 'deadweight' compares favourably with other forms of financial incentive and that selectivity helps minimize the problem (Armstrong 2001; Wren 2005). For the period 1991–1995, for example, one evaluation finds that around 80 per cent of projects receiving assistance would not have proceeded as they did without the incentive (Arup Economics and Planning 2000). In terms of employment additionality, evidence covering different periods of selective assistance indicates that around half the jobs created to some degree relied on the assistance given (King 1990; Wren and Waterson 1991; PA Cambridge Economic Consultants 1993; Armstrong 1995; Wren 1996). It also appears that foreign investors receiving selective assistance make more accurate predictions of their intended employment creation than investors not receiving assistance, possibly reflecting the greater scrutiny and possibility of clawing back assistance when targets are not met (Jones and Wren 2004: 511). Reducing or refusing grants to projects not dependent on assistance runs the risk of deterring projects that are reliant on the receipt of financial support. Consequently, as well as deadweight, the effectiveness of assistance should also be judged by the number of projects lost because of inadequate assistance. The impact gained has also to be judged against the intent of bringing jobs to lagging regions in a context when investors are free to pursue more favourable locations (Adams *et al.* 2003: 43).
- The cost per job produced through regional selective assistance has improved and it is at least as cost effective as other measures designed to reduce or alleviate unemployment, such as through grants to job seekers (Wren 2005). This outcome may be influenced by the declining expenditure on regional assistance such that assistance has been concentrated on relatively job-rich investment. In this regard, while the cost per job created may be judged favourably, the contribution to reducing regional unemployment has been modest. It should also be noted that since 1984 assistance has not been given to projects relocating within the United Kingdom, which has removed the possibility of supporting relatively labour intensive projects moving to assisted areas.

- The discretionary allocation of assistance has maximized the focus on manufacturing and services supplying non local markets. About 90 per cent of the value of grant offered during 1994–2002 went to manufacturing businesses (National Audit Office 2003). This achievement is significant in the context of a national picture of declining dependency on manufacturing, and also needs to be considered in relation to the direct employment outcomes. New investment can be capital intensive and directly it might reduce employment where new technology displaces labour but still bring economic benefits through enhanced competitiveness (Harris 1993). The scope to retain the manufacturing bias has been questioned, although further diversification to service and research activities has been judged desirable and of benefit in broadening regional economies (Adams *et al.* 2003).
- In the context of the United Kingdom and the greater integration of European economies, regional selective assistance has been one of the influences attracting investment from foreign-owned companies (Department of Trade and Industry 1995). Grants awarded to foreign investors tend to be concentrated among relatively few, large projects while funding to internal projects tend to go to SMEs (Taylor and Wren 1997). For foreign investors, one-off incentives will be judged against long term differences in corporate taxation and other business costs. Regional selective assistance is therefore likely to determine the choice of country when the location search is restricted to economies with otherwise similar business environments. Hence evidence that fiscal incentives have limited impact on the overall distribution of a country's outward flows of foreign direct investment (for example Hubert and Pain 2002) are not necessarily inconsistent with them influencing the investment going to an individual country. Nonetheless, there is a case for reducing the share of regional assistance going to foreign direct investment if this allocation mainly supports national economic objectives and is not managed to direct investment to lagging regions (Adams *et al.* 2003).

Changing evaluations of the branch plant

A concern with the use of financial incentives is that targeting mobile investment means supporting companies that have no long term commitment to the locality, giving eligibility to assistance. This echoes the widely shared perception that incoming investment based on branch plants of international companies tends to remain detached from the local economy (Phelps and Tewdwr-Jones 2001: 1269). Without forming linkages to local enterprises, the economic benefits obtained are limited and the possibility of relocation or closure is high. This spectre has been discussed in terms of a branch plant economy syndrome, in which external control and a tendency to focus on routine activity limit the ability of inward investment to address regional economic weaknesses (Firn 1975; Watts 1981; Hayter 1982) (Box 3.6). More recently the issue has been discussed in terms of the extent to which incoming investment becomes embedded in the regional economy, as indicated by the depth and quality of its relationships with co-located enterprises, and the extent to which it acquires autonomous development capacity as compared with being dependent on resources and roles allocated by its head office (Crone and Watts 2000).

***Box 3.6* The branch plant economy syndrome**

During the 1970s it became common to depict branch plants as providing low skill, routine and low paid jobs and as operating with little connection to their local economy, with the result that they failed to stimulate further economic growth. This impression was encouraged by surveys of recently opened branch plants confirming that they provided few 'white-collar' jobs and that plant managers operated under decision making constraints that limited their likelihood of expanding. In the United Kingdom, Townroe (1975) found that many new branch plants did not even carry out routine management functions, and that they rarely made use of local suppliers and services. In the USA, Bluestone and Harrison (1982) argued that conversion of a locally owned firm into a branch of an externally owned company resulted in a loss of local autonomy and other processes that heightened the likelihood of eventual closure. At the same time, branch plant research sometimes confounded the stereotype and other research pointed to a more complex pattern than a wholly negative assessment of branch plants. Ashcroft *et al.* (1987), for example, found that the conversion of independent companies to branch plant status could be beneficial to the enterprise and generate flow-on benefits for the regional economy. In their review of the branch plant literature Fothergill and Guy (1990) concluded that the only consensus finding is that conversion to branch plant status resulted in less local purchases of business services.

Scotland is traditionally one of the United Kingdom's assisted areas actively engaged in inward investment promotion as part of efforts to rebuild its economy away from declining heavy industries. These efforts were given a boost after the introduction of a degree of self government in 1999 that gave Scotland the ability to increase the value of the investment incentives it could negotiate compared with English regions (Raines 2000). Based on the examination of the electronics enterprises attracted to Scotland during the 1980s, one verdict was that regional policy was not working because incoming plants showed no sign of increasing their use of local suppliers (Turok 1993). Other researchers have also claimed to find evidence that in Scotland (unlike more prosperous parts of the United Kingdom) inward investment was leading to the displacement of local enterprise rather than providing it with new growth opportunities (Driffield and Hughes 2003). Others have questioned these conclusions, pointing out that the measurement of impacts is sensitive to the indicators used and timescale examined (McCann 1997). 'Silicon Glen' can be considered a regional policy success by taking note of the United Kingdom's larger decline in electronics manufacturing, the tendency for new arrivals to require time to build a local supply base, the absolute volume of local purchases as well as their share of output and comparisons with other manufacturing sectors. Ireland is another case where inward investment has diversified a previously struggling economy and resulted in the transfer of expertise into the local economy (Hochtberger et al. 2004).

A study has characterized overseas-owned plants in two parts of the United Kingdom (Wales and north east England) as 'extended enclaves', a status suggesting some degree of local attachment but still less than the ideal (Phelps et al. 2003). Many of the establishments in the study included the receipt of regional financial incentives as influences on their location, but it appears without bringing strong attachment to their new locality. Enclave refers to the tendency to be more connected to a home country economy than a host economy whereas the extended enclave has started to show some attachment to its host region. The relative unimportance of single-activity facilities, marketing and research responsibilities, a tendency to increase local sourcing, use of local education and training facilities and the incidence of further investment are indicators of branch plants becoming extended enclaves. Evidence of this transition concurs with an early study of multinational subsidiaries in the United Kingdom which identified the 'truncated miniature replica' plant (a category consistent with the enclave classification) as an approximation of the status of less than a third of the sample subsidiaries (Pearce 1999). Most branches had something more than an import substitution role for their parent company. By contributing in some way to the group's international production network the branch has more significance than a truncated replica, without necessarily becoming embedded within the host region.

A negative judgement is implied by the extended enclave classification as this is taken to indicate that overseas plants are not embedded into the regional economy. This evaluation benchmark implies that it is realistic to envisage that individual establishments affiliated to an international organization should be able to operate efficiently with predominantly local supply linkages and that they should internalize business support functions locally rather than drawing on resources from elsewhere within their own organization. This claim is not unique to the researchers as there has been much speculation about the emergence of a new type of branch plant that is simultaneously part of an international production network, has a high degree of managerial autonomy and is more integrated within its local economy than the branch plants of old (Box 3.7). In practice, there are costs and benefits of being locally embedded as compared with internationally networked and no reason to assume that one arrangement is always superior. In this context it has been observed that subsidiary upgrading relies on the successful blending of resources from within its parent organization with resources obtained from the host economy (Pearce 1999). Given the tendency for large organizations to distribute their operations over different types of establishment in different locations, the lack of embeddedness may not show a lack of long term commitment or mean that there are not economic benefits for the host economy beyond the plant's direct employment. For example, the study identifying branches established as truncated miniature replica also reported that managers of some of these plants expected their responsibilities to diversify in the future (Pearce 1999).

Box 3.7 **The new branch plant economy**

The emergence of a new type of branch plant has been speculated upon as a consequence of the growing scale of multinational business organizations and increased capacity to coordinate their subsidiary operation. Based on observations of some subsidiary companies gaining regional or even world product mandates, one extrapolation envisages a transition from branch to performance plants. Performance plants operate with greater strategic and operating autonomy than traditional branches and this is envisaged as bringing increased benefits for local economic development through locally managed outsourcing strategies. In practice new and old practices can overlap. In the automobile assembly industry, for example, some heightening of plant responsibility, some upgrading of functions and the introduction of new production techniques that offer enhanced but still limited benefits for local economic development have been detected.

Source: Pike (1998)

Looking at the reasons why plants have been closed is a way of gauging whether regional incentives encourage the opening of establishments in places that are inherently inefficient and hence prone to closure. The rationalization of manufacturing branch plants across the United Kingdom's assisted regions during the 1980s has been studied to examine this question (Fothergill and Guy 1990). This study examined branch plant closures in the context of a widespread rationalization of industrial capacity brought about primarily through long term shifts in demand accentuated by a period of recession. Consistent with other studies, the small size of a plant relative to others in the group and the particular product responsibilities mainly explain why an individual establishment closes, especially if a plant's product is toward the end of its market life (Kirkham and Watts 1998). The absence of office functions and limited capabilities are among other further influences, but their role and other explanations are variable and of secondary importance. In Fothergill and Guy's (1990) study the same dominant influences encourage closure wherever branch plants are located, but a geography to closure nonetheless exists partly as branch plants have different origins in assisted versus non assisted regions. Branch plants in areas eligible for regional assistance are disproportionately 'greenfield' operations, whereas those in more prosperous regions are disproportionately assets acquired from previously independent companies. By retaining some elements of their independence, branches in non assisted areas are less vulnerable to closure, although they tend to be in locations where site-related issues are more likely to be a reason for closure than in an assisted region. Importantly, the study finds no evidence that geography itself explains different rates of closure in the sense that it is harder to operate efficiently in one type of region than another.

Strictly, the reasons given for plant closure show whether a place has proved problematic for a business that once saw some advantage in the location otherwise it would never have opened the branch. In the case of Scotland it is documented that some enterprises saw problems with the location and declined to open a branch there (Cameron and Reid 1966). Closure evidence does not show that any type of industry would find a location in a lagging region suitable (McCrone 1969: 178). Based on interviews with business managers making the closure decisions, Fothergill and Guy (1990: 180) nonetheless judge that for most manufacturing firms the less prosperous regions need not be an inherently inefficient location. On this basis a case for regional policy remains, with the proviso that this should be based on discretionary assistance so that support goes to activities that are more than mere marginal, production-only units (Fothergill and Guy 1990: 180).

A similar conclusion emerges from a more recent investigation of why international companies have closed a plant in the United Kingdom while retaining or increasing activity at a plant located in another European country (Watts 2003). As within the United Kingdom, the small size of a plant relative to others under the same ownership is the main influence determining the selection of a plant for closure. A home-base effect is also observed with parent companies sometimes favouring own-country establishments over those located in other countries. No evidence is found of companies responding to national government support or differences in regulation.

Other regional policy experience

Determining how best to define the areas eligible for assistance is another regional policy experience, with implications for the local economic development policy. A broad consideration is whether to draw boundaries widely or tightly around the localities with the most severe employment problems. Over the history of UK regional policy both approaches have been tried. During the 1970s, large parts of the United Kingdom were encompassed by one of three levels of assisted area status. A policy experiment under the 1960 Local Employment Act, variously labelled a 'measles', 'black spot' or 'growth point' approach, focused assistance on localities with the most severe long term unemployment (McCrone 1969; Armstrong 1991). Since the late 1990s, the policy has reverted to drawing boundaries around localized high points of unemployment and deprivation based on Census wards (which in a large city might have an average population of around 20,000 residents and half this in less urbanized districts) (Adams et al. 2003). Targeting support in this way can overlook the fact that regional policy is demand-driven and reliant on the location choices of investors. When boundaries are drawn tightly it can result in localities that are wholly unattractive to investors, and especially to those investors with projects having long term growth prospects. Such an approach is not justified given that new employment opportunities are likely to be taken up by people who reside outside the boundary area (Box 3.8). For this reason regional policy incentives are most likely to influence investment decisions when aligned with broadly defined areas of eligibility including some comparatively prosperous localities (Armstrong 2001).

68 *Regional policy and inward investment*

> ***Box 3.8* Local economies as leaky buckets**
>
> Areas with the worst unemployment are those with the least favourable employment trends but this does not mean that they are two sides of the same problem. Higher local unemployment rates are explained by the distribution of people at most risk of being out of work (including single men, public housing residents, ethnic minorities and those with health problems). When job opportunities increase these high risk groups tend to be excluded from the initial uplift in opportunities: perceived shortcomings in skills, experience or commitment; lack of family attachments and residence in social housing reduce their access to employment. The overall population of these groups is much larger that those inhabiting specific neighbourhoods so that a policy response based on spatial targeting will miss many disadvantaged job seekers.
>
> Job openings near to pockets of high unemployment are competed over by more than those among whom unemployment is concentrated. This is compounded as previously employed people from outside get a share of the jobs and create vacancies elsewhere. It takes a large uplift in labour demand to affect a significant proportion of those most at risk of unemployment and under employment. At the local level, initiatives appropriately address social issues affecting employment outcomes (schooling, health, family support) and the ability of job seekers to widen their geographical search area. To get them employed requires a strong increase in labour demand, and as job opportunities ripple out through a regional labour market it is not necessary to site the initial new openings close to priority groups. Better to encourage investment where it is most likely to occur and reserve local area policies for social and mobility interventions to maximize participation in the employment growth that eventually diffuses.
>
> *Source:* Gordon (2000)

Regional policy experience includes the use of incentives to target specific preferred outcomes in addition to the use of investment incentives which bring variable outcomes in terms of the ratio of jobs to capital investment, multiplier benefits and long term growth potential. A regional employment premium (REP) is an example of attempted policy targeting in the United Kingdom. During the 1960s and 1970s it offered manufacturing industry in assisted regions (then called Development Areas) an annual wage subsidy valued at around 7.5 per cent of employment costs with the objective of encouraging employers to expand their activity (McCrone 1969: 192). At the time estimates of an additional 100,000 jobs being created were made, although it was recognized that the actual outcome would depend on how far REP was used to augment profits (and encourage re-investment) as compared with it uplifting wages (Brown 1967). In practice, by being extended to all manufacturing employers, the low level of subsidy had little impact on protecting or stimulating employment. Depending on the nature of the firm and industry the subsidy was potentially retained in a variety of ways that had no outcome in either increased wages or increased investment (Armstrong and Taylor 1985: 203). According to Fothergill (2005: 665) small levels of subsidy made available to all types of enterprise, as in the case of REP (subject to the manufacturing sector limitation), are simply prone to result in high levels of dead weight regardless of the activity that they target.

Local economic policy

There has long been recognized to be two broad explanations for the existence of spatial inequalities in economic well being within a national economy (McCrone 1969: 169). The interpretation that most influenced regional policy is that poorly performing regions have inherited an unfavourable economic structure. Current economic problems are primarily a legacy of past development rather than an indication that the locality is inherently disadvantageous for economic activity. Industrial structure is given attention as it is known that there are large differences in the value added by different activities, and hence in the ability to pay high wages. A tendency for multi site organizations to create a spatial division of labour as they put different types of job in different locations accentuates the impact of industrial structure (Massey 1984). These explanations influenced the UK support for regional policy and they continue to drive contemporary advocacy for a return to discriminatory regional policy (Barlow Report 1940; Fothergill 2005). The alternative perspective is that lagging economies face some endemic disadvantages which explain why the economic structure has not evolved and why policies designed to 'bribe' industry to move to these locations are unlikely to bring sustainable results. A contemporary manifestation of the location disadvantage interpretation points to the extent to which productivity differences account for a large share of the variation in regional per capita GDP (Department of Trade and Industry 1998; HM Treasury 2001). This can be seen to imply the existence of location disadvantages as businesses and workers appear to be much more efficient in one location than another. It can thus appear that poorly performing localities do not need an injection of additional jobs as much as support to raise the income earning potential of existing workers. This leads to an agenda focused on locally customized programmes in areas such as skills development, innovation, enterprise development and business competitiveness as well support for new investment.

Perceived shortcomings of traditional regional policy provided the initial impetus for change. In particular the argument grew that the focus on encouraging inward investment had resulted in too little attention to encouraging enterprise formation and growth from within the existing business population (Armstrong and Taylor 1985: 210). After many decades of giving primary attention to outside investment and of believing that economic development was inexorably favouring the concentration of business activity within large organizations (see Bolton 1971) a shift to promoting indigenous enterprise looked to offer promise. Optimism grew that the small-firm sector could play a significant role in rejuvenating local and indeed national economies (Storey 1982). Where multi-location enterprise was characterized as footloose and unattached, small enterprise owners were loyal to their region of origin as a consequence of their dependence on a localized network of associations. While individually of low employment significance, collectively small enterprise became seen as the engine of job generation (Birch 1979). Critics might point out that this contribution arose more when gross rather than net employment flows are examined (Fothergill and Gudgin 1979) but suggestions that large scale enterprise was becoming inflexible in relation to changing patterns of demand proved more compelling (Piore and Sabel 1984). These arguments foresaw a new industrial future in which ensembles of small enterprises utilizing modern computer-controlled technology would replace the concentration of activity within large, multi plant organizations. These organizational tendencies have provided the impetus for a 'new regionalism' (see Chapter 2) but the immediate consequence was the growth of policy interest in promoting new and small enterprise. As this is one of the few aspects of local economic policy that has been subject to systematic evaluation the results merit reflection as a guide to the relative potential of regional versus local economic development (Fothergill 2005).

Local economic policy for the small enterprise sector may focus on raising rates of new firm formation or strengthening the performance of established small firms or both these targets. Some forms of intervention may not specifically distinguish between new and established enterprises but there has been a tendency for policy to variously place the emphasis on the quantity of small enterprise or quality of small enterprises. In the United Kingdom, for example, the 1980s have been characterized as a decade where the policy emphasis was on the quantity of small enterprise while the 1990s saw a shift to the quality of established enterprises with a subsequent swing back to encouraging more enterprise (Greene *et al.* 2004).

The quantitative approach to promoting small enterprise is primarily concerned with increasing rates of new firm formation. Policy interest in encouraging more small firms commenced from the perception that this could be a substantial way of increasing employment and that support for start ups was a more effective job generation strategy than assisting older businesses. While there are reasons to believe that rates of new form formation are positively related with an area's economic prosperity there are equally reasons to doubt this (van Stel and Storey 2004). On the positive side, new firms are a direct source of employment, and while not all may survive some may be expected to grow eventually into substantial enterprises. The entry of new firms may also act to intensify the competitive pressure on existing enterprises that are consequently encouraged to improve their efficiency and diversify their activity (Disney *et al.* 2003). As well, new firms may introduce new ideas and new technology, with some observing that the opportunities for innovative small enterprise have been increasing (Audretsch and Thurik 2001). On the downside, there are also three reasons to doubt that increasing new firm formation can change a locality's economic fortunes (van Stel and Storey 2004):

- Over any period of time new enterprise can make only a modest contribution to a region's total stock of employment, particularly as most new enterprises do not increase their direct employment for several years after formation, if at all (Storey 1985).

- Most new enterprise formation involves 'ordinary' rather than innovative activity and this gives rise to the possibility of considerable displacement of existing enterprises when new firm formation increases.
- The employment significance of new start ups comes mainly through a few percent of ventures that survive and experience exceptional rates of growth (Storey 1985). The appropriate policy response is, therefore, to seek out new enterprises with high growth potential rather than on trying to increase the total sum of new enterprises.

In the case of Europe, increases in new firm formation have not been found to have a positive impact on employment (Acs and Storey 2004; van Stel and Storey 2004). This reflects how new firms partly displace established enterprises and that to have a marked impact on employment growth new firms need to grow substantially in size and to achieve this quickly, which most fail to do. The evidence is less clear in the case of the USA, where regions with the highest rates of new firm formation have been shown to have the highest rates of subsequent employment growth (Acs and Armington (2004). The European experience is different, which may be because of the different context for entrepreneurial activity including in the USA the 'survival of the fittest' mentality, comparatively regressive taxation and the absence of state 'safety nets' (Acs and Storey 2004: 876). While this may help explain the different employment significance of new firm formation there are other potential outcomes to be considered as well. It has been argued that there can be positive outcomes for productivity where new entrants displace older businesses based on outdated methods and technologies. Indeed in some UK industries most productivity change has been estimated to result from the process of enterprise churning (Disney et al. 2003). While these possibilities exist for newer industries undergoing organizational and technological change, the situation in less prosperous regions has been shown to be different.

Various studies indicate how efforts to raise new firm formation have least impact in the most distressed regional economies and that the inducement to enterprise churning in these regions can even have negative consequences for employment (Greene et al. 2004; van Stel and Storey 2004). In older industrial areas characterized by an existing domination of large enterprises and relatively low levels of highly qualified workers, new firms tend to concentrate in easy-to-enter sectors such as various types of personal service and construction. Assisting these start ups gives the new entrants a competitive advantage over incumbents and forces some of them out of business. Once the start-up support has expired, the new entrants are themselves exposed to competition from more recent entrants still enjoying their start-up assistance. At the extreme, this results in the churning of enterprise ownership that in the long run reduces consumer confidence in small enterprise and lowers total employment in the sector (Greene et al. 2004). Hence the strong conclusion that policies to increase rates of new firm formation discriminate against regions of high unemployment.

Rather than seeking to raise the overall rate of new firm formation, local economic policy might be advised to target those few enterprises with potential for high growth. Efforts to implement such policies have been made but they tend to underestimate the challenge of being able to identify the characteristics of better performing start-up firms (Box 3.9). A considered response is that such approaches rely on a judgmental talent that neither the research community based on evidence nor policy makers based on experience would find easy to exercise (Acs and Storey 2004: 876). Even if the selection capacity did exist, the problem remains that high growth enterprise are more likely to be discovered in the already fastest growing regions.

Box 3.9 **Selecting for high growth**

In the United Kingdom it is estimated that around one per cent of business start ups may eventually achieve sales valued at £1 million (US$1.6 million) a year. A sample of such high growth enterprises has suggested the possibility of public support agencies supporting their growth.

- More claim to recognize that they could have benefited from external support at start up than actually used it.
- A larger proportion (30 per cent) of the high growth start ups suggest that external equity would have been used at the start than actually used it (four per cent).
- More firms made use of external assistance post start up than during their start-up phase.
- Dissatisfaction with the support services used was high, particularly in terms of the limited financial support for product development and absence of free mentoring services for start ups.

Delivering support to high growth enterprises requires good referral systems to gather together cohorts of new enterprises for the cost effective delivery of support programmes; specialist advisers with credibility, resources and networks relevant to entrepreneurs with growth ambition; communication and information sharing platforms such as an intranet dedicated to programme participants. An ongoing uncertainty is whether all partners to the scheme will share an equal commitment to maintaining an 'elite programme for an elite group of enterprises' as compared with allowing in marginal cases to bolster programme numbers and build weight but ultimately damaging the exercise.

Source: Smallbone *et al.* (2002)

This leaves strategies to raise the quality and growth potential of established enterprise. Help of this sort may comprise 'soft' business support such as mentoring, advisory assistance, the dissemination of best practice and the encouragement of partnerships. 'Hard' business support may include training assistance, loan guarantees, support for innovation and grants to defray various business expenditures. Across this broad area of different policy initiatives five broad observations can be made:

- Despite the considerable investment of public resources in small firm policies the evaluation of their impact is undeveloped (Storey 1999; Roper and

Hewitt-Dundas 2001; Wren and Storey 2002). Storey (2006) identifies six kinds of evaluation that have variously been employed to assess the impact of small business support, but notes that the most rigorous approaches have rarely been used. He identifies a failure to adjust evaluation findings for selection bias as an especially serious shortcoming. This refers to the possibility that firms joining a support programme have different characteristics to those which do not. If this is not recognized it can result in a programme's impact being exaggerated, as Wren and Storey (2002) show in the case of an evaluation of a programme offering subsidized consultancy services to SMEs.

- Policy intervention has frequently proceeded on the basis of generalized objectives rather than the specific identification of the targeted outcomes. Ambiguous or vague policy targets may be a factor in weakening the impact of policy intervention. Commenting on the effectiveness of the advisory services provided by enterprise agencies in the United Kingdom, for example, Storey (1994: 290) notes that a tendency for agency staff to emphasize the number of clients seen as their measure of success militated against the goal of improving the performance of small business because agency resources were spread too thinly.
- It has proved harder for public policy to change the fortunes of the small firm sector than anticipated, partly as some types of support that were thought pertinent to small enterprise have had no discernible impact. Storey (1994) identifies training, the provision of information and advice and taxation incentives as areas where policy interventions have frequently failed to have any discernible impact on the growth or survival of small firms. The gains from administrative simplification ('cutting red tape') were also considered unclear with, among other indicators, evidence that a more beneficial taxation regime for the self employed had not encouraged an increase in work hours as might have been expected (Storey 1994: 304). Enterprise zones in the UK experiment were launched with the expectation that they would unleash free market dynamism in otherwise depressed local economies (Hall 1981). That experiment proved of limited effectiveness, with the main impact being the short distance relocation of existing enterprises to take advantage of financial concessions (PA Cambridge Economic Consultants 1995).
- Individual policy impacts tend to be concentrated among particular segments of the small firm sector rather than diffusing widely. Those capturing the benefits may or may not coincide with the priority groups for public policy intervention. Wren and Storey (2002) investigated the take up of a Consultancy Initiative scheme that operated in the United Kingdom from 1988 to 1994. The theory of the scheme was that SMEs have problems identifying and contracting external advice that could be reduced by offering selected firms subsidized consultancy services. The evaluation found that overall the policy had no effect on firm survival, but when the impact on different enterprise size classes is examined the policy was effective in assisting enterprise survival and growth for 'mid-range SMEs' with employment of from six to 80 employees. It is speculated that the policy did not benefit smaller enterprises

as they have limited capacity to act on consultant advice. In the case of larger enterprises they speculate it may have failed because it is mainly poorly performing enterprises that are drawn to the scheme among this size of enterprise. There remains a need to understand whether the apparent effectiveness for medium sized SMEs was because they would otherwise have found appointing outside consultants too daunting (as supposed by the scheme's designers) or whether the impact came through some other mechanism.

- The ability to affect small business activity can depend on national policy interventions and changes in national institutions rather than being entirely within the capacity of local agencies. Storey (1994: 305) rates the support given to high technology small enterprises as among the most important forms of intervention that have emerged since the 1980s. At the same time he sees that national government expenditure on science in higher education and in encouraging interest in science among young people ultimately controls the supply of potential high tech entrepreneurs.

One reason for the mixed outcomes of policy intervention is that little is known about the determinants of small-firm growth other than it is something to which many small firms do not aspire (Barkham *et al.* 1996). It is generally understood that the growth of small firms is governed by three interrelated influences (Storey 1994: 123):

- The characteristics of the entrepreneurs and owner managers: motivation, prior work experience, education, management expertise, age are among the factors that have been linked to the growth of small firms.
- The characteristics of the small firm: this includes attributes affected by decisions at the time of start up (sector, legal form, ownership structure and location) and the size and age of the enterprise.
- The business strategies implemented: this encompasses the actions that are taken by the small business owner and includes decisions over equity sharing, market positioning, new product introductions, customer diversification and management decision making structures.

According to Storey (1994) these three components cannot compensate for each other. To grow, a small firm is expected to display the desirable aspects of each of the three attributes. Research has yet to produce agreement over what the important aspects of each component are. Most investigations of small-firm growth have tended to explore a limited set of factors, partly as comprehensive investigations face respondent resistance to extensive questionnaires. One attempt to be encompassing of the influences identified in the threefold typology covered 172 small firms located in four UK regions (Barkham *et al.* 1996). The study gave some grounds to be optimistic about the ability of policy to influence small-firm growth as it identified investment in marketing and decisions about distribution (direct sales or the use of intermediaries) as important strategy decisions affecting growth. Encouraging market research and assisting enterprises to sell directly to end buyers are within the scope of public policy support, as suggested by the policy experience evaluated by Wren and Storey (2002). In the context of their study, Barkham *et al.* (1996: 143) consider the particularly extensive small-firm support offered by the small-firm agency for Northern Ireland to have been a factor in that locality having a high proportion of fast growing small enterprises. This came through what might be characterized as a saturation strategy in terms of the extent of the support effort rather than insight into the most cost effective approaches to small-firm development. The researchers also acknowledge that some of the growth experienced by Northern Ireland's small firms may actually have come about from constraints on the growth of small enterprises in other regions that left market gaps for them to occupy.

How to revive regional policy

A remaining question is how to adapt discriminatory regional policy to increase its effectiveness in the context of changes in the nature of economic activity and shifts in public policy priorities. Suggestions that have been made include extending regional policy to new and existing small firms with growth potential as well as inward investment (Taylor and Wren 1997; Adams *et al.* 2003). Such a diversification needs to confront the limited insight into how best to promote small enterprise, but there is a logic for so doing as small firms in less prosperous regions are at a disadvantage to those in more prosperous localities and there is evidence that regional assistance grants given to small firms have been more effective than those given to large firms (Hart and Scott 1994; Wren 1994). Particularly in the case of small firms, there can be a case for grant assistance. Compared with other ways of delivering financial incentives, 'up front' support addresses barriers to capital funding which can be a significant impediment to growth (Adams *et al.* 2003: 75). Delivering finance support through the taxation system may not lead to small business owners investing more in their enterprise, and unless this happens then business performance is unlikely to improve (Storey 1994: 317). Small firms might also be given greater recognition in regional policy by linking the allocation of investment assistance to the total jobs created by a firm receiving a grant, including those upstream or downstream of the assisted enterprise which may include small enterprise (Taylor and Wren 1997: 844).

A further diversification involves the question of whether the relocation of activity between regions merits support as well as wholly new investment. From a national perspective there is a case for prioritizing inward investment from overseas over activity that is transferring internally. This is consistent with the principle that assistance should be allocated according to the net impact of investment projects, but weakens the commitment to redistributing employment to the assisted regions. Supporters of regional policy nonetheless argue that there is a greater case for giving regional assistance to internal transfers than to incoming foreign investment (Adams *et al.* 2003; Wren 2005). For foreign investors, the availability of regional assistance mainly affects the choice of country rather than choice of region, especially when incoming investment has a preference to locate near to other investment from the same source country. This can be seen to indicate that regional assistance is mainly serving a national policy goal of attracting inward investment and so should be funded as part of national industrial development policy. In contrast, regional incentives can influence the destination of business relocating internally. Within a country regional incentives are a more important differentiating factor than when locations are compared across countries. For these reasons it has been argued that internal relocations should be given assistance as part of a strong regional policy (Taylor and Wren 1997).

The redistribution of public sector employment has been included in regional policy, but in the past this has tended to result in the relocation of secondary, back-office functions rather than senior management. In this way public sector relocation can still be viewed as having scope to redistribute employment opportunities and is potentially important in giving highly qualified workers opportunities in depressed localities. Adams *et al.* (2003) have also seen scope to address regional inequalities through a policy of making successful regions make a larger contribution toward meeting the increased costs of success. One application of this is to impose congestion taxes in areas suffering from the excessive utilization of roads (Taylor and Wren 1997).

An area of uncertainty is how far regional policy can be directed at reducing regional differences in innovation, affecting the rate at which enterprises introduce new products and services. There is no doubt that technical progress is important to a region's wellbeing. A regional policy perspective is that much of the inequality in innovative capacity results from the uneven distribution of research institutions and the unequal distribution of public expenditure on science and technology (Armstrong and Taylor 1985; Adams *et al.* 2003). The tendency for research institutions to cluster reflects many interlocking advantages, such as access to a large pool of highly qualified workers, access to markets, access to central government agencies and advantages of locating near to a concentration of other R&D facilities and company headquarters (Armstrong and Taylor 1985: 219). Scientific and research institutions provide much of the raw material for innovation. Proximity matters to the ability of innovators and entrepreneurs to use the ideas generated by basic research and apply them to commercial problems, as seen in the connections between the UK electronics industry in the south of England and government science institutions (Benneworth 2002; Adams *et al.* 2003: 65). This is partly because new enterprise 'spun out' of research institutions tends to stay close to its focal institution even though no functional linkage may remain (Oakey *et al.* 2001). Regionalizing scientific institutions risks damaging the international standing of a country's science base and faces considerable obstacles if it extends to changing the status of leading universities. Advocates of a revival of discriminatory regional policy recognize that there are limits to how far the capacity for innovation can be equalized (Adams *et al.* 2003). Potential steps are to encourage the relocation of scientific bodies that are relatively weakly attached to the scientific core and to make greater efforts to disperse parts of the public expenditure on science more evenly.

Conclusion

This chapter started with the claim that contemporary policy making for local economic development tends to overlook regional policy experiences. This omission is potentially serious as there is a long history to regional policy that has included systematic efforts to review its effectiveness and reflect on the experience of different regional policy tools. Three main influences may account for the tendency to overlook what can be learnt from regional policy. First, there is a tendency to view the promotion of inward investment as a failed policy on the grounds that the targets of the promotion exploit the competition for investment and rarely become attached to the places to which they are lured. Second, regional policy is associated with a time when governments were more willing to intervene in economc affairs and were more influenced by 'demand-side' explanations of economic malaise than they are today. Third, alternative policy approaches have appealed as they appear to promise much greater effectiveness, partly as they are more attuned to the nature of contemporary business organizations and the importance of local institutions in building competitive advantage.

The evidence and debate reviewed in this chapter points to the value of incorporating regional policy experience in contemporary local economic policy. At the broadest level, regional policy can be valued for its unambiguous objective of reducing regional disparities in unemployment. While there are always weaknesses in the ability of a single indicator to capture the full dimensions of a problem, policy is driven by a clear purpose and evaluation against policy objectives is possible. The contrast can be made, for example, with the promotion of small firms where policy has sometimes been driven by unclear objectives, making judgements of policy effectiveness hard. On the basis of the comparatively rigorous evaluations that have been conducted there is some confidence in being able to claim that regional policy can be effective. Regional policy has acquired a doubtful reputation partly through its association with a negative interpretation of branch plant economies. Evidence from the examination of branch plant closures suggests that past mass closure experiences need to be understood as episodes of industrial restructuring rather than a sign that investment was lured to inefficient locations. Going forward there are reasons to be positive about the potential for inward investment to support regional growth even without them attaining a high level of local embeddedness. With respect to policy design, regional policy has demonstrated how discretionary financial assistance can be cost effective and offer other advantages over automatic grants paid to qualifying activities or across-the-board subsidies. Another message is that the boundaries of assisted areas need to be drawn sufficiently wide to encompass relatively attractive locations as well as the places where those most in need of employment reside.

The promotion of new and small firms is one aspect of local economic policy where understanding has grown. This shows that raising the rate of formation and growth of new businesses is not easy. Small business growth is dependent on the alignment of multiple attributes, some of which are intractable to policy influence, such as the family and employment history of business owners. In depressed regions the tendency for small business support to result in the churning of enterprise ownership has been an unproductive outcome. Targeting the minority of new enterprises with major growth prospects remains a challenge and some doubt it will ever be possible to identify 'winners' in advance. As a source of growth to reduce regional disparities there are many reasons to doubt that small firms alone can replace the need for inward investment, although they may play a supplementary role.

Questions can still be asked about regional policy. Regional policy had its greatest impact in the context of a determined focus to redistribute employment and comparatively high levels of expenditure. In the United Kingdom, for example, expenditure peaked in the mid 1970s, since when it had reduced to around 10 per cent of that amount at the start of the new century (Wren 2005). Moreover, the effort was higher than the direct expenditure, as up to the early 1980s controls were maintained on the location of all new industrial investment involved in the construction of new plants above a specified floor area. These location controls were an important contributor to the movement of so many jobs to the assisted areas. In more contemporary circumstances of reduced expenditure and reduced effort to achieve a redistribution of employment it becomes harder to judge the effectiveness of remaining regional initiatives. Comparatively modest levels of expenditure can be concentrated on the 'best' projects, suggesting favourable cost per job outcomes that might not be sustained if expenditure was expanded. There are differences of judgement about the advantages of devolving the administration regional policy as compared with the benefits of centralized control. A shift to local administration can be encouraged by perceptions that this responds to the need for the strengthening of local institutions and development of distinctive economic environments. These possibilities are part of the subject of the chapters in the reminder of this book.

4 Learning regions

There is a widespread belief that knowledge diffuses more evenly and more rapidly among a localized community than among a highly dispersed community (Breschi and Lissoni 2001a; Pinch *et al.* 2003). As stated by one researcher, knowledge traverses corridors and streets more easily than continents and oceans (Feldman 1994: 4) so that even if knowledge ultimately diffuses, the first sharing of knowledge occurs locally (Feldman 2000). When combined with the perceived importance of knowledge and learning to business growth, a strong policy conclusion can result: economic development agencies should aim to build conditions that will maximize knowledge generation and learning, as these sources of competitive advantage are at low risk of immediate imitation. The ideas of the British economist Alfred Marshall are frequently cited in support of the possibility that an industry's secrets can be shared locally without risk of dispersing further afield. Among other judgements, Marshall observed that:

> When an industry has once chosen a locality for itself, it is likely to stay there long: so great are the advantages which people following the same skilled trade get from near neighbourhood to one another ... if one man starts a new idea it is taken up by others and combined with suggestions of their own; and thus becomes the source of yet more new ideas.
>
> (Marshall 1890: 332)

The implication frequently taken from this claim is of firms gaining from 'untraded interdependencies' that promote information sharing and learning (Storper 1995b). Technological trajectories are thus being traced to the development of localized pools of knowledge that support 'learning economies' (Lundvall and Johnson 1994) or 'learning regions' (Morgan 1997). Whatever the transition to a globalized economy and the increased capacities of electronic communication, key resources for competitiveness are claimed to come from people learning through sharing and exchanging information within localized business communities.

This aspect of the debate about knowledge economies is not about the attraction or importance of centres of public and private sector research activity or their role in seeding new enterprise. Local economic strategy grounded on the attraction of research-based activities on the premise that they can be encouraged to spin out new enterprise, generate positive regional multipliers and attract enterprises employing well paid knowledge workers is considered in the review of technology incubators (Chapter 7). Two main issues are at stake in the present chapter. First, that there is a strong negative spatial gradient to knowledge flows such that distance from the point of origin affects the ability to gain access to new knowledge. Those who believe this to occur see that the spatial clustering of knowledge producers and knowledge users provides powerful incentives for enterprises to concentrate in relative proximity to each other (Goldstein 2009: 241). Associated with this claim, which for economists can be a component of endogenous growth theory (Box 4.1), is the requirement that at least some new knowledge is 'non rival' and 'non excludable'. This means that one enterprise's take up of the knowledge does not exclude any other enterprise from making use of the same knowledge. In the terminology employed by economists, this makes knowledge a 'pure externality' or 'spillover' and results in the potential for gains to the local economy as a whole. Where knowledge is a proprietary good, access may not diffuse beyond the enterprises that own and control it, or it may be shared within selected networks, and this may lessen the justification for local agencies to support knowledge creation.

Box 4.1 Endogenous growth theory

A traditional neo classical economic explanation of regional development argues that provided there are no major barriers to the operation of market processes, regional economic disparities should reduce. This is an outcome of assuming that the demand for regional resources will increase in response to the movement in the price of labour and other business costs. Endogenous growth theory has developed to explain the persistence of regional economic disparities. This approach differs from earlier theories that explain why market processes do result in regional convergence (such as cumulative causation) by emphasizing the concept of 'increasing returns'. The existence of increasing returns explains why market processes should result in one group of enterprises continuing to grow without countervailing opportunities arising for the regions left outside the growth spurt. This makes regional disparities compatible with economic efficiency, whereas the proponents of cumulative causation had tended to see the need for regional policy intervention to correct regional inequalities. It is called endogenous growth theory because the opportunity to grow comes from forces internal to a group of enterprises, such as the way that growth permits specialization and specialization increases economic efficiency.

There are different versions of endogenous growth theory but they frequently rely on some form of knowledge spillover. This means that when an enterprise invests in technology and labour force skills the economic benefits diffuse to other enterprises, as when the efficiency gain to one enterprise is transferred to linked enterprises. Endogenous growth theories are used to build economic models of how regions will develop according to the assumptions of the model. There are reasons to question whether they fit regional development in practice:

- The theory is not able to explain why regions should experience sudden changes in their economic prosperity, for example endogenous growth theory

> could not explain why Silicon Valley became a focal growth of the semiconductor industry, neither do they recognize the danger of regions getting 'locked in' to an inefficient technology.
> - The models are not compatible with how industry structures tend to evolve over product cycles or how innovation can arise from economic diversity as well as increasing specialization.
> - Sources of enterprise growth are more varied than the mechanisms envisaged by endogenous growth theories. For example, studies of small firm growth tend to identify marketing decisions as a critical area of decision making (see Chapter 3) but these processes get little or no attention in endogenous growth models.
> - The policy application of endogenous growth theory is to encourage public sector investment in labour and technology. This results in a largely 'supply side' response to regional economic problems which can overlook the importance of demand: in other words, increasing the supply of skilled labour in a region may not assist regional development unless there is demand for their employment.
>
> *Source:* Martin and Sunley (1998)

The second and related issue under review is the alleged importance of knowledge that accumulates more widely within a community than just among those formally designated as knowledge managers and creators. This is captured partly by the distinction between tacit and codified knowledge. Tacit knowledge is generally understood as those aspects of understanding that defy codification or articulation in written and spoken words (Gertler 2003: 78). The person possessing tacit knowledge is not conscious of all the understanding that they have and they may be hampered from communicating their insight and skills by the absence of appropriate language. Consequently, observing, imitating and correcting others are said to be the primary means of transferring tacit knowledge and this suggests the importance of frequent, personal interaction. Spatial barriers to knowledge diffusion can be assumed and the advocacy of learning regions boosted if tacit knowledge is important.

Basing local economic development on the importance of a particular type of knowledge provides the main controversy to be considered in this chapter. Research on this issue tends to be polarized. At one extreme, it continues to be argued that proximity is a necessary prerequisite for learning because some knowledge (including, most importantly, new knowledge acquired in the course of research and not yet diffused through formal scientific reporting channels) is exchanged fully only in verbal, face-to-face communication (Balconi *et al.* 2007: 843). Whether it is craft skills or intellectual knowledge that is sought, access is held to depend on a location offering immediate, day-to-day access to a concentration of knowledgeable workers. At the other extreme are those who believe that it is not yet possible to say anything intelligent about the conditions under which tacit knowledge is most readily shared within a community (Gertler 2003: 95) or even that one form of knowledge is actually more important than another (Malmberg and Maskell 2002). Further scepticism has been offered by Martin and Sunley (2003: 17) who raise three sources of doubt:

- Distinctions between different forms of knowledge are not as sharp as those encouraged by the tendency to consider binary alternatives only (tacit versus codified; informal versus formal).
- The nature of the expertise existing as 'localized tacit knowledge' and how it creates a business advantage has not been sufficiently explained. To influence local economic development, knowledge of whatever type must be applied in business activities. In contrast, most accounts of the importance of tacit knowledge focus on 'territorial learning' and institutions other than individual enterprises.
- The role of tacit knowledge tends to be discussed in isolation from any account of innovation processes and how these influence the evolution of industries. Tacit knowledge is often linked to claims of a shared regional culture. The socializing processes that create a shared understanding can reduce non conforming outlooks and this has the potential to reduce the locality's capacity to anticipate and react to strategies that challenge established ways of working.

This chapter describes the learning region concept and explains forces that may give grounds for thinking that geography influences knowledge creation and learning. It then outlines the range of ways that the learning region concept has been applied. This shows how optimism in the scope for local learning can run ahead of conceptual clarity. A critical review of the conditions required for knowledge spillovers to disperse learning opportunities among co-located enterprises underlines the gulf between learning region theory and present evidence. The chapter finishes with the identification of four areas where reliable evidence exists and that offer some guidance on how to influence some form of localized learning.

The learning region

The idea of a learning region brings together two strands of thinking: that knowledge underscores business competitiveness and that the region is a platform for localized interactions that support the accumulation of knowledge. Both strands of interest have justification. The structure of older economies has been changing, and with it the basis on which business seeks to compete. The shift away from mass manufacturing to more customized areas of industrial activity, the growth of high-technology industry and increasing application of information technology all justify claims of the development of a more knowledge-based economy (Lundvall 1999). Interaction between firms (customers, suppliers and competitors), research organizations (universities, public and private sector research institutions) and other public agencies is now widely accepted as the basis through which much knowledge generation and application occurs. This has been referred to as 'learning through interacting' (Lundvall and Johnson 1994). As close proximity is thought to increase the likelihood of interaction, both because of the relative ease of face-to-face interaction and the common social context for communication, it becomes possible to present the region as an important arena in which knowledge is built, communicated and applied.

The concept of a learning region has developed from original interest in regional systems of innovation, which themselves grew out of the identification of national systems of innovation (Cooke 1998; Cooke et al. 1998; Bunnell and Coe 2001; MacKinnon et al. 2002). Freeman (1987: 1) defined a national system of innovation as the network of institutions in the public and private sectors whose activities and interactions initiate, import, modify and diffuse new technologies. This definition arose in the context of revealing distinctive aspects of the Japanese economy that had influenced its post war industrial growth. Lundvall (1992: 13) added to Freeman's definition by proposing five core elements of a national innovation system: the internal organization of firms; the nature of interfirm relationships; the role of the public sector; the institutional structure of finance; the intensity and organization of R&D activity. It was subsequently suggested that national systems might be more appropriately understood as a number of distinct systems identified by particular institutional or geographical affiliations, or both (Metcalfe 1995: 41). This led through to efforts to identify the existence of separate regional systems of innovation and efforts to integrate this analysis with a new regional science that sought to explain why regions might vary in their ability to innovate (Cooke 1998; Cooke et al. 1998).

A tendency to now talk about learning regions rather than regional systems of innovation can have a twofold significance. First, influential thinkers have proposed that learning rather than knowledge or innovation is the appropriate focus of research attention (Box 4.2). Modern thinking about technological change stresses the importance of cumulative and incremental problem solving rather than discrete acts of knowledge creation or innovation that are subsequently capitalized upon through changes in production. Knowledge generation is significant only as it feeds into a learning process and in so far as learning is a continuous process. Second, interest in learning regions is partly as a normative prescription of the policy agenda that development agencies should follow to maximize learning within individual regions (Bunnell and Coe 2001). Developing from this, the phrase 'learning region' is sometimes restricted to regions that are thought to have a high capacity for learning. For example, Hauser et al. (2007: 76) say that learning regions are 'locations with a strong social and institutional endowment that exhibit continuous creation and diffusion of new knowledge and high rates of innovation'. To understand how regions might obtain distinctive learning capacities, macro and micro forces can be distinguished building on Howell's (1999) top down and bottom up perspectives.

> **Box 4.2 From knowledge to learning economy**
>
> Knowledge is a crucial resource but learning is the most important process in a modern economy. This importance is an outcome of the development of information, computer and telecommunication technologies, reorganization of economic activity to facilitate flexible specialization and to changes in the process of innovation. Important sectors of economic activity are confronted with a steep increase in the costs of developing new products or systems of production. They must cope with an increased diversity of information sources and shorter product life cycles. This makes it crucial for firms to develop organizational forms that maximize learning ability. Such organizational changes include the reduction in management tiers within organizations and cooperation and alliances between firms to share financial risks and gain access to a diversity of information sources.
>
> *Source:* Lundvall and Johnson (1994)

Macro context for learning regions

The regional structure of a national economy provides part of the macro context shaping differences in learning patterns. The general pattern in older economies is that industries exhibit some degree of regional concentration. This is particularly evident in the attachment of heavy industry to parts of the national space economy that are shunned by new high tech activities: the rustbelt–sunbelt contrast. As well, industry that needs specialized infrastructure or has distinctive location requirements such as port access or large amounts of energy is frequently associated with one locality more than any other. Consequently, although the pattern in the USA has been for regional specialization to decline since the 1930s compared with earlier decades, some activities still exhibit a high degree of geographical concentration (Kim and Margo 2004). These regional specializations may have different dependencies on formal R&D, different rates of knowledge-worker employment and different opportunities for innovation among other sources of variation. As a consequence of this there may be little regional overlap in the institutions supporting innovation and learning (Nelson and Rosenberg 1993: 5). This difference might be expected to be especially strong where the region's attachment to a particular industry has a long history, although local specializations can be of recent origin too.

Intra industry differences are another reason for thinking that regions may have distinctive learning capacities. Howell (1999) discussed this in terms of the core–periphery divide. In most economies other than small city states there is a pronounced tendency for spatial divisions of labour to concentrate corporate control and associated business support services in a core economy. The periphery is distinguished by its dependence on branches of national and international organizations that tend to have little or no local management control, restricted responsibilities and no long term commitment. Such attributes are unsurprisingly judged negative for regional learning, but the changing characteristics of branch plants have lessened this aspect of the core–periphery divide (Chapter 3).

The structure of political systems is a third influence giving scope for distinctive regional experiences. Federal systems of governance and countries with strong local government can give significant regional control over education, environmental planning and infrastructure provision. Aligned with regional differences in political affiliation, the possibility arises for marked impacts on local business environments that have potential to impact on learning processes. For example, while the US government has not signed the Kyoto Protocol a large number of individual states have adopted the Protocol and enacted local climate change policies (Kruger 2005). This requires business in some states to learn about reducing carbon emissions and through this may come shifts in the perception of the environment as a business issue that may have broader impacts beyond meeting carbon reduction targets. Even in relatively unified political systems government expenditure is not distributed evenly across regions, with potential impacts on local learning capacities. Perhaps one of the most well known facets of this is the uneven distribution of military-related research expenditure, as this activity is frequently cited to have an influence in attracting other research activity and high technology industry to a region (Malecki 1991: 53).

Micro context for learning regions

The macro forces that may distinguish regional institutions and economic structures play a secondary role in learning region advocacy. This is partly because the way services are delivered and how they are received can vary where regions have similar institutional structures. In line with the focus on learning, most attention is paid to the social dimensions of regional differences. Some aspects of learning can be obtained through market relations such as the purchase of training and education services, but this is viewed as less effective than learning provided in an informal arrangement. It may, for example, speed up the learning process by avoiding the need to design and agree legal contracts (Lundvall 1999: 21). More importantly, where learning relates to 'know how' it is thought to have a large component of so-called tacit knowledge that is embedded in the production practices and accumulated experience of firms and workers rather than in a form that is readily written down, reported orally or 'codified' in some other form. In principle (but not necessarily in practice, as discussed below), codified knowledge can be traded or communicated through markets and management hierarchies and to this extent is readily transferred, whereas tacit knowledge is 'sticky' and dependent on close interpersonal and interfirm relations (Morgan 1997; Storper 1997; Cooke and Morgan 1998; MacKinnon *et al.* 2002). In this context the distinction between tacit and codified knowledge has come to play a central role in the claimed importance of localized learning economies (Breschi and Lissoni 2001b).

Proponents argue that close proximity between interacting parties increases the likelihood of tacit understanding being shared effectively, especially when combined with high levels of inter organizational and inter personal trust (Maskell *et al.* 1998: 44–49). Indeed, for some proponents of learning economy theory 'it is absolutely imperative that a minimum of respect and mutual trust exists for the transfer of knowledge to take place' (Lundvall 1999: 23). Trust is emphasized because it is seen to affect the ease of forming relationships and the extent to which interaction is likely to stimulate learning. When both parties have a high degree of trust in each other, a strong sense of mutual obligation regulates behaviour and guards against malfeasance without the need to rely on legal contracts (MacKinnon *et al.* 2002). On this basis, it is assumed that reciprocal exchanges of knowledge and joint working will be particularly conducive to learning. The perception that trust is a relatively scarce commodity is a further reason for giving it particular emphasis. Trust is not a commodity that can be purchased but rather is an aspect of widely shared understandings of expected behaviour and values that determine definitions of 'good' and 'bad' behaviour. If trust was everywhere abundant it could not explain why some regions had greater learning capacity than others. In this regard, Lundvall (1999) identifies the Nordic region as particularly well-endowed with trust as a consequence of strong welfare systems, social cohesion and relatively stable and homogenous populations. This claim was taken further by other Nordic scholars, who suggested that small industrial countries generally had an advantage in their levels of 'shared trust' (Maskell *et al.* 1998; Lundvall 1999: 23), a claim not substantiated when tested in New Zealand (Box 4.3).

Box 4.3 **No sharing of shared trust**

It has been argued that small countries have a relative advantage over large countries in fostering business cooperation (Maskell *et al.* 1998). This perspective points to shared backgrounds and the likelihood of mutual participation in activity outside the workplace (social, political or professional) as a basis for trust and the identification of joint interests. Like a village compared with a city, visibility and recognition among the population as a whole is claimed to be higher in a small country compared with a large country (Maskell 1998: 198). On this basis, smallness can facilitate interaction and information sharing, make informal sanctions such as social ostracism a viable sanction against opportunistic behaviour and encourage conformity and the acceptance of collective interests. Based on these ideas, Maskell *et al.* (1988) suggested that 'shared trust' had allowed the Nordic small economies to avoid the 'small country squeeze' otherwise arising from low economies of scale, limited economic diversification and the periodic relocation of business to larger overseas markets. These claims do not transfer to New Zealand, another small country that has neither matched Nordic economic success nor developed a business environment rich in shared trust (Perry 2001). This suggests that Nordic performance must be explained by other processes than its environment of trust, or that if trust has been significant this reflects conditions peculiar to the region rather than attributes shared with other small countries. A history of corporatist politics and Nordic economic integration are potentially more decisive sources of difference with other countries than any attributes common to small countries.

The Nordic experience refers to distinctive national influences on trust. Interest in learning regions was stimulated by the perception that just as countries had distinctive cultures that affected patterns of business development so might regions, at least within larger economies. The divergent economic performance of California's Silicon Valley and Boston's Route 128 during the 1980s after both had originally vied for leadership of the incipient computer industry has been seen as a demonstration of how regional cultures affect learning and economic progress (Saxenian 1994; James 2005). Baden-Württemberg was pointed to as another test case of the role that distinctive regional cultures could play in fostering learning and business innovation (Cooke and Morgan 1994). A further stimulus came from optimism that public agencies could play a role in changing the environment for business interaction even in less favoured regions without an inherited culture of trust that naturally fostered learning (Morgan 1997).

Learning region varieties

The learning region is a multi faceted concept that seeks to guide investigation of the relationships between regions, knowledge creation and competitive advantage and that is sometimes further developed into a prescription of how region economies should be organized. Being directed at a wide ranging agenda, the learning region has been used for a variety of purposes (Table 4.1).

Table 4.1 Learning region variations

Learning region perspective	Key claims	Main contribution	Unresolved issues
Embedded economic activity	Cultural attributes modify market processes.	Increased understanding of how the social environment affects economic activity.	Differences in culture may modify rather than fundamentally change economic processes; functionally equivalent conditions may reduce regional differences.
Learning and economic success	Advanced economies are knowledge based; learning is an interactive rather than linear process.	Identification of a transition in advanced economies to an increased dependence on knowledge intensive activity; knowledge relies on social interaction.	Unclear that all activities classed as knowledge based rely on high levels of learning; contribution of learning to breakthrough innovation unclear.
Region as the focus of learning	Regions have become important contexts for learning.	The existence of tacit knowledge and the role of social relations in transferring tacit knowledge.	Unclear that the distinction between tacit and codified knowledge is real or that proximity is a limiting factor on knowledge sharing.
Regional learning infrastructure	Specific economic institutions advance learning capacity.	Identification of alternative ways of structuring regional economies.	Advocacy of a preferred system of economic governance not supported by evidence that the favoured attributes explain differences in performance.

(*Continued*)

Table 4.1 Learning region variations (Continued)

Learning region perspective	Key claims	Main contribution	Unresolved issues
Strategy for regional development	Encouraging localized learning processes protects regions from the impact of globalization.	Distinctive knowledge is a source of regional competitive advantage.	Unresolved how the risks of 'lock in' to obsolete knowledge are avoided when the emphasis is on protecting regional knowledge pools and internal rather than external interaction.

At the broadest level, the learning region can be seen as a geographical application of Granovetter's (1985) claim that economic activity is embedded within a social context. The embeddedness thesis argues that culture shapes the operation of market forces so that it is misplaced to interpret patterns of economic development as the creation of a uniform economic logic. Granovetter (1973, 1983) first recognized this when studying a community dominated by strong social networks and revealing the importance of weak ties in providing access to novel sources of information. Developing from this kind of insight, it is argued that the workings of economic processes in a given place and time cannot be understood without simultaneously interrogating the social systems that underpin them, and this includes the capacity to learn (Block 1990). Thus the learning region has been defined as a theoretical orientation that emphasizes 'soft' factors such as interaction and cultural characteristics in the analysis of 'hard' outcomes such as innovative production and economic development (Hauser *et al.* 2007: 76). Sustaining this conceptualization of a learning region requires understanding of the degree of cultural distinctiveness needed to deflect economic activity from 'pure' market forces and the components of culture that modify market processes most strongly. There may also be a need to distinguish cultural differences that have an impact on economic activity from differences that are functionally equivalent to each other. For example, it has been argued that Japanese manufacturing plants in Europe and North America operate with functionally equivalent forms of trust to home country plants whatever the differences in national culture (Elger and Smith 1994). Similarly, while much stress is placed on trust as a socially embedded influence on economic development, this assumes an absence of trust is an impediment to effective business relations (Box 4.4). A further question of this perspective is whether culture overrides economic forces or whether it merely changes the incentives between buyers and sellers. For example, Williamson (1991, 1994) has proposed that culture can be treated as a 'shift parameter' that changes the costs of alternative business structures but does not fundamentally alter the basis on which decisions are taken.

> **Box 4.4 Trust and distrust**
>
> The perception that trust and shared backgrounds affect the disposition to join collective projects is challenged by some conceptualizations of trust. Implicit in interpretations of the significance of trust is the assumption that the absence of trust means the presence of distrust. An alternative assessment argues that the simultaneous existence of positive and negative sentiments is more likely to occur than the dichotomous existence of trust or distrust. In all but the most primitive and simplistic relationships, people relate to each other in multiple ways. People may engage with each other in different contexts with different intentions and different outcomes. A situation of low trust and high distrust exists where there are no expectations of beneficial actions by others and where there are expectations of harmful action by the other party. Where there are no expectations of harmful action, low trust can be combined with low distrust: resulting in a relationship where people have no reason to be confident or wary. A relationship of high trust and high distrust is possible, perhaps reflecting how in a multifaceted relationship there have been trust reinforcing experiences and distrust reinforcing experiences. In a business partnership, for example, it may be agreed to share technical and proprietary information while putting controls on the physical access of the partner organization's engineers to specified offices when they are on site.
>
> *Source:* Lewicki *et al.* (1998).

Following Lundvall and Johnson (1994), interest in the learning region concept may reflect a claim that the capability to learn has become critical to economic success. This is an argument about a transition in advanced economies in which knowledge has become the most important resource for business competitiveness and learning the most important process. With this perspective comes a specific understanding that learning relies on interaction among people in enterprises and other organizations and may be contrasted with learning-by-doing (Arrow 1962), learning-by-using (Rosenberg 1982) and learning-by-searching (Boulding 1985). The emphasis on interaction implies changes within organizations as well as between them. Internally, it challenges linear models of the innovation process that, among other aspects, tend to encourage the separation of R&D activities from other parts of the organization. Externally, a variety of processes, encompassing out-sourcing, joint ventures, strategic alliances and involvement in industry associations, are formal outcomes of increased interaction. The imperative to operate within business networks makes 'know-who' of growing importance to 'know-how' (Lundvall and Johnson 1994).

A focus on learning has been questioned from several perspectives (Hudson 1999). In the first place it is not established that there has been any change in the need for learning or adjustment for ways that the increased ability to access and process information may be changing the capacity to learn (Rallet and Torre 1999). The relationship between learning and radical, breakthrough innovation is not explored. Learning suggests an incremental process suitable for catching up to or moving beyond 'best practice' based on incremental improvements in business performance, whereas successful enterprises must also discover new products and services (Asheim 1999).

Lundvall's conception of a learning economy emphasized national boundaries as having most impact on geographical differences in learning capacity, as they tend to enclose networks of technological interaction and bring relative geographic and cultural closeness (Boschma 1999). In contrast, the learning region has been taken to indicate that the region has become the arena in which most learning occurs (Asheim and Isaksen 1997; Lawson and Lorenz 1999; MacKinnon et al. 2002) or at least is a key, necessary element for learning and innovation (Leamer and Storper 2001: 650). This claim is usually based on the importance of tacit knowledge and the belief that this form of knowledge is best transmitted and developed through close interpersonal and interfirm relations and so does not travel far (Storper 1997). It is not just that the parties need to know each other, they need a common membership of 'communities defined by cultural affiliation, language, ideology, desire, mutual identification, and other powerful forms of bonding' (Leamer and Storper 2001: 653). Learning is also informed by a collective sharing of knowledge through untraded dependencies or spillovers, as well as through bilateral cooperation. Access to the shared knowledge pool explains the importance of 'being there' in the sense of location among related firms and industries (Gertler 1995). The critical questions for this perspective on the learning region centre on the need to demonstrate the importance of tacit knowledge, proximity and spillovers and that these contributors to learning vary between regions. These connections are returned to in the following section.

The learning region can imply a particular regional infrastructure that needs to be put in place to maximize learning. Working from the perspective that it is possible to define the components of a successful regional economy, embeddedness is interpreted as 'the extent to which a social community operates in terms of shared norms of cooperation, trustful interaction and untraded interdependencies' as compared with a region based on competitive, individualistic, 'arm's length exchange' and 'hierarchical norms' (Cooke 2001: 960). This claim came from interpretations of regions such as Baden-Württemberg and Massachusetts and proposed four main components of a fully functioning regional innovation system:

- Regional financial competence over three areas of public and private finance: (i) the provision of finance to business; (ii) the setting and allocation of regional budgets, including authority to levy some forms of regional tax; (iii) infrastructure funding to enable regional control or at least influence over investment in hard (transport, telecommunications) and soft (universities, research, technology transfer) infrastructure.
- Institutional infrastructure that supports a cooperative culture, a learning orientation and a 'quest for consensus'.
- Organizational infrastructure refers to the employment relations models favoured by the region's enterprises and is expected to encompass trust within and between the senior management and 'shopfloor' levels of organizations,

welfare-orientated employment policies and openness in dealings with other enterprises.
- Governance of regional institutions is distinguished by the extent to which policy makers emphasize inclusivity, monitoring, consultation, delegation and networking.

This perspective converts the learning region into a specific public policy agenda, but as Cooke (2001: 961) acknowledges, regions close to these ideal characteristics are rare and newly discovered, which may have an implication that more has yet to be researched about the full origins of regional successes. For example, it is not clear how far the model depends on the presence of research-intensive multinational enterprise with large R&D expenditure: these are a feature of the model regional economies but they may also challenge the transition to a decentralized, networked economy that is seen to fit the 'new economy'. Others have questioned the claims that learning is associated with the empowering of employees and interpret the main changes in employment practices as more to do with multi tasking and new ways of intensifying the labour process (Hudson 1999: 66).

Finally, another shift of emphasis occurs with those who have presented the learning region as an antidote to globalization and a strategy for building regional advantage based on an optimal balance of competitive and cooperative forces. This is reflected in suggestions that the role of learning regions is to avoid 'ubiquitification' by protecting knowledge unique to individual localities (Maskell *et al.* 1998; Maskell and Malmberg 1999). Industrial location theory, as it first developed, recognized ubiquities as resources that are available to enterprises regardless of their location, and therefore of no influence on location. Access to a large domestic market, for example, ceases to be an influence on location when declining transport costs make it possible to reach that market from many more places. Developing from this, globalization is seen to be accelerating the conversion of once unique location factors into 'ubiquities' (Maskell 2001). Survival of local economies requires that enterprise location decisions respond to influences that are not susceptible to conversion into ubiquities. Three opportunities are identified to develop a learning advantage that guards against ubiquitification:

- Incremental 'low tech' learning and innovation is at least as important for economic development as the learning associated with formal R&D programmes, universities and other research bodies.
- The spatial arrangement of economic activity affects the capacity for incremental learning.
- Learning faster than competitors is a strategy for staying ahead of the competition.

This anti-globalization version of the learning region leads to the advocacy of the advantages of industry-specialized business clusters. These are recommended to comprise both large numbers of competing enterprises, to aid the transfer of knowledge between competitors, and large numbers of enterprises linked by

92 *Learning regions*

input–output connections. This arrangement is believed to maximize learning by concentrating enterprises that have sufficient differences to be able to learn from each other while retaining sufficient common ground for the results of interactive learning to be applied across different workplaces (Maskell 2001: 932). Other commentators may not go so far as to suggest that ubiquitification is the threat but nonetheless argue that globalization is homogenizing scientific, technological and marketing knowledge around the industrial world, and this makes tacit knowledge of increasing local economic significance (Morgan 1997; Gertler 2003).

The learning region as a finely balanced cluster of competitive yet collectivized enterprises needs to be reconciled with the need to maintain connection to external knowledge communities. Presumably, some connections are needed to provide access to international markets, to replenish technology and to avoid 'lock-in' to a specific business model (MacKinnon *et al.* 2002: 304). The need to reach out to the external economy is a universal challenge facing emerging business clusters and frequently the start of a process that leads to their disintegration, as seen in the transition that many of Italy's industrial districts have experienced since the 1980s (Chapter 2 Box 2.2) or the disintegration of many developing country clusters (Schmitz 1999). As discussed in Chapter 5, presentations of business clusters as comprising the perfect balance of cooperation and competition are based on idealized accounts not found in practice.

This sample of five divergent possibilities combined with other interpretations has not surprisingly led to doubts that the idea of a learning region has any validity (Lovering 1999; Markusen 1999; MacKinnon *et al.* 2002). Evidence tends to rely on a short list of oft repeated examples rather than a demonstration of similar processes being found in divergent environments (Bunnell and Coe 2001). Moreover, individual regional experiences can attract multiple interpretations (Box 4.5). Reviewing the basic propositions underlying the learning region gives further reason to search for more specific grounds on which learning processes might become sources of local economic advantage.

Box 4.5 **Silicon Valley stories**

The success of Silicon Valley and the relative decline of Route 128 during the late 1980s have been attributed to cultural differences that affected the willingness to share knowledge (Saxenian 1994). Unconventional, open-minded managers in Silicon Valley let their employees move between employers with benefits for individual enterprises and the strength of the cluster as a whole. Around Boston, conservative mangers sought to retain employees and frowned on 'job hoppers'. These attributes have given Silicon Valley the appearance of growing through knowledge spillovers.

One reaction to this claim is that particular conditions facilitated knowledge spillovers as well as the social environment of openness to information sharing:

- The basic technology was invented at the birth of the industry, providing a core technology which small firms could acquire at a reasonable price (Freeman 1982). Core technology was suitable for widespread modification into commercial products that could support large numbers of new firms (Oakey *et al.* 1990).

- In the early phases of the semiconductor industry university basic research lagged behind the work done by industry (OTA 1984; Daly 1985). This was an inducement to geographical concentration because university expertise tends to be highly dispersed whereas industry investment is comparatively mobile, enabling it to concentrate around an initial centre of expertise (Sharp 1990).
- There was a short lead time between the conception of an idea to the successful first sale of products and services. New companies could exploit small 'time windows' created by the hesitation of former industry leaders in identifying market potential (Oakey *et al.* 1990). The ability to earn profits quickly allowed new companies to become established before incumbents were able to react.

Another reaction is to recognize that information sharing is only one of many competing explanations for Silicon Valley's growth:

- Sustained public investment in defence-related technology development channelled to organizations that built up the electronics industry in California and the electrical engineering department in Stanford University and influenced companies to settle in the area before the semiconductor revolution took off (Prevezer 1998).
- A workforce attuned to rapid changes and unpredictability in the labour market relied upon a wide range of intermediaries including temporary help firms, employment agencies, recruiters, labour contractors and membership based associations. These agents responded to initial demands for flexibility but then moulded the behaviour of workers and employers to the needs of an information economy labour market (Cappelli 1999; Benner 2002).
- Venture capitalists willing to invest in new activities with a high risk of failure have been assessed as key to the Silicon Valley story through their entrepreneurialism and knowledge of scientific and technological advances (Prevezer 1998; Kenney and Florida 2000).
- Silicon Valley lawyers have provided more than a legal service and been credited with a decisive influence on the overall organization of business relationships by acting as 'gatekeepers to withhold community resources from inappropriately constituted deviants', as 'proselytizers to promote community transactions among uninitiated novices', and as 'matchmakers to sort and steer transaction seekers' (Suchman 2000: 94).
- The greenfield location created a new community in which 'nobody knows anybody else's mother' and the absence of intervening affiliations encouraged shared associations around the project of advancing a new technology (Saxenian 1994; Cohen and Fields 1999).
- In the 'Valley of the Boys' only 20 per cent of information technology professionals are women, partly causing and partly caused by 'a newly constituted masculinity that rationalized the loss of work-life balance' and that gave employers a dedicated workforce (Cooper 2000: 379).
- Silicon Valley commenced with enterprises that were unusually fertile in their rate of successful spinoff enterprises (Klepper 2009). Spinoffs respond to internal disputes and differences and the inability of senior managers to recognize the potential in the technology or individual, or both rather than to external conditions that may assist spinoffs such as the availability of venture capital.

Evaluating the learning region

The learning economy story relies on at least three related conditions being satisfied (Breschi and Lissoni 2001b: 980). First, inter-enterprise knowledge transfers are not dependent on business transactions: the originating party is not compensated and no investment is required by the absorbing party to gain access to the spillover. Second, the knowledge that transfers is a public good in the sense that it is freely available to all those who search for it or that become aware of it through their normal business activity. This means that the availability of the new knowledge is not diminished as it is taken up by others. Third, the form of knowledge being generated favours dissemination through direct, face-to-face contact and personal relations, as this can help explain why it flows more readily among a localized community than to more distant industry participants. These three conditions can themselves be interrogated from three perspectives.

Knowledge transmission mechanisms

The precise ways in which knowledge is transferred between organizations can have significant impacts on the path that local economic development takes. Knowledge may pass to some form of common knowledge pool or it may transfer among a restricted group or perhaps between persons linked to two enterprises. Alternatively, originators of new knowledge may apply it to their own activity and diffuse the benefit of it through their business transactions rather than sharing the knowledge itself. This may mean, for example, that knowledge is applied to improve the efficiency of an enterprise and then is transferred to other enterprises, to the extent that the efficiency gains translate into trading opportunities or affect the scale of individual enterprises, or both. A further diffusion may occur as the trading partners gain opportunities to raise their own efficiency. In the terms employed by economists, the transfer of raw knowledge to a common knowledge pool is a spillover (or pure externality) whereas transfer via business transactions is a pecuniary externality. Spillovers give every enterprise the opportunity to apply knowledge and this makes them potentially supportive of the survival of a diverse population of competing enterprises. Pecuniary externalities have the implication that new knowledge can support the growth of some enterprises at the expense of others.

The distinction between spillovers and pecuniary externalities has become crucial to economic models of local economic development. Commentaries on local economic policy by non economists frequently appear unaware of the distinction. Neither was it known to Marshall when he codified externality effects, although his description of industrial districts suggests he envisaged spillover processes (Fujita and Thisse 2000: 11). Marshall was examining industry at a time of comparatively modest forms of knowledge generation, open business populations in terms of the number and fluidity of business linkages and limited entrepreneurial resources (McCann 2001: 64). In today's world these assumptions are less easy to make. Some proportion of the locally generated knowledge may be given up to others, either deliberately or because it is difficult to withhold, but it is unrealistic to imagine that all knowledge of potential economic significance is simply released into the common knowledge pool. Moreover, that which does may be significant in facilitating 'catch up' learning and incremental improvements in business performance, whereas successful enterprise must engage in other forms of learning too (Asheim 1999).

A possibility is that public good research activity augments business contributions to the pool of knowledge. Indeed, correlations between investment in university research and the levels of innovative activity in neighbouring enterprise are sometimes the basis for claiming evidence of localized learning (for example see Jaffe 1989; Acs *et al.* 1992; Audretsch and Feldman 1996). This type of evidence can overlook the fact that universities may be linked to their surrounding business communities in at least three ways:

- University staff conduct publicly funded research and release the findings into the public domain.
- University staff transfer knowledge directly to individual enterprises or groups of enterprises through contract-based research, consultancy relationships and possibly by setting up new enterprises.
- Businesses recruit students graduating from the university and possibly faculty members as well.

The tendency to overlook the existence of alternative connections is not unusual for much of the evidence claiming to show the existence of knowledge spillovers (Box 4.6). Release of research into the public domain is most consistent with a knowledge spillover effect, but arguably the least likely to spread information of immediate commercial significance (Breschi and Lissoni 2001b). Much of the public good university research is of a relatively fundamental nature that is not immediately convertible to commercial applications. This type of new knowledge has potential to diffuse widely (for example through publication and conference presentations) before any take up in commercial application occurs. It is more likely that the university's impact is felt through research conducted specifically for clients and through labour recruitment. For example, a link has been found between the innovative performance of biotechnology firms and the total number of scientific papers published by the local university's eminent researchers (Zucker *et al.* 1998). It was also discovered that this link disappeared when papers written jointly with an employee of a business were excluded from the sample. This implies that university research does not flow freely but rather through specific purposeful connections between universities and business. Clearly individualized connections may still have important benefits for the local economy, but these are strictly not examples of knowledge spillover as they affect some enterprises more than others.

Box 4.6 **Evidence for spillovers**

Knowledge flows can be important to local economies without them existing in the form of 'pure' externalities or spillovers. Much of the research evidence interpreted as showing the existence of knowledge spillovers may actually be identifying more restricted knowledge transfer mechanisms. For example, association between the level of university research activity and the number of patents registered by other organizations in the same state does not indicate the existence of spillovers for at least three reasons:

- Existence within a geographical boundary does not show that location proximity causes information to flow between two entities: there may be a large physical distance between the parties and a need for deliberate action to access and comprehend university research findings.
- The technology classifications may exaggerate the possibility of local knowledge flows. An industry category such as electronics, for example, encompasses too many specializations for it to be inferred that any electronics patent taken out by a university will be of benefit to enterprises affiliated to the electronics industry in any particular locality.
- In the time between the origination of new knowledge and its fruition in commercial innovation there is the scope for many intervening events and actions that lead to information sharing, such as contracting university staff for expert guidance.

Source: Breschi and Lissoni (2001b)

Knowledge varieties

All knowledge may not be shared through spillovers, but if a part with particular significance is, there is scope to believe in the importance of localized learning. In this context the previously identified distinction between tacit and codified knowledge has come to play a central role in the conceptualization of learning regions. The tacit component of knowledge is portrayed as being contextual and difficult to communicate without face-to-face contact and personal relationships, whereas codified knowledge can be communicated through documentation and conversations conducted over distance. With less ease of distribution, tacit knowledge is thought to be of increasing importance as a source of local economic advantage (Gertler 2003).

Taking these points further, changes in the status of tacit knowledge may imply discretion in the form of knowledge needed to engage in any economic activity. Such a possibility is recognized in the distinction between uncodifiable knowledge and that which is codifiable but is currently uncodified (Gertler 2003). Technical and scientific insight, for example, can be reported orally and in text but the specific nature of the content requires a particular vocabulary to expedite communication (Cowan *et al.* 2000). Consequently, while much technical and scientific knowledge has the capacity to be codified in practice, the use of a specialized vocabulary requires the recipient of the information to understand a 'coded' language. This vocabulary could be compiled in a specific dictionary or code book, using Cowan et al.'s (2000) terminology. Frequently it is not, and even if it is tacit exchanges are still possible by discriminating between those who need to use a code book and those who do not (Breschi and Lissoni 2001a: 262). Communication of this form of tacit knowledge can involve formal exchanges (such as mails, scientific papers, conference presentations) because of the need for understanding of a specific vocabulary. Groups fluent in the language, or 'epistemic communities' discriminate between people on the basis of their ability to grasp the meaning of dialogue exchanged not on the basis of geographical proximity (Ancori et al. 2000: 278). In this way, communities of scientists, engineers and practitioners of some specialized task may be tightly linked while being physically apart (Breschi and Lissoni 2001a: 262; Rallet and Tore 1999). Co-location may not be without some advantage, especially during the early phases in the development of a new technology, although organizational proximity through membership of a professional community can compensate for geographical proximity (Boschma 2004b). Once the language has been settled spatial proximity may lose its importance (Balconi et al. 2007).

Of five types of tacit knowledge distinguished by Balconi et al. (2007: 841) only one is inherently uncodifiable: tacit knowledge in the form of physical, kinaesthetic or skill-like abilities. These can be understood as the type of knowledge that can only be acquired by 'flanking an expert' and observing his or her actions. While drawing attention to this inherently tacit knowledge variety, it is noted that the need for 'old type skilled workers' whose learning came from apprenticeship to an experienced worker has dwindled. Had it not, among other impacts, the explosive growth of manufacturing in the Asian countries could not have occurred (Balconi et al. 2007: 842). For most types of tacit knowledge, costs and benefits determine whether it is codified rather than the inherent characteristics of the knowledge itself. The process of codifying knowledge may be costly and it may be that there are insufficient incentives to invest the resources required, although advances in information technology have increased the possibility of converting some aspects of tacit knowledge into computer-mediated forms (Rallet and Torre 1999). Perhaps more importantly, the development of information technologies and social networking tools has increasingly allowed remote informal interaction. It is also claimed that some aspects of electronic communication mimic the processes utilized to transmit tacit knowledge (Nonaka 1994; Rallet and Torre 1999: 375). These possibilities may never entirely substitute for face-to-face contact (see Wellman et al. 1996), but equally the unique importance of spatial proximity is reduced by the possibility of temporary relocation and frequent IT-assisted communication. As well, temporary establishment within a localized knowledge pool may give access to less easily transmitted knowledge even without an invitation from the permanent members of the pool. A case of this was the relocation of design engineers attached to the Ferrari racing team from Italy to England's Motor Sport Valley for six months to facilitate access to the Valley's particular expertise in aerodynamics (Pinch et al. 2003).

Workers as knowledge bearers

Research has increasingly focused on the role of labour mobility in promoting knowledge spillovers (Cumbers and MacKinnn 2004; Kloosterman 2008). As knowledge and especially tacit knowledge is held by workers, the sharing of a common labour pool among co-located enterprises provides a potential conduit for the transfer of knowledge. When augmented by the tendency for founders of new enterprise to establish their start-up companies close to their previous place of employment, the case for localized learning can appear to be further strengthened (Oakey *et al.* 2001). In practice, neither local labour mobility nor local clusters of enterprise spun out of a focal organization can be taken to infer the spillover of knowledge.

Individuals moving between employers are agents for knowledge spillovers if this augments the common pool of insight and capabilities such that all past employers as well as the new employer have access to the employee's knowledge (Breschi and Lissoni 2001b: 991). If knowledge was simply being shunted from workplace to workplace as workers move this could only expand the common knowledge pool if all employers were affected by high levels of labour turnover and employees shared their knowledge with co-workers. This need for sharing would not be required if important aspects of knowledge were embedded in an organization's routines and practices, as is sometimes emphasized (Nelson and Winter 1982), but in this case mobility of individuals would have little impact on the common knowledge pool since it is being claimed that knowledge sticks to organizations. One line of investigation has explored how the movement of managers affects the markets served by the businesses that are moved to. This shows evidence that the markets of firms moved to tend to diversify in line with the markets served by the firms that managers are recruited from (Boeker 1997; Rao and Drazin 2002). This implies a one-direction knowledge flow and a process that ultimately might intensify competition as markets converge for businesses that share a labour pool. Such a possibility has led to a theory that localized labour pools may assist new venture creation but not business growth (Stuart and Sorenson 2003).

If it is accepted that high rates of labour mobility are required to disperse knowledge, some explanation for this flexibility is needed. It is difficult, for example, to present the acquisition of tacit knowledge as a factor in recruitment (Gertler 2003). The benefit of acquiring knowledge has also to be evaluated against the cost of labour turnover.

Employers that locate near to other employers of the same type of labour face a trade off between the benefits of labour market pooling and the costs of labour market poaching. The benefits of pooling rest with the opportunities for a firm to hire workers whose knowledge gained in other firms can be adapted to the profit of its own organization. The costs are that firms risk having their own knowledge workers poached and so feel obliged to protect themselves from this by raising their wages relative to other firms. It has been suggested that the degree of similarity between competing employers determines when it is most advantageous to belong to a labour pool (Combes and Duranton 2001). Assuming that wage increments act to deter employees leaving a workplace and that employers use them for this purpose, labour market pooling is potentially least attractive to enterprises that have most to gain from sharing their labour. This is because employers that raise wage levels to deter employees from leaving are most able to fully utilize the past work experience of people recruited from other enterprises in the labour pool. If enterprises in the labour pool are different to each other such that a new recruit's past experience is of only partial relevance to them, increased wage costs paid to encourage staff not to move are compensated for by the need to train and socialize new recruits to bring them to the same productivity level as experienced employees (in other words it makes sense to pay high wages if this saves on induction costs). Research conducted in the context of Italy's industrial districts can be interpreted as giving partial support for this economic modelling. While it is frequently thought that these industrial districts operate like Marshall's industrial districts, it has been found that workers moving between district enterprises do not get a wage premium over workers recruited from outside (Cingano 2003). This was seen as a sign that enterprises are sufficiently distinct in their specialization and work practices that they are no more able to utilize fully the skills and insight that a worker has obtained in another district enterprise than they are when workers are recruited from further afield.

Workers associated with new development projects have particular potential to transfer knowledge. Correspondingly, for the enterprise with defecting employees the impact can be costly. Indeed, an observer of Silicon Valley labour markets, which are generally rated as an exemplar of the benefits of an unattached workforce, has noted the potential for labour turnover to rip enterprises apart (Cappelli 1999). High turnover works in Silicon Valley only because the typical firm is always innovating and moving on from technology that supported previous activity. This creates less need for continuity in experience and employment than might normally be found (Cappelli 1999: 177). A further conditionality is that workers must be content to stay within a functional area of expertise rather than seeking to accumulate a diversified employment history that will assist movement up a management hierarchy.

Four areas where evidence exists

The review of knowledge spillovers suggests that much of the theory that would support the possibility of building learning regions remains incomplete. This is easy to understand in the context of an issue that is short of empirical evidence to inform theory building, particularly in the area of identifying and examining the mechanisms by which technical knowledge is shared (Breschi and Lissoni 2001a: 261). This final section summarizes four areas where empirical evidence exists and in each case this points to directions of research away from any widespread opportunity to promote learning regions.

Collective invention

Episodes of 'collective invention' have been identified at various points of time and in different industry contexts from which some generalizations are possible about circumstances encouraging knowledge sharing. Collective invention refers to a process through which the form of the technology that endures is discovered over time through the sharing of incremental improvements made by independent users building on each other's experiences (Meyer 2003). This mode of invention was identified first in a study of the development of the blast furnace in England during the nineteenth century (Allen 1983). The process of technological discovery leading to the optimization of blast furnace technology had two distinct features: information sharing and the absence of formal R&D efforts. Iron producers shared information about the design and efficiency of the blast furnaces they operated by allowing independent researchers to visit their plant, observe production and measure efficiencies. To hasten the possibility of discovering how best to design and operate blast furnaces the information was published and made available to all producers. The development of blast furnace technology thus came about through the exchange and free circulation of knowledge rather than the inventive success of one enterprise or any individual genius. Allen (1983) explained this collective approach to invention as an outcome of calculations by individual mill owners that they could reasonably expect to obtain more insight by learning from their competitor's experiences than they could glean for themselves. With this outlook, each firm preferred to be open rather than risk being shut out of the knowledge exchange. The ability to reduce internal R&D was an incidental outcome, as part of the rationalization was that individual investigation would be less effective than the collective sharing of individual experiences.

In a more modern context, a form of collective learning has been identified in the USA's speciality steel and mini mill industry (Schrader 1991). This study built on the observation that knowledge trading frequently occurred between the technical managers of individual plants. The context was an industry undergoing considerable incremental advances with, for example, the average person-hours per ton of steel produced falling by almost half from 1975 to 1985. Such improvements relied on continuous smallscale adjustments. This offered scope for valuable informal information exchange across mills to take place while at the same time questioning the worth of individual R&D programmes to discover marginal adjustments in technology and production methods. Information supporting small, incremental adjustments would be cumbersome and costly to seek through formal contracts. Enterprises not finding some other method for gaining information were, therefore, at a potential disadvantage and this was reflected in widespread participation in one-to-one knowledge trading that was managed informally by those involved. Shared information helped to improve rather than invent a technology but participation still had a significant positive impact on firm performance compared with firms that traded knowledge less or not at all.

Sharing information usually involves a lag between one party's giving and another's reciprocal return of information. The gap leaves uncertainty as to whether cooperation will obtain the expected pay-off and Schrader's (1991) study also offered insight into how external conditions affected the willingness to give away knowledge. New competition coming from unfamiliar sources acted to lower the deterrent effect of uncertainty and to increase the willingness to engage in information trading. The strong attachment of technical managers to their employer was another contributing influence as this heightened sensitivity to obtaining a net benefit from information exchange. Schrader speculates that managers without intentions of a long term attachment, or whose contributions to firm performance are less transparent, may not be as motivated to participate in reciprocal knowledge sharing.

The knowledge trading was a collective process as individuals might share information with multiple parties rather than through an exclusive one-to-one exchange. Something closer to the original model of collective invention has been claimed in the early years after the first production of semiconductor chips (Meyer 2003). In the 1970s, individuals started to experiment in using semiconductor chips to build crude home computers and clubs of hobbyists formed to share experiences. The Homebrew Computer Club (Box 4.7) is perhaps the best know because it has been well documented, is credited with having influenced the information sharing culture of Silicon Valley and was a learning ground for important entrepreneurs (Freiberger and Swaine 1984; Saxenian 1994; Levy 2001). Another modern case is open source software development such as LINUX (Cowan and Jonard 2003; Meyer 2003). Like the iron and steel examples, open source software developers share technical information so that individuals can add to the advances made by others on the basis that they give back the modified software for others to add to. The example differs in that programmers working on LINUX are located around the globe linked by Internet. In practice communication is usually through mailing lists and bulletin boards which are read by sub groups. These sub groups may have a dominant regional affiliation but acceptance of the network rules as well as location is required to stay in the group, and some members may participate in multiple groups and bridge geographically separate mail list populations.

Box 4.7 **The Homebrew Computer Club**

The first newsletter of the Homebrew Club reported how 32 enthusiastic people had met on 5 March 1975 in 'Gordon's garage' (located in Menlo Park, Santa Clara County). The newsletter says that after a quick round of introductions, the questions, comments, reports, information on supply sources poured forth in a 'spontaneous spirit of sharing'. Six of the group were reported to already have home computers up and running, others were in the process of building them. At the first meeting it was asked what it was thought people would do with a computer in their home. Suggestions reported in the newsletter included private secretary functions (meaning text editing and storage), control of house utilities, games, small business applications and neighbourhood memory networks. The newsletter editor concluded that he expected home computers would get used in unconventional ways, most of which had yet to be thought of.

> The hobbyists at the first meeting were a mix of hardware experts and software programmers. The scope of the club as it started was to help the hobbyist. The Club philosophy was that people met because of their common interest in computers rather than to gain insight that might be applied for commercial advantage. Nonetheless, from among the many hundreds who participated as the club got better known were the founders of many microcomputer companies including Bob Marsh, Adam Osborne, Steve Jobs and Steven Wozniak.

The common point in these stories is that information sharing occurred when there was an incentive to be cooperative. In the case of the English blast furnace industry and semiconductor chips, the incentive came from technological uncertainty; for speciality steel and mini mills it came as well from the presence of an external threat and the efficiency of informal information sharing for the type of insight being traded. Of course, there is always uncertainty with respect to technology forecasting. These cases deal with uncertainty arising from recent innovation that is seen to need further development, and where there is no clear view of the end point or what research and development activity will reveal it. The willingness to share information reduces once uncertainties have been resolved, or at least diminished to a point where there is confidence to commit to a form of the technology or particular line of improvement. After this point, the incentive for individual knowledge holders to guard their insight and pursue their own R&D increases. This process of gradual evaporation of collective invention processes has been captured in the case the Homebrew Club. When the early participants had evolved from building computers at home to establishing manufacturing companies, club rules about sharing techniques, refusing to recognize secrets and being open became a challenge. As reported by one former club member:

> People would ask you about your company and you'd have to say 'I can't tell you that'. I solved that the way other people did – I didn't go. I didn't want to go and not tell people things. There would be no easy way out where you would feel good about that.
>
> (Levy 2001)

These and other episodes of collective invention have a number of implications for proponents of localized learning. First, instances of knowledge sharing which at first appear as cases of knowledge spillovers are in reality cases where knowledge is exchanged on the basis of reciprocal obligations. Acceptance of the rules of engagement rather than physical proximity determines who gets access to information. Second, the origins of knowledge sharing regimes are to be found in the technological challenges and business environments associated with the new technology rather than in the characteristics of the communities in which the learning takes place. Many areas of new technology are not amenable to collective learning experiences as there are not fundamental uncertainties, or at least the direction of future development is known, and because individual enterprises feel that private R&D efforts can be justified.

Personal relationships

The ability of personal relationships to heighten the likelihood of information being shared and to increase the effectiveness of communication is frequently part of the case for claiming that learning is a localized phenomenon (Maskell 2001). The study of knowledge trading in the US speciality steel industry discussed above provides evidence that personal ties can be unimportant (Schrader 1991). This study found that individual technical managers calculated whether to give information to their counterparts in other plants by balancing an assessment of the worth of the information given up against the value of the information that they might obtain in return. The study found that friendship was not an influence on the willingness to share information: although it might influence who was approached for information (this was not tested in the study), it did not affect the willingness to give information away. For managers willing to trade information considerations were whether the information related to something that either party drew competitive advantage from and whether it was information that might be obtained from other sources, in which case there was no loss in releasing information even to a competitor (Schrader 1991: 165). The entry of new competitors from outside the traditional boundaries of the industry and from overseas outweighed the need for personal relationships or face-to-face contact for information trading to occur.

The emphasis on personal relationships arises because of its assumed importance in encouraging trust and shared understanding. It may be that face-to-face contact delivers important additional dimensions to communication, as it is capable of detecting lying, allowing intentions to be judged and of leading to the development of shared values between the communicating parties (Storper and Venables 2004). A need for face-to-face contact does not point to physical proximity as a necessary requirement for the success of interaction. Once relationships are established, a limited number of meetings combined with the use of electronic communication can support ongoing relationships (Malecki and Oinas 1999). An exception may be project-based business services that require frequent interaction among multiple parties (Grabher 2002). More generally, it is evident that the relative ease of meeting implied by physical proximity does not mean that face-to-face contact actually increases. A study of 70 small firms in the Sheffield (UK) metal work cluster found that purchasing transactions with neighbouring firms were no more likely to bring face-to-face meetings ('embodied transactions') than were transactions with non local firms (Watts *et al.* 2003). Buyers were reluctant to hold meetings with suppliers wherever they were located. The median frequency of face-to-face meetings with representatives of principal suppliers was three times a year. A fifth of respondents had no meetings in the previous 12 months with their principal suppliers. Two firms met their suppliers more frequently than once a week, contributing disproportionately to the total number of meetings. The frequency of meetings was not explained by the duration of trading relationships or whether the transaction involved standardized or customized inputs, so that no evident rationale existed to explain why

104 *Learning regions*

face-to-face meetings took place. Nonetheless, even while contact was scarce most buyers claimed to have a personal contact in their supplier firms who they knew well, and this contributed to them rarely using formal contracts to manage their transactions.

Moreover, much of the discussion of the role of personal relations can suggest that enterprises are passive and without capacity or inclination to develop relations as they are needed. In contrast with this assumption, an investigation of the optoelectronics industry (one of the breakthrough industries of the 1990s that was concentrated in regional clusters) found that to exploit new opportunities firms sought out collaborations wherever the relevant expertise was located (Hendry *et al.* 1999, 2000). As a consequence, companies were frequently more connected to customer industries located away from their home region than they were to same-industry enterprises with which they shared a location. The same observation of enterprises forming connections widely has been made in the context of other high technology industries (Oakey 1995; Oakey *et al.* 2001). Somewhat differently, but again illustrating creativity in the formation of business connections, 'flagship' enterprises in the information technology sector have been shown to pursue a two-tier relationship strategy (Cecil and Green 2000). First-tier relationships are formed on the basis of business strategy; second-tier networks are constructed with local partners and may be influenced by personal relationships, but are generally of minor importance to the business compared with the first-tier relationships.

Regional culture

The learning advantage to enterprises of being embedded within a distinctive regional culture has been subject to little direct investigation. An exception is James (2005) who studied firms embedded in Utah's Mormon regional culture and how the performance of Mormon-managed enterprises differed from non Mormon firms in the same North American state. The study focused on the computer software industry, which has a large representation of Mormon-founded enterprises in Utah and is an industry that has grown strongly in the state as elsewhere. The context is a regional culture based on shared religious beliefs and subscribed to by the majority of the state's population, making it sufficiently strong and demographically large to support an 'enclave' economy as well as residents and businesses that have varying degrees of integration into the mainstream economy. Mormon culture has aspects that contrast sharply with the values normally associated with private enterprise, such as a commitment to a balanced work–home life (compared with a long work hours ethic in the mainstream software industry); self sufficiency (rather than utilization of external resources); avoidance of debt (rather than acceptance of external funding) among other components.

On four of five standard business performance measures, Mormon firms under perform their non Mormon counterparts. James (2005: 1212) concludes that the study shows how regional culture can affect business performance. Given the scale of Utah's Mormon population, under performance can continue as the internal market is protected from the full force of market competition and insiders may have some offsetting advantages such as staff and customer loyalty. The larger observation is that regional culture can impede conversion to the modes of behaviour promoted by standard local economic development prescriptions. So, for example, recommendations that firms engage in interfirm cooperation and utilize external funding to gain access to the expertise of venture capitalists have little relevance to a business community that is willing to forgo business practices that compromise their cultural preferences. This experience might be dismissed on the grounds that more frequently encountered regional cultures are less at odds with business self interest. Alternatively, it implies a need to re-think the role of regional cultures in promoting learning economies where these are interpreted as implying that enhanced economic performance arises from a superior learning capacity. Rather than simply claiming the benefit of economic activity being embedded in a shared culture, it is necessary to shift the agenda to embedding economic activity in the 'right' kind of regional culture as judged by policy makers. This is a problematic proposition as it is by no means clear that there is a 'best' culture (see Chapter 2). As in the case of Salt Lake City, exhorting firms to modify their behaviour will have little impact where business behaviour is shaped by strongly held religious beliefs that are reinforced by social institutions and the importance of family relationships.

Firm learning

The logical starting point for designing strategies to promote learning within local economies is an understanding of how enterprises learn. Accounts of the learning region tend to be dominated by two ideas: that social relations enhance the capacity to learn from other parties and that most learning takes place within the context of enterprise routines (see Chapter 2). These ideas are related to theories of regional and enterprise development rather than being based on investigations of how learning takes place in individual enterprises. Studies that attempt to gather such insight can lead to a conclusion that enterprises learn in a variety of ways and have choices about the emphasis given to different learning processes. DiBella *et al.* (1996) provide such a perspective based on case studies of how learning takes place in four organizations: Fiat's engineering division responsible for the design of new cars, an organization of approximately 3,000 managers and professionals; the Investment Funds Group, a division of the USA-based Mutual Investment Corporation; France's nuclear power plant operator *Electricite de France* that generated 75 per cent of the country's electricity; a selection of Motorola's senior management teams, each comprising 20–25 executives from across the electronic equipment and services group. The study was based on each organization having had significant, identifiable learning needs and achievements in the years prior to the study. The researchers then set out to determine how the learning had occurred.

The results were presented in terms of seven learning orientations, expressed as bipolar continuums with the ends of each spectrum representing a 'pure' application of the individual orientation:

- Knowledge source: this identifies the extent to which an organization prefers to develop new knowledge internally versus the extent to which it is more likely to seek guidance from external sources.
- Product-process focus: enterprises vary in their preference over any period of time to focus on learning related to products and services versus enhancing their understanding of basic processes that support business operations.
- Documentation mode: organizations vary in the systems for storing knowledge and acceptance of what constitutes knowledge, for example in the way that some enterprises may perceive that knowledge resides in individuals and is lost when employees leave the workplace.
- Dissemination mode: organizations vary in their emphasis given to establish an organizational 'atmosphere' for learning (for example, consistent with developing 'communities of practice') versus structured and formal approaches to learning that include training courses and the acquisition of qualifications.
- Learning focus: at the extremes learning may be concentrated on methods and tools to improve what is already being done, or it may be directed at testing the assumptions that underlie current activity.
- Value-chain focus: this identifies which if any part of the organization's operations are the main focus of learning activity, as differentiating between targeting areas of design and manufacture versus targeting marketing and distribution.
- Skill development focus: organizations may support individual learning or prefer to stress teams and groups as the main conduit for learning.

DiBella *et al.* (1996: 375) argue that their framework does not measure how well an organization is learning, rather it facilitates description of how organizations differ in their preferred ways of learning and has implications for what is learnt. Other researchers have made use of the framework for this purpose (Coetzer and Perry 2008). Learning styles may not be an outcome of deliberate decision making and so there is a role for the framework in helping organizations reflect on their current approach to learning. The significance of the framework for the debate over the existence of learning regions is to recognize that among any community of enterprises there is scope for different approaches to learning to emerge. As well, it provides an alternative to the tendency to proscribe how organizations should learn and what institutional arrangements are needed to maximize learning. Rather than presume that there is one form of organizational culture and one way of organizing regional economies to maximize learning, there is a need to develop further understanding of the relationships between learning orientations, organizational contexts and other organizational processes.

Conclusion

The debate around the learning economy is essentially about the identification of conditions that encourage knowledge and learning to diffuse across a local economy. The idea of the learning region assumes the existence of local institutions and culture that promotes mutual trust in a way that stimulates and enhances information exchange. These attributes are given priority on the assumption that knowledge can be categorized into different types that are distinguished partly by the extent to which direct face-to-face contact provides the most effective and efficient means of communication. Further, that an important part of the knowledge needed by business exists in the form that relies most on face-to-face communication. With constraints on the communication of important parts of knowledge, it is then possible to explain why insight can accumulate locally and build an advantage for co-located enterprises. Such claims confront a number of contradictions.

The learning economy story relies on a further assumption that has so far attracted relatively little consideration. It implies that knowledge is like a physical good with certain immutable properties, of which one is a component that favours direct communication. An alternative perspective is that the form knowledge takes depends on the decisions of those with an interest in the knowledge. Depending on the incentives that exist, knowledge may or may not remain as a public good and may or may not be codified and transmitted between members of a widely dispersed network. For example, while learning is sometimes linked to the existence of social proximity (perhaps generated through common past experiences) these strong ties are apparently not sustainable if people move away, as surely some do. Equally as surely, no region can maintain and neither should it seek to maintain an absolute monopoly of knowledge. Learning region theory then implies the compatibility of one set of mechanisms for accessing knowledge internally and an alternative set of mechanisms for external knowledge acquisition, despite the former implying that the latter are ineffective.

One way forward is to move from viewing regions as learning entities built on knowledge spillovers to seeing regions as the potential hosts of multiple separate learning groups (or epistemic communities) that devise rules for information sharing and learning according to their individual circumstances. This perspective acknowledges that knowledge holders and users may regulate information sharing and make decisions about the form that knowledge takes (more or less codified or tacit). The instances of collective invention reviewed in the chapter show how, for example, knowledge sharing occurs in circumstances where enterprises are either unable or unwilling to devote resources to the discovery of new knowledge. This generally is the case where the future path of technological development is unclear, as with uncertainties about what form of consumer technology application the newly invented semiconductor was going to support. Other influences also appear important in shaping the form that collective invention takes, as in the way that the entry of new industry players can disturb established patterns of competition and encourage incumbents to lower their reluctance to trade information. The wider message from these experiences is that the willingness to share knowledge and support a collective learning process is explained by the business environment more than by the social environment.

5 Enterprise clusters and regional specialization

Investigation of enterprise clusters opens a potentially large area of investigation. The term cluster has been applied to geographical scales ranging from part of a single urban economy to a group of neighbouring economies. The 'new economic geography', for example, relates clustering to the tendency for economic activity to concentrate in extensive metropolitan regions rather than to diffuse evenly across national economies (see Brakman *et al.* 2001). 'Old' economic geographers, on the other hand, are most likely to reserve the term for pockets of economic specialization within a city or shared among neighbouring settlements. At the extreme, they may even set uniform boundaries to distinguish clusters from other forms of concentration (May *et al.* 2001). In the context of a book that is concerned with local economic policy, this chapter is most aligned with the old geography interpretation of a business cluster. While new economic geography has played a significant role in convincing policy makers that enterprise policy should include a spatial dimension, leading proponents recognize that their methods are still too abstract to yield policy guidance. As one prominent economic geographer has put it, this branch of economics is still in the Wright Brothers' phase of learning to fly (Fujita cited in Stelder 2002). In contrast, the old economic geography conception of clusters has been extensively promoted and highly influential within the field of local economic policy. Indeed, encouraging business clusters in the sense of localized concentrations of enterprise specialization was one of the biggest ideas in local economic development to emerge in the final decades prior to 2000 (Martin and Sunley 2003). This resulted in efforts by public agencies to increase awareness of the existence of business clusters (Department of Trade and Industry 2001) and in many industry-based projects to promote membership-based cluster groups (Sölvell *et al.* 2003).

The popularity of clusters among local economic policy makers can be explained in many ways, some of which have been identified in Chapter 1. Three reasons are worth noting as they raise issues that are given attention in this chapter. First, enterprise clusters appear to be amenable to local influence as they are associated with fostering geographically concentrated communities (Benneworth 2002; Raines 2002; Pinch *et al.* 2003; Rosenfeld 2005). Second, clusters are presented as a way of defending local economies against the ravages of globalization. They are claimed to 'embed' enterprise and reduce the inclination to pursue 'weak' competitive strategies based on cost minimization that ultimately result in relocation overseas (Hudson 1999). Third, cluster advocates promise an optimal balance of competitive pressures and cooperative opportunities that facilitate 'rapid best practice improvement' and opportunities for 'distinctive competitive positions' (Porter 2000: 265). Indeed seemingly perfect conditions for business growth are envisaged:

> A concentration of visible rivals encourages the search for ways of competing that are not head on. Niche opportunities overlooked by others can reveal themselves. Ready access to suppliers and partners provides flexibility to configure the value chain in a variety of ways. A more positive-sum form of competition can result when customer choice is widened and different customers are served most efficiently.
>
> (Porter 2000: 265–266)

In contrast to such optimism, there is evidence that clusters have no necessary impact on business performance (Malmberg *et al.* 2000; Beaudry and Breschi 2003; Braunerhjelm and Johansson 2003; Cingano 2003) or that they have significance for independent firms only (Beardsell and Henderson 1999) or that they encourage enterprise start up but not survival (Sorenson and Audia 2000; Stuart and Sorenson 2003). Equally, it is apparent that many of the public agency efforts to enhance business and local economic growth through clusters have failed (Kotval and Mullin 1998; Schmitz 1999; Huggins 2000; Perry 2004; Tambunan 2005; Bayliss 2007).

This chapter provides an overview of the arguments underlying the alleged growth of business clusters, examines alternative ways that clusters are being identified and reflects on the contradictory claims being made about the opportunity for and importance of promoting business participation in clusters. An appropriate starting point is to consider how industrial location trends may have influenced the formation of clusters. The discussion then shifts to the identification of enterprise clusters and the contrast between 'top down' and 'bottom up' approaches. The centrality of agglomeration theory in the explanation of cluster advantage can then be explained. Agglomeration economies offer a mechanism that may create business advantage but it is important to have some means of differentiating business clusters and appraising their prospective ability to sustain competitive advantage. Policy implications vary according to the understanding of how clusters come into existence and what their impact on business performance is.

Industrial location trends

Two accounts of the major trend in industrial location and regional specialization exist with sharply contrasting implications for cluster formation.

A long view of regional specialization has been presented for the USA (Kim 1995; Kim and Margo 2004). It finds a modest decline occurred from 1860 to

1890, then rose substantially and flattened out during the interwar years. Regional specialization then fell substantially and continuously from the 1930s to 1987 (the limit of the data analysed). The net outcome was that regions were less specialized at the end of the twentieth century than they were in 1860. Alongside the increased diversity in regional economic structure, industries became more dispersed than originally. These trends were interpreted as showing that the geography of business activity is driven by patterns of resource usage and the pursuit of economies of scale. Typically resource availability has become less constraining on where industry locates, although it can still help explain the relative dispersion of individual industries. Average plant size (measured by employment) in most industries peaked in the 1930s or 1940s and subsequent falls have assisted the dispersion of activity.

From this long term perspective, any advantage of being located near to like firms appears to be a minor influence on the distribution of activity. If important industry knowledge 'spills over' from one firm to its neighbour, it might be expected the activities most dependent on knowledge would have a greater propensity to concentrate than less knowledge sensitive activities. Kim (1995) does not identify this impact. Over time, most industries have seen an increase in their proportion of non production workers and an increase in research and development expenditure. This has not been associated with more spatial concentration or regional specialization. Looking at contemporary industry, activity defined broadly as high tech tends to be more dispersed than low tech activity.

The distribution of structural materials used in manufacturing illustrates how industrial location choices have expanded. Initially wood was the main structural material used by industry and this was available throughout the USA. As markets expanded and the materials utilized to iron and steel, transport cost and logistics encouraged use close to the source of these manufactured inputs. As a consequence, industry activity tended to concentrate and regional specialization tended to increase. More recently, many substitutes for wood and steel have been developed, including light metals, alloys, plastics, plywood and particle board. Diversification of the sources of supply and reduced transport costs allowed industry to disperse and regional specialization tended to decline as a result of this.

The alternative pro cluster view of industrial location trends tends to rely on the flexible specialization thesis (Scott 2006a; Storper and Scott 2009). According to this thesis, economic activity has entered a period of increased market uncertainty and high rates of technological change. This environment reduces the advantages of internal economies of scale and scope and favours business strategies based on horizontal and vertical disintegration. Consequently, enterprises are expected to replace their ownership of production capacity with a network of linkages to suppliers, supporting services and business partners as well as developing close relations with their customers. It is not simply a case of using subcontractors. External relationships must be configured to cope with market instability, meet customer expectations for distinctive products and services and be adaptable to shifts in technology. This means cooperative partnerships rather than the 'arms length' relationships that characterized outsourcing in the past. In turn, spatial agglomeration is encouraged as it is easier to form and maintain cooperative linkages with enterprises that are geographically as well as functionally close to your own (see Scott 1988; Scott and Storper 1992). The specialization of local economies is a further outcome as it makes economic sense for activities that do not generate mutual linkages to avoid each other (Henderson 1974, 1988). So, for example, if film production and automobile assembly generate few mutual external linkages they should locate in different places. This way they avoid generating congestion and high land rents for each other.

The flexible specialization thesis responds to some large changes in industrial economies but tends to simplify their impact on business environments. Around the industrial world, organizations have faced new economic, political and social conditions but this does not mean that business behaviour has coalesced around the globe (Whitley 1999). Pressures for change include reducing trade barriers between countries, the internationalization of economic activity, rapid technological change associated with the information revolution, the deregulation of markets, privatization and the ending of state monopolies, broadening conceptions of organizational stakeholders, demographic transitions such as ageing populations and changes in consumer demand (Holman and Wood 2003). These diverse pressures are experienced with varying degrees of intensity between countries, industries and businesses. Organizations are being pushed in various directions and only modestly toward increasing homogeneity in organizational practice (Djelic 1998; Zeitlin and Herrigel 2000). Business strategies offering flexibility in one aspect of their operations tend to bring inflexibility in another (Box 5.1). Moreover, common organizational responses are encouraged by social pressures to conform to prevailing business fads more than actual evidence of effectiveness (Burke 2002).

Box 5.1 **Inflexible flexibility**

The flexible specialization thesis continues to be influential despite longstanding claims that it is too sweeping and simplistic. The suggestion that relational contracting or supply chain partnering improves on arm's length contracting is one illustration, as many issues need to be optimized when managing the acquisition of inputs. Buyers may, for example, calculate that increasing the use of standardized inputs increases their flexibility by reducing the reliance on suppliers that are customized to their specific needs (Phelps 1993; Perry 1999). This strategy widens the pool of suppliers that can be selected from and reduces the concern a buyer may have about their proprietary technology diffusing to competitors via their outsourcing partners. Standardization counteracts the influence of supply partnering as it facilitates 'off-the-peg' sourcing rather than the need to rely on customized supply (Perry and Tan 2000: 46). This is a preferable outcome for many organizations as it reduces the risk of buyers having an obligation to support suppliers during market downturns (Miles and Snow 1992). Similar evaluation exists about the recommendation for business to concentrate on their 'core competencies' (Hamel and Prahalad 1994). The problem with this recommendation is that businesses need to retain their capacity to move into new areas while also preserving their core competencies (Christensen 1997).

> This means maintaining a broad conception of their unique expertise, otherwise the ability to test and protect new innovations is reduced. In line with this, many organizations nominate general skills such as technology or their market position ('being number one or two in the industry') as their core competency rather than radically slimming down their activity. This limits externalization to services such as property management, transportation, selected human resource functions, IT management and standardized component manufacture.

The flexible specialization thesis can also be criticized for its disregard of historical literature. This is unwise, as the fate that befell yesterday's clusters helps put present day clusters in context and cautions against seeing them as a resolution to business development challenges (Wilson and Singleton 2003). The English West Midlands was home to some strong industry clusters for much of the first half of the twentieth century, including some that formed the basis of influential studies in industrial geography that have more recently lapsed from citation (see Taylor and Plummer 2003 for a review of these studies). Accounts of a West Midlands motor industry cluster centred on Wolverhampton as it existed during the 1920s and 1930s show the need to evaluate clusters in terms of their compatibility with changes in industry structure. This cluster emerged from a history of engineering expertise out of which grew the skills to design and make motor vehicles. Even so, business in the West Midlands was unable to capitalize on its potential advantages. A skilled labour force was hard to adapt to the less demanding requirements of mass production, which instead went to places without any previous connection to the car industry. The engineering enterprises of the West Midlands were more inclined to keep on innovating rather than make the jump to large scale production. Mass production developed its own techniques and opportunities that were unfamiliar to the increasingly bypassed craft-based enterprises in the West Midlands cluster. This story makes a point that continues to be relevant today: clusters that look strong during a particular phase of industry development may impede adaptation to new industry conditions. The case of Manchester and the cotton industry is another historical example illustrating this (see Perry 2005: 51).

Counting clusters

It might be thought that industrial location trends could be established objectively by counting the changing incidence and scale of business clusters. In practice this is not straightforward as there is no agreed method of identifying clusters even as far as whether it implies the development of specialized local economies. Some cluster advocacy is not predicated on this outcome but on a more general interest in recognizing the interdependence of business activity. The two perspectives can result in opposing assessments of the significance of enterprise clustering (Perry 2005). A failure to distinguish between them has caused much confusion and it is, therefore, important to be clear whether a 'top down' or 'bottom up' evaluation of clusters is taking place.

Clusters and regional specialization 113

The top down or 'mode of inquiry perspective' makes use of input-output data to trace the linkages between industries (Feser and Bergman 2000; Feser and Luger 2003). By identifying groups of industries with high amounts of inter industry trade, it is possible to divide an economy into groupings of inter-connected activity. On this basis, using 1992 data, the manufacturing sector in the USA has been reduced to 23 'clusters' (Feser and Bergman 2000). These clusters comprise various major final market producing sectors with their key first, second and third tier supplier sectors. Close to 90 per cent of manufacturing was attached to the 23 national clusters. They vary in composition from 116 separate industries (defined at the three or four digit SIC level) in the case of metalworking to four in the case of tobacco. The researchers present these national clusters as templates that may be compared with the industry profiles of regions or local economies. From a top down perspective, such comparison reveals the relative strengths of sub national economies as well as the gaps in their industry structure in terms of missing cluster components. As discussed in Chapter 2, Porter (2003) has devised a similar approach to identifying business clusters that is based on the incidence of business co-location as well as input-output data.

For proponents of the top down approach, it makes sense to search for clusters using national templates, as the actual structure of local economies does not reveal what has potential to exist. National templates provide a way of assessing where opportunity exists to strengthen linkages in the locality of interest. Applied to North Carolina, for example, industries that form part of Feser and Bergman's vehicle manufacturing template cluster are discovered to account for 15 per cent of the state's employment. As the state did not currently have a vehicle assembly industry, Feser and Bergman (2000) argue that the presence of potentially linked activity reveals gaps in the existing range of activity compared with the national template. These gaps might represent specializations to be filled to help attract final assembly as well, although fuller investigation is needed to establish this. In this way, the top down approach is presented as a tool that local economic policy makers can use to identify latent clusters, although further investigations are recommended before implementing the results of template analysis (Box 5.2).

Box 5.2 **Implementing cluster templates**

Cluster templates divide a national economy into groups of relatively self contained and interlinked industries or clusters. The implication may be that if one component of the cluster is present in a local economy there is a good opportunity to attract the missing components so as to fill the cluster out. A number of reasons explain why this approach may provide a misleading impression of the scope for cluster building:

- Templates imply that local economies can become miniature replicas of their national economy. If the chemical industry nationally exhibits connections with a range of suppliers and customers, for example, the assumption is that these connections have the potential to exist wherever the chemical industry is located. Such potential overlooks the existence of economies of scale in production that limit the localization of supply networks.

- Aggregate industry linkages revealed in a national template need to be checked against the scope of activity in the industry locally. At the extreme, for example, food and drink production is conducted by organizations from boutique manufacturers targeting local markets to global multinationals. At the national scale, linkages reflect the activity of dominant scales and types of production. Locally, economies may specialize in market niches that do not give rise to the connections as identified for the economy as a whole.
- The spatial scale at which the national input-output template is applied is undetermined from the analysis. This means that gaps in the range of activity that the national template suggests exist in a locality that may appear to exist only because of the spatial scale to which the template is applied.

The bottom up approach starts with the assumption that business clusters are a locality with an unusual concentration of a particular type of economic activity that is not explained simply by the presence of a single, large establishment. Among other applications, this perspective has influenced the identification of Italy's industrial districts (Sforzi 1990; Burroni and Trigilia 2001; Paniccia 2002). The national statistics agency – *Istituto Nazionale di Statistica* (ISTAT) – uses two main indicators to count an industrial district (Perry 1999). First, the locality (identified by travel to work area boundaries) must have an above national average employment dependency on manufacturing. Second, geographically concentrated sectors must have an above average proportion of small and medium sized enterprises (defined as firms with fewer than 250 employees). These criteria capture what some see as the minimum conditions for a business cluster: geographical concentration of an industry in a local economy based on the presence of a large number of independent enterprises.

Compared with the top down approach, the bottom up perspective is more selective, as specified criteria must be met to count as a cluster. Indeed, when the Italian criteria are applied to other economies the incidence of clusters is low. In the case of the United Kingdom, for example, it was necessary to drop the requirement for an industry to be disproportionately present in a travel to work area and reduce the industry participation to 20 separate establishments before large numbers of 'clusters' were identified (Crouch and Farell 2001). When a bottom up approach was applied in Germany, no clusters were identified in one study (Glassman and Voelzkow 2001). The German researchers concluded that resources supporting competitive advantage were distributed evenly across the economy so that no one location offered a particular location inducement over another. In contrast, the top down approach can attach the label cluster to any geographical scale, from a single city to a group of neighbouring countries, as ultimately all economic activity is interconnected to some degree. For those who start from the belief that a cluster is a unique geographical phenomenon based on local specialization, the interdependence perspectives make clusters an infinitely elastic concept and a reason for doubting the claimed importance of business clusters (Martin and Sunley 2003).

Agglomeration economies

Agglomeration economies are the cost savings to a firm that result from the concentration of production at a given location (Parr 2002). Most accounts of business clustering are based on the existence of agglomeration economies, but as with other aspects of cluster theory there is much debate over their precise importance. A fundamental question is whether it is possible for a concentration of economic activity to exist without individual enterprises in the concentration gaining any agglomeration advantage. It has been argued that this is impossible since benefit from agglomeration does not rely on deliberate decision making. Clustering can be taken as a source of universal advantage if co-location alone causes enterprises to gain from concentration. In contrast, if certain qualifying conditions need to be satisfied it is incumbent on advocates of cluster advantage to identify the context and the mechanisms that jointly give rise to the benefits obtained. This was something that Alfred Marshall, the 'founding father' of agglomeration economies, recognized but that many have subsequently failed to do (Box 5.3).

Box 5.3 **Marshall's cluster realism**

Marshall's interest in agglomeration economies was stimulated by the need to explain how some activities survived in industrial districts during a time when most industry was dispersing across increasingly diversified urban economies. He judged that industrial districts associated with two types of goods had most chance of survival: goods in general use that were 'not very changeful in character' and goods that could be represented effectively in illustrated catalogues or samples distributed to wholesale and retail dealers (Marshall 1923: 288). Market stability meant that there was 'no particular time at which strong incitement is offered to open up the industry elsewhere' (Marshall 1923: 227). Even then Marshall thought that district survival relied on the attraction of 'new shrewd energy to supplement that of native origin' so as to avoid the risk of 'obstinacy and inertia' among established entrepreneurs (Marshall 1923: 227). In modern day terms, following the interpretation of Pawson and Tilley (1997), it might be argued that Marshall had a realist assessment of cluster survival. Agglomeration advantages provided a mechanism to offset the disadvantages of small scale enterprise but they worked only under conditions of relative industrial stability and open business populations.

To understand the sources of controversy further it is first important to recognize that agglomeration benefits may accrue to firms, industries or cities (Ohlin 1933; Hoover 1937, 1948; Parr 2002).

- *Internal scale economies*: these arise from the expansion of a single establishment. In detail, they may be of three types: (i) economies of horizontal integration (the form usually thought of as arising from the fall in the unit cost of production with increased output); (ii) economies of lateral integration (or internal economies of scope, occurring when a firm's joint output of two or more products involves less cost than the same product range produced by single-product firms); (iii) economies of vertical integration (or internal economies of complexity, obtained by integrating steps in the production chain in a single operation). The ability to purchase in bulk, use specialized equipment, optimize the deployment of worker skills and equipment are all potential sources of internal economies. In many cases, organizations can realize these economies without consolidating activities on a single location (in which case, these agglomeration advantages do not lead to geographical agglomeration). This is reflected in the advantages that multi site enterprises can obtain over single site competitors and is reflected in the dominance of multinational organizations in many branches of industry (Dicken 2007).

- *Localization economies*: these refer to the cost savings that accrue to a group of firms within the same or related industry, located in the same place. Strictly, localization advantages are those external economies that are immobile and are a function of the scale of the industry at a particular location (Parr 2002: 719). Localization economies from industry concentration may arise in four ways: (i) *information spillovers* (for example through direct observation of other industry participants and the frequency of face-to-face contact); (ii) *specialist suppliers* (specialist support may take longer to emerge for a dispersed industry than a concentrated one, partly due to the effort in ascertaining demand or identifying the market opportunity); (iii) *non traded local inputs* (for example a shared testing or certifying service established by and for co-located enterprises); (iv) development of a *local skilled-labour pool* (McCann 2001). Localization economies are referred to as external economies to emphasize how they are beyond the control of individual firms. Some researchers prefer the term 'untraded interdependencies' to stress those benefits that are not dependent on financial transactions between enterprises.

- *Urbanization economies*: these economies arise where benefits are external to both individual establishments and the industry, being sometimes referred to as external economies of scope. Sharing of infrastructure and services among diverse firms are examples. Their magnitude is a function of the size and diversity of an urban concentration. Traditionally, as with the so-called incubator hypothesis (Box 5.4), it has been thought that small and new firms obtain most benefit from urbanization economies. Activity-complex economies are a specific variety of urbanization economy. These are the benefits of proximity among the members of a production-chain sequence such as transport cost savings, reduced inventory and energy savings. Industrial ecology provides a modern context for the possibility of activity-complex economies (see Chapter 8).

> *Box 5.4* **Inner city incubators**
>
> The incubator hypothesis can be applied to any environment that helps promote new enterprise formation. It has been applied to enclaves of ethnic enterprise and educational institutions that spin out enterprises started by academics. The original formulation identified the importance of long established industrial areas within cities (Vernon and Hoover 1959). This was based on the observation that new firms will be attracted to areas offering services essential to their operation that they, because of their small size and limited resources, would be unable to provide internally. Old industrial areas in the inner city, for example, may provide new firms with a supply of buildings of various sizes and cost with access to cheap accommodation, suppliers, markets and a variety of supporting business services. By concentrating close together, it was envisaged that new and small firms create external economies by buying and selling among one another and sharing close access to transportation and storage facilities. Inner city locations were seen to provide access to a labour pool encouraged by the access via public transport. Interest in the inner city as an enterprise incubator declined as evidence grew that they had lost their special advantages for new enterprise (Fagg 1980).

Based on this classification, different sources of agglomeration are traded off, as it is not possible to maximize each source simultaneously. Consequently, claiming the importance of business clusters prioritizes localization economies over internal or urbanization economies. One study to attempt the measurement of their relative importance examined the impact on the export performance of manufacturing firms in Sweden (Malmberg *et al.* 2000). It estimated that the gain from localization was from 40 to 80 times smaller than the gain from urbanization and from 50 to 100 times smaller than the effect of internal economies, depending on the sectors examined. The conclusion was, therefore, that the clustering of similar firms in individual labour markets was of little importance to export activity (a key performance indicator in an open economy such as Sweden) relative to other sources of agglomeration advantage.

Another research approach examines the relative performance of a branch of activity when located in a city that is specialized in that activity compared with the same activity located in a city with a diversified economy (Duranton and Puga 2002). This evidence should reveal the importance of localization versus urbanization economies, although there are some dangers of reading too much into the evidence (Box 5.5). One widely quoted study based on US data found that employment growth in a city industry is positively correlated with the initial diversity of industry employment in the city, but not with initial own-industry employment in the city (Glaeser *et al.* 1992). The study concluded that geographical specialization reduces growth ('specialization hurts') while city diversity helps employment growth, and it gave the example of the steel industry to illustrate this (Glaeser *et al.* 1992: 1140). Foreign competition and displacement by alternative construction materials led to a period of decline in steel production from the 1970s that was especially severe for the main centres of steel production in the

United States. The steel industry located away from the specialized centres of the industry adapted best to the changing business environment. While the Glaeser study did not directly reveal this, it appears that steel producers in diversified cities benefited in some way from their location away from competitors. It may, for example, have made them more willing or able to seek out non traditional markets or sources of information than their peers in a steel town (see also the discussion of collective invention in Chapter 4). Certainly a tendency for heavy industry clusters to get locked in to established ways of working and to fail to respond to changing markets has been noted in other contexts (Grabher 1993).

Box 5.5 Specialized versus diversified cities and questions of evidence

If localization economies are important, industries in specialized cities can be expected to outperform the same industry located in a diversified city. The results of studies examining this proposition are sensitive to the number of cities examined, how urban boundaries are determined and how specialization is measured. In the USA it has been shown that city diversity tends to increase with the size of the city. This can mean that differences in city performance are associated with size as well as the level of economic diversity. Places are classified as diversified or specialized according to the share of city employment in an industry compared with the industry's national share of employment. Cities may be specialized in an industry without this being a dominant part of the urban economy. Consequently, evidence based on specialized versus diversified cities is not capturing the position of clusters that involve a high degree of locality concentration on a single activity or set of related activities. Similarly, industries may be so broadly defined as to encompass a wide range of activities.

Source: Duranton and Puga (2002)

A direct source of evidence about the operation of localization economies has come from studies by Sorenson and Audia (2000) and Stuart and Sorenson (2003). These studies are based on data for the USA that indicates the location and other details of each establishment relative to all other establishments in the same industry. The database records annual establishment openings and closures and this allows changes in industry geography to be linked to the density of establishments. This test of how the performance of individual plants is affected by the density of same-industry plants around them gives some insight into the importance of localization economies. The findings are of particular interest in covering two contrasting industries: footwear and biotechnology.

In both industries, it is found that establishments located among a high density of own industry establishments are more likely to close down than are relatively isolated establishments. In contrast, openings are most likely to occur in locations with an existing high density of establishments. These observations are used to propose an interpretation of agglomeration that views it as helpful for new entrants but as disadvantageous to incumbents. This interpretation is built upon three claims:

- The current distribution of production determines the opportunity structure for new entrants. Dense clusters of like industry maximize the ability of individuals to accumulate the knowledge, social ties and confidence needed to form a new venture. Potential employees, investors, customers and collaborators assume greater risk in dealing with a new enterprise compared with an established enterprise with a known track record. Social capital helps would-be entrepreneurs overcome the advantage held by established organizations. It is built through personal relationships and tends to be concentrated among geographically localized contacts.
- Organizations located among other industry affiliates face stronger competitive pressure than isolated organizations. The pressure is intensified by a tendency for the business strategies of clustered firms to converge. Increased similarity between enterprises is considered especially likely where there is a high level of labour migration between firms and where enterprises occupy structurally equivalent positions within buyer–supplier networks (meaning identical ties to identical actors).
- The benefits to an individual enterprise of being in a cluster dissipate over time as managers' networks expand geographically. Market growth, participation in industry associations and industry-centred conferences facilitate the formation of ties among dispersed industry participants.

The Sorenson studies lead to a theory of clustering based on the social structure of opportunity: localization promotes new firm formation but detracts from the performance of established organizations. The test of this proposition is that high founding rates rather than low failure rates sustain clusters, which is found to be the case for the footwear and biotechnology industries. In effect this is a variation on the incubation hypothesis (Box 5.4) which suggested that certain environments were favourable for new firm formation. Indeed, given that plant densities may be expected to be highest in industrial cities, the Sorenson findings may be reaffirming long known-of processes rather than being entirely novel, but the results nonetheless remain important given the assumption popular among other researchers. A note of caution is that conditions specific to the industries studied need to be considered in applying the ideas more broadly. Biotechnology, for example, is not representative of other new technology-based sectors (see below and Chapter 7).

A two stage model of cluster development proposed by Schmitz (1995) and Schmitz and Nadvi (1999) is consistent with the Sorenson evidence and is of additional interest in addressing the question of whether deliberate decision making is needed to sustain any gains from clustering. The evidence it has given rise to is particularly valuable in that has caused researchers to examine the development of clusters over time (Box 5.6). As noted above, the failure to do this has been noted to be a particular gap in many contemporary cluster studies. The Schmitz model arose from studying low income countries where clustering is typically widespread at the early stages of industrialization and where the key question is whether this inhibits or advances development.

Box 5.6 Sinos Valley transitions

At the end of the 1960s, importers from the USA began scouting Brazil for shoe suppliers and identified the Sinos Valley as a potential source region, on account of its existing footwear industry and regional support for the sector including a national annual shoe fair. Around 20,000 pairs of shoes were produced annually in the Sinos Valley in the late 1960s, all for the domestic market. By 1984, production had grown to around 160,000 pairs with roughly 100,000 of these exported. A decade later, growth slowed as the Sinos Valley shoe industry lost market share to China and other low cost locations. By improving quality and adjusting to 'just-in-time' delivery schedules the industry had recovered its export volumes by the end of the 1990s. Large producers determined that their interests were best served by cooperating with their overseas buyers rather than supporting strategies designed to ensure the survival of the Sinos Valley industry as a whole. This support might include exporting shoe leathers to manufacturers in other overseas production centres, assisting the strategies of their buyers but not smaller Sinos Valley producers.

Source: Schmitz (1999)

In the Schmitz model, clusters commence on the basis of individual decisions that create unplanned advantages for any business locating in the cluster. Responding to the resource constraints at the outset of industrialization, enabling smaller amounts of investment than where production commences in isolation or among dissimilar activities is the key unplanned advantage obtained (Schmitz 1995). For example, producers can concentrate on a specific task and leave others to complete the process. Specialized workshops to repair and upgrade equipment further reduce the barriers to entry. In effect:

> the enterprise of one creates a foothold for the other ... ladders are constructed which enable small enterprise to climb and grow. It is a process in which enterprises create for each other – often unwillingly, sometimes intentionally – possibilities for accumulating capital and skill.
>
> (Schmitz and Nadvi 1999: 1506)

Being unplanned, clusters are easy to form, but while there is equality of access to cluster benefits they are unlikely to stimulate significant business growth (Schmitz and Nadvi 1999). Open access implies that no business can sustain an advantage over any other and the cluster as a whole has limited capacity to withstand competitive shocks. The main impact of stage one clustering is to reduce the scale of investment required to gain entry to the cluster.

A second stage of cluster development is needed to realize significant outcomes for business growth. In the second stage, dominant enterprises emerge with greater entrepreneurial capacity and ambition than 'ordinary' cluster firms (Schmitz 1995). Dominant enterprises make deliberate decisions about the use of cluster resources and selectively work with other cluster firms. According to these decisions, differences emerge between enterprises with respect to their size, resources, markets and pursuit of growth. Business heterogeneity has the potential to change the character of the cluster. Leading enterprises may, for example, start to build business networks beyond the cluster and lessen the opportunities for the original cluster enterprises left outside these networks (Box 5.6). Initially, it was considered possible that public agencies could play a role in ensuring that opportunities to participate in planned action were not controlled by a few dominant enterprises. More recently it has been recognized that the scope for clusters to assist business upgrading is frequently restricted by the organization of the supply chains that cluster enterprises depend upon (Humphrey and Schmitz 2002; Schmitz 2004, 2007).

This two stage model was developed from the evaluation of clusters in developing countries, but it has equally been applied to Italy's industrial districts (Rabellotti and Schmitz 1999). Widely seen as the exemplars of business clustering, Italy's industrial districts emerged during the 1950s when the country's post war revival fed through to increasing demand for many consumer products that could be supplied by small scale, family enterprise (Bamford 1987). With markets expanding rapidly, individual firms could operate without entering rigid relations with other enterprises and on the basis of opportunistic marketing strategies (Nuti and Cainelli 1996). Post 1980, the districts entered a second stage of development as market growth slowed and informal ways of working were replaced by more selective and structured inter-firm relationships (Brusco *et al.* 1996; Cossentino *et al.* 1996). Typical outcomes for individual districts included the internationalization of leading cluster enterprises, more reliance on non cluster businesses and the increased concentration of production within fewer, larger enterprises. The 'classical' district comprising many independent small enterprises and supporting agencies is now a minority among the local economies still recognized as an industrial district (Chapter 2 Box 2.2).

The picture painted by the Schmitz model, therefore, is that clusters evolve through a stage of relatively homogenous enterprise to a more heterogeneous business population. It is against this context that the frequently claimed ability of clusters to deliver an optimal mix of cooperative and competitive business relationships needs to be assessed (Box 5.7). Such idealized harmony is incompatible with an environment in which enterprises have different opportunities and different dependencies on their business neighbours. This is understood by researchers who have developed typologies of cluster varieties (Coe 2001). The hub and spoke cluster is worth special mention as it is a generic type that explains how the significance of clustering changes when a dominant enterprise emerges, an outcome that matches clusters such as aircraft manufacturing in Seattle (Gray *et al.* 1996). Such clusters comprise a central coordinating institution and satellite enterprises that are linked to the hub but not directly to each other. This structure has a number of implications for enterprise development in the cluster:

122   *Clusters and regional specialization*

- The spokes from the hub firm to suppliers and subcontractors may extend far beyond the local economy. This can assist local development by facilitating access to ideas or techniques that are new to the region, but it can also act to raise the pressure on local linkages where performance is now judged across a wider range of potential suppliers.
- The economic growth of hub and spoke districts is regulated by the position and success of hub organizations and their continued commitment to production and procurement within the district. This contrasts with the small-firm district where cooperation to share risk, spread the cost of innovation and reduce the vulnerability of the locality to economic change.
- There may be little cooperation within the hub and spoke network, especially if the hub enjoys dominance in an oligopolistic industry as this suggests its suppliers will have a high dependence on its custom. In this context communication between firms may not extend beyond product specification, quality standards and delivery schedules.
- Labour markets in the hub and spoke district are primarily controlled by the hub. Where the hub offers better pay and more stable employment, labour turnover will tend to be low, with workers strongly inclined to stay within the dominant organization. This differs from the situation envisaged in small-firm networks where labour is committed first and foremost to the district rather than an individual firm. Where the hub organization has multiple locations, movement of employees into and out of the cluster is facilitated and this can further reduce the extent to which a shared labour market develops for the district as a whole.
- Business and financial services in the hub and spoke district may not provide the specializations and interests that support local entrepreneurship. Dominant firms, for example, may have ties to national trade associations and have minimal interest in supporting the ambitions of local companies to expand beyond the cluster. Similarly, local government may centre its promotion and regulation on the dominant employer rather than on encouraging local entrepreneurship.

Box 5.7 **Cluster idealism**

Italy's industrial districts are frequently given as justification for believing that competition and cooperation can develop side by side. Close investigation of actual districts shows how business relationships are sensitive to the precise production and marketing environments operated in. A case study of two shoemaking districts in Emilia-Romagna, Fusignano and San Mauro Pascoli, shows how apparently similar business communities are associated with business relationships that are either cooperative or competitive.

Fusignano developed to supply cheap articles for tourists visiting the Adriatic 'Riviera'. San Mauro Pascoli has its origins in a number of medium sized firms specializing in high quality women's footwear. Apart from slight differences in style and market destination, high quality shoes are a relatively unvarying product. This stability has enabled some firms to specialize in component manufacture, for example soles and heels. The larger producers seek strategic associations with such specialists as a way of balancing the demands of quality and skill retention. With products that are relatively price inelastic what matters is the reliability of production partners, some of which may be exporters in their own right.

In Fusignano 'conventional' subcontracting is dominant: most firms are self contained except for a few minor tasks that are given out to subcontractors. Their middle to low quality products are made with technology that requires comparatively large amounts of fixed investment. Managing uneven market demand and avoiding the need to add to internal capacity motivate the use of subcontracting. Contracting links are made and broken according to prevailing needs and opportunities and as a further distinction with San Mauro Pascoli may involve subcontractors located outside the district. Faced with a shrinking market, in Fusignano subcontracting is mainly as a cost reduction strategy and gives few of the opportunities for cooperation.

Source: Nuti and Cainelli (1996)

A small example of the conflicts potentially arising in hub and spoke type clusters arose in the context of an investigation of four regional clusters in the New Zealand forest processing industry (Perry 2007b). These clusters had all been supported under a government cluster promotion scheme through financial support to formalize the cluster enterprises in a network association with an independent facilitator. Of the four groups, only one sustained participation and a significant programme of activity. It was distinguished by a business population that had a relatively high level of internal transactions as well as comprising businesses of broadly similar size and activity. The cluster group with some of the characteristics of a hub and spoke cluster raised the possibility that promoting the cluster might disadvantage small enterprise linked to the hub (Box 5.8).

Box 5.8 Conflicts in a timber cluster

In a cluster where there was a dominant producer and many smaller enterprises, the responses of managers to public agency support of a formal cluster group met varying responses. Firms with business relationships, directly or indirectly, with the large firm but predominantly dependent on their own marketing capacity were the most likely to report positively on the cluster. These firms can be working in a synergistic relationship with the dominant enterprise, purchasing services or material from it and selling material or services of its own back to the company. This offers mutual advantages and provides a context in which the opportunity provided by the cluster group to discuss business issues informally is valued. Smaller firms have benefited from the success of the large firm as well as retaining their own business development capacity. As well, the cluster has addressed shared issues such as promoting the industry as a source of employment to job entrants and seeking to encourage a positive attitude toward the industry among local politicians. In contrast, firms that relied predominantly on the large firm for their main business activity viewed the cluster project as something that reinforced their dependency and reduced their chances of being able to pursue other markets. Activity pursued by the cluster has to attract wide support, but with particular influence exerted by the large firm and directed at supporting its interests. Those enterprises seeking to reduce their dependence on the large firm saw the cluster project as something that added to their difficulty breaking away.

Source: Perry (2007b)

Agglomeration without agglomeration economies

A further weakening of the significance of business clusters arises if it is possible to show that clustering involves physical proximity only. Following a distinction proposed by Oakey (1995) and Oakey *et al.* (2001), physical clustering exists where businesses locate in proximity to each other, without any functional linkages between them and without deriving any special benefit from their location. This may be distinguished from functional clustering, from which firms gain some benefit from being close to each other, and these benefits explain why the co-location occurs. Against much of the reason for cluster enthusiasm, physical clustering is argued to be particularly prevalent among high technology activities. In practice, these activities comprise a mix of often technologically sophisticated but functionally heterogeneous enterprises (Oakey 1995). The inputs and outputs on which high tech companies rely are frequently of international origin and destination (Hendry *et al.* 2000; Oakey *et al.* 2001: 403). Politicians and planners tend to treat high tech activity as a single industry but in reality there is little in common between, say, a high tech electronics company and a high tech pharmaceutical company. As Oakey *et al.* (2001) investigate in the case of the non-broadcast visual communications (NBVC) sector (communications organizations utilizing Internet, multimedia, video conference and related media) in southern England there can even be much diversity within particular high tech activities. Consequently, although NBVC firms are frequently clustered, the benefits obtained from this are often minor.

Clustering arose partly from the frequency with which firms in the study had their origins in some large organizations such as a research centre and near to which they remain located. It is a common assumption that these origins induce functional clustering, through linkages between the spun-off firms, the incubator organization or other local enterprises. In practice, the clustering is consistent with the Sorenson theory and the tendency for new enterprises to start up close to the founder's prior place of residence. In Oakey *et al.*'s (2001) NBVC sample, the availability of relevant labour market skills was the main observable cluster benefit, but this had played no part in encouraging or sustaining the concentration of start ups. Other high tech clusters question whether even this advantage is obtained, as in the case of the opto-electronics or photonics industry (based on computer, laser and optic fibre technologies).

The photonics industry emerged in geographical clusters in four countries (Germany, Japan, United Kingdom and USA) and at the end of the 1990s comprised in the order of 5,000 firms worldwide (Hendry *et al.* 1999, 2000). Investigation in three of these locations revealed that local relationships played little role in the development of the individual clusters for five main reasons (Hendry *et al.* 1999, 2000):

- *Strong internal labour markets*: partly as there is a reliance on developing skills through in-house experience there is little mobility of scientists and engineers between work places.
- *Market diversification*: technological breakthroughs require firms to seek out collaborations wherever the relevant expertise is located rather than sticking with their original partners.
- *Complex firms*: even relatively small firms in a high tech industry engage in merger and acquisition activity, partly as it is necessary to assemble a range of expertise to develop a complete product or service.
- *Hub and spoke networks*: business networks are largely controlled by the activities of large or otherwise powerful firms rather than through the collective action of small firms.
- *Spin offs merely indicate inertia*: new firms frequently set up close to their former employer but this does not mean that functional linkages to the parent organization remain.

Perhaps even more surprising is the possibility that Silicon Valley is equally unaffected by localization economies. Such a claim has been made from research that has reconstructed the development of the Silicon Valley cluster by examining which firms spawned spinoff enterprises, the location of the parents and their spinoffs, the relationship between the performance of spinoffs and their parents and the reasons for the split (Klepper 2009). Underlying this investigation is the recognition that this regional experience captures the development of an industry during a period of intense technological change. Such experiences are not unique and indeed earlier investigations of the development of the car industry in and around Detroit are the basis for the method applied to Silicon Valley (Klepper 2006). The spinoff process is given prime attention in explaining the growth of industrial clusters, as it is expected that spinoffs result when motivated and talented employees find their project ideas are blocked as a consequence of senior management failing to recognize the potential of the idea or the employee or both. With the assumption that the performance of firms is based on the quality of their employees, leading companies have the most potential to generate spinoffs. The rate at which spin outs emerge from top companies will depend on the ability of their mangers to judge new ideas and identify employee talent. Once spinoffs emerge the process has potential to accelerate, as the ownership of ideas taken from the parent company is unclear and this facilitates subsequent diffusion, both back to the original parent and to other spinoffs. In Klepper's account Silicon Valley came to dominate the semiconductor industry because of the fertility of its first wave of spin out enterprises in generating their own spinouts and because stronger companies disproportionately gave rise to spinouts.

Reflecting on both his examinations of Silicon Valley and Detroit, Klepper (2009) concludes that conventional agglomeration economies related to knowledge spillovers, labour pooling and specialized input suppliers are not needed to explain the existence of an industry cluster. If they exist they are an outcome of other processes rather than a reason for the industry concentration. Two sources of evidence suggest that agglomeration economies may in practice be of little importance:

- The leading enterprises in the cluster tend to remain those with origins as a spinout from companies that continue to be or at least were at one stage among the industry top performers. A tendency for spinouts to be the creation of above-average employees working in the best enterprises can explain why location concentration occurs and why industry expertise does not emerge in many places.
- Companies such as Texas Instruments and Motorola have competed successfully from a location outside Silicon Valley, as have spinoff companies that they have spawned.

In essence, what explains the cluster is the location of a parent enterprise that at some point led new technology and that gave birth to equally strong spin outs. In the case of Silicon Valley, Fairchild filled that role, being itself the result of defection from Shockley Laboratories, and that was subsequently affected by some of its own staff being frustrated by the investment choices made by Fairchild. The Fairchild spinoffs were then affected by their own internal debates and sources of friction that provoked further spinoffs. The existence of spinoffs has always been recognized in accounts of the Silicon Valley cluster (for example Saxenian 1994); Klepper's perspective differs in viewing them as the primary driver of such industry concentrations. Rather than agglomeration processes being of causal significance, the location of early, highly successful entrants to a new area of industry opportunity and their spinoff fertility determines the incidence of spatial clustering. This interpretation of the origins of clusters still leaves scope for public policy intervention, given the desirability of unleashing the process of technological development that can result from the creation of spinoffs. Potential public policy changes relate to removing or at least reducing the ability to include 'restraint of trade' and 'non compete' clauses in employment contracts and reducing the ability to pursue litigation over 'trade secrets' where this might impede new enterprise formation. At the local level, the main policy message may be to include spinoff potential in the list of attributes prioritized in inward investment promotion programmes, as well as ensuring that financial support is available to spinoff enterprise (although spin out entrepreneurs are frequently well connected enough not to require assistance).

One qualification can be added to the spinoff interpretation of clusters. Neither of the industries studied by Klepper had much dependence on university research once the basic technology had been invented: semiconductors in the case of Silicon Valley and the internal combustion engine in the case of Detroit. While there was much improvement to be undertaken there was wide access to the basic technology and the forms of development required remained within the reach of individual companies. Development patterns differ where technology development is controlled by basic research going on in universities (Freeman 1982). University expertise tends to be highly dispersed, whereas business investment in the early phases of a new industry is comparatively mobile, facilitating clustering around an initial centre of expertise (Sharp 1990). The significance of such influences is seen through comparison between semiconductors with biotechnology (Gray 2002).

In computing, the key links and information flows were between engineers in different companies; in biotechnology, the important relationships have been between the science base and companies (Prevezer 1998: 128). In the case of biotechnology, partly because of the need for regulatory approval, a long time frame from scientific discovery to commercial application results in a particular relationship between established companies and new start ups. Incumbents with activity potentially affected by biotechnology innovations could maintain a 'watching brief' over prospective competitors, knowing that breakthrough companies would need the assistance of a large-firm partner to bring their innovation to market (Oakey et al. 1990). Thus it was not until the 1990s that commercial products started to emerge from the new biotechnology discoveries arising from scientific advances in genetics and molecular biology of the early 1970s (Audretsch 2001). Commercialization proceeded as large pharmaceutical companies selectively took up the products of biotechnology start ups and began to make strategic choices about their own investment (Sharp 1999). These companies do not depend on a location near to the original centres of expertise.

Theory informed practice

The discussion above has raised the possibility that the incidence of localization economies is less than the incidence of geographically clustered industry. One line of investigation recognizes that localization economies are of modest assistance to business development and of significance only up to the point where a more differentiated business population emerges. Ultimately, business success tends to concentrate in a small number of growth-orientated enterprises. Once the cluster divides among firms of unequal scale and ambition the access to localization economies is no longer based simply on location. Another line of investigation recognizes that spinout processes can result in clusters without the influence of localization economies. This may arise where the focal organization is a research centre and the spinouts pursue separate areas of technology specialization. Equally, where the spinouts continue the development of a core technology, the process through which spinouts arise can explain the relative unimportance of localization economies. Spinouts are likely to arise from the strongest enterprises and be established by individuals with high levels of technological insight and business ambition; this tends to reduce the reliance on external resources, although the availability of finance is a necessary precondition.

These ideas need to be reconciled with those accounts of clusters that appear to show the advantage gained from localization economies. Three general responses can be made that are consistent with seeking explanations for business clusters that are not based on the existence of localization economies.

First, there is a need to separate existing attributes from the underlying causal processes. The tendency for clusters to emerge in economically advantaged regions is one indicator of the presence of influences other than localization economies (Benneworth 2002). The examples of England's Motor Sport Valley, the Öresund medical cluster spanning Denmark and Sweden and biotechnology in Rhône-Alpes have been given as examples of clusters forming in privileged locations (Lagendijk 1999). As pointed out from the experience of Sophia-Antipolis, the benefit of accumulated exceptional levels of public funding over many locations explains this cluster rather than the gains from the proximity of agencies and enterprises (Longhi 1999). A comparison between Silicon Valley and 'second wave' IT clusters in other parts of the world (such as the clusters of IT activity in England, Finland, Ireland and Taiwan as well as other regions within the USA) also makes this point (Bresnahan et al. 2001). It found that even among other IT clusters experiencing high growth a large gap tends to remain between them and Silicon Valley. Bresnahan et al. (2001) judge that newer clusters remain confined to technology and market gaps that have not already been exploited by any other cluster, and this leaves them at a continuing disadvantage to Silicon Valley. For the researchers, this drew attention to how many of the advantages thought to accrue to cluster participants are not able to exist at the outset of a concentration. There are not, for example, other firms around in sufficient numbers to generate external economies. Rather than 'new economy' localization economies, 'old economy' attributes such as the sustained investment in education and research explained the emergence of second tier clusters. Getting to the point where a cluster stakes a claim on a new technology depends on years of firm and market building effort and long term investment in education and skill development. Even then, identifying a technology able to support a new concentration of business activity was seen to involve luck as well as foresight.

Second, where localization processes appear to have been important this can be explained by unusual circumstances. Motor Sport Valley in southern England is an example of a cluster which is thought to exemplify localized learning and benefits of a shared labour pool among other localization advantages. It has given rise to a theory of learning that associates business clusters with the accumulation of 'architectural knowledge' (Pinch et al. 2003). This theory argues that architectural knowledge tends to be acquired collectively among participants in a cluster, as in the way that designers in Motor Sport Valley became expert in aerodynamics while the Italian-based Ferrari team concentrated on engine power. When it was established that aerodynamics was the more fruitful line of development for producing faster racing cars, to catch up Ferrari found a need to locate a design office within the Valley and recruit engineers from English-based teams. This story is worth attention as Motor Sport Valley is a large business cluster of world significance. In the late 1990s, around three quarters of the world's single seat racing cars were designed and assembled in the cluster that employed over 50,000 people, most of them highly skilled engineers and designers (Pinch and Henry 1999). Breaking down the making of a Formula One car into four components (design, base, chassis and engine), nine out of 14 racing teams had three or four of these located in Motor Sport Valley. This case is an unambiguous illustration of the benefit that clustering can bring, but it still needs to be asked whether any additional influences are at work.

While Motor Sport Valley is involved in more than the production of racing cars this is a focal activity that attaches the cluster to an unusual industry. Cars are produced for races that are conducted against a uniform set of rules wherever the race takes place. A race in a tropical country such as Malaysia may have to contend with different weather conditions than encountered in Europe, but such differences do not require design expertise to be located close to each race track. Design and construction teams can stay in one place while racing occurs around the globe. The appearance of the cluster has also to be seen as an outcome of the extensive regulation of car racing, which for some codes is managed from the United Kingdom. Regulation produces the duplication of activity across race teams rather than the consolidation of ownership that would arise if cars were produced for the open market. For example, to prevent domination by one manufacturer, each team has to produce its own chassis (Pinch and Henry 1999). Regulation has also to be seen as a limiting factor on innovation since all teams operate within rules governing permissible technology. This is presumably a factor in allowing the accumulation of industry insight among a shared labour market as there is much public knowledge and common technology and visibility at the race track, although teams may seek to keep things hidden (see Combes and Duranton 2001: 8). Neither has there been pressure to locate where business costs might be minimized as sponsors are more motivated to see their logo on a winning team rather than to improve the efficiency of car racing (Pinch and Henry 1999: 819). Consequently, there are reasons why the industry has remained concentrated in the United Kingdom that are unconnected to localization economies. It is also worth noting that the Ferrari team office opened in Motor Sport Valley closed within a year (Pinch *et al.* 2003). It can be speculated that this was either because it was judged to be unnecessary or that the role it was set was accomplished quickly.

Third, there is much confusion over which business arrangements maximize localization economies. In some accounts it is envisaged that advantage arises when small firms are linked in comparatively stable networks, whereas other accounts envisage the possibility of enterprises continuously exchanging business partners and specializations (Breschi and Lissoni 2001a: 266). In practice, the effectiveness of business structures encouraged by localization economies needs to be assessed over time, with awareness that the form of advantage obtained can rapidly become redundant. The semiconductor manufacturing equipment industry provides an example of this (Chon 1997). Originally, close integration of the production of semiconductor manufacturing equipment with the manufacture of semiconductors was a source of strength to Japan's electronics sector. The direct transfer of knowledge about trends in the market for semiconductors helped equipment producers innovate more quickly than their competitors in the United States, where equipment manufacturers were independent of users. The balance of competitive advantage changed when North American equipment manufactures reorganized through strategic alliances. Working in cooperation with competitors, high tech manufacturers combined resources, shared risks and learned to better link their knowledge of production processes with research and development. Firms in the United States became leading suppliers of equipment to Japan, and in Japan ties between equipment users and suppliers have been cut. More recently, equipment makers have shifted to prioritize economies of scale matching the increasing consolidation of the semiconductor manufacturing industry. This example illustrates two general propositions: first, that the precise source of localization advantage influences the form clustering may take; second, the source of industrial advantage derived from localization can be short lived.

Accepting that the formation or survival of business clusters does not depend on localization economies downgrades the case that can be made for promoting business clusters. This is because it suggests that the gains experienced by cluster enterprises by virtue of their proximity to each other are less than expected. At the same time, two dangers of encouraging increased specialization remain. Increasing a commitment to particular technologies, products and markets may impede the long term adaptability of the local economy and make it more vulnerable to short term instability and external shocks concentrated in a particular sector. The case for supporting emerging areas of business specialization needs to be made on clear evidence that there is opportunity to develop the collective capacity of a group of related enterprises. This means providing a rationalization for policy intervention on the grounds of providing public goods that are missing due to market failure. Four types of such goods have been identified as relevant to cluster promotion operating on this basis (Martin and Sunley 2003):

- The creation of cooperative networks that encourage dialogue between firms and between firms and other agencies, with the result that firms can more easily pool resources, design collective solutions to shared problems and develop a strong collective identity.
- The development of collective marketing of an industry specialization and shared investment in the opening of new markets.
- The local provision of services for firms such as financial services, marketing, design and component production in place of remotely obtained services. Through local provision, such services can become customized to the particular industrial specialization of the cluster.
- Weaknesses in existing cluster value chains can be addressed by helping to rationalize activity among existing firms and by efforts to attract investment and businesses to fill the gaps and strengthen demand and supply links.

Simply identifying a shortfall in collective resources is not sufficient to justify intervention. The perceptions of industry participants must be recognized as it affects their willingness to support their development and this is frequently where cluster promotion fails (Perry 2007a; 2007b). Policy makers may succeed in identifying a cluster but mistake their ability to influence its development direction. A small but notable example of the way cooperative opportunities are frequently less than anticipated is reported in the case of the New England (USA) town of Barre (Kotval and Mullin 1998).

At various times since the late nineteenth century Barre (Vermont, population around 10,000) has been promoted to be the granite capital of the world. It is located above extensive granite deposits that in the late 1990s were mined by around 60 companies, with many of the rest of the town's businesses supplying transport, machinery or equipment repair services to the miners. Most of the businesses have been in family ownership for generations. Fear that the industry was continuing to lose market share led town officials and some industry leaders in Barre to turn to cluster thinking for help in reviving business growth while remaining as the 'granite town' (Kotval and Mullin 1998: 314). Strategies adopted including the relaxation of zoning controls, more effort to ensure infrastructure and land was available for business growth, keeping taxes down, regulation to require the use of granite in all Vermont public buildings and encouragement for education and banking institutions to focus on the industry's needs. None of these strategies brought the desired upgrading of the stone industry away from comparatively low value rough cut stone and grave memorials. A key obstacle was that Barre's biggest firm was more inclined to act like a multinational corporation than a home-grown firm (Kotval and Mullin 1998: 315). It is a good citizen, participating in community events and operating a visitor centre, but its business strategies suggest greater interest in remaining the dominant business in the industry rather than in helping to grow the industry as a whole. Without its inclination to join, the effort to lever advantage from the concentration of activity was stymied. The final conclusion then becomes of wider significance: the opportunities for gaining advantage from the presence of an industrial cluster frequently assumes a willingness among individual enterprises to sacrifice their business aspirations in the interests of growing the cluster a whole. Except under conditions of crisis it is unrealistic to imagine that such a shift in priority will be supported.

A market failure justification for cluster intervention leaves unresolved the scale of the public benefit required to justify intervention and how much attention needs to be paid to the distribution of the benefit obtained. It is well known that even in the case of clusters based on advanced sectors, not all constituencies share in the prosperity (Crang and Martin 1991; Benner 2002). The growth of industrial concentrations can encourage congestion, increased land costs and labour shortages, and these outcomes tend to fall first on those gaining least benefit from the core activity of a cluster. Firms with lower margins may be forced out of the area, along with workers on lower incomes who find it more difficult to afford housing in the cluster. Rosenfeld (2003) has argued that unless distributional issues are addressed in policy initiatives there is a risk of cluster promotion widening economic disparities. Clusters create a capacity for industry participants to network and learn from one another but potentially raise the barriers for firms outside the cluster. The more clusters are defined by formal membership and the more business activity depends on personal networking, the higher the hurdles can become for outsiders to gain entry. To enable clusters to reach and serve the interests of weaker economies and small businesses, Rosenfeld (2003) suggests that cluster policy should have low entry requirements and impose conditions on the access to cluster assistance. These recommendations are unlikely to appeal to policy makers. Low entry requirements imply a flexible definition of clusters to encompass of wide range of situations, whereas policy makers are likely to prefer a precise definition that imparts a specific status to resulting interventions. The suggested conditions include representation from labour unions and 'third sector' organizations with interests in the environment, civil society and equity.

Conclusion

Most explanations of clustering start with a list of advantages that firms can enjoy from a location among their industry peers and supporters. The presence of these advantages is simultaneously the explanation for clustering. Such an approach has three problems. First, it leaves a gap in explaining how the activity accumulated to the point where the advantages emerged. Presumably, up to the time when an activity started to assume importance, future cluster members were small in number and part of a diversified economy. Second, the advantages ascribed to clusters are numerous and partly in competition with each other. A cluster that offers a gain through the sharing of tacit knowledge is unlikely to be simultaneously one that gains from the stimulus of intensified competition. If there is intensified competition it suggests a high degree of similarity between businesses and consequently not much new information to be gained from neighbours. Similarly, heightened competition does not seem compatible with the long term survival of diverse population of enterprises. While the worlds of business and ecology differ it is instructive to recall Gause's law of the principle of competition exclusion: no two organisms that compete in every activity can coexist indefinitely in the same environment (Thorngate 1976: 122). Third, it suggests that all activity should be located in clusters. If clusters are simply about the pursuit of advantages, it would seem that organizations not availing themselves of them will fall behind those that do. In practice there is no undisputed evidence that patterns of industrial location are changing in favour of clusters, or that businesses that are located in a cluster gain an advantage over those that do not.

Perhaps the greatest challenge to the interest in business clusters comes from the most influential exemplar, Silicon Valley. Recent interpretation of the development of Silicon Valley as the creation of spin out enterprises managed by gifted entrepreneurs moving out of leading ventures is about to account for clustering without reference to the existence of localization economies. This shifts the public policy significance of such enterprise clustering away from local economic policy to national issues related to the legal impediments that might exist to entrepreneurial spin outs. Even then this interpretation depicts processes that arise only in the context of episodes of substantial technological discovery and that encompass selected enterprises working at the forefront of technological innovation.

Other evidence dealing with more 'ordinary' business sectors also suggests that the importance of enterprise clusters is mainly in their impact on new enterprise formation. Barriers to new enterprise formation can be lowered when enterprise is clustered. It maximizes the capacity for new entrants to gain a foothold by exploiting their personal connections to offset the disadvantages of newness. Unlike the spin out process associated with Silicon Valley, however, enterprise formation can simply add to competitive pressure on incumbents rather than being a basis for local economic development.

These comments deal with business clustering in the sense of localized concentration of business specialization that might be identified on the basis of criteria such as those employed in the official survey of industrial districts in Italy. This chapter has distinguished this perspective on clusters from the interest in business interdependence and ability to identify another form of cluster through national templates. A top down approach to cluster analysis has a role in assisting local economic development agencies to investigate their locality and understand the linkages that might exist between activities in their economy. Many local development agencies may discover pockets of business specialization below that which might be confirmed as a cluster using the qualifications such as those employed by Italy's statistical agency. The doubts this chapter has raised about the importance of localization economies should temper the investment in promoting small scale clusters, but local development agencies may still have justification for wanting to support groups of enterprise. Experience suggests that such intervention needs to be explicit about at least three matters prior to launching any form of cluster promotion. First, the interpretation of cluster development guiding the proposed intervention needs to be resolved and checked for its consistency with the proposed measures. For example, if the collection of enterprises is diverse in scale and dependency on other local enterprises the opportunity for developing collective resources is less than where the group of enterprises are similar in scale and have some interconnections. Second, investigation of the particular opportunities existing is needed rather than a justification based on localization economies or the possibility of replicating aspects of exemplar clusters. Third, public agencies need to respond to the potential distributional consequences of cluster promotion, explaining how unequal gains will be mitigated or how the intervention has been designed to allow for a wide range of participation. It is naive, for example, to assume that collective projects suggested by a cluster group will necessary suit all enterprises.

6 Urban success and the creative class

New perspectives on urban success have developed from the simple observation that people vote with their feet and move to the places with the best amenity and the strongest labour market. This is something that has always been a possibility, but it has tended to be dismissed for two main reasons. The freedom of people to move from areas of relative economic distress to areas of relative economic buoyancy is held back by the devaluation of personal assets in a declining region. This can apply to physical assets such as property as well as to the worth of work skills and experience where they are linked to a declining sector of activity. Entry barriers have been a second reason for believing that the distribution of population adjusts sluggishly to the changing geography of opportunity. Access to job opportunities in a growing region is constrained by housing shortages and the pressure on urban infrastructure. The successful city may offer better long term economic prospects than a lagging locality but immediately it may mean acceptance of reduced living space, increased commuting effort and broken social networks. From the perspective of the economy as a whole, the value of relieving infrastructure pressure in the local economies that are growing is balanced against the underutilized resources in the localities that people move from. Hence the focus of regional policy in the past on moving jobs to the people rather than people to the jobs (Chapter 3 Box 3.3).

The new interest in personal mobility reflects specific claims rather than a general belief that mobility has become less restricted than it was. One innovation proposes that some types of worker have a larger influence than others on the success of city economies, and that some people's ability and inclination to relocate has grown more than others. These talented and mobile city workers, collectively known as the creative class, are found across occupations including science, engineering, arts, culture and entertainment and the knowledge-based professions of management, finance, law, healthcare and education (Florida 2002a; Florida *et al.* 2008: 616). This argument has proved highly attractive to many policy makers despite academic doubt over the identity, mobility and precise contribution of the creative class to urban economic success (Peck 2005; Markusen 2006; Scott 2006b). A second shift in the argument is to recognize that the increasing openness of the international economy has broadened the pool of potential migrants capable of significantly affecting city prosperity. This opening of the city gates to international migrants means that there are now more potential recruits and more ability to select from among the top talent. It has been claimed, for example, that Ireland's economic boom during the 1990s would not have been possible without the ability to draw from the Irish emigrant population located around the globe (Krugman 2005). Whereas this might be thought to reinforce the creative class approach, a lack of consideration to the role of foreign-born migrants and ethnic entrepreneurship has become a further source of critique (Thomas and Darnton 2006).

The creative class thesis makes the location decisions of key city workers the determinant of local economic development. Creative workers are judged to be the creators and users of knowledge and the mechanism for bringing new information and learning to places (Hansen and Niedomysl 2009). Among innovation-based theories of local economic development, this may be contrasted with arguments that organizations and institutions are the core components of regional innovation systems (see Chapter 4). The creative class thesis is built on the high mobility of talented workers, but city managers are advised to improve their attractiveness so as to restrain the desire of their own key workers to move to cities with more favourable living environments. This advice answers a longstanding question in regional studies about whether economic growth is stimulated by people moving to jobs or, through jobs, moving to where people are most plentiful. The creative class approach recommends that local economic agencies work on the assumption that business will move to where talented workers are most plentiful. As cities are made more attractive to creative workers they signal their openness and inclusiveness in ways that can attract other talented individuals, and so the process can be made to feed on itself (Florida *et al.* 2008). Evidence for this is mainly in the form of an association between the highest rates of urban growth and the highest levels of specific forms of urban amenity to which creative workers are held to be particularly sensitive (Florida 2002a).

The policy recommendation to focus on improving urban amenity and the evidence from which it is derived have become the source of controversy, as it seems to imply that urban policy can be decoupled from a city's industrial legacy and how that shapes future growth potential (Storper and Scott 2009). Some have even referred to the 'curse of the creative class', seeing the advocacy of creative localities as a burden rather than a boon for business (Malanga 2004). Others argue that given a free choice amenities may influence the location preferences of key knowledge workers, but location selections are rarely unconstrained and amenity preferences are highly variable (Peck 2005). In any case it is not clear that creative workers are as mobile as is claimed, at least in the context of smaller industrial economies where creative occupations tend to concentrate in one or a few cities (Hansen and Niedomysl 2009). Irrespective of whether knowledge workers are shown to gravitate to the most successful urban economies it can be wrong to claim a causal connection. People may move to places where their skills are most effectively employed and most rewarded, but such movement responds to business growth as well as augmenting it. At the least it is necessary to recognize that the influences initiating economic growth can be different from the influences that sustain growth (Bresnahan *et al.* 2001). Put more practically, people are unlikely to move from one location to another unless relevant employment opportunities are actually or potentially already available (Storper and Scott 2009: 161). On the other hand, even if this proves to be a small contributor to urban success, making cities attractive to creative talent can be justified as long as it is not at the expense of social inequalities that accentuate other constraints on urban growth.

The review of the debate commences with further explanation of the creative class thesis and how this links to other human capital theories of urban economic success. To provide a context for evaluating these ideas it is first necessary to contrast them with other approaches to understanding urban economic development. Specific doubts that have been raised against the thesis are identified and evaluated, which leads to a concluding discussion on what current evidence indicates is the appropriate response to the claimed role of a creative class in supporting urban economic development.

The creative class and human capital theories of urban economic growth

The starting point for the creative class thesis is the more general claim that the availability and quality of human capital shapes differences in regional economic performance. Florida et al. (2008) identify a stream of literature dating back to Solow (1956) that they see as developing a case for putting human capital at the centre of explanations for differences in regional growth. Solow's starting contribution was to note the effect of technology on economic growth, but this led followers to develop theories about how technology developed. Credit is given to the work of Jane Jacobs (1961, 1969) in emphasizing the role of cities with diverse populations and economic activities in facilitating the transfer and diffusion of knowledge that stimulated the generation of new ideas and innovations. Romer (1986, 1987, 1990) developed an endogenous growth model which indicated how processes of economic concentration and enterprise specialization connected technology to human capital, knowledge and economic growth (Chapter 4 Box 4.1). Lucas (1988) argued that urban concentration and the improvement of human capital are the crucial components of endogenous growth processes. People develop insight and generate knowledge and are able to share this more easily when part of an urban concentration that facilitates knowledge transfer and the rapid circulation of new ideas. A number of more recent studies are then identified which are taken to confirm these theoretical models by showing that a relationship exists between human capital and national growth rates (Barro 1991; Rauch 1993; Simon 1998) and with regional growth rates (Glaeser 2000). Florida et al. (2008: 618) conclude that theory and empirical evidence demonstrate that firms locate in areas of high human capital concentration to gain competitive advantages, and that accessibility to suppliers and customers is now a comparatively minor influence on location decisions.

A further observation underlines the interest in the creative class: the most talented sector of the workforce is becoming more concentrated in fewer, larger cities (Florida 2002b; Berry and Glaeser 2005). The uneven availability of talented workers challenges the tendency for economists to assume that human capital is a fixed stock or endowment which belongs to a place in the same way that a natural resource might (Florida et al. 2008: 619). Instead, talented workers should be treated as a flow resource with high mobility and a strong motivation to optimize their place of residence. The consequent crowding of workers with most capacity to contribute to business development justifies attention to their residential preferences, as it appears many places are in danger of being depleted of a key resource for urban growth. With this as background, Florida's main concerns are to determine how best to measure and account for human capital and to advise city managers how they can best retain and attract creative workers.

On the first of these issues, the creative class thesis seeks to promote a particular way of identifying that component of the workforce of most significance to economic development. Prior to Florida (2002a) the value of human capital was linked to the extent of training and education completed. As with the influential studies of Glaeser (1994, 1998, 2004), human capital had been differentiated according to the share of the workforce holding at least a bachelor degree. The rationale was that education qualifications captured the most important investments made to increase the value of human labour. Four reasons are given to support the use of occupation as an indicator of creativity rather than the level of qualification (Florida et al. 2008):

- Well known examples of highly successful entrepreneurs who have not completed undergraduate degrees, such as Bill Gates and Michael Dell, show how educational achievement is a poor indicator of ability and creative drive.
- Educational achievement captures a broad population that does not permit a focus on specific occupational groups, whereas the creative class is readily analysed as a whole and in terms of its component parts.
- Education measures potential talent or skill but this underlying capability has an impact on economic activity only to the extent that educated persons have an occupation.
- The benefits of education may be reflected in enhanced productivity but attributes such as creativity, intelligence, on-the-job knowledge and accumulated experience provide at least equivalent impact.

The creative class comprises occupations that are judged to require 'complex problem solving that involves a great deal of independent judgement and requires high levels of education or human capital' (Florida 2002a: 8). They are identified through a sequence of judgements that starts by selecting occupations demanding educated workers and offering knowledge-based jobs, adding selected occupations not already included because of their particular merits and expanding the group with workers in the arts. The commonality is the possession of a job that requires thinking rather than simply the carrying out of prescribed processes. The selected occupations (Table 6.1) were counted to comprise around 30 per cent of the total US workforce: this is similar to the proportion of the workforce that has completed a college degree. Within the full creative class a 'super creative core' are identified by their especially high levels of creativity. A modified occupational classification

Table 6.1 Creative class occupations

Super creative core
• Computer mathematical occupations
• Architecture and engineering occupations
• Life, physical and social science occupations
• Education, training and library occupations
• Arts, design, entertainment, sports and media occupations
Creative professionals
• Management occupations
• Business and financial operations occupations
• Legal occupations
• Healthcare practitioners and technical occupations
• High-end sales and sales management

Source: Florida (2002a: 328)

proposed by McGranahan and Wojan (2007) has also been given attention, recognizing that this may more accurately reflect the skill content of creative occupations than the original grouping of occupations (Florida *et al.* 2008).

According to the theory, the tolerance and openness of places along with the location of universities and the quality of urban amenities are key influences on the residential selections made by creative class workers (Florida 2002a). In a context where the mobility of talented workers is thought to be increasing, it is suggested that these influences play complementary roles in influencing the distribution of talent and promoting regional development: universities are a necessary aspect of a locality with a good concentration of creative talent but not a sufficient condition as their graduates may choose to move away (Florida *et al.* 2008: 616). Similarly the role of amenities is not dismissed, although Florida (2002a) measures it through a 'bohemian index' (Box 6.1) rather than in terms of a concentration of consumer and personal service industries as suggested by Glaeser *et al.* (2001). The novel measure – tolerance and openness to diversity – is added in the belief that a diverse population provides opportunity for complementary skills to be combined in ways that will support creativity and innovation. In this claim, Florida assumes that openness to people enables places to capture a higher quotient of skills and ideas and that his 'gay index' provides a good proxy for this quality of a city (Box 6.2).

Box 6.1 **Bohemian index**

The bohemian index is a measure of the extent to which artistically creative people are over or under represented in a given metropolitan area relative to the USA as a whole. It includes authors, designers, musicians, composers, actors, directors, painters, sculptors, artist printmakers, photographers, dancers, artists and performers. The original calculation of the bohemian index was based on 1990 Census data.

Source: Florida (2002a: 333)

> *Box 6.2* **Gay index**
>
> The gay index is a measure of the over or under representation of coupled gay people in a metropolitan area relative to the USA as a whole. The data is derived from a Census question that allowed respondents to identify that they lived with an unmarried partner. This information was combined with sex of the respondents identified as belonging to a household to compute an estimate of the number of gay and lesbian couples.
>
> *Source:* Florida (2002a: 255, 333)

With these innovations, Florida goes on to construct a larger explanation of the sources of regional economic success as measured by regional wage and income levels (Box 6.3). This explanation centres on the '3Ts' of economic development: technology, talent and tolerance. All three must be substantially present: individual components are necessary but insufficient in themselves to generate regional development (Florida 2002a: 249). Welcoming, diverse and open-minded cities attract creative people and concentrations of creative people attract investments in high tech industries which lead to economic growth. As technology and talent, when measured by educational attainment, have previously been canvassed as the sources of regional growth, the most novel aspect of the theory relates to the claims about tolerance and diversity. Florida supports his innovation in regional development theory by identifying how openness can be linked to urban productivity levels (Florida *et al.* 2008).

> *Box 6.3* **Measuring economic success**
>
> Florida (2005) measures metropolitan economic performance as either an index of the presence of high technology industries, drawing on the Milken Institute's high tech index (www.milkeninstitute.org) or the level of regional income. Creativity is associated with high technology and because high technology and total job growth often go together the use of Milken scores is seen to be an appropriate measure of economic success. Florida accepts that creativity may be a feature of any industry rather than a high technology monopoly and argues that a high Milken score often means growth in other industries too. Wages comprise around 70 per cent of average total personal income in the USA, with the other income sources including rents, interest and capital gains. Income provides a fuller measure of regional wealth but includes sources that may be unconnected to the region of residence. Florida *et al.* (2008) recognize this shortcoming and test for the impact of the creative class on regional income and separately wages.
>
> As well as the overall regional performance, levels of income inequality can be a concern to public agencies as high average income can exist alongside extreme poverty and the need to manage attendant social issues. With this in mind, Thomas and Darnton (2006) propose four alternative ways to measure the economic performance of a region:
>
> 1. Overall relative income growth, growth in key industries (as compared with a single sector) or overall job growth.

2. The creation of clusters of activity based on ethnic enterprise, specific industries or occupations that offer economic potential and address the needs of specific communities.
3. Progress eradicating economic sinks and locations characterized by high segregation from the larger urban economy and a concentration of poverty.
4. The extent of economic distress as revealed by poverty, unemployment and related indicators.

Four mechanisms are at the centre of the explanation of urban economic success offered by the creative class approach:

- A concentration of bohemian and gay populations indicates that the community is open to accommodating a diversity of racial, ethical and other social groups. Citing Page (2007) as evidence, diversity is associated with the greater likelihood of a group generating new perspectives and, in turn, with innovation and growth.
- Bohemian and gay populations and other component segments of a diverse population establish networks that disseminate ideas across firms and industries. It is claimed that a study of the connections between bohemian communities and the mainstream technology community (Stolarick and Florida 2006) supports this contention, as does the work of other researchers who have studied links between the arts and urban economies (Markusen and Schrock 2006; Currid 2007).
- Openness to gay and lesbian populations indicates society's overall tolerance, and tolerance measured by self-expression values is correlated with GDP growth (Inglehart and Norris 2003; Inglehart and Welzel 2005). This is explained by psychological studies that have established a link between self expression and higher levels of creativity, innovation and entrepreneurial behaviour.
- Artistic and gay populations gravitate to places that do not impede their full participation in society. The openness that attracts and retains these populations equally supports entrepreneurship and new firm formation by giving creative people full access to mainstream economic institutions.

Critical reflections on the creative class

The reaction to the creative class explanation of urban success has included three levels of critique: the appropriateness of seeking human capital explanations of regional development; the particular interpretation of human capital in the creative class approach; the effectiveness of the public policy recommendations. Individual commentaries may combine elements of each perspective, but to simplify the debate around key areas of concern there is value in explaining each line of critique in turn. The three levels of critique are not inclusive of all commentaries on the creative class. They overlook those that react more to the support for selected social groups than to a concern with local economic development theory (for example, see Lehmann 2003 and Malanga 2004 for contrasting assessments) and does not explore concerns with the evidential base drawn upon (for example, see Marcuse 2003). Neither does it consider the existence of non conforming cases or debate the relative merits of alternative indicators (Box 6.4). The focus is on issues that are thought to have most significance for larger controversies in local economic development practice.

Box 6.4 **The Las Vegas critique**

Las Vegas is one locality that stood apart from the creative class claims that economic success comes from bohemian environments. Prior to 2008 Las Vegas was among the USA's fastest growing local economies, but based on gambling and gaudy tourism more than creativity and artistry. Such exceptions to the claim that bohemianism begets prosperity do not end the argument. Florida presents his ideas as an unfolding agenda to be further explored rather than as a scientific theory which leads to mechanistic laws about the sources of urban growth, although clearly he wishes it to be seen as more than merely an interesting possibility.

The Las Vegas critique may encourage the development of alternative indices based on indicators that match its experience. For example, Malanga (2004) suggests a range of business friendly indicators as alternative, more accurate predictors of urban economic success. This level of critique does not address the more important issue as to whether correlating any urban league table with selected measures of urban economic success gives insight into the causes of urban change. The limitation is that league tables can capture outcomes of urban growth as well as, if not more than, the underlying sources of urban growth. The latter tend to be multi faceted, interrelated and hard to measure.

Starting with the most fundamental critique, doubts have been raised that labour availability of any form can explain regional growth (Scott 2006b; Storper and Scott 2009). This doubt is based on the assumption that a convincing theory must be able to explain the core processes accounting for urban growth. As they believe that places must have achieved a degree of economic dynamism before people shift to them in significant numbers, this relegates the creative class and other human capital theories to at best explaining marginal or intermediate adjustments. This critique prefers a theory of urban growth that can explain why economic activity gets locked into an initial location and that incorporates agglomeration economies and cumulative causation processes. The combination of agglomeration and cumulative causation is seen to explain three features that are central to most industrial economies: (i) dominant urban centres grow over long periods of time through adaptation to changing economic opportunities; (ii) there is an increasing concentration of economic activity in urban regions, despite high land and labour costs relative to non urban locations and despite the declining cost of transport and communications; (iii) organizational and geographical fragmentation of production increases as economic growth permits increasing business specialization.

With cumulative causation and agglomeration economies, a growth of output has a positive impact on further output growth (for example by facilitating more efficient scales of production and more specialization) and leads to an expansion of the labour market that, in turn, allows a further round of output expansion, and so on. From this perspective, the amenities available at any locality should be viewed as the creation of urban growth processes rather than independent drivers of that growth. Even climate and physical environments can be looked on as resources created by economic development since, with the possible exceptions of the retired and super-rich, these goods are usually consumed in combination with urban facilities and work opportunities.

Periodic shifts in technology may be seen as opportunities for human preferences to come to the fore and deflect the path of urban growth. Such a 'window of opportunity' (Scott and Storper 1987) has been created by the growth of information and digital technologies which have directly created new industries and reshaped the organization of older industries. It has been associated with a shift from rustbelt to sunbelt regions. Even so, Storper and Scott (2009) question how much of this changing geography can be attributed to individuals acting on their residential preferences. Places such as Silicon Valley were not constructed in a desert but rather their emergence was linked to pre-existing activity (Prevezer 1998). As these clusters developed and the locality's reputation grew, people moved in response. A cumulative development process occurred as workers in the emerging industries learnt from one another within relationships mediated by their organizational affiliations. Evolving expertise supported business growth and business growth drew in workers, facilitating further expansion of human skills and business growth and so on.

Correlating labour movement to the contemporary features of urban areas such as the quality of their amenities, climate or population profile assumes that people are free to move. It assumes that decisions to move or stay are made independently of the availability of income earning opportunities, and that accumulating concentrations of creative workers will of itself stimulate creative interaction. Both assumptions are questionable. It seems implausible that labour force participants move without regard to their income and career prospects, or that enterprise growth can be explained without reference to organizational strategies, resources and business opportunities (Storper and Scott 2009: 149). Evidence to this effect is given in a study of graduate migration patterns across 31 metropolitan areas in the USA (Gottlieb 2004). Areas revealed to be poor at retaining and attracting science, technical and engineering graduates suffered from a lack of job opportunities rather than residential amenities. It followed that strengthening the availability and conditions of employment would have more influence over graduates than seeking to change city ambience.

Florida relies partly on a relationship between patenting activity and the population density of cities, showing that rates of patenting are highest in high density cities (Knudsen *et al.* 2008). This is claimed to show how the crowding of creative workers helps to stimulate innovation on the grounds that 'density is what enables frequent, unpredictable, serendipitous meetings and interactions' (Knudsen *et al.*

2008: 474, footnote 2). There is no demonstration that such forms of encounter are actually taking place or that they play any role in patent activity. Patent data respond to the perceived incentive to register intellectual property claims and are an imperfect measure of either creativity or innovation (Pakes and Griliches 1984; Feldman and Audretsch 1999; Nelson 2009). Where patents are registered is affected by the uneven distribution of company head offices and R&D facilities and the tendency for these to concentrate in long established cities with a high density of economic activities and supporting institutions. Innovation leading to patents is supported by vast expenditure on research and deliberate, programmed activity. Gaining connection to new sources of insight is an aspect of creative innovation, but formal and programmed encounters are the dominant way that information is shared (Cohen et al. 2002).

Florida's claim that firm location is now shaped by the availability of creative workers and that accessibility to suppliers and customers has ceased to be a constraint on business location decisions has also to be considered against the extent to which cities have de-industrialized. Urban economies in most Western industrial economies have ceased to be major centres of manufacturing employment and are now dominated by service sector employment. Urban manufacturing employment has not only been lost to countries overseas, it has shifted to smaller towns and rural areas where space is most readily available (Fothergill et al. 1985). Services vary in their industrial organization but the faster growing parts tend to be highly constrained in their location choice because of the extent to which face-to-face contact with their clients is an aspect of their normal business activity. The world of manufacturing has globalized but labour-intensive business services frequently continue to serve markets that are highly localized when considered in terms of the respective location of providers and clients. The alleged freedom of enterprise to shift to where key workers prefer to locate does not recognize how urban growth has become dominated by enterprises that are more constrained in their location choice than the types of enterprise that once dominated cities.

The second level of critique takes issue with the measurement of human capital. One aspect of this debate has already been alluded to: whether education levels are a better indicator of the component of human abilities that affects regional growth or whether this is better captured by some measure of creativity. Glaeser (2004) argues that an education-based measure is an effective predictor of regional economic growth. Others point out that being based on broad occupational categories, the grouping of nominally creative workers encompasses jobs with varying educational and creativity demands including some that appear to require little of either (Markusen 2006; McGranahan and Wojan 2007). Florida et al. (2008: 619) refer to Swedish and Dutch studies endorsing the creative class definition (Marlet and van Woerken 2004; Mellander and Florida 2006). Wojan et al. (2007) have proposed an alternative classification more focused on occupational skill levels, while Donegan et al. (2008) raise questions about the creative category however constructed (Box 6.5). Nonetheless, it seems that education-based, creative class and a modified creative class definitions are all capable of being correlated with economic growth. This reflects how they identify overlapping rather than radically different groups. It is also a product of the way that growing parts of the economy have a different employment profile to the less well performing segments. The profile of newly recruited workers differs from that of long established workers, for example, because of the higher proportion of people entering the workforce with university degrees and the tendency for new recruits to be younger than the average age of all workers (Child 1974). In this sense, employment profiles differ as a consequence rather than as a cause of growth. The mobility characteristics and residential preferences of the creative workforce are equally in doubt.

Box 6.5 Indicators of performance in the USA

Donegan *et al.* (2008) contrast measures of regional creative capacity, as developed by Richard Florida, with more conventional competitiveness factors in terms of their association with regional economic performance. Using data relating to metropolitan areas in the USA, the researchers make two comparisons:

- The Florida talent (creative class) index is compared with a traditional measure of human capital (the proportion of adults with bachelor's degrees).
- The tech pole index (used by Florida to indicate the presence of high tech employees in an area) is compared with measures of industry mix (these separately assess the sector profile and entrepreneurial activity).

The results of the regression analysis show that differences in Florida's measures of creativity are not generally associated with differences in metropolitan economic performance. Indicators of human capital and industry composition perform as well or better than talent, tolerance, and technology in explaining metropolitan job and income growth and job instability. The conclusion is that measures derived from Florida's creative class hypotheses are no more associated with positive economic outcomes than traditional competitiveness measures. Consequently, it is considered wrong to replace traditional economic development strategies with those based primarily on attracting the creative class. Programmes supporting education, business creation and industrial diversity are considered more likely to promote economic well-being than are initiatives aimed at trying to attract creative class professionals. job growth, income growth and job instability.

A high degree of residential sensitivity and a high level of mobility are claimed for creative class workers. This impression has been gained from correlation measures and indices that study settled populations rather than from direct observations of mobility and residential selection processes. A Swedish study provides an exception made possible by a unique official data series that enabled a representative sample of 10,000 internal migrants to be surveyed (Hansen and Niedomsyl 2008). The study modifies some aspects of Florida's approach but the reasons for this are in themselves of some significance. Location attributes are measured through a 'people climate' score that omits the issues encompassed by the gay index on the grounds that Nordic acceptance of homosexuality makes it ineffective as a means of distinguishing the openness of places to new settlers. Tolerance is based on a comparison of the employment rates of Swedish and non Swedish born people. This is considered a more rigorous assessment of integration than Florida's measures as it captures an aspect of actual behaviour. Florida's measures are criticized as, while purporting to measure tolerance, high scores can be returned by places with high levels of racial segregation.

Applying their customized indicators, Swedish experience offers a mixed endorsement of the assumptions underlying the creative class. Four findings question the theory:

- There is a low margin of difference in the annual rates of migration across labour markets for highly educated workers (the study's proxy for the creative class) and for lesser qualified workers: 4 per cent versus 2.8 per cent.
- Highly educated people tend to move to places with a lower people climate ranking than the place they depart from. A preponderance of migration up the people climate hierarchy is a feature only of younger, lesser educated workers.
- High and low educated workers express similar motives for relocating except that employment reasons are more dominant for highly educated migrants, especially in the case of long distance migration.
- Migration for an improved 'living environment' accounts for 10 per cent of moves and encompasses diverse judgements on the components delivering an improvement. The category encompasses responses that variously indicate a desire for change, better urban/cultural facilities, rural amenities or a preference to live in a more urban or more rural environment.

The overall significance of migration is the main endorsement coming from the study, especially when the annual rates of movement are summed over a decade or more. As well, the study finds that the two largest labour markets in Sweden (Stockholm and Gothenburg) have positive inflows of highly educated workers, against the larger pattern for places with a high people climate ranking to lose creative workers. The researchers speculate that the USA's large number of similar sized big cities may be conditioning a creative class effect in that country (Hansen and Niedomysl 2009: 202). Large cities have the potential to combine good employment opportunities, including capacity to support dual career households, responding to the main influence driving migration. At the same time, large cities can have a high people climate, providing amenities that are valued by some of those migrants who move for non employment reasons. The Swedish evidence highlights that the USA may give unusual opportunity to combine movement for work and movement for an improved people climate. In small countries, people are forced frequently to optimize on only one of these attributes, and faced with the need to choose it is employment that typically takes precedence.

The migration to lower ranked people climate destinations in Sweden is explained partly by movement associated with the commencement and completion of university education and the changes in residential priorities over an individual's life cycle. Further exploration of this phenomenon was recommended as the researchers concluded that the migration aspect of the creative class theory as presented by Florida is wrong. The role of organizational migration is an aspect of internal migration that was not explored in either the original or Swedish studies. This is migration made at the request of and supported by an employer and can involve relocation between cities where branches of a national or international organization are located. Even in a small economy where business activity is concentrated in a few centres, organizational migration can account for around a quarter of annual internal migration (Perry 2003). Creative workers figure highly among the types of employee multi location employers may wish to relocate and such movement reflects organizational strategies rather than personal preferences.

The third level of critique addresses the policy agenda promoted by attention to the creative class. Peck (2005) has pointed out three shortcomings that are broadly endorsed by other critical commentaries (Box 6.6). First, participation in zero sum competition is encouraged, in which cities compete for a share of a limited pool of mobile, creative workers based on identical strategies. When focused on a limited pool of potential targets the risk is that the multiplication of projects aiming to encourage mobility simply facilitates ongoing movement and limited attachment of creative workers to any single place. Second, the policy diverts attention to issues that disregard urban poverty and may even intensify social differences, as creative occupations frequently exist within a social division of labour that also generates large numbers of low paid, insecure jobs. A response that attending to the creative economy will expand opportunities for people to join overlooks the fact that this in itself will not change the circumstances of those at the lower end of the labour market. Third, the recommendation to promote artistic neighbourhoods and street level diversity may conflate consequences of urban growth with causes. Fashionable neighbourhoods and urban renewal projects have followed the wealth obtained by city residents, and especially those working in highly remunerated financial services. As became evident in the wake of the world financial crisis that unfolded during 2008, this expansion was to do with a specific regulatory environment and financial globalization. Lax banking practices that facilitated a housing market bubble temporarily made viable the transformation of formerly neglected neighbourhoods. Urban renewal as a strategy to promote growth will mirror the experience of an earlier phase of local economic policy targeted at encouraging cities as places as consumption. This saw the renewal of waterfront areas and the development of cultural districts. The first wave of projects achieving some impact through their novelty but the impact rapidly diluted among the many imitations that followed (see Levine 1987).

Box 6.6 **Creative doubt over the BBC's look north**

The British Broadcasting Corporation (BBC) is the United Kingdom's main public broadcaster and producer of television programmes. An 'out of London' initiative has been started to relocate parts of the BBC's activity away from the capital, partly in the belief that this will help to make the corporation representative of the United Kingdom as a whole. The northern city of Salford has been earmarked for the site of a regional headquarters and media city. In making their case for this development, the BBC and local officials echoed themes advanced by the creative class agenda. Planning documents envisage that with the BBC as a creative core other creative talent and enterprises will be encouraged to cluster in and around media city. Planning documents envisage a world-class environment designed to be the springboard for ongoing creativity by offering amenities and ambience that stimulates 'conversations' among artistic workers. This image justifies ambitious plans and investment support to assist the BBC's relocation to Salford.

Drawing on a larger critique of the creative class approach to urban economic development, Christophers (2008) identifies three uncertainties with the case being made by supporters of the relocation:

- The geographical reach of the economic benefits that might flow from the core project are unknown. Claims vary from a project that may transform a part of Salford to a project capable of transforming the entire north of England. Deliberate over optimism and a development agenda without demand constraints explain the inflation of expectation. The fruits of creative talent are always in demand.
- The distribution of project benefits among different social groups is overlooked. High levels of deprivation in parts of Salford, the project's dependence on public money and involvement of parties that have received public funding directly or indirectly should make the distribution of benefits central to the project's evaluation.
- The project shares much in common with previously attempted efforts to regenerate urban environments through entrepreneurial strategies that prioritize private sector decision making over democratic processes, utilize large amounts of public subsidy and accommodate consumption rather than production activities.

Finding space for the creative class

The creative class agenda has gained prominence through convincing policy makers more than through convincing academics with an interest in urban and regional development that new insights are arising. Peck (2005) sees it as an example of 'fast policy circulation', an idea that has been taken up in haste through the appeal of the prescriptions rather than the weight of underlying evidence. This appeal has been linked to the accessibility of the ideas and how working within the grain of existing city obligations and desires to promote art festivals, culture and gentrified neighbourhoods can be given a new significance with relatively modest adjustments in strategy. The linkage of culture to the '3Ts' of local economic development – technology, talent and tolerance – further helps in the endeavour as it converts something once placed more on the cost side of public budgets into an agent of economic growth. Indices and league tables add to the appeal of the approach, especially when constructed in ways that allow for frequent changes in position. Public agencies might, for example, track the immediate return on activity and gather evidence to maintain action.

Policy-maker friendliness is wrong if the friendliness is bought at the expense of the rigour of the underlying ideas and without due attention to the costs as well as potential benefits, which is the implication of Peck's (2005) commentary. It is less clear that policy attention should be criticized for not addressing the core processes that might ultimately explain the origins and development of cities. Storper and Scott (2009: 153) suggest that it is a shortcoming of the thesis that it can at best attend to marginal and intermediate adjustments to urban economies rather than to core processes. They have proposed an alternative agenda that aims to influence the fundamental causes of urban development (Storper and Scott 1995, 2009: 164). This involves policies to support the enhancement of agglomeration economies, collective action to internalize externalities (which may encompass efforts to retain knowledge spillovers within the urban economy), building effective norms of economic interdependence and avoiding adverse path selection. Such initiatives have not been ignored by the policy community and are at least partly represented in many cluster promotion strategies (Chapter 5). Of course, this alternative agenda is itself controversial and has equally been accused of confusing development outcomes with the causes of urban growth (see Bresnahan *et al.* 2001). Agglomeration economies, knowledge spillovers and social networks may be aspects of successful urban economies but they cannot explain how the economy grew to acquire these attributes.

Policy application does not have to be justified by a complete theory of urban economic development. Marginal adjustments in urban growth are generally the target of policy intervention. Influences shaping incremental change may differ from those affecting the origins and long term development of urban economies. Practically, urban managers are constrained by the need to demonstrate the effectiveness of their policy interventions over short term timescales consistent with annual budget setting, and for this reason also may be well advised to maintain a portfolio of initiatives addressed variously to aspects under immediate policy influence as well as attending to issues shaping longer term development of the city. In this context a case can be made for policy that seeks to deflect rather than fundamentally shape urban development. A question is whether seeking to influence the location of people judged high in creativity has the potential to make this kind of impact. In line with the argument that it takes more than a people concentration to alter the path of urban development, Wojan *et al.* (2007) find evidence in US Census data for a 'weak' definition of creative milieu: above 'normal' concentrations of creative people tend to encourage the movement of additional creative people to the same locality. They do not find evidence for a 'strong' definition of creative milieu in which a high concentration of creative people is associated with a faster rate of new firm formation and employment growth, except in the case of rural, small-town counties.

The core challenge for the creative class approach is to demonstrate that the openness and tolerance of communities is the causal agent of enhanced business performance. Creative class supporters know of this challenge. A need for evidence of actual interaction is recognized between, on the one hand, creative people and activities and, on the other hand, entrepreneurship and business growth

(Wojan *et al.* 2007). Correlations between variously constructed indices and selected measures of economic performance do not substitute for this insight. At best they identify an indicator variable: an attribute of a locality that can act as a proxy for the form of economic performance that is of interest. Indeed, the literal interpretation of the gay index would be at odds with the claims about openness and tolerance.

Gay and lesbian events such as festivals and parades are the most evident direct impact on economic development of homosexual-based enterprise, promoted because of their potential for increasing visitor expenditure and augmenting destination marketing (Thomas and Darnton 2006). As well, city neighbourhoods dominated by homosexual and transgendered residents are sometimes transformed into visitor attractions for similar motives. These possibilities have a doubtful link to tolerance given the instrumental motive for the celebration, the encouragement of voyeurism and disregard of difference among those that become the target of tourism. Florida's approach is justified by reference to claims that openness to gay and lesbian populations is the best indicator of society's overall tolerance of self expression and that this tolerance is correlated with GDP growth (Inglehart and Norris 2003; Inglehart and Welzel 2005). Transfer of the indicator to urban success assumes that the distribution of the homosexual population responds to differences in city tolerance. As noted in the study of internal migration in Sweden (see above), this indicator loses significance when society as a whole is comparatively tolerant and open.

A case study of linkages, or what are called 'spill-acrosses', from the bohemian to the traditional technology community has been taken as justification for the ongoing research agenda (Florida *et al.* 2008). For this reason the study by Stolarick and Florida (2006) bears close examination. It centres on interviews with 34 individuals residing in Montréal and employed in an organization that relies on some form of creativity with respect to art, design, software or technology development. In essence, the intent is to show how environments that enable creativity to be practised outside work transfer that creativity to the work environment. Montréal is presented as a good test of the creative class approach; indeed it may even be seen as a critical case given the claimed suitability for processes central to the thesis.

- The scope for creative interaction among residents is believed to be especially high in a city such as Montréal that has a high population density as this facilitates face-to-face contact.
- There is a large concentration of creative class occupations with the most reliance on creativity, the so-called 'super creatives'.
- There is an internationally recognized cluster of arts activity including festivals, performers, venues, societies and art sector promotion.
- As a bilingual and multicultural city with connections to the rest of North America and Europe, it draws in a diverse population of migrants partly because of its distinctive culture and geographical connections.

Stolarick and Florida (2006) interpret their interview responses as showing how creative companies benefit from operating within an environment attractive to creative workers (Box 6.7). They also suggest that creative workers may be attracted to a city perceived to be culturally diverse and tolerant of diversity. It is acknowledged that these processes are not equally advantageous to all companies and that the cultural diversity has drawbacks as well as advantages for business activity. For example, while some respondents believe that bilingualism is a benefit, others emphasize the costs of language duplication, impediments to labour recruitment and association with a negative political image. There is also difficulty determining how much of the arts effect is a product of the size of the city's art scene rather than processes that can be replicated in smaller centres. Montréal is the home of major arts events and institutions and the demand for art by artists themselves can help to sustain the sector. These issues are recognized by the researchers, but other aspects of the responses are not reflected upon. For example, in the male-dominated software and digital technology industries after-hours socializing has been viewed as something that tends to be based upon and reinforcing of a 'boys only culture' (Cooper 2000).

Box 6.7 **Bohemia and business in Montréal**

Florida *et al.* (2008: 621) suggest that a case study of creative processes in Montréal by Stolarick and Florida (2006) shows how bohemians and the traditional technology community are connected through so-called 'spill-acrosses'. These are said to spread economically significant ideas in a wider ranging way than spillover processes. Interviews with 34 representatives of creative organizations identified different types of connection:

- Respondents from the 22 private sector businesses represented indicate that on average almost 50 per cent of their co-workers have an outside part time job, hobby or passion related to arts, design or culture.
- Interviewees mention that Montréal's artistic and cultural environment helps attract 'technical talent'.
- One respondent mentioned encouraging employees to indulge in the city's nightlife to increase their attachment to the region.
- When a person resigns to pursue his or her own venture, some firms market the business to potential recruits by celebrating the lost employee's move to independence.
- Companies, and especially small ones, frequently engage outside independent designers supporting a fringe of creative talent that can be enabled to combine dual interests in art and business.
- Services or business products designed for an arts event or artistic company in the city find other applications and become sources of business growth.

Other responses are presented as indicative of the advantages that may arise operating in a culturally diverse city and the value of cultural capital:

- Montréal's status as a bilingual (French and English) and multicultural city makes it a good market laboratory and testing ground for business ideas.
- Companies can variously present an American or European identity depending on which is most advantageous.

- Multilingual speakers have enhanced creative capacity and Montréal's bilingualism is therefore good for business.
- A multicultural community and the associated image of 'neutrality' can comfort foreigners and help to attract international students.
- Scientists have ready access to research reported in multiple languages.
- Montréal permits migrants to the city to retain their home country culture without losing the opportunity to connect with others in the city.

As well as the difficulty of identifying the net balance of positive and negative forces, the evidence falls short of demonstrating precise causal connections. Many of the processes identified through the interviews appear contingent on labour market and business conditions attendant on a period of industry and employment expansion. The suggestion that creative workers, which may include software engineers and scientists as well as designers and artists, participate in arts activity outside work hours is among the more direct ways that artistic and business activity is claimed to be linked. It can suggest that art activity outside work in some way informs and strengthens contributions at work, but the Montréal study does not demonstrate that this is actually occurring. Similarly, there is an implied superiority to arts activity that gives it potential to have greater economic significance than out-of-work participation in sport, gardening, church going, home maintenance or other activities that may engage people during non work time. Social capital theory stresses the importance of out-of-work activity in providing connections between people that otherwise would not engage with each other (Granovetter 1973; Hauser *et al.* 2007). Strong overlap between work and non work activity may not be helpful in this respect. Florida (2004, 2005) equates social capital with traditional communities that are unattractive to many creative professionals, and so must have some other mechanisms in mind. Neither is it clear whether a unique association is being claimed (creative occupations become filled by people with unusual artistic talent in cities that attract this segment of the creative workforce) or whether some aspect of the work and city environment unleashes the artistic talents that reside within everyone privileged to hold a creative job. In reality, a range of possible explanations for the out-of-hours arts activity exist, with different implications for its economic significance:

- Relatively high incomes facilitate the consumption and practice of art activities helped by the availability of art events and groups in large cities.
- A broad conception of art activity exists that merges with entertainment, as when employees' 'passion' for some branch of the arts means frequent cinema and theatre attendance.
- The workforce profile includes a preponderance of young, single employees without household commitments and whose interest in the 'arts' is associated with the search for a mate as much as if not more than an intrinsic interest in the arts.

- The social environment of workplaces assigns status to participation in the arts and correspondingly stigmatizes those declaring preference for other pursuits.

As acknowledged by Stolarick and Florida (2006), further insight is needed. A close look at the artistic workforce, its links to economic development and the larger group of creative occupations raises some doubts while not closing the door entirely to aspects of Florida's agenda (Markusen 2006; Markusen and Schrock 2006). Interestingly, Florida cites this work in support of his own stream of investigation (Florida *et al.* 2008: 621).

Markusen (2006: 1932) points out that it is not raw agglomerations of artists and related occupations that ensure synergies develop among them. Rather, attention needs to be paid to the infrastructure supporting arts activity in the form of spaces and organizations, including museums, theatres and other artist-employing and -presenting organizations. Artists attached to large arts institutions such as major theatres, galleries and museums designed as regional flagships tend to inhabit a different arts world to those attached to neighbourhood scale venues and centres. Outside the cities that house national theatre companies and orchestras, locally based artists may gain little from the big art venues as they tend to be used by national and international touring acts and exhibitions. The local population of artists is characterized as dependent upon a mosaic of small scale art centres that support experimental and controversial work as well as that which is locally informed. Markusen's (2006) informants advise that artists affiliated to neighbourhood art places tend to be supportive of liberal political agendas and to be critical of big-business interests. They are also influenced by different residential preferences to those favoured by holders of other occupational groups to which they are linked in Florida's creative class grouping. Within cities, artists gravitate to the denser, more central and often seedy and transitional neighbourhoods. Their urban preferences, politics and impacts on urban form and community life make it hard to envisage commonality with the other creative occupations. Artists respond to different features of places and are inclined to be more liberal than other professional workers. On the other hand, efforts to enhance the impact of the arts on business activity are seen to have their role, and so some aspects of the creative class approach can survive interrogation. Markusen (2006: 1683) suggests that there is a case for cities to nurture their artistic populations and that this can be done partly through neighbourhood strategies allowing art spaces to flourish. As well, artists can be viewed as talent available to help companies design a better product, produce written material, solve management problems through simulation and prepare marketing materials. Encouraging these connections could bring benefits to business while helping to sustain artistic livelihoods.

The tendency of many artists to be self employed contractors rather than business employees gives scope for individual preferences to influence where they concentrate. In the USA, urban based artists tend to consider a restricted range of cities, choosing between the arts capitals (New York, Los Angeles and San Francisco) and smaller arts-rich cities, trading off 'being where the action is' against liveability, artistic networks and philanthropic support for the local arts sector (Markusen 2006: 1929). Influencing local support for the arts has the chance of modifying location selections for this occupation group.

Just as a close look at the arts sector gives some scope for aspects of the creative class agenda, so does consideration of the changing context in which the migration of younger professional workers more widely is occurring. As discussed above, doubts about the creative class agenda have arisen from a study of labour migration in Sweden that found people tended to move away from places with a good people climate (Hansen and Niedomysl 2009). This is based on migration patterns in a single year. When long term trends in labour mobility are considered, a different picture emerges (Smith 2005; Sheller and Urry 2006).

Since the 1990s in industrial economies some traditional labour exporting regions have been attracting more of their lost skilled workers back. This is seen, for example, in the increasing flow of Scottish born residents returning to Scotland from London and the surrounding South East region of the United Kingdom (Findlay *et al.* 2008). This return reverses the traditional pattern of skilled workers moving to the United Kingdom's core economy. The reverse flow concentrates on Edinburgh, the Scottish financial capital and seat of the Scottish parliament since 1999, but it is not a simple case of employment-induced migration. At the same time that career opportunities have grown in the home-country capital and selected other Scottish cities the Scots who remain in the UK capital region continue to outperform their labour market peers. The particular propensity for well qualified younger professionals to return to Scotland provides further suggestion that lifestyle and residential rather than career preferences are influencing the reverse flow. Younger workers on the first steps of a career ladder may be thought to be the most concerned with gaining experience in the core region, but in practice they are the most open to other possibilities (Findlay *et al.* 2008: 2182). Encouraging for the creative class approach, the researchers suggest that aspects of contemporary society may be allowing immediate job opportunities to be acted upon with less concern over the implications for long term career prospects. Reduced costs of short haul air travel, the easy access to Internet-mediated information and web-based social networking may be behind the willingness to move away from places with the strongest labour market. Migration may no longer have the risks once perceived when a move away does not weaken social networks and is not perceived to close future career options. The enduring significance of such innovations has still to be established, but they are suggestive of the way that some barriers to migration may be reducing. If so it does suggest that city managers will be well advised to give more attention to their strategies for attracting talented labour, which is a further avenue for keeping open some aspects of the creative class agenda.

Immigrant and minority enterprise is a third aspect of the creative class approach that deserves further attention. Florida (2002a) reported that economic development was less associated with the proportion of foreign-born residents in a metropolitan area (his melting pot index) than it was with the gay and bohemian index scores. The melting pot index was correlated with population growth but not with his measure of innovation or the presence of high tech firms. This led to the conclusion that 'leading edge' centres did not have a high proportion of racial minorities (Florida 2002a: 80). In the follow up edition of the original study, racial integration was measured using an index of the geographical distribution of the 'non white' population (Florida 2004). Against the larger thesis about tolerance, some of the localities with high tolerance scores on Florida's other indices are also the most racially segregated communities. Rather than questioning his research design and methods, the ambiguity of the results are played down and racial diversity is discussed largely in problematic terms connected to the enduring divide between the white and non white populations in the USA. A need to rationalize and protect a larger research agenda and results may have skewed this discussion and resulted in too little consideration of the potential role of immigrant and non white entrepreneurship.

Three aspects of immigration have been shown to be positive for local economic development: the attraction of high skilled migrants; the attraction of low skilled migrants and the development of ethnic enclaves (Thomas and Darnton 2006). A study of Asian immigrants to Silicon Valley identified how their strong networks provided connections, practical advice and possibly some business funding to new immigrant entrepreneurs (Saxenian 2002). A one per cent increase in the number of first generation immigrants to California was estimated to boost state exports by nearly 0.5 per cent. Silicon Valley is able to attract highly skilled migrants and its high tech industries offer considerable scope for growth, but more generally it has been argued that population diversity in the form of immigrants increase regional productivity (Ottaviano and Peri 2005). This possibility has been endorsed by Florida *et al.* (2008: 620), who interpret it as showing how immigrants can benefit economic activity by their possession of complementary skills.

Other research has found that the increased availability of skilled labour attracts firms to the cities where skilled immigrants concentrate and that these cities then benefit from the international connections of their workforce (Koser and Salt 1998). The attraction of low skilled immigrants can also have positive economic effects, although perhaps of a more problematic nature. Immigrant workers can compete for work at the bottom of the labour market with some gain to the urban economy as a whole, but possibly at the expense of displaced local workers (Saiz 2003a). The increased demand for housing resulting from an influx of immigrants can also boost the urban economy (Saiz 2003b). The certainty of these outcomes is less than in the case of skilled migrants, as the ability to absorb migrant workers and their ability to enter the housing market and contribute to neighbourhood revitalization will vary with the precise volume of migration and national economic conditions. The extent to which immigrant communities can build an enclave economy can also condition the impact of migration.

Enclaves are different to ghettos partly in the extent to which participation is voluntary, with membership replenished by new arrivals some of whom can augment the resources available to the community as a whole and increase the ambition to succeed. On this basis, enclaves can be perceived as an opportunity for advancement or at least as a route to a satisfactory standard of living (Peach 2005; Qadeer 2005). Enclaves result partly through the preference of participants to retain their ethnic association, as well as through barriers to participation in the mainstream economy. The possibility of workforce attachment to individual employers based on shared ethnicity and the possibility of future advancement supports a low cost structure that can enable market expansion outside the enclave. These possibilities contrast with the involuntary isolation of ghettos that heightens the impact of discrimination by physical separation that restricts access to resources and markets. Consequently, racial segregation in the United States results in persistent economic sinks that damage the economy and society (Fischer and Massey 2000; Squires and Kubrin 2005).

Florida acknowledges that the creative economy does little to ameliorate the economic divide between white and non white segments of the American population and indeed may even accentuate it (Florida 2004: 263). Equally, the forms of diversity and methods to promote them recommended by Florida are not directed at changing this situation. Two potential routes out of the ghetto have been identified: education and the acquisition of credentials that give access to professional career paths or efforts to revive African American enterprise that once provided a flourishing 'middleman' role (Butler 2005). Interest in diversity and tolerance is potentially of support to both paths, but it would need to involve more specific initiatives than enhancing the qualities of cities deemed attractive to creative workers. The risk is that by encouraging economic development to be equated with high technology development the creative class agenda may prioritize forms of economic development that have the least prospect of affecting the opportunities of people who reside in a low income, racially segregated neighbourhood (Thomas and Darnton 2006: 162). Lagging education systems and other aspects of the digital divide are barriers to minority participation in a high technology economy.

Conclusion

Three main forms of evidence are needed to substantiate the creative class perspective. One comprises demonstration that the processes deemed to influence economic development are linked to superior business performance. This type of evidence comes from correlation and regression analysis and requires agreement that valid and reliable indicators are being employed. A second form of evidence substantiates the causal mechanisms that explain why the processes deemed to affect the level of economic performance have the power that they are claimed to possess. Whereas the former type of evidence may be based on the use of already collected data, the confirmation of causal processes requires the collection of new information and may involve intensive investigations of individual participants in the urban economy. The third form of evidence provides understanding of the context in which the processes work, and is important, as economic development is multi faceted. There are both immediate causes of urban success and a larger context that make those processes of importance. To date the creative class approach has assembled more of the first of these types of evidence than that which informs the existence of causal mechanisms or that explains what other conditions are required to make the mechanisms effective. As Florida *et al.* (2008: 643) state, 'while out theory and model posit a strong set of underlying mechanisms for the effects of tolerance on regional development, our empirical models and evidence do not specify the precise nature and direction of causality'. For example, the coincidence between homosexual populations and successful cities may reflect the greater availability of employment appealing to gays and lesbians rather than indicating that openness is rewarded by enhanced economic performance. The statistical correlations between the Bohemian and Gay indices and certain measures of economic success are able to justify keeping the approach on the policy agenda but it is important that the search for other forms of evidence increases before the policy commitment intensifies.

The core thesis is surprisingly under explored. Precisely how people with enhanced creative capacity are able and motivated to gravitate to particular places and how the concentration of creative talent changes business performance remains largely a matter of conjecture. The study of creative workers in Montréal recognizes the importance of gathering this insight and has made some suggestions as to how creative environments inside and outside workplaces may be linked. Much of the evidence may be explicable by the labour market conditions prevailing at the time of the study, and is further limited by its reliance on employer interpretations of employee behaviour. The conclusion from a study of the artistic workforce is that most insight is obtained from studying individual occupations rather than diffuse groups of workers held together only by a common need to exercise some form of creativity at work. Individual occupations tend to vary in their opportunities for mobility, the diversity of job roles offered and the dominant outlooks of participants. From the investigation of artists reviewed in the chapter it appears that the creative class agenda has relevance, but that opportunities and strategies need to be customized to the circumstances arising in a particular occupation. Indeed this is partly acknowledged in Florida's later work that finds the linkage between the '3Ts' of urban development – tolerance, talent and technology – is stronger for some creative occupations than others, and barely evident in the case of education and healthcare (Florida *et al.* 2008).

The context in which it is possible to manipulate the residential choices of key city workers has received least attention of all. Internal labour migration has traditionally been studied as a process variously responding to negative aspects of existing locations, positive attributes of destination locations, life cycle stages and the strength of frictional forces that impede free movement. In comparison, the creative class approach has been viewed as simplistic in its assumption that key cities workers move according to their affinity with places demonstrating openness and tolerance. Large numbers of people with significant incomes at stake are unlikely to shift location with disregard for their employment prospects. Moreover, it would need explanation that people inclined to disregard their career prospects when leaving one locality come to exert significant influence over the economic dynamism of the place moved to. Rather than simply responding to the relative attractiveness of places there is a suggestion that younger, migrant professionals perceive different risks in moving away from places where their long term career prospects may be greatest. The reduced cost of long distance travel and participation in computer-enabled networks may be increasing the motivation to optimize lifestyle and employment prospects. How far these incipient trends will continue post the 2008 international financial crisis is unclear, and if they do it remains to be explained whether they are consistent with creative class processes. In the context of the United Kingdom, new influences on internal migration have been observed in the flow of professional workers away from the cosmopolitan capital of London to cities in the relative economic periphery.

Finally, reducing racial disadvantage and encouraging immigrant enterprise offer opportunities for urban economic growth where openness and tolerance can make a difference. The creative class approach has not focused on these aspects of diversity, partly as when measured by a melting pot index racial diversity has not correlated well with the measures of innovation or the presence of the creative occupations. The disjunction between the creative economy and openness and tolerance of ethnic groups is even greater when examined in terms of residential integration. This raises perhaps the most serious objections to this area of work, as it can be questioned whether it is possible to claim economic success when this may be associated with the persistence of large disparities in income that give rise to large social costs. From the perspective of seeking to raise the economic performance of cities, a balance needs to be struck between encouraging the already well functioning parts of the economy and activity directed at more intractable issues. Reducing racial segregation and ethnic differences in entrepreneurial activity needs to be included in the efforts to promote economic development through encouraging diversity.

7 Technology incubators
Hothouse accelerators or life support shelters?

Business incubators provide environments for aspiring entrepreneurs to draw on assistance and mutual support as they implement a new business venture. The broader economic development objective is to seed the local economy with new start-ups of high growth potential that maintain allegiance to their place of birth (Phan et al. 2005). Assistance in developing business and marketing plans, building management teams, obtaining financial capital and access to a range of other more specialized professional services may be included in the incubation process (Sherman and Chappell 1998). The incubator provides workspace on flexible lease terms with the opportunity to draw on shared office and perhaps other business services. A graduation policy may set a maximum period of stay reflecting the intent of supporting a transition to becoming a standalone commercial enterprise. Incubators aim typically to accommodate a cohort of new enterprises with growth potential and over time rotate occupants and do this with a high post-incubator survival rate, including a proportion that develop into substantial businesses. To achieve these outcomes, incubator managers are expected to have good links to the wider business community, including providers of business finance, centres of R&D expertise and universities, and to advance the reputation of entrepreneurial activity more broadly. The broad case for this activity rests on the perceived barriers to new enterprise formation and growth. This means that while intended to deliver measurable impacts for their local economy, incubators are also of interest as laboratories for testing theories of the constraints on enterprise development.

Incubator sponsors differ in the objectives they set and this has created a heterogeneous mix of projects (Sherman and Chappell 1998; Aernoudt 2004). The first wave of incubator projects established up to the 1980s were conceived mainly as contributions to the revitalization of declining industrial regions. Incubators for technology-based enterprise emerged in the 1980s as tools for improving the competitive strengths of local economies and differed from earlier incubators in their physical proximity and frequently in their operational ties to higher educational and public research institutions (Aernoudt 2004: 128). The National Business Incubation Association (NBIA) counted around 950 incubators in the USA in 2002, of which 37 per cent were classified as technology incubators, with around two thirds of these sponsored by academic institutions (Linder 2003). In Europe, technology incubators comprise around one third of all those identified in a European Union evaluation, having been the fastest growing component of the incubator sector during the previous decade (Centre for Strategy and Evaluation Services 2002). This group of incubators is further distinguished by their reliance on public funding, making it important to be precise about what they are intended to achieve and how far they deliver these outcomes.

Technology incubators are generally viewed as effective support mechanisms for new entrepreneurial firms (Smilor and Gill 1986; Barrow 2001; McAdam and McAdam 2006). This endorsement extends to the larger population of incubators, which have been presented as the creators of future wealth and employment (Wynarczyk and Raine 2005). Controversy arises when evaluation moves beyond the ability of incubators to provide an environment of support and encouragement. By allowing entrepreneurs to focus their effort on key business development challenges it should be expected that enterprises residing in an incubator gain an advantage over their peers on the outside that do not receive equivalent support, although this does not always happen (Lumpkin and Ireland 1988). Uncertainty remains over the justification for selectively distributing support to those that gain entry to an incubator and which ventures most merit support. Incubators that are assigned the job of accelerating enterprise growth can be expected to produce a higher graduation rate of enterprises, with stronger post-exit performance than those aiming to bring a start-up venture into existence. The case for incubators needs to specify how the boundary between efficient (acceleration of enterprise formation) and inefficient (life support) outcomes is set and managed. This is a challenge for all types of incubator but is particularly evident in the case of technology incubators. Technology incubators linked to research-orientated universities have potential to attract outside entrepreneurs who value the status of a university-linked address but that do not necessarily need special access to university resources to further develop their venture. Equally, technology incubators may attract academic entrepreneurs who see value in a research discovery but that need further time to commercialize the technology as well as help in developing business management skills. Determining which, if either, of these roles is best taken on by technology incubators remains to be established.

The evaluation question is whether the 'right' group of enterprises are selected for incubation as well as whether incubator occupants become successful enterprises at a greater rate than outsiders. Determining which type of venture is the most appropriate to support relies on a clear understanding of the market failures that frustrate new enterprise formation and the local economic development goals to which incubators are to be directed. Support for incubators tends to be a component of larger institutional interests in technology transfer, justified by generalized perceptions of the impediments of converting research into enterprise development. A specific theory of the market failures that incubators are designed to overcome and why they may be an appropriate solution to those failures has yet to be developed (Mian 1997; Hansen et al. 2000; Phan et al. 2005). Without a clear mandate and agreed measures of performance some observers argue that it is premature to endorse technology incubators (Phan *et al.* 2005: 170).

Research evidence informing the operation of technology incubators is scarce, particularly as it relates to the interaction between incubator support and venture development. This chapter offers a broad assessment of the potential contribution of technology incubators to local economic development. It commences by examining an underlying assumption that innovation is a source of high growth enterprise. Sponsors of technology incubators may view the initial commercialization of university research as their primary goal, rather than enterprise growth, but support of the outside economic development community is based on optimism that at least some incubated enterprises have high growth potential. The broad case for technology incubators is also considered in terms of the reasons why new technology-based firms fail. The larger changes affecting efforts to encourage the commercialization of university and other public research are then considered. This is important, as the interest in technology incubators is connected to other developments that have increased the pool of potential projects to incubate without necessarily indicating that barriers to new enterprise formation have increased. The chapter then turns to the operation of technology incubators. It focuses on the two most frequently cited advantages imparted by technology incubators: (i) enhanced access to scientific expertise and research results, including the possibility for direct participation by academics in commercialization projects; (ii) help in developing business networks that support the new entrepreneur during and beyond his or her time in the incubator. The emphasis throughout the chapter is on guidance to the evaluation that local economic development agencies should make of technology incubators. University and research institute sponsors of technology incubators have multiple reasons for their involvement, including creating goodwill in their local community, attracting public funds and providing a 'shopfront' for their ongoing research activity (Barrow 2001). Such roles do not depend on substantial contributions to enterprise growth, which is the outcome of main interest to this chapter.

Innovation and high growth enterprise

A case for incubation support can be found in the evidence that young and small enterprises have faster rates of growth than established enterprises. A general perception may be that young, technology-based firms are more innovative, proactive and risk orientated than older firms, partly as new firms emerge to take advantage of a new opportunity. This entrepreneurial model of enterprise growth contrasts with a more prosaic explanation of enterprise growth rates: the availability of under-utilized resources. This idea has a long heritage based on the claim that indivisibility of production inputs requires enterprises to acquire larger quantities of production capacity than are needed for current levels of activity (Penrose 1959). This observation leads to the interpretation of business growth as a sequential process in which periods of rapid expansion follow each round of investment (Pettus 2001). Small enterprises are most affected by the indivisibility of resources and this gives them an unusual incentive to grow. A 'theory of learning' interpretation of young enterprise growth adds to the incentive (Box 7.1). This perspective argues that accurate matching of business capacity with market demand depends significantly on learning within individual enterprises rather than simply being based on analytical calculation (Moreno and Casillas 2007: 74). Managers of new enterprise are most at risk of miscalculating investment costs or the level of demand or both, and are consequently most likely to be under particular pressure to rapidly increase their business activity. For long established enterprises accumulated insight gives discretion over their rate of growth in contrast to the 'liability of newness'.

Box 7.1 **A theory of learning**

In a dataset of 6,814 SMEs located in Andalusia (Spain), high growth enterprises were distinguished from other growing enterprises based on an enterprise's four year sales growth relative to the median for the firm's sector. Enterprises exceeding the median were classed as high growth enterprises and these amounted to slightly over 10 per cent of the sample. Of the options tested, the factor that most distinguished high growth enterprises was consistent with the theory of learning: the smaller the enterprise the greater the likelihood of acquiring assets in excess of current needs and of growing at the highest rate. The researchers could not distinguish how far this result was a product of the indivisibility of assets or a preference to 'invest for growth', but either way high growth was not linked to innovation.

Source: Moreno and Casillas (2007)

Accelerating entrepreneurial learning offers a justification for incubators, but a question remains as to how access to the support should be rationed. From the perspective of contributing to local economic development it has been argued that incubators should focus their support on fast-growing enterprises or 'gazelles' (Aernoudt 2004). In the context of technology incubators, such selectivity requires that innovation generates high growth enterprise. Evidence of this association is perhaps surprisingly thin (WPSMEE 2007). Certainly, it is hard to envisage high rates of enterprise growth without some form of innovation in strategies, actions or behaviours being necessary, but this may simply be adjustment to accommodate accelerated growth (Markides 1998; Moreno and Casillas 2007). More uncertain is whether new technology is the impetus for the growth spurt. This is partly an issue of empirical investigations tending to encompass relatively trivial as well as more substantial forms of innovation, whereas a narrower focus is needed to explore the sources of high growth. Nonetheless, even where studies have attempted to isolate substantial forms of innovation, an impact on enterprise growth rates has not been detected.

A study of small and medium-sized enterprises in part of the United Kingdom comes close to presenting the ideal evidence in distinguishing types of innovation, the originality of the innovation and three measures of enterprise performance. Using data from a survey of 1,347 SMEs based in Scotland and Northern England, Freel and Robson (2004) examined the relationship between product and process innovation and three measures of growth (employment, sales turnover and productivity). This study incorporated a distinction between novel (new to industry) and incremental (new to the enterprise) innovations and reported results for manufacturing and service enterprises. Few significant associations were discovered. They found a positive relationship between novel (new to industry) product innovation and employment growth in service and manufacturing enterprise. Sales growth, on the other hand, was found to be negatively associated with both types of product innovation in the case of manufacturing. For incremental (new to the enterprise) innovations, a positive association was found for service firm sales growth and productivity, but data for the other patterns tested was inconclusive. The inability of their methods to control for the impact of 'super' performers or underperformers in determining the strength of the associations searched for was acknowledged to be a limitation of the findings (Freel and Robson 2004). Nonetheless, the mixed results do at least serve to challenge any necessary impact of innovation on enterprise growth, with the absence of a connection between product innovation and manufacturing sales growth being especially counter intuitive.

Oke et al. (2007) also separate incremental and radical innovation among a sample of UK SMEs that in this case are identified by an expression of interest or actual participation in a government programme supporting business growth. For the purposes of the study, enterprises are assumed to be high growth based on their interest in the government programme. The sample enterprises were surveyed to identify their actual business activity and the frequency of individual activity patterns are taken to indicate which are most likely to induce high growth. The study finds that incremental innovation is more likely to promote enterprise growth than radical innovation, but neither form of innovation is a major source of business expansion. Overall, the researchers suggest that a focus on existing core markets ('sticking to the knitting') is a more certain growth path than pursuing wholly new markets through radical innovation. Earlier research on the distinguishing features of successful small high technology firms also finds that the most strongly growing ventures enhance their core technology rather than diversify into wholly new areas (Roberts and Berry 1985). Similarly, there is evidence that new technology-based ventures are more likely to succeed when the enterprise is attached to the same industry as the founder previously had experience of (Feeser and Willard 1989).

Another lens on the link between innovation and high growth is provided by exploring the attributes of high growth enterprise; if the link is strong this should be evident in the profile of high growth enterprise. This approach pits innovation against other potential sources of high growth such as marketing strategies, financial commitment, entrepreneurial skills and the use of business alliances. Some doubt that much research insight has been gathered on this topic (Box 7.2). A carefully constructed UK study provides important insight in being based on a sample of independent, medium-sized enterprises that were tracked over a four year period (Parker *et al.* 2006). The starting sample were taken from a larger database on the basis of their high rate of sales growth (average 36 per cent over 1992 to 1996), qualifying them as 'gazelles'. The study gathered insight into the strategies pursued over the four year observation period to test the relative impact of five alternative management strategies:

- *Competition focus*: decisions made in respect of the emphasis on business-to-business markets, international sales and product diversification.
- *Human resource management*: encouraging workforce participation, investment in workforce training and having a human resource manager appointed to the board.
- *Innovation*: the launch of new products and services, new product development and having a R&D director appointed at board level.
- *Administration and governance*: represented by being a single corporate entity, management by director-owners and the level of institutional ownership.
- *Marketing and sales strategies*: the use of customer surveys, taking customer complaints seriously and having a separate marketing department.

Box 7.2 **Spinning the wheel**

According to Greene (2009), a researcher in the University of Warwick's Centre for Small and Medium Sized Enterprises, very little is known about high growth firms other than their rarity. He pins this lack of insight on three observations about much of the research directed at determining the origins of high growth:

- A reliance on what entrepreneurs say is the secret of their success despite them being an unreliable research informant. Their recollections are affected by cognitive biases, such as over optimism, hindsight bias and the halo effect. This tends to lead entrepreneurs to see their success as too much a product of their own agency.
- A tendency to 'backcast' rather than forecast as hindsight fails to explain why some firms grow and others do not. Being educated and incorporating a business are among the few factors that have been consistently related to growth, but the overall variation in enterprise growth remains unexplained.
- The search for explanation overlooks the fact that luck is central to fast growth and that much success is simply an outcome of being the 'right' person, in the 'right' place at the 'right' time. An indicator of this is that success does not typically breed success, as evidenced by the performance of serial entrepreneurs.

The best analogy for understanding high growth firms is that it is like the few who come out of casinos as big winners. They may be keen to share their 'strategy' and have some common attributes but ultimately it was merely chance that resulted in their good fortune.

Source: Greene (2009)

Each of the strategies under investigation had prior research evidence indicating that action in that area of management discretion has been positive for business growth. The study compares the relative strength of the five approaches on their gazelle sample. Data analysis controls for some measurable ways in which external environments vary in ways likely to influence business success (including demand growth, market concentration and number of competitors). It finds that the management strategies most helping gazelles to become or remain large (in terms of turnover) are having a marketing department and having a main product that is a major contributor to overall income, indicating that enterprises keep a focus to their business operations. When performance is examined in terms of growth, the most successful strategies are using customer surveys to guide decision making, avoiding diffuse ownership (including worker participation in ownership) and refraining from developing new products or services. Another finding suggests that business success is not based on deliberately replicating the practices that it is thought produced growth in the past. Successful business need to adapt their strategies to changing business conditions but it appears not to be necessary for product innovation to be part of this.

Sector characteristics and new enterprise survival

The survival of a start-up enterprise depends on more than a viable technology. New entrants must withstand the reaction of incumbent industry participants, some of which may be large companies with substantial resources for technology development. A general insight is that new technology-based firms are most likely to survive when they are based on a radical new technology that undermines the competencies of potentially more powerful competitors (Tushman and Anderson 1986; Shane 2001). Survival can otherwise depend on the new entrant exploiting technology that is not of interest to the major customers of established businesses (Christensen and Bower 1996). Either way, the perception is that new entrants need a window of opportunity to ramp up their marketing and manufacturing capacity before established enterprises have time to react (Teece 1986; Merges and Nelson 1990; Shane 2001).

Ideas about the chances of survival for a new technology start-up have developed mainly from examining how well established companies cope with technological change. This generally shows that incumbents defend incremental innovation much more successfully than they withstand radical changes in technology. When the focus shifts to examining start-up survival rates, the ownership structure of existing industries emerges as an important influence on start-up survival chances. In addition to the possession of radical technology, Nerkat and Shane (2003) argue that start-up success is more likely when industry ownership is fragmented, as this indicates that relatively small enterprises can be competitive. Innovative technology can be outdone by the marketing and manufacturing resources that large incumbents can invest to combat the strategies of new entrants. Fragmented industries are therefore more favourable to start ups than concentrated industries (Box 7.3).

> **Box 7.3 Entry points to fragmented industries**
>
> To survive, new technology-based firms must build an organization and acquire assets to enable the exploitation of their innovation. This process faces fewer challenges in a fragmented industry compared with a concentrated one:
>
> - Suppliers of marketing and manufacturing assets are less likely to be controlled by existing large customers than in an industry where existing activity is concentrated in a few dominant enterprises. This can make it comparatively easy to source relevant resources.
> - The scale of production that new entrants are required to match is comparatively modest, reducing the capital requirements to attain a competitive volume of activity.
> - There is less risk of new entrants being thwarted by the market power of large incumbents, such as market pricing designed to make entry unprofitable for the new firm.
> - New firm entry does not necessarily impact the efforts of market leaders to serve their customers because the target customers of the new firm can belong to small, established players. In a concentrated industry, new entrants may be required to target the customers of market leaders who are provoked to react to the new competition.
>
> *Source:* Nerkat and Shane (2003: 1394)

The constraints on start-up survival are demonstrated in the case of a study of 128 new technology companies founded from 1980 to 1996, based on inventions originating in or linked to Massachusetts Institute of Technology (MIT), among the most prolific generators of university spin-out companies in the USA (Nerkat and Shane 2003). For the analysis, start-up successes include cases of acquisition by an established company as well as survival as an independent enterprise. This is justified on the grounds that acquisition is a preferred exit route for some start-up owners and because it can mean that the original venture continues in some form. Failure is clear cut: the cessation of operations, including cases of bankruptcy. Industry concentration is measured by the market share taken by an industry's four largest companies, with account also taken of the total number of industry participants. The evidence indicating how industry structure differentiates start-up survival rates is supported by arguments presented by other researchers explaining how large firm incumbents build barriers to new entrants. When an industry is concentrated start up companies must have capacity to:

- Raise large amounts of capital to fund investment in a scale of production that can compete with large companies before the value of their intellectual property is nullified (Acs and Audretsch 1987).
- Respond to cost and market power advantages enjoyed by incumbents that may override the demand for novel alternatives (Acs and Audretsch 1989).

- Take customers from large established firms and counter the potential for market retaliation as companies seek to protect their customer base (Romanelli 1989; Eisenhardt and Schoonhoven 1990).
- Acquire assets from the few established firms that dominate the market, such as recruiting some of their experienced managers and technology specialists (Teece 1986).

Two further points of interest in the MIT study are worth noting. First, many of MIT's start ups were based on discoveries funded by established firms that had declined to participate in further development work (Nerkat and Shane 2003: footnote 1). The study does not identify how the innovations rejected by big firms are distributed between concentrated and fragmented industries. Assuming that small firms are most likely to pick up a rejected innovation in a concentrated industry and these decisions are based on informed insight, the origins of spin out ventures may contribute to the high failure rate of projects directed at concentrated industries. The MIT outcomes may therefore result from a particular selection process as well as the competitive processes stressed by Nerkat and Shane (2003).

Second, biotechnology start ups were separated from others in the MIT sample. This reflected a judgement that biotech start ups have an unusual reliance on university-created technology and high capital requirements compared with other start ups that can cause them to become public companies prior to having a commercial product. These features mean that their time to market differs from that expected of other start ups and that public capital raising may not indicate commercial success. These were problems for the form of analysis adopted in their study but other researchers have viewed biotechnology as illustrative of how large incumbents in concentrated industries control new firm entry. Particularly in the area of biomedicine, the long time to commercialize products allows industry incumbents in the form of large pharmaceutical companies to maintain a 'watching brief' over prospective competitors, knowing that breakthrough companies would need the assistance of a large-firm partner to bring their innovation to market (Oakey *et al.* 1990). This can be interpreted as showing how the existence of biotechnology start ups is explained by the behaviour of established enterprises rather than entrepreneurial endeavour (see Chapter 5).

Implications for incubators

A number of implications for the operation of technology incubators arise from the links between innovation and high growth enterprise and the role of industry structure in influencing start-up survival:

- New technology is not a major source of high growth enterprise. Small enterprises that have achieved exceptional rates of growth tend to be distinguished by their marketing and management capacities rather than the possession of innovative technology. This evidence relates to the attributes of enterprises

that grow and survive as independent enterprises. It implies that support for incubators should recognize that much new technology transfers to established enterprises rather than being the basis for a new generation of independent enterprises. For example, an analysis of the commercialization of biotechnology products shows that the resulting jobs are captured by large pharmaceutical organizations rather than by the places or ventures that first developed the product (Gray 2002).
- With the exception of academic entrepreneurs without prior involvement in a new venture and new entrants to the labour market, entrepreneurs typically do not start from cold. Incubator proponents need to be clear how their support fits with other environments in which would-be entrepreneurs gather expertise and resources. An entrepreneur's prior place of employment is another type of incubator environment. Success has been shown to increase where start-up entrepreneurs are able to make use of expertise and networks developed in a prior place of employment. Encouraging entrepreneurs to maximize this learning opportunity while developing their venture proposal can be another incubator strategy.
- Large established enterprises interact with start-up ventures in ways that need to be acknowledged in the justification for incubator support. The research from which commercialization projects develop may have been funded by or at least implemented in cooperation with a large enterprise. This can mean that there has been prior screening of the technology rather than a total impasse to new ventures. When picking up these projects, incubators may see their role as developing technology with niche market potential, or judge that their insight into technological opportunities is greater than those who decline to take up the venture, or that they have a role in challenging the inertia of established companies. All these roles can be justified, but they suggest different demands on incubator resources and different outcomes.
- The industry context matters in evaluating the likelihood of a sustainable venture graduating from an incubator. Industries vary in the time it takes for research findings to be converted into commercial ventures and in the scale of production that new entrants must attain for survival. The ability of incumbents to block start-up ventures in concentrated industries suggests a barrier more amenable to competition policy than incubator support. Where the time between discovery and commercialization is long drawn some start-up activity exists while large enterprise awaits its further development. If the ultimate target is an increase in innovation and economic efficiency this impact need not be a concern, but it does imply a contradiction with the intention to use incubators as mechanisms to launch start-up activity in competition to established enterprise.

Knowledge generated from research going on within universities and other public research institutions can help to underpin new rounds of economic activity without them being significant sources of spin-out enterprise. The contribution is made through fundamental research, training and consultancy and occasionally through the discovery of new breakthrough technologies. Consequently, the direct connection between universities and new technology-based enterprise is frequently less than imagined. The Cambridge Science Park, founded in 1970, has been viewed as one of the greatest successes of university-linked business incubation in the United Kingdom (Siegel et al. 2003). Undoubtedly, it serves as a leading example of the development of a high tech cluster, but academics leaving Cambridge colleges to translate scientific findings into commercial reality played little role in the cluster's formation (Hamilton 1998). Rather, the status of a location close to a prestigious university drew in entrepreneurs and enterprises that succeeded without developing any connection to activity in the university. This experience is not unusual among the larger population of university-linked enterprise incubators (Aernoudt 2004). The Internet's origins as a computer-based discussion group designed for a community of physicists in Switzerland, and Columbia University's role in the development of nuclear fission and fusion, encourage the perception that universities spawn the next generation of growth enterprises. These examples help explain why there is support for efforts to commercialize the results of university research, but there is still need for a precise explanation of the need for and scope of technology incubators.

Public knowledge and private enterprise

Over the time that technology incubators have been in existence the broader environment for university-linked innovation has been changing too. Results at first ascribed to incubator initiatives may in practice be a product of larger changes in the innovation system (Nelson 2001). Up to the 1980s, universities were generally not seen as significant generators of spin-off enterprise with the exception of a few outstanding institutions (Bruno and Tyebjee 1984). Even then, the contribution was skewed to particular sectors rather than widely dispersed across different industries (Feeser and Willard 1989). Biotechnology has long been recognized as a particularly fertile sector for university spin-out companies (Kenney 1986) whereas in Silicon Valley only six of 243 firms founded in the 1960s had one or more full time founders who came directly from a university (Cooper 1971). The semiconductor industry developed largely on the basis of expertise that rapidly concentrated within private industry and had comparatively little dependency on university research resources (Sharp 1999). As explained above (and see Chapter 4 Box 4.5), biotechnology has played a significant role in the changing perception of the university contribution to new enterprise formation, although it is mainly the incidence of intellectual property claims that has changed.

In the USA prior to 1980 few universities had established a technology transfer office to assist the commercialization of their institution's discoveries: by 2005 few major universities had not done so. Involvement in technology transfer is now viewed as a necessary aspect of being a research-orientated university (Thursby and Thursby 2007). In 1965, 28 universities in the USA registered a total of 96 patents: in 1992 over 1,500 patents were granted to over 150 of the USA's universities (Henderson et al. 1998). A more recent survey conducted by the Association of

University Technology Managers (AUTM) in the USA reported 3,090 patents registered by 158 universities and three times this number under application (AUTM 2004). The same survey reported that the average number of inventions disclosed by university staff grew by 72.5 per cent comparing 1996 and 2004 among 109 organizations responding to surveys in both years. The number of patents issued and licences executed among universities in the United Kingdom has increased similarly when the period pre and post 2000 is compared (Wright et al. 2003; HEBCI 2007). In absolute terms rates of patenting among UK universities are substantially below those in the USA (Siegel and Wright 2007: 533). Whether this should be viewed as a relative failure by UK institutions to match the research productivity of their North American counterparts depends partly on what lies behind the changes.

Policy makers have been cautioned against using the assertion of intellectual property rights and the number of technology licensing agreements to judge university performance (Nelson 2001). In the context of the United Kingdom, a government-appointed review has argued that universities tend to over value their intellectual property (Lambert 2003). With the establishment of technology offices, universities have tended to over emphasize the search for revenue rather than recognizing that public funding of much of their research activity is intended to ensure that the results of research benefit the economy as a whole. Rather than increasing the supply of commercial ideas from universities into business, the Lambert Review considered that the more important issue is to raise the overall level of demand by business for research from all sources.

Developments in the USA have been conditioned by a specific regulatory regime rather than necessarily indicating economic or social progress. The 1980 Bayh-Dole Act established the right of universities in the USA to presume an entitlement to take out patents on discoveries arising from publicly funded research. Without such a presumption, specific permission from the funding agency would be required to enable a direct commercial benefit to be obtained from work assisted by public funds. Designed specifically to encompass publicly funded research, the Act helped legitimize university presumption of intellectual ownership rights more broadly. The increase in patenting and licensing subsequent to the Act encourages the perception that universities have become more important components of the innovation system. Drawing on insight into activity in the three universities in the USA generating most income from technology licences, Nelson (2001) gives four reasons to doubt that changes in intellectual property regulation influenced the commercialization of research findings:

- The growth in patenting and licensing commenced prior to the Bayh-Dole Act and this implies that the legislation did not release previously existing constraints on technology transfer.
- University contributions to technology advance in industry have grown through the progress attained in the new fields of biotechnology and biomedicine and more broadly in the application of computing to established areas of research activity. While viewed as offering great commercial promise there is typically considerable post-license development work required to

establish this. For example, it took until the 1990s for commercial products to emerge from the scientific advances in genetics and molecular biology that were achieved in the early 1970s (Audretsch 2001).
- Scientifically inspired research tends to remain fundamental in nature rather than being readily converted into income generating activity. Fundamental research need not play an initiating role or perhaps even any role in industrial innovation (Cohen *et al.* 2002). The increased contributions of university research to industry arise in many ways other than the application of university initiated research, such as through consultancy relationships and graduate training.
- Judicial decisions outside the Bayh-Dole Act have allowed the patenting of discoveries that in the past would probably not have been considered patentable. This applies particularly to the patenting of natural organisms and processes.

Effective technology transfer does not have to rely on or be facilitated by university patenting and licensing. Immediately, it shows that universities have responded to an environment where the ability to claim ownership of intellectual property has grown and in which there has been optimism in the commercial significance of certain areas of university endeavour. Once it appears that technology transfer is important these processes feed on themselves, as not doing so risks being viewed as being research inactive and otherwise 'behind the game' (Thursby and Thursby 2007). Underlying processes need to be examined to judge the importance of universities rather than the growth in intellectual property claims.

Any long term benefit that results from university patent registrations and licensing agreements has to be weighed up against the potential impacts on the larger contribution of universities to 'open science' (Nelson 2001). This contrasts patents and licenses with the free availability of university research (Box 7.4). In the debate that followed the passage of the Bayh-Dole Act, open science was associated with embryonic research findings that require further testing and development before their commercial value can be evaluated. Patenting and licensing enables a university to grant an exclusive right of development to an individual entity. This exclusiveness can appear to increase the chances of research being taken up as it offers protection to those willing to invest in the application of the discovery. An open science regime does not provide this certainty over the ability to capture the rewards of successful development and was judged to be a deterrent to commercializing university research findings (Nelson 2001: 15). In contrast to these arguments Nelson suggests that a need for further development gives the possibility of patent or other protection of the invention as it is actually released to the market. Consequently, it is possible that much commercialization effort would have existed without the growth in university patents and licenses and without the intervention of technology transfer offices. A direct benefit to universities, that licensing may provide an additional revenue stream to fund ongoing research activity, can also be discounted. In the USA it appears that most technology transfer offices are a drain on university resources rather than a net contributor to the funding base (Thursby and Thursby 2007: 629). It is a similar situation in the United Kingdom, where few universities have more than a handful of license agreements that generate a net income for their institution (Siegel and Wright 2007).

> **Box 7.4 Open science**
>
> Open science is based on the perspective that the production and verification of new knowledge is best conducted through a transparent and open process. Rather than relying on direct financial gains, researchers are rewarded through public awareness of their research activity and its impact on their reputation and ability to undertake further research. Open inquiry and complete disclosure are an efficient basis for developing new knowledge as they facilitate the validation of findings and reduce excess duplication of research efforts. Sharing of knowledge should ensure that new insights are accessible to those who can put it to use on their basis of their expertise, imagination and material resources that might not be available to the original discoverers and inventors. This enables the incremental additions to the stock of knowledge to be combined with existing and new areas of enquiry, promoting knowledge spillovers between individual research endeavours. Underlying an open science regime is the importance of individual recognition and peer esteem in maintaining the willingness of researchers to share the results of their work.
>
> *Source:* David (2003)

This context is relevant to the evaluation of university involvement in technology incubators. Part of the basis on which university-linked incubators obtain occupants is by awarding exclusive rights to develop the technology on which they are based (Rothaermel and Thursby 2005). The allocation of rights to develop should not overlook the considerable challenges in commercializing university research (Thursby et al. 2001; Thursby and Thursby 2003). The growth of university patents and licenses can obscure the fact that many are far removed from immediate commercial application (Box 7.5). Where there is uncertainty over how best to apply scientific discoveries, an exclusive right of development needs to be justified against the possible weakening of the strengths of an open science regime. As noted above, exclusivity maximizes the financial incentive of the holder of intellectual property rights by putting enterprises in a favourable position to appropriate the returns from the inventions licensed (Kitch 1977; Dechenaux et al. 2003). This can be less important than allowing multiple lines of exploration, especially where the path to something of practical use is long and has many potential destinations (Merges and Nelson 1990). Ensuring successful innovation may then rely more on universities marketing the potential applications of scientific research through the traditional mechanisms associated with open science and placing discoveries in the public domain to be taken up by any party motivated to pursue their commercial potential. It is, therefore, important to explain how technology incubators are expected to affect the formation and ongoing existence of new enterprises.

> **Box 7.5 The long road from university to market**
>
> University inventions are typically embryonic and this means that further investment in their development carries a high risk of failure. Based on a survey of 62 universities in the USA, three quarters (77 per cent) of university-based inventions require some inventor involvement in the further development of the technology (Thursby et al. 2001; Thursby and Thursby 2004). From the same survey, the gulf between scientific claim and commercialization is frequently wide: 48 per cent of inventions are no more than a 'proof of concept' when licensed to a commercial partner; and three quarters are no more than a laboratory-scale prototype. The failure rate of inventions that are licensed is high. Among 113 businesses licensing technology from the sample universities, 42 per cent believed that university-sourced licenses failed more frequently than those licensed from other businesses, while 11 per cent had the opposite assessment.

Evaluating technology incubators

Since incubators are configured to keep enterprises in existence, characteristics of enterprises under incubation give little basis for judging the value of incubator support (Phan et al. 2005). Incubation may encourage overconfidence in projects with limited chances of long term survival and among individuals unfitted for entrepreneurship (Camerer and Lovallo 1999). These risks are especially prevalent in the early stages of a new industry (Colombo and Delmastro 2001). A full evaluation of incubator activity must, therefore, account for both the additional level of enterprise formation and technology commercialization beyond that occurring in the absence of incubator support and any slowing of economic adjustment caused by protecting ventures that were based on inflated expectations (Bearse 1998; Hackett and Dilts 2004: 73). This evidence is hard, if not impossible, to assemble but some insight can be obtained by comparing like groups of enterprises participating in different types of incubator, or that exist inside and outside incubators. Such 'matched pairs' analysis has been applied to technology incubators following its use to determine how far a location in a science park affects the input and output characteristics of on-park enterprises compared with off-park peers (Monck et al. 1988; Quintas et al. 1992; Westhead and Storey 1994; Westhead 1997).

A 'matched pairs' research design is a recognized quasi experimental method (Robson 2002). These methods mimic an experimental research design and are generally envisaged as being used when it is not possible to randomly assign research subjects to separate experimental and control groups. This clearly applies in the case of allocating admission to a technology incubator, but some limitations of the method still need to be noted (Box 7.6). In the case of Colombo and Delmastro's (2002) investigation of Italian ventures, a group of enterprises located in a technology incubator are 'matched' with enterprises located elsewhere in terms of their similarity of activity, location and age. A cross-sectional comparison of the respective levels of employment suggests that in-incubator enterprises outgrow off-incubator enterprises. This is reinforced by evidence that the in-incubator enterprises outperform the off-incubator enterprises with respect to their workforce qualification level, the use of innovative information and communications technology, participation in European Union sponsored research projects, ability to utilize scientific and technical services and the likelihood of formal cooperation with a university or other entities. Colombo and Delmastro (2002) contrast their evidence, as well as that from a study of technology incubators in Germany (Sternberg 1990), with the results of matched pair studies of science parks. Overall they suggest that technology incubators have the more positive impact on occupant performance.

Box 7.6 **Limitations of quasi experiments**

A quasi experiment is a research design involving an experimental approach, but where random assignment to treatment and comparison groups has not been used. They are frequently considered a second-best method: a fall-back to consider when it is not possible to randomize the allocation research subjects. Evaluating business incubators or science parks by comparing similar enterprises located inside and outside the facility of interest raises risks common to non randomized comparisons. The biggest risk is that initial differences between groups prior to the entry to the incubator environment are not recognized by the matching. A further problem may be that the access of 'off location' enterprises to resources is affected by the incubator. This might occur, for example, if the time of university staff is absorbed by incubator enterprises to the loss of their availability to assist other enterprises.

Source: Robson (2002)

Matched pairs evaluation recognizes that a critical test of technology incubators is their impact on enterprise performance, but the evidence has its limitations. Regardless of the issue addressed, the reliability of the method requires that the samples are matched on relevant criteria. Colombo and Delmastro (2002: 1120) acknowledge that their study design may not achieve this. Citing Storey (1999), two selection steps are identified that can result in a group of enterprises entering incubators with characteristics which their own study did not take into account and which other studies would find equally hard to construct matched samples around. First, the ventures that seek to locate in an incubator may do so because of predilections that would be followed regardless of location, such as an interest in establishing a collaborative relationship with a university research team. Second, managers of technology incubators have the opportunity to select enterprises with aspirations that their support is most focused upon and that have latent characteristics judged most likely to convert into outputs sought by the incubator's sponsors. This may mean that enterprises entering incubators disproportionately comprise those with a high certainty of commercial success and with most uptake of innovative technology. To control for these sources of selection bias the ideal matched pairs study would evaluate the relative performance of in-incubator firms with like outside ventures that have been admitted for entry on the same basis of those in occupation. Such a group might, for example, be assembled from a waiting list.

Quasi experimental design improvements are part of the challenge confronting the evaluation of technology incubators. Prior to judging the effectiveness of technology incubators it is first necessary to agree their purpose. At the broadest level some technology incubators may limit their ambition to developing new technology rather than nurturing entrepreneurial talent and commercial enterprises (Bøllingtoft and Ulhøi 2005). Another perspective links incubators to a stage model of enterprise evolution and identifies how support needs to address progressive hurdles in the way of transforming scientific discoveries into successful ventures (Box 7.7). Whichever of these approaches is taken, the overall purpose of incubation support needs to be defined. Is the role of incubation to guarantee a successful transition from technological discovery to commercial venture for those projects of highest potential, or is it about strengthening the chances of marginal cases making it to market, or some combination of these roles? Most comment assumes a compromise role of targeting 'weak but promising' ventures: weak due to resources limitations and promising in their business case (Hackett and Dilts 2004: 62). A different perspective puts the emphasis on the nature of the locality in which projects originate rather than the nature of the project itself. According to this view incubation is a process designed principally for localities without an existing entrepreneurial environment (Roberts and Malone 1996; Clarysse et al. 2005). In a high tech region the suggestion is that existing industry participants can be relied upon to take up promising technology developed within the locality's research institutions. Correspondingly, the need for incubation support arises where the chances of 'business pull' are low and it is left to research institutions to provide venture creation and development support. Such a clear demarcation breaks down where scientific research relates to new areas of technology and where business does not have the scientific insight to appraise or develop university research findings. On this basis, some of the earliest technology incubators were established in support of emerging clusters of high technology industry (Aernoudt 2004).

Box 7.7 **Stage models of enterprise formation**

The establishment of technology incubators is consistent with a stage model of the evolution of new ventures (Clarysse et al. 2005). Stage models recognize a number of characteristic phases through which a project evolves from scientific discovery to commercial realization, with each stage filtering out projects proving unviable for further development. A basic stage model of the start-up process distinguishes three steps: invention, transition and innovation (Clarysse and Moray 2004). The transition phase takes the project from a starting point, where there are still uncertainties over the ability of the technology to perform as required, to the point where the uncertainty has been resolved and a business idea is validated. The innovation phase encompasses the period when the growth expectation is tested. The stage model depicts the challenges to be overcome at each phase in the start-up process. Incubation is the process through which support is provided to assist ventures as they move through the three phases and may need the support of the parent research institution. Where a parent research institution is involved, this support may be directed at ventures occupying a specific incubator building, but key forms of assistance are potentially provided to a larger group of projects. This assistance is generally expected to deliver four types of benefit to the ventures receiving support: enhanced credibility of the project; shortening of the entrepreneurial learning curve; business decision making support; access to an entrepreneurial network (Smilor 1987).

The diversity with which technology incubators interpret their role means that little insight is obtained from studies that do not acknowledge their individual context and objectives. For example, a sample of seven European technology incubators revealed three distinct types (Clarysse et al. 2005). This study drew on seven base examples from incubators located in regions of scientific excellence, as measured in the European Report on Science and Technology Indicators (1994), and that shared three characteristics: established pre 1997; a documented record of spin-out activity; with claims to be regarded as an exemplar in managing enterprise generation from their linked research institution. Even with this commonality, three distinct types of project were identified according to the emphasis given to attributes typically expected of technology incubators, namely:

- The extent to which incubated enterprises are positioned to receive external capital at spin-out and the extent of venture capital received.
- The utilization of own patented technology.
- The product orientation and target market of the spin-out enterprise (for example whether they aim to sell a proprietary product or service).
- The forecast time to commercial solvency as a measure of the readiness of incubated enterprises to survive in the open economy.

The *low selective* incubator is directed primarily at creating immediate employment options in the context of an economically depressed (but still scientifically strong) region. The long term survival or growth potential of ventures supported is of little concern compared with the goal of assisting graduates and researchers into self employment. Among these spin-out enterprises there is little use of technology developed in the sponsoring research institution and little use of external capital. Typically, businesses are low entry enterprises that provide consulting or other services.

The *supportive* incubator is motivated to assist spin-out enterprise as a preferred alternative to licensing technology to an outside entity. This arises from the perceived benefits to the research institution, such as the attraction of entrepreneurial researchers and ongoing relationships to commercial enterprises whose start-up they can claim to have assisted. Spin-out ventures are supported on the basis of an acceptable business plan, but the rate at which projects are supported exceeds the selectivity that might be expected of private venture capitalists. Projects tend to rely on public–private partnership funding rather than on commercial finance.

The pure *incubator* is focused on supporting spin-out ventures that can attract substantial external funding. Acceptance of projects for incubation depends on this being judged most likely to maximize the project potential, otherwise alternative technology transfer mechanisms will be preferred. Incubation is associated with expectations of assisting the realization of 'explosive growth' based on a strong technical foundation and global orientation to marketing.

Each of the three models has its own combination of organizational, human, financial, technological, network and physical resources. Adding to the variability, Clarysse *et al.* (2005) identify two suboptimal types according to whether the incubator lacks the requisite resources or competences to deliver the mission aspired to. Competence-deficient organizations have sufficient resources but insufficient capabilities to realize their ambition; resource-deficient organizations seek to provide support to start-up enterprises but lack the financial capacity to do this effectively. They find that in a sample of 43 incubators slightly over half need to adjust their mission if they are to match their capacity with a level of service that they have a prospect of delivering. Meanwhile, the combined variability gives three reasons to question previous claims about the effectiveness of technology incubators:

- Success needs to be judged against the intended goals and operational environment of individual incubator projects. Their performance cannot be judged against generalized assumptions as to how these projects operate.
- The results achieved by incubators are a product of the organizational culture within the associated research institution and the broader local environment for entrepreneurship as well as the incubator's own efforts.
- Incubator experiences are location specific, and this makes it doubtful that incubation experiences can be replicated across different regions (see Chapter 2 Box 2.9).

Inside technology incubators

A systematic case explaining how technology incubators respond to specific impediments faced by new enterprise seeking to commercialize research findings has yet to be presented (Phan *et al.* 2005; Link and Scott 2007; Thursby and Thursby 2007). A general claim is that various market failures impede the ability of new technology-based firms to access resources needed to develop their enterprise (Colombo and Delmastro 2002). Acquiring consultancy services is a potential instance due to high search costs in locating and selecting service providers focused on their specific concerns. This is disputed by evidence that small companies make widespread use of external advice (Robson and Bennet 2001), although there is some policy experience suggesting that facilitating access to some types of consultancy advice is an effective way of helping small enterprise growth (see Chapter 3). A justification for technology incubators exists in four broad claims about technology-based entrepreneurship:

- Scientific and technical knowledge is an important resource for technology-based entrepreneurship (Rothaermel and Thursby 2005: 1077). As discussed in Chapter 4, there is a strongly held belief that the uptake of the knowledge and research resources held in universities is highly localized. This claim is used to justify technology incubation in close proximity to universities. In this way, technology incubators are a manifestation of the larger belief in the localization of knowledge spillovers (Rothaermel and Thursby 2005: 1077; Link and Scott 2007: 664). Proximity to academia is, therefore, expected to accelerate the commercialization of new enterprise by maximizing the opportunity to acquire new knowledge, especially that of a tacit or experiential nature. The clustering of multiple organizations around research universities is believed to consolidate the incubator's ability to gain from knowledge flows (Link and Scott 2007).
- Incubators are believed to respond to the resource needs of emerging technology-based start ups. Sophisticated users of new technology are potentially to be found in and around a university, reducing the search costs for locating users of the products and services being developed by start ups in the incubator (Link and Scott 2007). On the supply side, incubator enterprises can gain access to a highly specialized labour pool and a presumed advantage in the ability to recruit university graduates and expertise for short term assignments such as by appointing university staff as consultants.
- Attachment to an incubator can perform a quality signalling role, particularly where there is competitive selection of incubator occupants or at least a stringent selection process overseen by skilled assessors (Bugliarello 1998). A track record of incubating successful graduates may further assist incubator enterprises to gain third party support that is otherwise difficult to access because of the perceived high risks associated with technology start ups. This may be particularly important in increasing access to finance (Storey 1994; Oakey 1995). The perception that a university connection adds credibility to an enterprise has been identified as the main incubator benefit perceived by occupants (Hackett and Dilts 2004; Mian 1996).
- It has been observed that incubator occupants tend to form relationships with other incubator residents (Sherman and Chappell 1998). On the basis that organizations with diverse network connections are advantaged over isolated enterprises, assisting enterprises to form relationships has become seen as a further way that incubators reduce impediments to enterprise formation (Bøllingtoft and Ulhøi 2005).

Even accepting these propositions it needs to be established that incubators are uniquely able to overcome impediments to new technology enterprise, or at least that they can do this more efficiently than other institutional arrangements. This recognizes that there is the possibility of incubators substituting for other mechanisms as well as being complementary to them (Siegel and Wright 2007: 538). For example, venture capital providers, virtual networks and online marketplaces may provide some of the network benefits that may be supplied by an incubator. In the same way that an incubator might confer status, the receipt of venture capital has been shown to bestow legitimacy on a new venture (Stuart et al. 1999).

As discussed in Chapter 4, proximity in itself may not affect access to knowledge, as this often depends on formal interactions and individual relations (Cohen et al. 2002). As in the case of an engineer seeing an article and then contacting the author about how the research may be used, a combination of reading published literature and direct exchanges are frequently what happens in practice (Gibbons and Johnston 1975; Faulkner and Senker 1995; Walsh and Bayma 1996). Further development of technology licensed from universities typically requires ongoing input from the university-based inventor (Jensen and Thursby 2001). This raises the possibility that technology incubators can be important in giving start-up ventures privileged access to the staff and resources of the parent research institution and in providing an environment that supports academic entrepreneurship.

Little is known about the extent to which university academics are involved in incubator firms, but their role in the broader commercialization of university innovation has been investigated. This work merits comment, as close contact with university staff is potentially one of the main distinctive features of a technology incubator. The role of technology incubators in developing entrepreneurial networks is a related possible outcome that has been investigated and is commented on below.

Academic entrepreneurs and start up success

The task of commercializing university discoveries may be given to the academic responsible for the discovery or to an independent or 'surrogate' entrepreneur. If the primary responsibility falls to the surrogate entrepreneur the possibility still arises for the related academic to participate in the venture's development as a member of the senior management team, a consultant contracted for specific tasks or as an informal advisor. Whichever form of association is opted for, the question is whether this assists the development of a viable business venture. The academic entrepreneur is more likely to lack entrepreneurial experience than those recruited from outside and prior experience of developing a new enterprise matters to the likelihood of ventures reaching the market (Daniels and Hofer 1993; Radosevich 1995). The academic entrepreneur may compensate for this through a strong commitment to the technology and their ongoing involvement with the underlying science. Nonetheless, reflecting their relative strengths, academic entrepreneurs may have a tendency to focus on the technical aspects of the innovation to the neglect of developing a commercial enterprise. Ventures led by outside entrepreneurs have thus been found to outperform those managed by the academic-inventor (Chrisman et al. 1995). This supports the more general contention that the person who first identifies an innovative opportunity is frequently not the most appropriate person to carry it forward, as this depends on a separate set of skills (Venkataraman *et al.* 1992).

Given conflicting evidence over the relative effectiveness of academic and surrogate entrepreneurs, it is inviting to suggest that combining their involvement will increase the likelihood of success (Franklin *et al.* 2001). Retaining the inventor's involvement in the venture's development alongside an outside entrepreneur would make up for any lack of insight into the technology, which is a potential shortcoming of the surrogate option. A risk is that a clash of business and scientific cultures arises (Samson and Gurdon 1993). A focus on common values and the overall goals of the venture can reduce the risk of culture clash. Interestingly for the value of technology incubators, it is also suggested that having the academic partner retain his or her university position alongside involvement in the start-up venture can help develop the shared outlook necessary for the blending business and scientific priorities.

An evaluation of the Georgia Institute of Technology's Advanced Technology Development Centre (ATDC) provides some clarification of this tangled debate and what it means for the importance of technology incubators. The study examined how links to Georgia Tech's staff affected the progress of ventures in the incubator (Rothaermel and Thursby 2005). The ATDC has existed since 1980 and is among the first technology incubators established in the USA. Occupants may be ventures based on technology licensed from Georgia Tech or new ventures recruited from outside the parent institution, some of which may have connections to other universities. Rothaermel and Thursby (2005) looked at the progress of 79 ventures over the period 1998 to 2003 that were incubator tenants at some stage from 1998 to 2000, giving the possibility of discovering graduation, failure or continued presence in the incubator as the main outcome. These enterprises were differentiated according to whether they were founded to commercialize a technology licensed from Georgia Tech and whether there was some form of involvement from a university academic, and if so what form it took. The key part of the study examines how strong links to the sponsoring institution affect the incidence of successful graduation from the incubator. A strong link is judged to exist where the venture is based on a technology licensed from Georgia Tech or where an academic linked to the prior development of the technology is part of the senior management of the venture.

Strong links were found to reduce the probability of an incubator venture failing while also acting to reduce the likelihood of graduation within three years of entering the incubator. A reduced likelihood of failure was most affected by the holding of a licence, whereas the retarded rate of graduation was most affected by the senior management involvement of university staff. Where the involvement of university staff was as a contracted or informal advisor there was no measurable impact on the venture's likelihood of outright failure or failure to graduate successfully. The researchers interpret their findings as evidence for an agency effect in which founders maintain a higher commitment to their project than would an entrepreneur not associated with the initial discovery and claim of commercial potential. Others have seen such commitment as a sign of 'bold optimism' in the eventual chances of commercial application (Camerer and Lovallo 1999). The persistence with projects may be further encouraged where the venture holds an exclusive license to develop the technology, as this holds out the prospect of controlling future income should they succeed. Whether the persistence is foolhardy or ultimately justified is unknown. Rothaermel and Thursby (2005: 1088) speculate that the slow rate of graduation among ventures that are strongly linked to the university is an outcome of the ability of academics to combine dual roles of university researchers and start-up managers. The need for this flexibility arises in the context of the rudimentary nature of the technology that is licensed most frequently by universities.

The Georgia Tech study indicates that strong links to academics do not accelerate the emergence of high growth enterprises. Some further insight into this issue has been obtained from examining the perceptions of technology transfer managers in UK universities with a track record of successful start-up ventures and those without such a record (Franklin et al. 2001). The study considered whether more successful universities are predisposed to using surrogate entrepreneurs. In the context of the study, a successful track record was based on securing some degree of private sector funding for more than five start-up ventures over a five year period. Less than a quarter of universities providing information for the study met the 'high success' cut off, indicating how most UK universities have had few spin-out companies although they have established technology transfer offices.

A difference of outlook was identified, with the more successful universities being least concerned about the risks associated with the release of university assets to an outside entrepreneur. Positive experience of the relationship with surrogate entrepreneurs partly explained the difference in outlook. Universities with a record of successful spin-out companies were more likely than others to recognize the attributes brought by an outside entrepreneur as advantageous for venture development: this includes the motivation of making capital gains (as compared to the motivation of perfecting technology) and the resources accessed through the entrepreneur's network. This led the investigators to suggest that many of the difficulties in developing university spin-out companies may arise from the 'less creative and more rigid approaches adopted by the less successful universities' (Franklin et al. 2001: 138). While suggesting this it was noted as well that all universities have similar perceptions of the main barriers to using surrogate entrepreneurs: the difficulty of luring people to champion new ventures that had yet to secure funding and of identifying people to approach for this role.

While the review of university perceptions of the relative merits of academic and surrogate entrepreneurship point to the value of maximizing the use of outside entrepreneurs, the researchers offered a less clear cut conclusion. They prefer to emphasize the variability in commercialization projects and consequently recommend against the use of standardized approaches. A flexible approach to spin-out companies is encouraged, utilizing both surrogate and academic entrepreneurship as appropriate (Franklin et al. 2001: 139–140).

Incubators as network builders

More broadly than the interaction with the parent research institution, technology incubators may assist emerging enterprises to build a supportive business network (McAdam and McAdam 2006). Such an outcome would be important, as it is generally agreed that a rich network of connections can give an enterprise significant advantages in meeting its need for external resources (Uzzi 1997). Entrepreneurs typically exploit the opportunities and contacts immediately available to them rather than constructing their networks through purposeful investigation (Schutjens and Stam 2000). Incubators that assist occupants to build a network of business contacts have, therefore, been viewed as the most effective (Hansen *et al.* 2000).

The case for network incubators seems to be strengthened by the straightforward strategies recommended to fulfil the role (Box 7.8). A note of caution is that these strategies reflect the context of a particular type of incubator existing in the USA, where the ability to concentrate on 'good prospects' may be unusually high (Box 7.8). Hansen *et al.* (2000) drew on incubators established by venture capital companies whose previous investments include high profile Internet and IT successes. These incubators are able to leverage their connections to past investments and the prestige of the venture capital sponsor. The examples informing the role model of a networked incubator may also be distinguished by them having a financial stake in their member enterprises, making them even more of an extension of a venture capital business, and in the member enterprises having the resources to purchase various support services. Consequently the achievements influencing the assessment made by Hansen *et al.* (2000) derive from both the quality of their incubators' member companies and the effectiveness of the networks facilitated for member companies. When attention turns to a 'normal' university-linked incubator there is still a need for evidence of their impact on the development and effectiveness of entrepreneurial networks.

Box 7.8 **Network building tools**

Incubator managers can assist their member companies establish connections and relationships by formalizing the incubator's links to organizations and individuals that are likely to be important sources of advice for their member companies. In particular, incubator managers are advised to consider the following mechanisms for institutionalizing network development support:

- Create formal links with external experts, for example by appointing them to an advisory board.
- Bring outside experts on site by offering work space to companies that supply relevant services.
- Schedule occasional but regular meetings between the incubator manager and outside executives that may be potential partners of or investors in the incubator's resident enterprises.
- Establish processes for exchanging information and know-how across companies, such as through the exchange of board representatives associated with

> member companies and through databases that allow incubates to share information.
> - Implement economic incentives by the incubator organization investing in member companies.
> - Hire specialized deal brokers whose role is to work with member companies to develop their network connections and investigate potential partnerships.
>
> *Source:* Hansen *et al.* (2000)

A small scale investigation of a technology incubator located on a university science park in Ireland provides a source of evidence of how network development can be influenced (McAdam and McAdam 2006). This case study incubator aims to accommodate small high technology business for a period of up to three years, after which enterprises relocate to the university's science park. During their time in the incubator enterprises have access to an integrated package of new business development support services, facilities and expertise. The associated impact on the networks of 12 resident enterprises was tracked by McAdam and McAdam (2006) over three years. The overall findings reveal how positive effects are offset by certain limitations or even outright disadvantages of developing networks from within an incubator:

- The incubator assisted enterprises to form a network of professional relationships through the added credibility arising from their university-linked address as well as through practical considerations, including a stable location adaptable to changing needs (compared with outside peers who over the same period might occupy two or more premises) and the use of reception and meeting space. As well, the incubator could give an impression of being a larger enterprise than its actual resources merited and this was also seen to help give the venture added credibility. On the downside, academic entrepreneurs risk being viewed as trying to keep attachments to two camps rather than being 'real' entrepreneurs with serious business intentions.
- A shared location with other ventures at similar stages of development encouraged shared outlooks that helped transfer experience and mutual encouragement between members of the incubator. This outcome can be sensitive to precise physical locations that bring people into regular contact rather than being a product of the joint location alone. Some incubator occupants expressed feelings of isolation. Moreover, shared outlooks did not necessarily overcome the reluctance to share significant information at the heart of the individual business's challenges and ambition. Information exchange among member companies tends to be about generic start-up issues such as marketing, venture capital and accommodation matters.
- A number of member companies make use of the university connection and deepen their capacity to absorb research findings and enhance their technical expertise. Such outcomes depend on individual inclinations to search out and use university resources, and this partly arises from prior associations with

the university rather than being something that results from affiliation to the incubator.

Beyond these incubator influences on networking, McAdam and McAdam (2006) found that 'normal' network accumulation processes open to all enterprises continue to be important for members of the incubator. This includes the use of personal networks, previous work contacts, the recruitment of staff with desired connections and conference participation. Consequently, rather than highlighting how the incubator enhanced their business network, the study gives a more unambiguous endorsement of practical assistance such as telecommunications facilities. Such support is regarded highly as it enables owners to concentrate on developing their business. As to the possibility of network support fundamentally changing enterprise prospects, the diversity among new technology businesses is a major challenge to delivering effective assistance. High technology activities comprise a mix of often technologically sophisticated and functionally heterogeneous enterprises (Oakey 1995). Politicians and planners tend to see these activities as a single industry, but in reality there is little in common between, say, a high tech electronics company and a high tech pharmaceutical venture.

Conclusion

Technology incubators now form a large part of the business incubator sector. The expansion of incubator projects has occurred without it being clear how their effectiveness is to be measured. The immediate impact in terms of the success in graduating start-up enterprises that grow in the mainstream economy can be identified, and when it is the record is generally positive. The limitation is that projects entering incubators vary in their chances of successful commercialization and incubator managers have varying degrees of discretion to accommodate projects with good prospects of success. An address in a university-sponsored incubator can be valued for the credibility it adds to occupants as well as, if not more than, because of the access to the services offered to occupants. For this reason incubator performance must be measured against the extent of the challenge taken up and the effectiveness of incubator services in facilitating the commercialization of projects that otherwise would not have progressed beyond the laboratory. It is also necessary to evaluate project outcomes relative to the overall outcomes of university research efforts.

Technology incubators have grown in number in the context of larger initiatives to extend the involvement of universities and other research institutions in the commercial application of scientific discoveries. Research institutions and especially universities have become more active in protecting their intellectual property and in devising ways to generate income from it. This is partly in response to developments within various areas of science and technology that have increased the flow of knowledge that is perceived to have commercial application. As well, government actions have frequently encouraged universities to become more aggressive in asserting their ownership of scientific discoveries through patents, licences and associated measures. These developments can obscure the fact that the most important contributions of universities and research institutions to economic development come through their contributions to open science, consultancy services and training. Direct involvement in technology transfer can be at the expense of open science. As a consequence, the evaluation of technology incubators needs to be expanded to consider how they affect access to technological discoveries and the possible long term benefits of allowing multiple development programmes to take up the results of scientific research.

The broad purpose of technology incubators is to enhance the likelihood of scientific discoveries being converted into viable commercial enterprises. There is less agreement over the specific market failures impeding this transformation that technology incubators are an effective response to. Further research is needed to ensure resources are focused on the issues that can have most impact in increasing the commercialization of research findings, and that support is concentrated on activities that would otherwise lie dormant or fail, but hold potential to become viable ventures. The particular importance of university-linked incubators is their potential to enhance the access to knowledge-based assets that are needed by technology-based start ups. It remains to be established that companies in incubators actually change their use of university resources or that incubators provide an environment that accelerates the conversion of academic projects into commercial ventures. The results from one incubator show that those enterprises with strong links to the sponsoring institution are less likely to fail than those without connection, but that they are also less likely to graduate into the mainstream economy. This is suggestive of technology incubators simultaneously acting as business accelerators and shelters for projects of least interest to outside entrepreneurs. Outcomes are a product of the ventures entering the incubator rather than being a consequence of incubator intervention. The acceleration benefits are captured by ventures with the highest likelihood of progressing outside an incubator. Projects at the technological frontier are potential long term residents kept in existence through the supportive environment and because sponsoring agencies perceive benefit to their institution from the effort to commercialization technology. It can, for example, provide a demonstration of university commitment to the application of their research activity, offer learning opportunities for the staff involved and be the basis for attracting support from government programmes. For the present it seems that technology incubators should be appraised as more likely to bring institutional benefits to the sponsoring agency than immediate local economic development outcomes.

8 Local economic development and ecological modernization

The possibility that promoting good environmental practices can simultaneously encourage business growth has become the inspiration for a new set of local economic development policies (Gibbs 2002; Cohen 2006). Eco-industrial parks (Gibbs *et al.* 2005); local environmental taxes (Brady and Jackson 2003); 'buy local' campaigns (Midmore and Thomas 2006); and assisting the uptake of 'clean' technologies (Gibb 2002: 120–122) are some of the initiatives in this vein. Targeting 'win-win' outcomes of improving environmental sustainability while promoting local economic development, or even 'win-win-win' outcomes (simultaneous environmental, economic and social gains) frequently centres around encouraging some form of increased regional self reliance. In the extreme, it has been argued that all goods and services that reasonably could be provided locally should be (Hines 2000). Others, sympathetic to the desirability of greater local self sufficiency for environmental and economic advantage, recognize that the case for increased localization frequently relies on arguments that are 'over simplified' and 'over romantic' (Gibbs 2002: 86). Efforts to build more self reliant regional economies have reinforced rather than resolved the uncertainties associated with this agenda (Midmore and Thomas 2006). Within any locality some opportunities for increasing local linkages may exist, but as these opportunities are revealed so are the reasons why self reliance is unattainable.

The presentation of the environment as a win-win opportunity for business and the quality of life raises questions about how to measure a 'win' and how well balanced the returns to both sides must be. The linkage of economy and environment is frequently combined with particular conceptions of what constitutes development. Measuring economic progress through changes in local income, investment volumes and employment may not be the target of some who espouse double wins. A qualitative change in aspirations, including the willingness to moderate material standards of living by accepting the full the costs of environmental externalities, may be part of the agenda (Daly 1996; Curtis 2003; Wells and Nieuwenhuis 2004). At the other end of the spectrum, modest adaptations of existing business practice may be counted as a gain for the environment (Epstein 2008). Such a range of views parallels the debate about the nature of the environmental risks facing society and the requirements for sustainable development. Beyond the broad acceptance that sustainable economic development means giving consideration to resource flows, resource flow impacts, stakeholder analysis and carrying capacities, there is little agreement over what is needed (Birkin 2000; Blowfield and Murray 2008: 241). Some assessment of the larger consequences of economic activity and some willingness to change behaviour is agreed, but a wide difference remains over the extent to which this must lead to a radical rethinking of business's purpose.

The divergence in agendas is partly captured by the demands for 'eco-efficiency' compared with the call for economic activity to become 'eco-effective' (McDonough and Braungart 2002). The former is consistent with strategies that reduce negative impacts; the latter involves conscious striving to enhance environmental conditions by rethinking technologies, products and the whole relationship of business and society. Using this terminology, local economic development may be eco-efficient when it promotes clean technology to a group of enterprises or supports ecological entrepreneurialism. The same initiatives may not meet the standard of eco-effectiveness if the increased income and employment transfers demands to other environmental resources (Jänicke *et al.* 2000). The dilemma of the '*N* curve' (Box 8.1) captures this concern. For some commentators, local initiatives that result in a 'greened' locality expanding its environmental footprint at the expense of other regions are not acceptable, rather a radically restructured economy is needed to deliver a genuine double dividend (Gibbs 2002: 87).

***Box 8.1* The *N* curve dilemma**

Incremental increases in environmental efficiency can be wiped out by subsequent growth processes or rebound effects. Reductions in car emissions, for example, can be neutralized by increases in road traffic – a problem recognized as the 'dilemma of the *N* curve'. On a larger scale, Industry in Japan achieved remarkable savings in the use of energy and raw materials from 1973 to 1985 but these were subsequently offset by strong industrial growth during this period.

Source: Jänicke (2008)

One way through this conceptual maze is to differentiate how win-win gains are to be realized. One possibility is that improving environment performance offers a continuous opportunity for strengthening the profitability of enterprise. Evidence of this relationship can be obtained from examining the performance of businesses that have invested most in improving their environmental performance relative to the performance of other businesses. This possibility is frequently understood in terms of the existence of a business case for individual enterprise to become more environmentally responsible. It is more likely to be measuring the economic value of eco-efficiency than eco-effectiveness. Some insight into the ability to combine profitable enterprise with eco-effectiveness is obtained from examining local economic projects that seek to promote new ways of organizing economic activity rather than simply helping conventional enterprise add a green component to their operations. This chapter has selected two types of project that optimistically are claimed to combine opportunities for business growth and absolute reductions in environment impact. These are projects encouraging the localization of food production and consumption and eco-industrial projects inspired by industrial ecology principles.

Incremental 'win-wins'

The performance of businesses taking a lead on environmental responsibility relative to enterprises with less investment in environmental initiatives provides one test of the scope for 'win-win' local economic policy. This evidence evaluates the impacts of marginal shifts in business practice. It potentially captures how far enterprises are able to profit from pollution-prevention strategies without having to fundamentally rethink how business is conducted. Opportunities for an incremental shift toward a greener economy are seen to arise through at least five processes (Dryzek 1997):

- Reduced pollution and waste production can result in greater business efficiency.
- Avoiding future financial liabilities, such as the potential cost of clearing up contaminated land.
- Creating a better environment may have workforce benefits by, for example, encouraging employee commitment and assisting recruitment.
- The marketing of products and services on the basis of their comparatively favourable environmental performance.
- The sale of environmental control technology and services.

Through these opportunities, environmental leadership shifts from being a responsible but potentially high risk aspiration to being a sensible step for profit-seeking enterprise. The perception that enhancing environmental performance is simultaneously profit enhancing is reflected in claims that strong environmental regulation is good for national competitiveness. Porter (1991), in an influential *Scientific American* article, proposed this relationship with the qualification that turning environmental concern into competitive advantage depends on the 'right kind of regulation'. It must stress pollution prevention rather than abatement or clean up; it must not prescribe one form of technology over another and it should not impose standards but rather encourage environmental improvement through market incentives. Such qualifications are consistent with most current thinking on environmental management (see Gouldson and Murphy 1998; Gibbs 2002) and so have little dented the frequency with which the existence of a business case for environmental responsibility is claimed.

An equal conviction exists that increasing investment in environmental initiatives damages business performance. Porter applies his argument mainly to how a country might gain a competitive advantage through strict environmental policies. For individual companies, environmental impacts and the costs of mitigation can vary significantly (Jaffe et al. 1995). Similarly, there is not a consistent willingness among consumers to contribute to the costs of environmental improvement. In some countries, for example, consumers are more willing than in others to pay a high premium for organically produced food (Saunders et al. 2004). Whatever the country, the actual willingness to pay an environmental premium tends to exist only for a limited range of household products such as detergents, paper and certain food items (Eden 1996).

Pulling a 'rabbit out of the hat' and delivering win-win outcomes depends on business income increasing at a faster rate than the costs of environmental mitigation, whereas in practice the opposite has tended to occur (Walley and Whitehead 1996). In economic language, there are diminishing marginal returns from investing in mitigation efforts. It is usually possible to find some easy wins when the search to reduce environmental impacts commences without specific prior efforts in this endeavour. As the drive continues, companies are likely to come up against increasingly complex environmental problems that involve increasing amounts of expenditure (Box 8.2). For example, during the late 1980s expenditure on environmental mitigation for a sample of oil and gas companies grew at six times the rate of their direct labour costs in response to the need to attain higher levels of environmental performance (Walley and Whitehead 1994: 40). Overall, the costs of pollution control to industry grew at an estimated nearly 300 per cent 1972–1990 in the USA (Jaffe et al. 1995). The tendency for business to be given increasing choice in how it responds to environmental pressures through the shift from old-fashioned command-and-control regulation to various forms of market-based incentive compounds the cost of environmental mitigation efforts (Sterner 2003). Freedom to choose can be justified by economic theory but it assumes that business managers make optimum decisions, and this is far from assured.

Box 8.2 **Escalating environmental demands on dairy farms**

In New Zealand, dairy cow numbers have risen from 3.1 million in 1983 to 4.2 million in 1996 and 5.4 million in 2005. Agricultural pollution from dairy shed effluent (particularly nutrients and pathogens) poses a serious threat to the quality of the environment. With the development of understanding, new technology and more demanding regulations, the recommended methods for treating this effluent have become increasingly expensive and complicated.

The first mitigation measure involved the construction of barrier ditches for storing effluent before its discharge into a waterway. Next came oxidation ponds, initially for holding before water discharge, and later regional councils encouraged application to land because of the mixed performance of ponds. Neither method is now seen as adequate. Effluent needs to be well treated before being applied to land to be entirely safe for humans and the environment. To meet this need, advanced pond systems and anaerobic digester technology is being developed to provide the means for upgrading effluent treatment. Anaerobic digester technology gives the possibility for resource recovery but brings an additional demand in the need for mechanical scraping rather than flushing with water. Even with the potential of this

> technology, the combination of nutrient and faecal contamination in effluent is seen to require farmers to increase efforts to reduce access of grazing livestock to waterways and to make use of nitrification inhibitors that enhance the capacity of soil to retain nutrients.
>
> *Source:* Parliamentary Commissioner for the Environment (2004)

Resolving how far local economic development can rely on a business case for lessening environment impact draws us to two areas of investigation: first, the relationship between environmental and business performance; second, reflection on how and by whom business cases are constructed.

Evidence of a business case

It is not in doubt that pollution prevention can sometimes make good business sense for an individual enterprise. For organizations that have previously done little to address their environmental impacts, some opportunity frequently exists to lessen those impacts while raising production efficiency and keeping their basic approach to business intact. This was the experience of many businesses during the 1980s and the origins of the win-win mindset (Walley and Whitehead 1994). Simply updating production equipment can offer a double dividend, which is partly why so many businesses are able to claim they are getting greener while aggregate environmental conditions deteriorate (McDonough and Braungart 2002). The unresolved issue is whether an ongoing commitment to improve environmental performance is reflected in ongoing gains in business performance. As expressed by one advocate of eco-industrial development, the issue is not about doing the same with less but rather about doing far more with far less (Cohen-Rosenthal 2003: 22).

Case studies of high profile companies such as Dow Chemicals, Unilever and Wal-Mart (Steger 2004) and of individual industries (for example Porter and Van der Linde 1995) show how environmental and business performance can be linked. Companies increasing their reliance on environmentally certified raw materials, working with suppliers to reduce packaging or extending their production of 'environmentally friendly' consumer items such as energy-efficient light bulbs are shown at the same time to be reaping considerable financial and competitive advantage. Companies are doubtless making the changes reported and individual projects may offer business advantages but it is the combined weight of individual stories that counts, and this is where the evidence gap opens. Case studies report a variety of measures of business performance and relate to different types of environmental initiative (Székely and Knirsch 2005). Without standardization little guidance is produced about which dimensions of environmental action are related to which aspects of business performance, or what influences the strength and direction of this relationship (Blowfield and Murray 2008: 134). It is also interesting to note that most focus on business opportunities obtained rather than the net gain adjusted for the opportunities forgone, although there are exceptions (Box 8.3). Generally, valuing events that have not occurred is considerably harder than valuing the impact of negative consumer reaction to dramatic downgrades in a company's standing with consumers.

> *Box 8.3* **Co-operative Bank sustainability downside**
>
> In 2001, the UK-based Co-operative Bank developed a method for measuring how its sustainability practices affect revenue and growth. From information gathered in a survey of customers, it ascertained that 53 per cent of personal current account customers regard sustainability as one of a number of influences that had caused them to open or maintain an account at the Bank; 31 per cent said it was the most important consideration. These responses were used to develop a sustainability factor that allocates profitability from Bank products according to the weight given to sustainability by customers. These gains are offset by a valuation of the business opportunities foregone as a result of the application of its ethical principles. In 2009, it estimated that adherence to its ethical principles had cost the Co-operative Bank a potential £1 billion (US$1.7 billion) in lost business over the past 15 years. The ethical code had brought offsetting gains too. For example, the bank reported that Bob Dylan allowed them to make use of one of his songs in its advertisements, apparently because of the company's impressive ethical track record. The ability to report gains and losses may be helped by the organization's cooperative status. A 'mainstream' bank has fiduciary responsibilities to its shareholders, including the pursuit of income maximization.
>
> *Source:* Epstein (2008: 191); www.co-operativebank.co.uk

Further questions can also be asked of case study evidence. Aggregating case studies can overlook how the motives for acting vary and the fact that the paybacks being looked for may be hard to value. Companies act in response to specific challenges and have a particular business case that they are looking to fulfil (Steger 2004). For example, for a supermarket company environmental actions may be embarked upon to offset criticism arising from the monopolistic character of their industry and threats of regulation to introduce greater competitiveness. In contrast, case study evidence may focus only on the output of the action taken (for example, the proportion of environmentally certified suppliers utilized) rather than the outcome actually being looked for (maintenance of market dominance) (see Plambeck and Denend 2008). Outputs are easier to achieve than outcomes, but it is the attainment of outcomes that will determine the valuation of the returns and the enduring commitment to environmental initiatives. For many companies the outputs may be environmental, while the outcomes may be longstanding business concerns such as retaining brand loyalty and increasing market share (Smith 2003).

The complexity of the business case for enhancing environmental performance is reflected in the inconsistent results of quantitative studies. According to Salzmann *et al.* (2005) it is difficult to conclude much about the link between business and environmental performance from existing empirical studies. As well as a general failure to test definitions and concepts, three shortcomings in research design have produced conflicting results:

- The use of a wide variety and sometimes poor indicators of environmental action. Frequently, studies rely on composite indicators of an enterprise's environmental commitment, such as corporate reputation index scores, rather than multidimensional measures based on perceptual and objective data.
- Sample designs that cannot capture internal competencies, external pressures, degrees of public visibility, stakeholder configurations and regulatory concerns as factors explaining activity. Either from data limitations or lack of prior conceptualization, the tendency has been to rely on large, pan sector populations, whereas more insight would be obtained by focusing on a single industry or combining plant and industry level data (as attempted by Greening 1995; Moore 2001: Simpson and Kohers 2002).
- The use of accounting (for example return on assets) and market-derived measures (for example share value) with any individual set of measures being an incomplete assessment of business performance. For example, as recommended by the use of a balanced scorecard, there should be a mix of short and long term impacts (Epstein 2008: 137).

On the larger relationship of social (including environmental) and financial performance, reviews of the evidence find little to support the contention that doing good for society means doing well financially (McWilliams and Siegel 2000; Margolis and Walsh 2003). Similarly, there are over 100 studies showing that company share prices are not affected either upwards or downwards by their inclusion in a social investment fund (Vogel 2005). These results suggest that the most that can be concluded is that investment for environmental gains need not damage a business's financial performance.

Most research has assumed either a positive or negative relationship between environmental and financial performance or some form of synergistic interaction (Preston and O'Bannon 1997). This is reflected in the tendency to present the purpose of investigations as seeking to choose between the possibility that corporate responsibility diminishes shareholder value (frequently benchmarked against Freeman 1984) or that it enhances business competitiveness. An inverted U relationship is an alternative way that environmental investment may be related to business performance (Salzmann et al. 2005). At any time, this implies that an optimum level of investment in environmental projects exists rather than the possibility of ongoing returns from continued enhancement of the business's environmental performance. A number of studies suggest that this form of relationship most approximates business experience (Bowman and Haire 1975; Sturdivant and Ginter 1977; Lankoski 2000). A further complication is that what comprises 'excessive investment' cannot be determined by the nature of the environmental initiatives alone (Salzmann et al. 2005). The same environmental actions undertaken in different locations can have quite different cost implications according to local circumstances (Arnold 1995: 208). For example, the manufacturer of low energy electric light bulbs selling to consumers in a locality with high energy costs and developed recycling facilities has an easier business case to make than a manufacturer supplying a less supportive market. Similarly, the idea that actions need to be carefully attuned to opportunities has also been suggested in the context of firms seeking a first-mover advantage (Box 8.4).

Box 8.4 **What is required for a first mover advantage?**

To obtain a first-mover advantage a firm must be sustainable in the sense that it is not easy for competitors to replicate or catch up. They may arise because of existing resources or because a firm obtains an opportunity to build unique resources that result in 'asymmetries' between the firm and its competitors. The first-mover advantage may be based on the possession of resources, learning-curve effects and customer commitment, possibly induced by high switching costs to later market entrants. There is some evidence that first movers are more likely to realize their advantage through increased market share than other aspects of business performance. Offsetting the advantages can be late-mover or follower advantages, as when later entrants achieve distinctive product or service attributes identified from the first-mover's experience. Corporate social responsibility initiatives most likely to produce a first-mover advantage are central to the firm's strategic mission, result in firm-specific benefits and are visible to external stakeholders.

Source: Sirsly and Lamertz (2008)

Salzmann *et al.* (2005) suggest that the best available evidence points to considerable within-industry variation in the ability of plants to combine environmental improvement with increasing business success. An implication is that the business case is easier to establish for a whole industry than it is for individual enterprises within the industry. An industry may be reconfigured to combine improved environmental and business performance, but there will be winners and losers in the process of adjustment both in terms of companies and localities. For example, at one stage it was estimated that the top ten oil companies in the USA had environmental expenditures that varied from slightly over five to slight over one per cent of annual sales, reflecting their different situations in meeting similar environmental standards (Walley and Whitehead 1996).

What influences the business case?

Evidence of the relationship between business and environmental performance is of some importance to the ecological modernization thesis (Box 8.5). This thesis believes that encouraging business to recognize the opportunities for profitable enterprise is ultimately the way environmental challenges will be overcome (Gibbs 2002: 9). This is the root of the claim that 'the way out of the ecological crisis seems only possible by going further into the process of industrialisation'

(Spaargaren and Mol 1992: 14). The qualification to this claim is that businesses must be given the right market signals to identify and profit from their environment impacts. In economists' terms this means that a price is put on environmental externalities and that this price is incorporated in market prices (Huber 1985; Gouldson and Murphy 1996). Until 'ecology is economized' it can be argued that the lack of return on environmental investments reflects the failure of the market to price externalities. In this way, the notion of a business case is misleading if it is intended to imply some freely arrived at evaluation without reference to the context in which decisions are made.

Box 8.5 **Ecological modernization**

Ecological modernists argue that it is possible to develop economically and socially, equating negative environmental impacts with inefficiency (Morad 2007: 29). Ecological modernization offers a way of countering the argument that economic growth is inherently in contradiction with the aspiration for sustainable development (see, for example, Daly 1996). Its origins are generally linked to the contributions of Huber (1982) and Jänicke (1985). The central argument is that the way out of the ecological crisis is to accelerate processes already evident with the progress of industrialization (Spaargaren and Mol 1992). Huber (1982, 1985) expressed this in terms of the need for an ecological switchover in which environmental criteria become more integrated within production and consumption processes. A precedent for this is seen in the way that economic activity has already been modified through social policy and employment regulation to accommodate other welfare concerns. In a similar way, ecological modernists foresee a need and opportunity to elevate the attention to environmental welfare and envisage that this can be achieved through changes in the sectoral composition of economies and the technology employed by individual enterprises. This optimistic perspective offers a potential rationalization for action, but it is important to recognize the internal differences among modernists as well as the larger challenge from those who believe that it underplays the nature and scale of social change required for truly sustainable forms of development.

Business cases are influenced by the perception of the need to change practices, and the opportunities for so doing. These perceptions are socially constructed rather than being based on a straightforward cost–benefit calculation (Hannigan 1995; Liberatoire 1995). At present some environmental issues gain wide attention while others are neglected. A large scale example of this is seen with the way that climate change has become a major motivation for action while other environmental issues remain neglected (Carr and Mpande 1996), and while the debate about the anthropogenic contribution to global warming continues (Byatt *et al.* 2006; Carter *et al.* 2006). Similarly, it has been shown how the motivation for environmental action varies between industries (Sterner 2003: 122). Some proactive 'green' companies operate in industries with an inherent interest in environmental awareness (such as health products, cosmetics and travel), some may be driven by motivated managers but other times going green is more of a pre-emptive business strategy. Indeed, it is frequently observed that much of the business willingness to invest in environmental initiatives is driven by the belief that this will assist them to shape government actions and future regulatory regimes rather than the pursuit of direct income (Labatt and Maclaren 1998; Hoffman 2005; Kruger 2005). Business cases involve political choices and consequently, presentations of the environment as offering opportunities for mutual advantage have been judged technocentric and overly simplistic (Murphy and Gouldson 2000: 43). In this regard it is important to consider how the business–environment agenda has been reshaped to make it appear that it offers opportunity for profitable enterprise.

Generally, the debate about environmental responsibilities and opportunities is driven by issues that are widely perceived rather than as a response to the weight of objective data. This is partly because participants generally find it difficult to evade the latest dogmatic fad when selecting matters to place on their agenda (Soyez 2002). This is especially so when popularly perceived issues are translated into regulatory priorities, as regulation, actual and potential, can be critical in forcing or facilitating the adoption of innovations that enable significant changes in business practice. Regulation can establish the imperative for improvement and reduce the barriers to action. Requiring groups of enterprises to act simultaneously enables supporting infrastructure to be developed and can imply markets must adapt to the new business environment. Left to market forces alone, it may be only in the medium to long term that innovation produces environmental and economic benefit, and this raises a major barrier to action without regulatory pressure. Public policy can be decisive in encouraging the take up of environmental technologies, such as the way clean air legislation forced automobile manufacturers to invest in the development of catalytic converter technology (Blowfield and Murray 2008: 137). In the light of this some ecological modernists pin their hopes on the development of 'smart regulation' rather than market forces (Jänicke 2008).

The possibility of clever regulation needs to be judged against the capacity of regulatory agencies to change business calculations. Regulation can change the viability of adopting a specific technology, but it is not clear that regulators have the capacity to fundamentally change the willingness of business to incorporate environmental concerns into their long term strategy. Murphy and Gouldson (2000) arrive at this conclusion based on an analysis of the effort to encourage participation in integrated pollution control in England and Wales. This form of control involved intensive interaction between representatives of the regulatory agency and environmental managers in individual companies. The aim was to negotiate solutions fitted to the circumstances of individual plants as part of an effort to shift business perception of the pay back from addressing their environmental impacts. Through the programme pollution inspectors were tasked to negotiate the 'best practical environmental options' for minimizing emissions from plants regulated under the empowering legislation. This was envisaged partly as an opportunity to encourage a search for 'win-win' investment based on clean technology rather than 'end-of-pipe' responses. Murphy and Gouldson (2000) suggest that inspectors stimulated some willingness to prioritize specific environmental actions that had a short to medium term impact, but that they were unable to influence the way companies tended to look on environmental investment as a compliance cost rather than a business opportunity. While this outlook persists the likelihood of seeing a business case is less than what it would be if environmental responsibilities were integrated within a long term business strategy.

The extent to which ecology will be economized and whether this will have the stimulus intended has also to be considered. Particular hope has been placed on the ability of market-based solutions (such as emissions trading, transferable quotas and environmental offsets) to provide ways of pricing environmental externalities and ensuring that environmental leadership can be rewarded in the marketplace (Epstein 2008). There has been a significant shift in public policy toward the use of these tools and this contributes to some of the optimism that business will support green initiatives. There are two main ways to explain the change in approach to environmental policy with different implications for the willingness to continue to trial market-based instruments (Stavins 2003). A normative approach focuses on the choice that ought to be made according to policy theory and evidence of how policies have operated in practice. A political economy approach looks at how choices have been made in practice, noting that the preferences of interested parties (politicians, public agency staff, environmental campaign groups and affected businesses) has a big influence on environmental management choices.

One assessment is that thus far a collective desire to believe in the superiority of market-based instruments better explains their diffusion than evidence of their greater effectiveness in practice (Stavins 2003). Thus, although it is possible to point to some successful uses of market-based instruments this does not indicate that other forms of regulation have become redundant (Sterner 2003; Box 8.6). A smooth path to a future where environmental impacts are integrated within business decision making is a distant prospect.

***Box 8.6* Controlling sulphur dioxide emissions**

The control of sulphur dioxide (SO_2) emissions from power generation in the USA is frequently the main example given of a successful use of tradeable permits. Responding to a growing acid rain problem, the SO_2 emissions reduction programme aimed to cut the annual SO_2 emissions from power plants by 10 million tons under phase one (1995–2000) and by a similar amount in phase two (2000–2010). It set a cap, allocated permits and allowed trading in permits among any party that wished to buy or sell them, including environmentalists seeking to reduce the availability of permits. The scheme was softened by allowing offsets (allowing emissions to be exceeded in some localities); bubbles (allowing a group of plants to be treated as one unit); and banking (allowing permits to be saved for future years) and did not seek to be comprehensive of all pollution sources.

Phase one targets were achieved helped by favourable supporting conditions that suggest the trading scheme may have been incidental to the outcome:

- The cost of abatement technology such as air scrubbers fell significantly after the programme started.

- Simultaneous deregulation of the rail industry decreased the cost of freight and increased the commercial availability of low sulphur coal.
- Some states introduced local environmental regulations that added to the pressure on power plants to cut emissions.

Source: Sterner (2003); Kruger (2005)

An appealing possibility is that business cluster development offers a way for local economic development agencies to enhance the willingness and capacity of business to support environmental initiatives. As well as the assumption that close geographical proximity of enterprises and supporting business services enhances the capacity for innovation, other attributes might be thought to encourage business in clusters to demonstrate environmental leadership (Weiss 2008: 22):

- There are a large number of potential partners to support collaborative projects and to share research costs and industry research facilities. The likelihood of effective collaboration is increased as shared traditions, shared problems and shared ties to the locality encourage mutual trust and interaction between industry participants through deliberate and chance encounters.
- There are a large number of potential users of newly developed technologies with demand further enhanced by the tendency for cluster enterprises to share similar problems. To the extent that cluster enterprises are relatively similar to each other, an approach adopted by one firm is likely to be relevant to others.
- Clustering can raise the economic significance of an industry and encourage government efforts to assist it to address environmental issues in ways that will enhance its competitiveness. At the extreme, where a country's main export sector is spatially concentrated the locality attracts policy attention on grounds of national and regional importance.

These possibilities are consistent with idealized accounts of business clusters (such as Porter 2000) and in practice need to be balanced against the possibility that a community's high dependence on an industry may reduce the pressure to address environmental impacts. As well, based on evidence reviewed in the discussion of business clusters (Chapter 5), the knowledge sharing encouraged by a cluster may not be positive for the environment. It may result in an industrial culture that is resistant to taking new approaches to old problems or that is resistant to technologies that threaten to upset established industry structures.

A study of the Swedish pulp and paper industry in the 1980s concluded that the main impact of a cluster on industry knowledge came through the enhanced capability of regulatory authorities as a consequence of frequent dealings with cluster enterprises (Soyez 1985 cited in Weiss 2008: 29). The local population were considered passive in their relationship to the cluster industry rather than either being a force for change or strong defenders of their industry. The lack of community pressure to address environmental issues that resulted was reinforced by Swedish geography (industrial activity being dispersed at low density in regions that were perceived to maintain a high level of environmental amenity) and by the dependence of the local population on the pulp and paper industry for their livelihoods. The tendency for communities that are dependent on a specific industry to accept environmental risks rather than encourage their eradication has been observed in other contexts (Wynne 1992) and in the extreme can even lead communities to see a future in dirty industry (Perry 1985).

In the more recent context of Germany's kraft pulp industry, it was similarly concluded that industry clusters had no consistent impact on increasing a locality's perception of or ability to address environmental issues (Weiss 2008). This study examined how clusters of industry expertise affected the willingness of a locality to accept a new sulphite pulp plant. With best environmental practice, production of this raw material can be relatively benign, but it is perceived popularly to be a highly polluting activity. The possibility existed that an industry cluster would have most likelihood of capturing a new plant based on its understanding of how the environmental impacts can be minimized and because of the community's existing links to the pulp industry. The analysis of local reactions to a prospective new plant revealed that local debates were informed primarily by national-level discussions of environmental problems. The relatively uniform perception that sulphite pulp is always dirty was not challenged by industry insight existing within clusters or by the larger community living within the clusters. Fear of drawing attention to their existing pulp industry and being perceived as 'job killers' if they raised awareness of the industry's environmental issues partly explained the quiescence. In the case of one pulp cluster, there was evidence of local expertise informing discussion of the environmental technology that could be employed, but this did not continue into efforts to attract a new plant. Overall, the conclusion was that a weak industry cluster might prove the most likely to encourage informed debate (Weiss 2008: 29). This claim is based on two assumptions: a weak concentration of industry expertise is sufficient to identify how technology can be modified for environmental gains; communities with a weak economic specialization are open to the possibility that high pollution industries can be rendered environmentally benign. For the present these assumptions are speculative. A cluster of economic expertise in itself does not mean that local agendas can be divorced from national perceptions of business impacts on the environment.

Eco-effective development

The linkage of local economic development and the environment takes on a more active form in various projects designed to encourage the greater localization of business transactions. The idea that building local self reliance is a route to a more prosperous local economy has a long heritage based on the simple proposition that importing goods and services drains income away from a locality (Midmore and Thomas 2006). This concern has found new applications when linked to a concern about the state of the environment. These projects offer a different kind of evidence about the extent of 'win-win' opportunities related to the success of schemes that proactively seek to support environmentally conscious enterprise. Depending on the form that projects take, a higher test is placed on what counts as an environmental win than when incremental business decision making is evaluated. Much of the commentary about the opportunities for eco-industrial development is based on the principle that 'greened' localities should not be able to grow by expanding their environmental footprint (Gibbs 2002). To achieve this requires substantial changes in business practice and significant changes in the composition of local economies.

Eco-localists (Box 8.7) can be viewed as occupying a strong sustainability extreme on the spectrum of views about how far economic activity must change to provide a net environmental dividend (Curtis 2003). As well as encouraging regional self containment, eco-localism seeks a return to forms of commerce that existed before the development of integrated national, and more recently international economies. It is the perspective that sees new opportunities in local currency systems and barter, food and housing cooperatives, farmers' markets, permaculture, car sharing, home-based working and micro enterprise ventures (Curtis 2003). Whether local economic agencies need to work with such an agenda and go backwards to a green future is unclear. Inspired by industrial ecology, other agendas seek to combine modern technology with environmental and economic improvement. The central component is a move away from linear to closed loop industrial systems in which the effluents and wastes from one process serve as the input materials for other processes, or are recycled for further production (Gibbs and Deutz 2005). This technological re-engineering is not universally seen to depend on increased local self containment of industrial activity as much as the development of a form of 'super-industrialization' that lessens the dependence on resource intensive and environmentally burdensome sectors (Mol 1997). Nonetheless, encouraging linkages between co-located enterprises is viewed frequently as a way of facilitating the use of specialized environmental services and transfers of energy and materials between producers (Dunn and Steinemann 1998; Allenby 1999). Examining this agenda raises different issues about the desirability and practicality of greening local economic development.

Box 8.7 **Eco-localism**

'Eco-localists' advocate locally orientated, import substitution, linkage-building policies over long distance trade, especially with regard to the supply of everyday needs. They see value in an 'in my back yard' (IMBY) effect. IMBY argues that innovation is stimulated when the environmental side effects of producing and consuming goods and services stay where they are created. Long distance trade is one of the processes through which environmental impacts are transferred in a way that lessens the incentive to reduce pollution and resource depletion. Eco-localists support the cutting back of non essential consumption and less private ownership of resources that can be obtained through shared ownership and services. Locally owned businesses are seen to gain strength from their reliance on human relationships, cultural distinctiveness and employee commitment. It is believed that place-based businesses are more likely to protect local environment resources than businesses without particular dependence on any one locality. Eco-localism is thus presented as an antidote to the perceived economic vulnerability and environmental damage created by globalization.

Source: Curtis (2003)

Eco-localism – staying home to eat

The possibility of securing a double dividend from encouraging increased local production of food for local consumption has been taken up in many localities. The motivation may sometimes be driven by concerns about the rise of capitalist agriculture, the ethics associated with globalized food production and the loss of local distinctiveness (Friedmann 1994; Murdoch and Miele 1999, 2002; Murdoch *et al.* 2000; Hendrickson and Heffernan 2002). An economic motivation arises where the emphasis shifts to the concern to reduce 'food miles' (Paxton 1994), the value of short food supply chains (Marsden *et al.* 1999; Renting *et al.* 2003) and the opportunities for promoting ecological entrepreneurship (Adams 2002; Marsden and Smith 2005). These agendas overlap in practical projects such as local branding, support to farmers' markets and buy-local campaigns.

As with the larger suggestion that addressing environmental concerns offers business opportunities for profitable enterprise, supporters of localized food production suggest it fits with a number of social trends collectively indicating that a counter-revolution in food production and consumption is underway (Suzuki and Dressel 2002; Guthrie *et al.* 2006):

- Affluent consumers are paying less attention to cheapness and quantity and more to quality, rarity and esteem for artisan production methods (Fernandez-Armesto 2001).
- There is increased desire to eat 'real' rather than synthetic foods and to reject the products of industrialized agriculture (Adams 2002; Szmigin *et al.* 2003; Hinrichs *et al.* 2004).
- Conscious consumption is displacing conspicuous consumption and 'slow food' is displacing 'fast food' (Honore 2004; Hamilton 2005).
- Inner city areas and small rural towns that have lost retailing and service functions to shopping malls and retail parks are being repopulated by locally owned enterprises that are valued for their business offerings and connection to social networks (Guthrie *et al.* 2006).

These processes provide the context in which it is argued that local producers of quality food products are able to secure premium prices, and local economies are able to retain an increased share of the enhanced profits obtained by food producers. Thus, in their review of farmers' markets in New Zealand, Guthrie *et al.* (2006) repeat a number of indicators of the economic advantages of localized production. They suggest, for example, that growers do not have to sell as much produce to make the same income as they can capture more of the final price received compared with when using market intermediaries. A four fold increase in the profit margin on each unit of sales is considered reasonable and only part of the gain, since local producers utilize local resources. Overall, it is suggested that every $10 spent on local produce can return in the order of $24 to the local area, whereas the same expenditure at a supermarket would generate $14 (Guthrie *et al.* 2006: 569). If such attractive economic advantages exist, a new wave of agricultural entrepreneurship can be envisaged. The likelihood of this occurring has been assessed in terms of competition, replicability and uneven development (Goodman 2004).

In open economies, it can be assumed that opportunities for increased income will attract the attention of competing producers. This means that to sustain the initial income advantage there must be something about the product and its production that maintains barriers to market entry. In contrast, elements of an apparently alternative food production model are comparatively easy to replicate in terms of qualities such as 'traditional', 'fresh', 'local' and 'organic'. Indeed, supermarket chains have frequently acted quickly to source 'local' foods and in some respects are strongly positioned to take advantage of any growth in demand for non conventional food products (Banks and Bristow 1999). For example, the UK supermarket chain Waitrose now reports sourcing local produce from close to 500 suppliers, with two-thirds of products delivered directly to individual supermarkets and over 150 of their stores having dedicated regional display areas for local produce (John Lewis Partnership 2009: 8). Similarly, the international supermarket chain Tesco reports substantial growth in the sale of local regional product lines (Hawkes 2008). In the minds of many consumers, conventionally produced foods are as likely to be considered local products as are organically produced foods (Winter 2003). Particularly where consumer interest is motivated by food quality concerns, corporate food retailers have modified their supply chain management to incorporate heightened product traceability, which includes more recognition of the source locality and methods of production. Similarly, locality branding schemes may put the emphasis on locality characteristics rather than specific methods of production, with a consequence that conventional enterprise can benefit, as well as enterprises adhering to strong sustainability practices (Box 8.8). Moreover, long surviving regions of artisan production, such as the Parmesan cheese cluster (van der Ploeg and Renting 2000; Roest and Menghi 2000) exist under a constant cost-price squeeze that originates in the plentiful availability of close industrial substitutes.

Box 8.8 **Product labelling**

The French *appellation d'origine controlee* (AOC) is the oldest form of regional product labelling in Europe and is regarded as the strictest of its kind. Products covered by AOC labels are controlled by the state to assure both their territorial origin and their conformity to precise rules for production and processing that are intended to guarantee their distinctive character. The system is guided by the concept of *terroir*, which translated crudely refers to how production in specific places results in unique product qualities. This is typically seen to depend on a combination of specific environmental conditions and methods of production perfected and handed down over many generations. Originally applied mainly to wine and spirits, product labelling based on claims of *terroir* have expanded to a growing range of land-based products, including cheese and meats.

AOCs are credited with helping to maintain agricultural profitability in areas that are marginal for industrial farming methods. Natural environmental qualities are given most attention in the decision to award an AOC, but this does not mean that production is beneficial for the environment. It may, for example, limit the varieties of crop planted. It may help preserve traditional hillside terraces that protect from erosion but that nonetheless maintain a modified rather than natural environment. Boundaries may reflect historical associations rather than ecological transitions and the process through which they are agreed is affected by lobbying. Tasting panels set up to monitor product conformance are political as well as gastronomic arbitrators. Certification changes are influenced by an increasing range of stakeholders, whose interests include tourism and rural development linked to the cachet and draw of speciality products and the cultural events that can be constructed around them.

Source: Barham (2003)

Positive community development impacts of locally based food production have equally been questioned (DuPuis and Goodman 2005). Advocates of locally based food production see opportunities for 'recovering a sense of community' (Esteva 1994), basing food production on an 'ethic of care' (Holloway and Kneafsey 2004) and aligning food production with local ecologies (Murdoch *et al.* 2000). The assumption that locally based food systems are inherently more socially just than food systems controlled by international food companies has been interpreted as little more than the 'politics of conversion' (Childs 2003; DuPuis and Goodman 2005: 361). A small, unrepresentative group asserts preferences as to what is in everyone's best interest and then seeks to change the world by converting others to its point of view. This contrasts with the 'politics of respect' which avoids the presentation of idealized communities as attainable entities. In their place the ideal is to encourage debate between persons representative of different sections of society on the directions of change that might be pursued. One indicator of the politics of conversion at work is the tendency for local food systems to be most strongly supported by a narrow range of consumers who might broadly be characterized as elitist and that may give more priority to ecological sustainability over social justice (Allen *et al.* 2003). A study in New Zealand of the affinity between Mäori and the country's largest discount retailer has suggested similar evidence of elitism in the claimed damage to community wellbeing from externally owned enterprise (Box 8.9).

Box 8.9 **Red sheds and Mäori**

The Warehouse Group owns New Zealand's largest chain of discount general merchandize stores. The group's 'red sheds' have spread from cities to smaller towns, frequently in the face of opposition from local retailers. Sayers *et al.* (2008) assessed what Mäori organizations and individuals in three small towns felt about the red sheds. Mäori are New Zealand's 'first nation' people, now accounting for around

15 per cent of the country's population but much more than this in some small towns. While represented in all socio economic categories, a disproportionate share of Māori have low incomes, experience of unemployment and poor health.

In the small towns studied, Māori make more frequent trips to a red shed than do other ethnic groups, are more positive about the service provided, more responsive to special promotions and more inclined to include a visit to the store as part of a 'day out'. From these and related observations, the investigators suggest that Māori have 'appropriated' the store as a social and cultural addition to their life rather than being passive victims of the consumerism that the store encourages. One reason for this is that the Warehouse stores employ Māori and are regarded by them as a good place to work compared with other retail chains. Some Māori informants also comment on their comfort when shopping in a warehouse store layout compared with a traditional store where there can be a feeling that 'someone is watching you'. These endorsements lead to the suggestion that critiques of 'big box retailers' such as Wal-Mart are affected by romantic and nostalgic ideas about what constitutes a community that overlook the fact that not everyone was happy with the Main Street of old.

The environmental benefits of local provisioning do not escape serious questioning, particularly when linked to the claimed benefits of reduced 'foodmiles' (DEFRA 2005; Wyen and Vanzetti 2008). This phrase originated in the early 1990s to refer to the distance that food products travel between their place of production and final sale to end consumers (Paxton 1994). The inference was that the further the distance travelled the greater was the environmental impact, a message that was taken up by environmental campaign groups and academic proponents of eco-localism (Curtis 2003). In the context of public concern over global warming, the association between distance and environmental impact attracted wide attention, partly as it offered concerned households an intuitively appealing way to combat climate change that was easy to comply with. The concept has since been discredited as a meaningful measure of environmental impact for three main reasons:

- The environmental impacts of transporting food products capture only part of the food production life cycle. The impact of long distance freight can be offset by comparatively low environmental impacts during the production and harvesting phases. It has been shown, for example, that the energy consumed in the production, distribution and sale of diary products, lamb, apples and onions from New Zealand in the United Kingdom is less than that associated with more locally sourced alternatives even after taking into account the difference in freighting distance (Saunders *et al.* 2006). Similar calculations have been made when comparing the energy used in the production of lambs in New Zealand and Germany (Schlich and Fleissner 2003) and when comparing roses grown in Kenya with those grown in the Netherlands (Williams 2006).
- Distance travelled does not take into account the relative impacts of different travel modes. Carbon emissions from long haul air freight are over 100 times larger than those from sea freight (DEFRA 2008). Excluding

localized pollution impacts around major sea ports, there can be environmental gains when relatively short distance air freight is replaced by long distance sea freight.
- The focus on food miles overlooks how distribution in the end market can account for a large share of the environmental costs. A standard British shopping trip by car of 6.4 kilometres to collect a weekly purchase of groceries (20 kilograms) can use the same energy required to transport the same weight over 8,500 kilometres by sea (Heyes and Smith 2008). Consequently, up to two thirds of the total environmental impacts can be accounted for when environmental assessments focus on final distribution to the point of sale, shopping trips and on-farm production externalities.

Bearing in mind the extent to which a focus on foodmiles alone is misleading, any shift in consumer purchases responding to this issue has the potential to cause a net increase in environmental externalities and a loss of income in food producing nations that are distant from their markets (Ballingall and Winchester 2009). These losses might have some justification if environmentally sensitive local production grows to replace more conventional methods of production. In practice, much of the popular concern with foodmiles is driven by market protectionism, opportunity for conventional enterprise to obtain commercial advantages and food security concerns.

Industrial ecology and localization

Industrial ecology encompasses a large set of ideas that in various ways emphasize how science, technology and the power of the state can engineer a change in the relationship between the economy and ecology (Gibbs 2000). The recent history of the concept is traced to the late 1980s but is linked to the longer interest in finding ways to minimize waste (Korhonen 2002). Moving away from linear to closed loop industrial systems is central to the agenda, with the objective of turning the effluents and wastes from one process into the input materials for other processes if they cannot be eliminated entirely (Gibbs and Deutz 2005). Waste and pollution are indicators of uneconomic and harmful practices that should be minimized by dovetailing them with the supply of raw materials (Barrow 2006).

Parallels with natural ecology are drawn partly in the appropriate scale of analysis (Frosch and Gallopoulos 1989). An industrial system as a whole should aim to conserve raw materials by minimizing waste rather than this target being given to individual companies. Indeed, seeking to minimize the waste of individual enterprises may be counterproductive as volumes may be too small to attract processes that can utilize it as a raw material. Accumulated into large volumes it is more realistic to envisage the appearance of 'niche species' that can transform wastes into useful inputs (Dunn and Steinemann 1998). Producer–consumer–recycler linkages in current industrial systems are small scale and flow from producers and consumers to recyclers (Korhonen 2002). In natural ecosystems, the largest flows are from producers (plants) to recyclers (micro organisms, bacteria, fungi) and this gives direction to how industrial ecosystems can evolve. The analogy to natural ecosystems becomes more challenging when the process of change is considered. Rather than the 'survival of the fittest', trust and cooperation among members of an eco-industrial network is generally thought to be essential (Brand and De Bruijn 1999; Gibbs 2002: 133). In the industrial ecosystem world, symbiotic relationships rely on partnership and interdependence in place of the emphasis on independence and competitiveness in the traditional view of industrial systems (Côté and Cohen-Rosenthal 1998).

In an ideal industrial ecosystem, there would be complete or near complete internal recycling of materials and 'zero waste'. Advocates see this as an aspiration that identifies a target to work towards rather than something that can be realized in practice. Nonetheless, most advocates envisage that a substantial change is possible over a timescale of 'several decades' to interconnect large parts of the industrial economy in ways that will benefit participating firms financially while reducing environmental impacts (Tibbs 1992; Graedel and Allenby 1995; Cohen-Rosenthal 2003). In addition, industrial ecology is seen as a way of improving life styles by shortening commuter distances as cleaner industrial practices permit increased co-location of different land uses (Deutz and Gibbs 2004).

The eco-industrial park has emerged as the major application of industrial ecology principles in local economic development policy (Erkman 1997; Gibbs et al. 2005). The first wave of such parks emerged during the 1990s, predominantly in North America but examples are now found in many regions of the world (Gibbs et al. 2005). The necessary attributes of an eco-industrial park are debated, with some perspectives expecting them to be relatively self contained industrial communities while others see them more as a node within a larger network of inter-connected businesses (Chertow 1999; Schlarb 2001). Generally, they are intended to be something more than a collection of environmentally responsive organizations, or simply a collection of enterprises sharing an environmental technology (for example common reliance on solar power), and more than a concentration of resource recovery and recycling enterprises. At the same time, the initially tight focus on high levels of inter-company partnering among the enterprises co-located on a park has been watered down in preference to a more permissive definition in which park occupants show a willingness to gradually deepen their own range of environmental commitments. This approach is unsatisfactory to those who expect as a minimum that some form of waste and energy exchange between park occupants is required (Gibbs et al. 2005: 180).

One potential controversy with eco-industrial parks as they have been implemented can be dismissed. Even among sympathetic observers it is accepted that they have yet to demonstrate their ability to foster latent industrial ecosystems (Cohen-Rosenthal and McGalliard 1998; Korhonen 2002; Deutz and Gibbs 2004; Gibbs et al. 2005). The claim being made for eco-industrial parks is that they are an experiment worth persisting with, as gradually over time they have scope to demonstrate the viability of industrial ecology as an organizing strategy.

Two sources of this optimism provide issues for debate. First, a precedent exists for localized eco-industrial development that indicates the opportunity for replication, although it may take longer than envisaged originally. Second, the underlying principle is sound even if there are challenges to its practical implementation.

Much of the work on eco-industrial parks has drawn upon the experience of Kalundborg, Denmark (Box 8.10). Many have believed the town provides evidence of what can be achieved by applying industrial ecology principles to local economic development (Lowe 1997; Brand and De Bruijn 1999; Gibbs 2002; Jacobsen 2003; Gibbs et al. 2005). A number of limitations and aspects of this story need to be considered before judging it a model industrial ecosystem:

- The network was built on one-to-one deals (16 bi-lateral contracts existed in the mid 1990s) rather than network-wide decision making. Individual deals have responded to immediate shared economic opportunities and have not relied on modifications of technology or the costing of environmental impacts. For example, the transfer of steam from the power plant to the refinery enabled the refinery to avoid the need to replace its own steam boilers.
- The supply of flare gas to Gyproc and the power station ceased in the early 2000s.
- National environmental regulations governing sulphur emissions introduced in 1992 required the refinery to install a sulphur recovery unit. This had the impact of increasing the quality of refinery gas to make it useable by the power plant. Similarly, the district heating system enabled the replacement of domestic oil furnaces that were a source of local air pollution.
- The network has many leakages. The power plant mainly burns coal rather than the refinery sourced gas; sulphur goes outside the town for use in the manufacture of sulphuric acid; Gyproc uses imported as well as locally sourced gypsum.
- Only a small proportion of industrial by-products are consumed by the network. In terms of material flows the volume of exchange is large only by including the use of sludge from Novo Nordisk's processes and the fish farm's water treatment plant as fertilizer or pig food by farms neighbouring the town. For use as fertilizer, imported lime is added to the waste and it is supplied free of charge.
- Core parts of the network – the power plant and refinery – are continuous processes with a high degree of reliability in the ability to maintain the supply of their by-product. A network may be harder to create around enterprises in 'footloose' industries affected by continuous competitive pressures.

Box 8.10 Kalundborg, Denmark as prototype industrial ecosystem

Kalundborg is a small coastal town (population around 16,500) seen as an example of spontaneous self organization into a web of waste and energy exchanges. This network evolved over a period of over 20 years, apparently confirming that time is required for industrial ecosystems to develop. The network is usually described as having five main participants:

- Statoil Refinery, Denmark's largest oil refinery.
- Asnæs Power Station, Denmark's largest electricity generator that is primarily coal-fired but that also burns gas created as an oil refinery by-product and in return supplies the refinery with steam.
- Gyproc, a manufacturer of plasterboard that utilizes gypsum produced by the power plant's desulphurization process.
- Novo Nordisk, a biotechnological company producing pharmaceuticals and industrial enzymes that utilizes steam from the power plant for some of its energy needs.
- The City of Kalundborg receives steam from the power plant to supply heating to local houses.

In addition, in some accounts a fish farm and neighbouring farms are included in the network. Some of the heated salt water created through the power plant's cooling system is utilized by the fish farm. Neighbouring farms are supplied with fertilizer and feedstock. The origins are traced to the city council's construction of a water pipeline from a local lake to avoid the refinery's need to draw on ground water supplies. Gyproc's location in Kalundborg in 1972 added to the network as it was established to use the refinery's flare gas as a low cost source of power.

Rather than a pointer to the future, the willingness to view Kalundborg as a demonstration of industrial ecology at work may better illustrate some shortcomings in the underlying concept. Indeed, the secondary uses of power station steam and heated water and the agricultural use of industrially produced compost and feedstock is not unusual. Moreover the context of a small, densely populated sea-bordered country is important in bringing together a largely chance juxtaposition of non competing operations with complementary wastes. The case does not indicate any major step forward in industrial orgernization or any overall reduction in environmental impact for Denmark as a whole. For the present, it appears that industrial ecology is a catchword encompassing many agendas rather than being restricted to a specific programme of action (O'Rourke *et al.* 1996).

Industrial ecology as environmental strategy

Distinguishing how industrial ecology differs from pollution prevention strategies provides one perspective on its likelihood of producing effective local economic strategies. Pollution prevention strategies are broadly understood as efforts to reduce the amount of any hazardous substance, pollutant or contaminant entering any waste stream or otherwise released into the environment so that hazards to public health and the environment are minimized (Oldenburg and Geiser 1997: 103). Industrial ecology, on the other hand, emphasizes the role of linked up industrial systems in making possible the conversion and re-use of wastes, with less concern placed on the production of pollution and wastes in the first instance. While there is scope for the two concepts to overlap, there are at least three ways that industrial ecology creates additional environmental and business risk (Oldenburg and Geiser 1997):

- Industrial ecology encourages recycling and the transfer of materials from one place to another. Liability issues arise with the storage and transfer of industrial by-products. Recycling wastes from one firm to another often involves some degree of 'downgrading' compared with the quality of the original material. With the exception of a few materials (for example glass and aluminium) there are limits to the number of rounds of recycling possible. In some cases, such as plastic food packaging, regulation can forbid the use of recycled material for the original use.
- With pollution prevention economic gains can be captured by a single enterprise, although as discussed earlier there are limits to the lowering of production costs that can be achieved. Industrial ecology implies that equivalent gains are shared among a network of enterprises. Extending the life of materials through exchanges among enterprises may offer efficiencies for the economy as a whole, but these may not provide incentives to individual enterprises. The costs of preparing wastes for onward delivery, complying with regulation and establishing appropriate facilities, need to be weighed up against the price of virgin materials. Moreover, the investment in a 'waste-to-input-material' network has the potential to stifle future innovation so as to maintain the resource flows that have been committed to.
- Risk minimization is given little attention in discussions of industrial ecology. A network of material transfers should help to contain environmental risks but the building of exchange networks gives priority to the transfer of materials rather than the prioritization of risk. Indeed, it has been argued that industrial ecology initiatives have the potential to increase health and safety risks for employees as a consequence of the concentration and transfer of wastes and adaptations to industrial processes that may be made to facilitate exchange (Ashford 1997). By their nature pollution prevention strategies should at least target the reduction of pollutants.

The viability of materials interchange on any large scale has yet to be demonstrated, but it is likely that the costs of closing loops will frequently exceed the benefits for the enterprises involved (Esty and Porter 1998). This can suggest a role for public agencies in supporting the establishment of exchange facilities, but formidable barriers seem likely to persist. Such barriers have been recognized in the case of Kalundborg, with one study reflecting that it is possible that industrial ecology makes partners too dependent upon each other and creates an inflexible situation in which there is a danger that inefficiencies within the companies are not dealt with (Brand and De Bruijn 1999: 230).

The extent of these economic barriers to realizing an eco-industrial network depends partly on the geographical scale to which interactions are confined. Localized exchange networks such as eco-industrial parks provide the greatest contrast with pollution prevention strategies and the greatest increase in business risks (Boons and Baas 1997). Applied at the level of product and material life cycles encompassing dispersed enterprises there can be less reliance on stable, one-to-one business partnerships which are a particular source of economic risk. Indeed, some versions of industrial ecology give primary attention to encouraging 'extended producer responsibility' in which manufacturers are expected to manage environmental impacts across the life cycle of their products (Rainey 2005). Even at this more flexible scale there are challenges to attaining the 'win-win' outcome of more profitable enterprise and reduced environmental impact (Opoku 2004).

Discussion

The claim that it is possible to design local economic strategies that provide a double dividend of business growth and environmental improvement is problematic, as there is no agreement over what constitutes a 'win' for the environment. Most discussion of the greening of local economic development assumes that the world faces some form of environmental crisis that requires substantial changes in the organization and nature of business activity. A reflection of this is the assumption that environmental outcomes are countable only if they are realized across the economy as a whole, or even the planet as a whole. Environmental gains limited to the immediate locality do not count if it merely means that impacts are displaced, either spatially, temporarily or both. This may suggest that local economic strategies are subject to a severe test, but paradoxically it can also result in little critical scrutiny. Where the target is contributing to a radically new form of economy, bold strategies can be justified on the basis of the perceived need for change. Evidence of immediate business resistance can be rationalized on the grounds that it will take time to gain support for the new ways of working, and that further public policy coordination is required to provide business with incentives to participate. In this context there is a role for judging environmental wins against criteria that can be measured over the short and medium terms. Some will question the value of environmental gains that cannot guarantee an ongoing net improvement in environmental conditions. This uncertainty needs to be balanced against the greater ability to evaluate progress where projects have specific goals to be achieved over specific time frames.

To evaluate the ability to combine local economic and environmental development it is helpful to distinguish a pollution-prevention-pays perspective from an ecological-modernization perspective (Table 8.1). A pollution prevention perspective is here distinguished as one requiring that individual enterprises find reason to participate in green initiatives because of positive impacts on their individual business performance. A 'green initiative' is loosely defined as a project designed to offer some environmental gains over equivalent activity that does not make the same investment in environmental improvements. The ecological modernization perspective sees a need for some form of 'ecological switchover' that changes the relationship between the economy and the environment in favour of the latter. For this perspective a green initiative is one that contributes to the rebalancing of the economy and the environment as distinct from activity that may merely shift the incidence of environmental impacts. Something like this distinction has been

Table 8.1 Evaluation frameworks for green initiatives

	Pollution prevention pays	Ecological modernization
Environmental wins comprise	Eco-efficiency – reductions in ecological impacts and the resource intensity of individual business operations.	Eco-effectiveness – aggregate business activity operates with reduced environmental footprints
Economic wins comprise	Enhanced business performance reflected in financial, reputation and business growth indicators.	Changes in economy composition favouring activity with low environmental demands.
Eligible projects	Individual business initiatives that can reduce the intensity of energy and resource usage, increase the dependence on renewable resources and shift output to the more environmentally friendly options.	Projects designed to bring changes in industry practice and organization by including ecological criteria in business decisions.
Current evidence	Win-wins most likely to be captured at the industry level.	Large gap remains between current and required business practice; promoted models as yet unproven.
Dependence on regulatory change	Works within existing policy settings.	Requires an economic value to be put on nature.
Focus of change	Individual enterprises	Industrial systems and national economies
Assumption of environmental challenge	Environmental issues can be managed with incremental improvements in business practice.	Limits to growth require an ecological switchover.
Time horizon	Short term.	Long term.
Main purpose	Measures short time change and enables monitoring of policy intervention; may guide strategy designed for larger environmental wins.	Promotes a vision of long term change and coordinates action to realize society-wide change.

applied to the evaluation of eco-industrial parks (Deutz and Gibbs 2004). That study contrasted green initiatives with a place promotion motivation from those with the motivation of promoting industrial ecology: the former using eco-industrial parks as a tool to attract new investment in competition with other localities, while the latter aims to attract investment and encourage changes in industrial organization that deliver net environmental gains. Use of eco-industrial parks as a place promotion tool was judged unsatisfactory as it provides no guarantee that any substantial change in business practice is being encouraged.

Many of the contributions reviewed in this chapter develop from the ecological modernization framework. This framework can be questioned on at least four grounds:

- There is an enormous degree of uncertainty about the immediacy of the environmental limits to growth. In response to this uncertainty, the ecological modernization framework offers a normative and prescriptive theory (Blowers 1997: 852). It can be applied as a theoretical concept to analyse change (as in the way industrial ecology provides a model to judge developments against) but it is also a political programme based on judgements about what is desirable and feasible (Gibbs 2000: 12). The political programme is characterized by a mix of technological optimism, certainty in the need to amend the path of industrialization to fit within environmental limits and the relative neglect of the social and ethical context of change (Blowers 1997). Ecological modernization is premised on the assumption that environmental crisis is inevitable if economic trends do not change, but the response it offers provides no clear picture of the political institutions necessary to deliver a society that is able to develop sustainability. Ecological modernization can thus be seen as an incomplete standard by which to judge local economic development.

- Ecological modernization is targeted on the long term development of economies and is not readily applied to the evaluation of projects seeking to provide immediate opportunities for employment and business growth. A danger is that focusing on what might be desirable and feasible in the long term justifies initiatives that have little immediate prospect of success. Such a claim can be made in the case of eco-industrial parks. Initial evidence of a lack of adherence to the principles outlined by industrial ecology is explained by the complexity of the challenge rather than questioning of the underlying concept (Deutz and Gibbs 2004; Gibbs *et al.* 2005). Similarly, existing evidence that enterprises investing more than others in environmental initiatives generally do not gain a performance advantage can be dismissed on the grounds that this merely indicates a need for environmental costs and benefits to be more fully priced than they are at present. These types of judgement militate against critical evaluation of the underlying concepts and leave local agencies without guidance on how to determine whether projects are on track.

- Defenders of ecological modernization suggest that, compared with an agenda built on the goal of sustainable development, it offers analytical rigour and precision in exactly what needs to be done (for example Dryzek 1997:143). This claim is challenged by the existence of at least two streams of argument within the modernization movement: one emphasizes the ability of science and technology to resolve environmental challenges in combination with market decisions informed by the fuller pricing of environmental externalities; the alternative stream believes that social justice, income redistribution and increased democratization require equal attention (Hajer 1993; Christoff 1996).

- Local projects designed as contributions to an 'ecological switchover' must be coordinated with national and perhaps international initiatives. Placing an economic value on nature and modifying fiscal policies are central to the agenda of ecological modernists (Huber 1985; Gouldson and Murphy 1996). This reform cannot be instituted through local projects, but it critically affects the extent to which the environment can become a source of profitable enterprise. Innovations of the type being looked for by ecological modernists are not adopted on the basis of their individual characteristics alone (Kemp 1993;

Murphy and Gouldson 2000: 35). They must also be compatible with the larger network of institutions and aligned economic activities that are needed to facilitate the adoption of clean technologies. This indicates the role that ecological modernization can play in setting a long term strategic target and coordinating local action. The incremental steps open to local projects are nonetheless appropriately judged against incremental objectives whatever ambiguity this leaves about the real substance of the environmental gain.

The lesser test implied by a pollution prevention framework of merely requiring local initiatives to gain business support on the basis of immediate, individual business advantage has its shortcomings too. At the least, localized projects need to be coordinated if they are to build momentum to the attainment of higher policy goals (Dryzek 1997). If projects are designed with weak environmental objectives the distinctiveness of this area of activity tends to reduce. Framing projects in the context of ecological modernization or some other transformation programme offers a long term vision that may help to motivate participation and retain commitment to delivering environmental as well as economic goals. Where eco-industrial developments combine place promotion and larger environmental goals the more easily realized objectives might well displace more challenging eco-objectives (Gibbs and Deutz 2005: 462). Equally, setting overly ambitious policy goals may ultimately discredit projects and cause the abandonment of any attempt to promote some form of more environmentally responsible economy. A pollution prevention framework has the benefit of encouraging more learning from action within the scope and time horizons of local agencies.

The argument is not that one framework should replace the other. Rather, just as companies are recommended to develop a portfolio of environmental strategies differentiated by their ambition and certainty of realization (Rainey 2005) so local eco-industrial strategies might be differentiated by their mix of immediate and long term goals. Something like this separation has been proposed in the context of applying industrial ecology to current local economic development strategy. Schlarb (2001) and Chertow (1999) identify a range of intermediary steps on the way to the ultimate target of building local economies around materials and energy interchanges. Thus, in the initial phase in the development of an eco-industrial park they suggest that business use of environmental management systems, provision of sustainable buildings, job training, public participation and attracting an anchor tenant such as a power plant that has potential for providing resource transfers are among appropriate first stage targets. Such an approach is not liked by those who want assurance that the target will remain the fostering of industrial ecology and symbiosis based on inter-organizational networking (Gibbs and Deutz 2005: 456). For the present it remains to be discovered whether incremental steps will build into a larger transformation or whether aiming high from the outset will bring a swifter evolution in industrial practice. Another possibility has also to be considered: that the development and wide adoption of radical new technologies will have most impact in encouraging a step change in the relationship of the economy and the environment rather than the deliberate efforts to promote new models of industrial organization. Public policy has a role in this third possibility in facilitating or forcing the uptake of new technologies that imply changes within and between organizations, but this is primarily a role for national and international agencies rather than individual localities.

Conclusion

This chapter has explored the scope for 'win-win' local economic strategies that seek to encourage opportunities for business growth based on improved environmental performance. When examined in terms of the business case for environmental responsibility there is no consistent evidence that business and environmental performance are linked. This may reflect the increasing cost faced by individual businesses that continue to invest in environmental initiatives once the easy options for making pollution prevention pay have been exhausted. The evidence is not conclusive, as the business case perceived by managers may be hard to detect, being mostly linked to the reduction of downside operational risk and to measures that increase 'eco-efficiency' and that are hard to separate from 'normal' good management practice. The returns to business may materialize over the long term and affect issues such as employee and customer loyalty that are hard to value. Moreover, whatever the strength of this evidence, it is capable of being dismissed by those who advocate the promotion of 'eco-effectiveness'. Both these perspectives may agree that full returns from business investment in environmental responsibility will be evident only once environmental impacts are more fully reflected in market prices than they currently are. In this context it may be premature to search for evidence of 'win-win' outcomes until the business environment has become more supportive of environmental initiatives.

Promoting increased self containment has been a theme common to local economic strategies linked to the environment. This has been illustrated in the case of localized food production and consumption and the interest in applying industrial ecology to local economic development. Both areas of endeavour have yet to illustrate the delivery of the double dividend. Efforts to support the consumption of 'local' foods have yet to establish that conventional enterprise is not able to capture the opportunities arising from consumer interest in 'local' produce and are criticized for the extent to which it is assumed that all consumers have the same preferences. Industrial ecology remains a distant prospect and potentially more applicable at the level of product life cycle management than localized materials exchange.

Whatever the immediate evidence, ecological modernization theory provides a rationalization that encourages continued belief in the possibility of marrying economic and environmental development. This theory is claimed to offer a specific agenda for action, but in practice is supported by a broad church. The core projects to be realized are generally agreed, but the mechanisms for progressing change and timescale over which results are expected are not. This context is a challenge to the delivery of evidence that can resolve the scope and best opportunities for linking economic and environmental development. In particular, the willingness to support intermediary steps with modest environmental gains, as compared with requiring more ambitious environmental strategies to be pursued, divides ecological modernists and highlights the present uncertainty with the claim of 'win-win' opportunities. One interpretation of this claim is that the incremental steps on the road to a more sustainable future offer a continuous set of opportunities for profitable enterprise. Another interpretation is that the adjustment to a new, more environmentally benign form of economy will ultimately provide the opportunity to combine profitable and environmentally responsible enterprise. These alternatives have quite different implications for local economic development. The incremental approach is potentially an opportunity for local action but it is an approach that remains unconvincing to many ecological modernists.

9 Making progress in local economic development

There is a perspective that local economic development suffers from too little theory (Rowe 2009a). This claim is based partly on the judgement that much of the practical effort to promote local economic development is not well informed and consequently not particularly effective (Rowe 2005: 230). Others would agree that local economic development agencies frequently achieve little with their programmes, perhaps only 'tinkering on the margins of massive market forces' (Isserman 1994: 94). As a consequence, generating job announcements can be given more priority than delivering positions that are actually filled (Beer *et al.* 2003: 163). For Rowe (2009b), a theory of local economic development could contribute to the improvement of practice in a number of ways. It might help unify local development activity that is currently rendered somewhat incoherent by the variety of disciplinary fields that practitioners are drawn from: economics, geography, resource management and urban planning being potential prior areas of study. A core theory of local economic development might help career entrants immerse themselves into the system of knowledge that informs practice (Gunder 2004). A theoretical reference point might guide development professionals as they adjust to changes in the nature of economic activity and the targets of local economic policy. To the extent that it gave professionals a clearer understanding of their role, it might help relieve the pressure to which they are exposed, including the frequent need to justify their role to funding providers. There may also be an argument that a theoretically informed profession would better manage the need to compete with other professionals over investment projects. It might give something akin to a code of conduct and reduce the risk of excessive competition between local economic development officials affiliated to different agencies.

Some further justification for Rowe's call for a theory of local economic development may be seen in an evaluation of how economic development professionals rationalize their activity. A tendency to follow courses of action that offer administrative certainty over risk taking and innovation has been claimed (Rubin 1988; Beauregard 1993). As officials working in public agencies are faced with considerable uncertainty over their ability to make a demonstrable difference to the state of their local economy, there is a tendency to focus on the demands that come forward from businesses rather than working to an independent agenda. Economic development professionals may feel that their role is not well understood by others, including the people that they report to and rely on for the continuance of their job. A response is to seek out some certainty in their task, even if this amounts to a philosophy of 'shoot anything that flies and claim anything that falls' (Rubin 1988: 237). Responding to immediate demands, whether that be assistance in obtaining regulatory permits, finding a site or influencing a utility provider to prioritize provision for a key industry, gives the economic development professional scope to see a set of concrete outcomes. Moreover, attending to what may be individually low key demands gives the professional a basis for dialogue and networking with the business community that they may also view as a tangible and useful outcome of their role. An outcome can be a tendency to devote considerable time to making concessions to business that may have little economic development impact. Rubin's conclusion was that providing professionals with more certainty over the task to be performed and greater confidence in their role might assist economic development agencies to make a more substantial contribution than he saw them making.

A different perspective is that local economic development is affected by too much theory. According to this view, the multiplicity of theoretical perspectives claiming to justify particular courses of action spreads confusion among practitioners given the lack of a compelling evidential base from which to assess competing policy recommendations (Beer 2009: 63). Among the theoretical agendas claiming policy relevance Beer includes regulation theory and its emphasis on the creation of appropriate institutions for regional and local development; neoclassical models that suggest the importance of attracting investment or labour or both; new regionalism and the possibility of encouraging growth locally; new institutionalism and a focus on reducing transaction costs through information and infrastructure provision that reduces impediments to new investment. As a consequence, economic development practitioners could make a case for policy interventions as varied as subsidizing inward investment, devolving the management of national programmes, cluster promotion, business incubators and new enterprise formation. Rather than judicious selection, Beer (2009) suggests that the absence of consensus is more likely to result in all being ignored as there appears no compelling case to prioritize any single agenda. The absence of any tradition of evidence-based policy facilitates this lack of engagement as well as the lack of priority among academics to produce research that can be readily translated into practice. As a consequence, while there is a profusion of theory about local economic development, much of it remains too underdeveloped to be useable in practice. Tellingly for Beer, the new ideas that have had most impact on practice are associated with academics (Michael Porter and Richard Florida) who have engaged directly with the policy community and have been willing to translate their ideas into strategies that can be readily understood. The implication of this is that academics should make more effort to communicate their work beyond the usual academic channels. Echoing the criticism that academic theories are frequently 'fuzzy ideas' (Markusen 1999), less separation of theory development and practical application would potentially subject academic theories to greater quality assurance than occurs when there is little concern over their translation into specific policy advice.

A further perspective is that the emphasis on developing new theories and ideas has resulted in too little attention being paid to past insights (Taylor and Plummer 2003). That judgement has been made in reaction to the way that an institutionalist model of local economic development has come to dominate thinking in economic geography. Taylor and Plummer (2003) see institutionalism's influence in the stream of ideas, starting with the claim of a second industrial divide, a shift from Fordism to flexible accumulation and the creation of new industrial spaces. This line of argument sees economic activity as being socially constructed in the sense of it operating through networked relationships shaped by regional culture and local institutions. With economic growth based on networked enterprises, trust-based relationships that stimulate knowledge generation and sharing, learning and innovation the implication appears to be that prosperity can be built on any economic base provided it is appropriately specialized and rich in social capital. For Taylor and Plummer (2003) such prescriptions for growth would have been cut off had more attention been paid to the findings of previous generations of economic geographers. Studies of specialized regional economies as they existed in the half century after the 1920s reveal that business success frequently depended on breaking out from local transactions and local conventions. An enduring message may be that places that are successful in incubating and commercializing new technology are not necessarily well suited to taking that technology into mass market production. Keeping in mind the fate that befell yesterday's industrial clusters might cause more circumspection in presenting modern-day clusters as the perfect places for enterprise.

One justification for not looking to the experiences of other times and places is that local economic strategies need to be customized to local characteristics and opportunities. This can explain why some researchers have not prioritized the development of a body of evidence-based theory: if places are sufficiently different from each other it means that policy experiences in one environment are not readily transferred to other localities. This argument was encountered in Chapter 2, including the claim that successful policy initiatives should serve as no more than a source of inspiration for what might be done elsewhere (Hospers 2006: 13). This argument was developed in the context of regional policy within the European Union, where there have been attempts to disseminate 'best practice' through the presentation of case studies of successful policy initiatives and through regional benchmarking exercises. Such an approach is considered dangerous, as the influences having most impact on regional competitiveness are connected to institutions and values that are local in their origin and effectiveness, and so policy successes are unlikely to be repeated when taken out of their home region. This perspective can also lead to another interpretation of why local economic development is frequently ineffective: while there is a need for locally developed policy, too much control remains with central government (Beer 2009: 66). Control is maintained, it is alleged, because central government seeks to avoid supporting local action that might have unanticipated outcomes. This also leads them to favour programmes that, while appearing to be substantial commitments to local development, in practice are selected because they have minimal financial implications and contain local action to 'approved' initiatives.

Learning from regional development

A reflection on these arguments around local economic development is to consider how some of the claims being made are harder to sustain when applied to regional policy. Using the distinction between these policy areas that was introduced in Chapter 3, this contrasts the understanding that has developed over the effectiveness of regional development grants versus the mix of variously untestable, untested or partially supported ideas about how otherwise to promote local economic development. Of course, the comparison is not between equals. There is a longer history to the use of investment subsidies as a strategy for addressing differences in regional prosperity than there is to local economic development. If inward investment policy were connected to the larger body of academic interest in regional development, the range of theoretical perspectives and competing policy prescriptions may not differ too greatly from discussions of local economic development. Nonetheless, there is something to be learnt from those who have continued to advocate traditional approaches to closing spatial inequalities, and reflecting on their contribution helps to assess some of the suggested reasons that advocates of alternative ways of promoting local economic development have frequently had little impact on policy.

The effectiveness of offering incentives to investors to modify location decisions or to influence the timing of projects is relatively well documented. For some countries at least, where this approach has been used over a long period of time, there has been an accumulation of comparable research evidence from which judgements can be made. Some of this has come from official evaluation reports and some from academic-initiated evaluations. Supporting this work has been the development of evaluation methodologies and academic debate over the appropriate ways to measure impacts. From this it has been possible to learn something about how to increase the effectiveness of incentives and how to evaluate investment projects in terms of their potential to promote regional development. A notable feature of this area of policy is the extent to which it has engaged academic research. This shows that the academic community is not structurally adverse to applied research, as some have suggested when considering the limited translation of local economic development theory into practice.

Two facilitating factors should be noted. First, the purpose of regional grants has been comparatively straightforward: the retention and generation of employment. This provides a comparatively unambiguous basis for determining effectiveness, although not without the ability to raise questions over the quality and duration of employment and upon the scale of impact expected. Indeed, there may be arguments that too little attention continues to be paid to the distributional consequences of regional investment grants. The message here is not to over burden initiatives with multiple purposes, as allowing tradeoffs can be akin to continually shifting the policy evaluation goalposts. Second, accumulating evidence about investment incentive programmes is relatively straightforward in the sense that the results of different studies can be compared with each other to build up a body of understanding. Unlike other areas of local economic development it is perhaps more likely to encounter references to research conducted several decades ago in the context of contemporary investigations. In discussing proposals for UK regional policy post 2000, for example, Fothergill (2005) makes the point that the inherited literature stretching back almost 50 years continues to have important messages for policy makers. Issues of context cannot be avoided entirely. As noted in Chapter 3, an uncertainty with claims in the United Kingdom about the continuing effectiveness of regional selective assistance is that impacts would not be maintained among a larger population of recipients. Similarly, the nature of investment projects and relationships of branch plants to parent organizations do change, with possible implications for the impacts of regional grants. The ability and inclination to conduct comparatively large scale investigations that encompass whole cohorts of grant recipients is something that has assisted to provide comparable research evidence. A policy approach that has been applied with some degree of consistency over many decades has more prospects of generating a capacity for evidence-based policy than piecemeal policies or approaches which are continually modified. The possibility of building a body of evidence-based understanding relevant to policy has also been noted in the case of promoting small enterprise (Storey 1999). This again is a relatively enclosed area of interest, although with potentially greater challenges where lessons need to be drawn from comparatively small scale programmes and influences on small firm performance are multi-faceted and interconnected.

The importance attached to empirically based studies is a further influence that has helped to develop an understanding of the impact of regional grants. Much of the research reviewed in this book can be characterized as theory driven in that it sets out to confirm a predetermined position. In contrast, it has been argued that existing theories of urban and regional change ought not to be treated with undue reverence if they are at odds with even a few pieces of empirical evidence (Fothergill and Gudgin 1985: 100). Such a standard would certainly address the concern expressed by Beer (2009) of too much theory in local economic development acting as a barrier to policy selection. Without seeking to close off a debate about alternative research philosophies, the point can perhaps be sustained that work of considerable value to the understanding of regional growth and decline has included essentially non theoretical work driven by the goal of being able to identify 'what actually happened'. This approach can make use of official statistics to compile comprehensive databases and accounting systems in which individual components sum to the total so that the relative importance of each can be ascertained. Accounting systems do not directly explain anything, and perhaps because of this have become an unfashionable aspect of much research potentially informing local economic development, but they can throw light on the matters of interest by disaggregating the components of change and drawing attention to potentially useful lines of investigation (Stone and Peck 1996: 66). A bias to this style of investigation, at least as a starting point for investigation, can have other methodological implications. It can facilitate the breaking up of a complex problem into discrete processes and lessen the chances of confusion arising. For example, Fothergill and Gudgin (1985) explain this in terms of their use of an accounting framework to study urban and regional change in which they analyse separately the influence of a region's industrial and urban structure on regional employment trends. Equally, they caution against the reliance on case studies because enterprises are highly variable and data relating to a small area may reflect the experiences of a few enterprises rather than more systemic processes. Supporters of the use of the case study method may point out that the purpose of their case study is not to establish regularities, but frequently findings are presented as having importance beyond the experience studied.

The significance of the research about regional grants and investment promotion is that in some respects it can viewed as a model of what is required to build an understanding of an area of applied economic development. It does not mean that researchers are necessarily satisfied with the use that policy makers have made of their research evidence. Indeed, research related to aspects of traditional regional policy has continued in the face of declining public policy interest in this form of local economic development. Researchers have nonetheless maintained their commitment to this area of study. Policy decisions are not tightly constrained to follow the results of research, partly as there is a need to balance the investment in different areas of policy and there is a desirable scope for experimentation. In this context, the contribution of local economic development research should not be judged by its actual influence on decision makers but by the extent to which it can claim to have assisted decision making. This might involve widening the range of options presented to policy makers or specifying the consequences of particular courses of action. A conclusion from the reviews presented in this book is that these types of contribution are held back by the limited evidence being brought forward and the difficulty of combining the evidence from individual studies.

References

Abbeglen, J. and Stalk, G. (1985) *Kaisha, the Japanese Corporation*, New York: Basic Books.
Acs, Z. and Armington, C. (2004) 'Employment growth and entrepreneurship in cities', *Regional Studies* 38(8): 911–927.
Acs, Z. and Audretsch, D. (1987) 'Innovation, market structure and firm size', *Review of Economics and Statistics* 71: 567–574.
—— (1989) 'Patents as a measure of innovative activity', *Kyklos* 42: 171–180.
Acs, Z. and Storey, D. (2004) 'Introduction: entrepreneurship and economic development', *Regional Studies* 38(8): 871–877.
Acs, Z., Audretsch, D. and Feldman, M. (1992) 'Real effects of academic research: comment', *American Economic Review* 82: 363–367.
Adams, J. (2002) 'The real food revolution: a snapshot of the Australian farmers' market movement', Market Forces – Farmers' Markets: The Real Food Revolution, Bathurst: Australian farmers' Market Conference.
Adams, J., Robinson, P. and Vigor, A. (2003) *A New Regional Policy for the UK*, London: Institute for Public Policy Research.
Aernoudt, R. (2004) 'Incubators: tool for entrepreneurship?', *Small Business Economics* 23(2): 127–135.
Allen, P., Fitzsimmons, M., Goodman, M. and Warner, K. (2003) 'Shifting plates in the agrifood landscape: the tectonics of alternative agrifood initiatives in California', *Journal of Rural Studies* 19(1): 61–75.
Allen, R. (1983) 'Collective invention', *Journal of Economic Behavior and Organization* 4: 1–24.
Allenby, B. (1999) *Industrial Ecology: Policy Framework and Evaluation*, Eaglewood Cliffs, NJ: Prentice-Hall.
Amphion Report (1996) Evaluation of the Network Co-operation Programme 1989–1992, Copenhagen, Department of Trade and Industry.
Ancori, B., Bureth, A. and Cohendet, P. (2000) 'The economics of knowledge: the debate about codification and tacit knowledge', *Industrial and Corporate Change* 9(2): 255–287.
Anholt, S. (2007) *Competitive Identity: The New Brand Management for Nations, Cities and Regions*, Basingstoke: Palgrave.
Armstrong, H. (1995) 'The evaluation of regional policy', in *Regional Policy*, Fourth Report, Trade and Industry Committee, Session 1994–95, HC 356-II, 157–165, London: HMSO.

—— (2001) 'Regional selective assistance: is the spend enough and is it targeting the right places?', *Regional Studies* 35(3): 247–257.
Armstrong, H. and de Kervenoael, R. (2000) 'Europe and the regions: the issue of equity versus efficiency', *Regionalism and Federalism Studies* 10: 78–106.
Armstrong, H. and Taylor, J. (1985) *Regional Economics and Policy*, Oxford: Philip Allen.
—— (1993) *Regional Economics and Policy* 2nd edition, Hemel Hempstead: Harvester Wheatsheaf.
—— (2000) *Regional Economics and Policy* 3rd edition, Oxford: Blackwell.
Arnold, F. (1995) *Economic Analysis of Environmental Policy Regulation*, New York: John Wiley & Sons.
Arrow, K. (1962) 'The economic implication of learning by doing', *Review of Economic Studies* 29: 155–173.
Arrowsmith, J., Sisson, K. and Marginson, P. (2004) 'What can "benchmarking" offer the open method of co-ordination?' *Journal of European Public Policy* 11: 311–328.
Arup Economics and Planning (2000) *Evaluation of Regional Selective Assistance 1991–95*, London: AEP.
Ashcroft, B., Love, J. and Scouller, J. (1987) *The Economic Effects of the Inward Acquisition of Scottish Manufacturing Companies 1965 to 1980*, ESU Research paper 11, Edinburgh: HMSO.
Asheim, B. (1999) 'Interactive learning and localized knowledge in globalizing learning economies', *GeoJournal* 49: 339–343.
Asheim, B. and Isaksen, A. (1997) 'Regional innovation systems: the integration of local "sticky" and global "ubiquitous" knowledge', *Journal of Technology Transfer* 27: 77–86.
Ashford, N. (1997) 'Industrial safety: the neglected issue in industrial ecology', *Journal of Cleaner Production*, 5(1–2): 115–121.
Ashworth, G. and Voogd, H. (1988) 'Marketing the city – concepts, processes and Dutch applications', *Town Planning Review* 59(1): 65–79.
Audretsch, D. (2001). 'The role of small firms in U.S. biotechnology clusters', *Small Business Economics* 17: 3–15.
Audretsch, D. and Feldman, M. (1996) 'R&D spillovers and the geography of innovation and production', *American Economic Review* 86: 630–640.
Audretsch, D. and Thurik, A. (2001) 'What is new about the new economy: sources of growth in the managed and entrepreneurial economies', *Industrial and Corporate Change* 10: 267–315.
AUTM (2004) *AUTM Licensing Survey, Fiscal Year 2004 Survey Summary*, Northbrook IL: Association of University Technology Managers.
Balconi, M., Pozzali, A. and Viale, R. (2007) 'The "codification debate" revisited: a conceptual framework to analyze the role of tacit knowledge in economics', *Industrial and Corporate Change* 16(5): 823–849.
Ballingall, J. and Winchester, N. (2009) *Distance isn't dead: an empirical evaluation of food miles-based preference changes*, New Zealand Institute of Economic Research Working Paper 01/09, Wellington, New Zealand.
Bamford, J. (1987) 'The development of small firms, the traditional family and agrarian patterns in Italy', in R. Goffee and R. Scase (eds) *Entrepreneurship in Europe*, London: Croom Helm.
Banks, J. and Bristow, G. (1999) 'Developing quality in agro-food supply chains: a Welsh perspective', *International Planning Studies*, 4(3): 317–331.

Barham, E. (2003) 'Translating terroir: the global challenge of French AOC labeling', *Journal of Rural Studies* 19: 127–138.

Barkham, R., Gudgin, G., Hart, M. and Hanvey, E. (1996) *The Determinants of Small Firm Growth*, London: Jessica Kingsley/Regional Studies Association.

Barlow Report (1940) *Report of the Royal Commission on the Distribution of Industrial Population*, CMND 6153, London: HMSO.

Barro, R. (1991) 'Economic growth in a cross section of countries', *Quarterly Journal of Economics* 106(2): 407–443.

Barrow, C. (2001) *Incubators: A Realist's Guide to the World's Business Accelerators*, Chichester: Wiley.

Barrow C. J. (2006) *Environmental Management for Sustainable Development* 2nd edition, London: Routledge.

Bayliss, D. (2007) 'Dublin's Digital Hubris: Lessons from an Attempt to Develop a Creative Industrial Cluster', *European Planning Studies* 15(9): 1261–1271.

Beardsell, M. and Henderson, V. (1999) 'Spatial evolution of the computer industry in the USA', *European Economic Review*, 43: 431–456.

Bearse, P. (1998) 'A question of evaluation: NBIA's impact assessment of business incubators', *Economic Development Quarterly* 12(4): 322–333.

Beaudry, C. and Breschi, S. (2003) 'Are firms in clusters really more innovative?', *Economics of Innovation and New Technology* 12(4): 325–342.

Beauregard, R. (1993) 'Constituing economic development: a theoretical perspective', in R. Bingham and R. Mier (eds) *Theories of Local Economic Development*, Newbury Park, CA: Sage.

Beer, A. (2009) 'The theory and practice of developing locally', in J. Rowe (ed.) *Theories of Local Economic Development – Linking Theory to Practice*, Aldershot: Ashgate.

Beer, A., Maude, A. and Pritchard, B. (2003) *Developing Australia's Regions: Theory and Practice*, Sydney: University of New South Wales.

Begg, I. (1999) 'Cities and competitiveness', *Urban Studies* 36: 795–810.

—— (2002) *Urban Competitiveness: Policies for Dynamic Cities*, Bristol: Policy Press.

Benner, C. (2002) *Work in the New Economy: Flexible Labour Markets in Silicon Valley*, Oxford: Blackwell.

Benneworth, P. (2002). 'Creating new industries and service clusters on Tyneside', *Local Economy* 17(4): 313–327.

Benneworth, P., Danson, M., Raines, P. and Whittam, G. (2003) 'Confusing clusters: making sense of the cluster approach in theory and practice', *European Planning Studies* 11(5): 511–20.

Berry, C. and Glaeser, E. (2005) *The divergence of human capital levels across cities*, National Bureau of Economic Research Working Paper 11617, Cambridge, MA: NBER.

Birch, D. (1979) *The Job Generation Process*, MIT Program on Neighborhood and Regional Change, Cambridge, MA.

Birkinshaw, J. and Ridderstråle, J. (1999) 'Fighting the corporate immune system: a process study of subsidiary initiatives in multinational corporations', *International Business Review* 8: 149–180.

Birkin, F. (2000) 'The art of accounting for science: a prerequisite for sustainable development', *Critical Perspectives on Accounting* 11(3): 289–309.

Block, F. (1990) *Postindustrial Possibilities: A Critique of Economic Discourse*, Berkeley, CA: University of California Press.

Blowers, A. (1997) 'Environmental policy: ecological modernization or the risk society?', *Urban Studies* 34(5–6): 845–871.

Blowfield, M. and Murray, A. (2008) *Corporate Responsibility: A Critical Introduction*, Oxford: Oxford University Press.

Bluestone, B. and Harrison, B. (1982) *The Deindustrialization of America*, New York: Basic Books.

Boddy, M. and Parkinson, M. (2004) 'Competitiveness, cohesion and urban governance', in M. Boddy and M. Parkinson (eds) *City Matters: Competitiveness, Cohesion and Urban Governance*, Bristol: Policy Press.

Boeker, W. (1997) 'Executive migration and strategic change: the effect of top manager movement on product-market entry', *Administrative Science Quarterly* 42: 213–236.

Boland, P. (2007) 'Unpacking the theory–policy interface of local economic development: an analysis of Cardiff and Liverpool', *Urban Studies* 44: 1019–1039.

Bøllingtoft, A. and Ulhøi, J. (2005) 'The networked business incubator – leveraging entrepreneurial agency?', *Journal of Business Venturing* 20: 265–290.

Bolton, J. (1971) *Report of the Committee of Inquiry on Small Firms*, CMND 4811, London: HMSO.

Boons, F. and Baas, L. (1997) 'Types of industrial ecology: the problem of coordination', *Journal of Cleaner Production*, 5(1–2): 79–86.

Boschma, R. (1999) 'Learning and regional development', *GeoJournal* 49: 339–343.

—— (2004a) 'Competitiveness of regions from an evolutionary perspective', *Regional Studies* 38(9): 1001–1014.

—— (2004b) 'Proximity and Innovation: a critical assessment', *Regional Studies* 39(1): 61–74.

Boston Consulting Group (1975) *Strategy Alternatives for the British Motorcycle Industry*, London: HMSO.

Boulding, K. (1985) *The World as a Total System*, London: Sage.

Bowman, E. and Haire, M. (1975) 'A strategic posture toward corporate social responsibility', *California Management Review* 18(2): 49–58.

Brady, S. and Jackson, T. (2003) 'Waste recovery using packaging waste recovery notes: a cost effective way of meeting targets?', *Journal of Environmental Planning and Management* 46(4): 607–621.

Brakman, S., Garretsen, H. and van Marrewijk, C. (2001) *An Introduction to Geographical Economics*, Cambridge: Cambridge University Press.

Brand, E. and De Bruijn, T. (1999) 'Shared responsibility at the regional level: the building of sustainable industrial estates', *European Environment* 9: 221–231.

Braunerhjelm, P. and Johansson, D. (2003) 'The determinants of spatial concentration: the manufacturing and service sectors in an international perspective', *Industry and Innovation* 10(1): 41–63.

Breschi, S. and Lissoni, F. (2001a) 'Localized knowledge spillovers vs. innovative milieu: knowledge "tacitness" reconsidered', *Papers in Regional Science* 80: 255–273.

—— (2001b) 'Knowledge spillovers and local innovation systems: a critical survey', *Industrial and Corporate Change* 10(4): 975–1005.

Bresnahan, T. Gambardella, A. and Saxenian, A. (2001), '"Old economy" inputs for "new economy" outcomes: cluster formation in the new Silicon Valleys', *Industrial and Corporate Change* 10(4): 835–860.

Bristow, G. (2005) 'Everyone's a winner: problematising the discourse of regional competitiveness', *Journal of Economic Geography* 5: 285–304.

Brown, A. (1967) 'The Green Paper on the Development Areas', *National Institute Economic Review* May: 26–29.

Bruno, A. and Tyebjee, T. (1984) 'The entrepreneur's search for capital', in J. Hornaday, F. Tarpley, J. Timmons and K. Vesper (eds) *Frontiers of Entrepreneurship Research*, Wellesley, MA: Babson Centre for Entrepreneurial Studies.

Brusco, S., Cainelli, G., Forni, F., Franchi, M., Malusardi, A. and Righetti, R. (1996) 'The evolution of industrial districts in Emilia-Romagna', in F. Cossentino, F. Pyke and W. Sengenberger (eds) *Local and Regional Response to Global Pressure: The Case of Italy and its Industrial Districts*, Geneva: International Institute for Labour Studies.

Bugliarello, G. (1998) 'Knowledge parks and incubators', in R. Dorf (ed.) *The Handbook of Technology Management*, Chicester: John Wiley.

Bunnell, T. and Coe, N. (2001) 'Spaces and scales of innovation', *Progress in Human Geography* 25(4): 569–589.

Bureau of Industry Economics (1995) *Beyond the Firm: An Assessment of Business Linkages and Networks in Australia*, Canberra: Australian Government Publishing Service.

Burke, R. (2002) 'Organizational transitions', in C. Cooper and R. Burke (eds) *The New World of Work – Challenges and Opportunities*, Oxford: Blackwell.

Burroni, L. and Trigilia, C. (2001) 'Italy: economic development through local economies', in C. Crouch, P. Le Galés, C. Trogilia and H. Voelzkow (eds) *Local Production Systems in Europe: Rise or Demise?*, Oxford: Oxford University Press.

Business Week (1976) 'The second war between the states', 17 May: 92–114.

Butler, J. (2005) *Entrepreneurship and Self Help Among Black Americans*, Albany, NY: State University of New York Press.

Byatt, I., Castles, I., Goklany, I., Henderson, D., Lawson, N., McKitrick, R., Morris, J., Peacock, A., Robinson, C. and Skidelsky, R. (2006) 'The Stern Review a dual critique: Part II: Economic Analysis', *World Economics* 8(2): 199–229.

Camagni, R. (1991) *Innovation Networks: Spatial Perpsectives*, London: Belhaven-Pinter.

—— (2002) 'On the concept of territorial competitiveness: sound or misleading?', *Urban Studies* 39(13): 2395–2411.

Camerer, C. and Lovallo, D. (1999) 'Over confidence and excess of entry', *American Economic Review* 89: 306–318.

Cameron, G. and Reid, G. (1966) *Scottish Economic Planning and the Attraction of Industry*, Occasional Paper 6, Glasgow: Social and Economic Studies, University of Glasgow.

Cappelli, P. (1999) *The New Deal at Work: Managing the Market Driven Workforce*, Boston, MA: Harvard Business School Press.

Carr, S. and Mpande, R. (1996) 'Does the definition of the issue matter? NGO influence and the international convention to combat desertification', in D. Potter (ed.) *NGOs and Environmental Politics: Asia and Africa*, London: Frank Cass.

Carter, R., de Freitas, C., Goklany, I., Holland, D. and Lindzen, R. (2006) 'The Stern Review a dual critique: Part I: The science', *World Economics* 8(2): 161–182.

Cecil, B. and Green, M. (2000) 'In the flagship's wake: relations, motivations and observations of strategic alliance activity among IT sector flagship firms and their partners', in M. Green and R. McNaughton (eds) *Industrial Networks and Proximity*, Aldershot: Ashgate.

Cellini, R. and Soci, A. (2002) 'Pop competitiveness', *Banca Nazionale del Lavoro Quarterly Review* 55(220): 71–101.

Centre for Strategy and Evaluation Services (2002) *Benchmarking of Business Incubators*, Final Report to the European Commission Enterprise Directorate General.

Chaston, I. (1996) 'Critical events and process gaps in the Danish Technological Institute SME structured networking model', *International Small Business Journal* 14(3): 71–84.

Chertow, M. (1999) 'The eco-industrial park model reconsidered', *Journal of Industrial Ecology* 2(3): 8–10.

Child, J. (1974) 'What determines organization performance? The universals versus it-all-depends', *Organization Dynamics* Summer: 2–18.

Childs, J. (2003) *Transcommunality: From the Politics of Conversion to the Ethics of Respect*, Philadelphia, PA: Temple University Press.

Chon, S. (1997) 'Destroying the myth of vertical integration in the Japanese electronics industry: restructuring in the semiconductor manufacturing equipment industry', *Regional Studies* 31(1): 25–39.

Chrisman, J., Hynes, T. and Fraser, S. (1995) 'Faculty entrepreneurship and economic development: the case of the University of Calgary', *Journal of Business Venturing* 10: 267–281.

Christensen, C. (1997) *The Innovator's Dilemma*, Boston, MA: Harvard Business School Press.

Christensen, C. and Bower, J. (1996) 'Customer power, strategic investment, and the failure of leading firms', *Strategic Management Journal* 17: 197–218.

Christoff, P. (1996) 'Ecological modernization, ecological modernities', *Environmental Politics* 5(3): 476–500.

Christophers, B. (2008) 'The BBC, the creative class, and neoliberal urbanism in the north of England', *Environment and Planning A* 40: 2313–2329.

Cingano, F. (2003) 'Returns to specific skills in industrial districts', *Labour Economics* 10: 149–164.

Clark, T., Lloyd, R., Wong, K. K. and Jain, P. (2002) 'Amenities drive urban growth', *Journal of Urban Affairs* 24: 493–515.

Clarysse, B. and Moray, N. (2004) 'A process study of entrepreneurial team formation: the case of a research-based spin-off', *Journal of Business Venturing* 19(1): 55–79.

Clarysse, B., Wright, M., Lockett, A., van de Velde, E. and Vohora, A. (2005) 'Spinning out new ventures: a typology of incubation strategies from European research institutions', *Journal of Business Venturing* 20: 183–216.

Coe, N. (2001) 'A hyrid agglomeration? The development of a satellite-Marshallian industrial district in Vancouver's film industry', *Urban Studies* 38(10): 1753–1775.

Coetzer, A. and Perry, M. (2008) 'Factors influencing employee learning in small businesses', *Education + Training* 50(8/9): 648–660.

Cohen, M. (2000) 'Ecological modernization, environmental knowledge and national character: a preliminary analysis of the Netherlands', *Environmental Politics*, 9(1): 77–106.

—— (2006) 'Ecological modernization and its discontents: the American environmental movement's resistance to an innovation-driven future', *Futures* 38(5): 528–547.

Cohen, S. and Fields, G. (1999) *Social Capital and Capital Gains, or Virtual Bowling in Silicon Valley: An Examination of Social Capital in Silicon Valley*, Working Paper, Berkeley, CA: Berkeley Round Table on the International Economy, University of California.

Cohen, W., Nelson, R. and Walsh, J. (2002) 'Links and impacts: the influence of public research on industrial R&D', *Management Science* 48(1): 1–23.

Cohen-Rosenthal, E. (2003) What is eco-industrial development?, in E. Cohen-Rosenthal (ed.) *Eco-industrial Strategies*, Sheffield: Greenleaf.

Cohen-Rosenthal, E. and McGalliard, T. (1998) *Eco-industrial development: the case of the United States*, Institute for Prospective Technological Studies Report 27, Saville: European Commission Joint research Centre.

226 References

Colombo, M. and Delmastro, M. (2001) 'How effective are technology incubators? Evidence from Italy', *Research Policy* 31: 1103–1122.

Combes, P-P. and Duranton, G. (2001) *Labour Pooling, Labour Poaching, and Spatial Clustering*, Centre for Economic Performance Discussion Paper 510, London: London School of Economics and Political Science.

Cooke, P. (1998) 'Introduction: origins of the concept', in H. Braczyk, P. Cooke and M. Heidenrich (eds) *Regional Innovation Systems: The Role of Governance in a Globalized World*, London: UCL Press.

—— (2001) 'Regional innovation systems, clusters, and the knowledge economy', *Industrial and Corporate Change* 10(4): 945–974.

Cooke, P. and Morgan, K. (1994) 'The regional innovation system in Baden-Württemberg', *International Journal of Technology Management* 9: 394–429.

—— (1998) *The Associational Economy. Firms, Regions and Innovation*, Oxford: Oxford University Press.

Cooke, P., Urranga, M. and Etxebarria, G. (1998) 'Regional systems of innovation: an evolutionary perspective', *Environment and Planning A* 23: 197–213.

Cooper, A. (1971) *The Founding of Technologically-Based Firms*, Milwaukee, WI: The Center for Venture Management.

Cooper, M. (2000) 'Being the "go-to guy": fatherhood, masculinity, and the organization of work in Silicon Valley', *Qualitative Sociology* 23(4): 379–405.

Corporation for Enterprise Development (1986) *Taken for Granted: How Grant Thornton's Business Climate Index Leads States Astray*, Washington, DC: Corporation for Enterprise Development.

—— (2009) *2009–2010 Assets & Opportunity Scorecard Executive Summary*, Washington, DC: CFED (see http://scorecard.cfed.org).

Cossentino, F., Pyke, F. and Sengenberger, W. (1996) *Local and Regional Response to Global Pressure: The Case of Italy and its Industrial Districts*, Geneva: International Institute for Labour Studies.

Côté, R. and Cohen-Rosenthal, E. (1998) Designing eco-industrial parks: a synthesis and some experiences, *Journal of Cleaner Production*, 6: 181–188.

Cowan, H., David, P. and Foray, D. (2000) 'The explicit economics of codification and tacitness', *Industrial and Corporate Change* 9(2): 211–253.

Cowan, R. and Jonard, N. (2003) 'The dynamics of collective invention', *Journal of Economic Behavior and Organization* 52(4): 513–532.

Crang, P. and Martin, R. (1991) 'Mrs Thatcher's vision of the "new Britain" and the other sides of the "Cambridge phenomenon"', *Environment and Planning D: Society and Space* 9: 91–116.

Crone, M. and Watts, H. (2000) 'MNE supply linkages and the local SME sector: evidence from Yorkshire and Humberside', *Local Economy* 15(4): 325–337.

Crouch, C. and Farrell, H. (2001) 'Great Britain: falling through the holes in the network concept', in C. Crouch, P. Le Galés, C. Trogilia and H. Voelzkow (eds) *Local Production Systems in Europe: Rise or Demise?*, Oxford: Oxford University Press.

Crouch, C., Le Galés, P., Trogilia, C. and Voelzkow, H. (2001) *Local Production Systems in Europe: Rise or Demise?*, Oxford: Oxford University Press.

Cumbers, A. and MacKinnon, D. (2004) 'Introduction: clusters in urban and regional development', *Urban Studies* 41(5–6): 959–969.

Cumbers, A., MacKinnon, D. and McMaster, R. (2003) 'Institutions, power and space: assessing the limits to institutionalism in economic geography', *European Urban and Regional Studies* 10: 325–342.

References 227

Curran, W. (2007) 'From the frying pan to the oven: gentrification and the experience of industrial displacement in Williamsburg, Brooklyn', *Urban Studies* 44: 1427–1440.

Currid, E. (2007) *The Warhol Economy*, Princeton, NJ: Princeton University Press.

Curtis, F. (2003) 'Eco-localism and sustainability', *Ecological Economics* 46: 83–102.

Daly, H. (1996) *Beyond Growth: The Economics of Sustainable Development*, Boston, MA: Beacon Press.

Daly, P. (1985) *The Biotechnology Business: A Strategic Analysis*, London: Pinter.

Daniels, G. and Hofer, C. (1993) 'Characteristics of successful and unsuccessful entrepreneurial faculty and their innovative research teams', in N. Churchill, S. Birley, W. Bygrave, J. Doutriaux, E. Gatewood, F. Hoy and W. Wetzel (eds) *Frontiers of Entrepreneurship Research*, Wellesley, MA: Babson College.

David, P. (2003) *The Economic Logic of Open Science and the Balance Between Private Property Rights and the Public Domain in Scientific Data and Information: A Primer*, Discussion Paper 02-30, Stanford, CA: Stanford Institute for Economic Policy Research, Stanford University.

Dechenaux, E., Goldfard, B., Sane, S. and Thursby, M. (2003) *Appropriability and the Timing of Innovation: Evidence from MIT Inventions*, National Bureau of Economic Research Working Paper 9735, Cambridge, MA: NBER.

DEFRA (2005) *The validity of food miles as an indicator of sustainable development*, report prepared by AEA Technology for the UK Department for Environment, Food and Rural Affairs.

Department of Trade and Industry (1995) *Assessment of the Wider Impact of Foreign Direct Investment in Manufacturing in the UK*, Cambridge: PA Cambridge Economic Consultants.

—— (2001) *Business Clusters in the UK – A First Assessment*, London: Department of Trade and Industry.

Deutz, P. and Gibbs, D. (2004) 'Eco-industrial development and economic development: industrial ecology or place promotion?', *Business Strategy and the Environment* 13(5): 347–362.

DiBella, A., Nevis, E. and Gould, J. (1996) 'Understanding organizational learning capability', *Journal of Management Studies* 33(3): 361–379.

Dicken, P. (2007) *Global Shift: Mapping the Changing Contours of the World Economy*, London: Sage.

Dicken, P. and Tickell, A. (1992) 'Competition or collaboration? The structure of inward investment promotion in Northern England', *Regional Studies* 26: 99–114.

Disney, R., Haskel, J. and Heden, Y. (2003) ' Restructuring and productivity growth in UK manufacturing', *Economic Journal* 113: 666–694.

Djelic, M-L. (1998) *Exporting the American Model: The Postwar Transformation of European Business*, Oxford: Oxford University Press.

Doel, M. and Hubbard, P. (2002) 'Taking world cities literally: marketing the city in a global space of flows', *City* 6: 351–368.

Donegan, M., Drucker, J., Goldstein, H., Lowe, N. and Malizia, E. (2008) 'Which indicators explain metropolitan economic performance best?', *Journal of the American Planning Association* 74(2): 180–195.

Driffield, N. and Hughes, D. (2003) 'Foreign and domestic investment: regional development or crowding out?', *Regional Studies* 37(3): 277–288.

Dryzek, J. (1997) *The Politics of the Earth: Environmental Discourses*, Oxford: Oxford University Press.

Dunn, B. and Steinemann, A. (1998) 'Industrial ecology for sustainable communities', *Journal of Environmental Planning and Management*, 41(6): 661–672.

Dunning, J. (1993) 'Internationalizing Porter's diamond', *Management International Review* 33(2): 7–15.

Dupuis, E. and Goodman, D. (2005) 'Should we go "home" to eat? Toward a reflexive politics of localism', *Journal of Rural Studies* 21: 359–371.

Duranton, G. and Puga, D. (2002). 'Diversity and specialization in cities: why, where and when does it matter?', in P. McCann (ed.) *Industrial Location Economics*, Cheltenham: Edward Elgar.

Eden, S. (1996) *Environmental Issues and Business Implications of a Changing Agenda*, Chichester: John Wiley & Sons.

Edgington, D (1997) 'Flexibility and corporate organization in Chukyo, Japan: a study of five industries', *Regional Development Studies* 3(Winter): 83–108.

Eisenhardt, K. and Schoonhoven, K. (1990) 'Organizational growth: linking founding team, strategy, environment and growth among US semiconductor ventures', *Administrative Science Quarterly* 35: 504–529.

Elger, T. and Smith, C. (1994) 'Global Japanization? Convergence and competition in the organization of the labour process', in T. Elger and C. Smith (eds) *Global Japanization? The Transnational Transformation of the Labour Process*, London: Routledge.

Epstein, M. (2008) *Making Sustainability Work*, Sheffield: Greenleaf.

Eraydin, A. (2001) 'New forms of local governance in the emergence of industrial districts', in D. Felsentein and M. Taylor (eds) *Promoting Local Growth*, Aldershot: Ashgate.

Erkman, S. (1997) 'Industrial ecology: a historical view', *Journal of Cleaner Production*, 5(1–2): 1–10.

Esteva, G. (1994) 'Re-embedding food in agriculture', *Culture and Agriculture* 48: 2–13.

Esty, D. and Porter, M. (1998) 'Industrial ecology and competitiveness', *Journal of Industrial Ecology* 2(1): 35–43.

European Report on Science and Technology Indicators (1994) EUR 15897 EN, Directorate-General XII, Science, Research and Development, Brussels: European Commission.

Evangelista, R., Iammarino, S., Mastrostefano, V. and Silvani, A. (2002) 'Looking for regional systems of innovation: evidence from the Italian innovation survey', *Regional Studies* 236: 173–186.

Fagg, J. (1980) 'A re-examination of the incubator hypothesis: a case study of Greater Leicester', *Urban Studies* 17(1): 35–44.

Faulkner, W. and Senker, J. (1995) *Knowledge Frontiers: Public sector research and Industrial Innovation in Biotechnology, Engineering Ceramics and Parallel Computing*, Oxford: Oxford University Press.

Feeser, H. and Willard, G. (1989) 'Incubators and performance: a comparison of high and low growth high tech firms', *Journal of Business Venturing* 4: 429–442.

Feldman, M. (1994) *The Geography of Innovation*, Dordrecht: Kluwer.

—— (2000) 'Location and innovation: the new economic geography of innovation, spillovers, and agglomeration', in G. Clark, M. Feldman and M. Gertler (eds) *The Oxford Handbook of Economic Geography*, Oxford: Oxford University Press.

Feldman, M. and Audretsch, D. (1999) 'Innovation in cities: science-based diversity, specialization and localized competition', *European Economic Review* 43: 409–429.

Fernandez-Armesto, F. (2001) *Food: A History*, London: Pan.

Feser, E. and Bergman, E. (2000) 'National industry cluster templates: a framework for regional cluster analysis', *Regional Studies* 34(1): 1–20.

Feser, E. and Luger, M. (2003) 'Cluster analysis as a mode of inquiry: its use in science and technology policymaking in North Carolina', *European Planning Studies* 11(1): 11–24.

Findlay, A., Mason, C., Harrison, R. Houston, D. and McCollum, D. (2008) 'Getting off the escalator? A study of Scots out-migration from a global city region', *Environment and Planning A* 40: 2169–2185.

Firn, J. (1975) 'External control and regional development: the case of Scotland', *Environment and Planning A* 7: 393–414.

Fischer, M. and Massey, D. (2000) 'Residential segregation and ethnic enterprise in U.S. metroplitan areas', *Social Problems* 47(3): 408–424.

Florida, R. (2002a) *The Rise of the Creative Class: And How It's Transforming Work, Leisure, Community and Everyday Life*, New York: Basic Books.

—— (2002b) 'Bohemia and economic geography', *Journal of Economic Geography* 2(1): 55–71.

—— (2004) *The Rise of the Creative Class: And How It's Transforming Work, Leisure, Community and Everyday Life*, 2nd edition, New York: Basic Books.

—— (2005) *Cities and the Creative Class*, New York: Routledge.

Florida, R., Mellander, C. and Stolarick, K. (2008) 'Inside the black box of regional development – human capital, the creative class and tolerance', *Journal of Economic Geography* 8(5): 615–649.

Foster, J. (1999) *Docklands: Cultures in Conflict, Worlds in Collision*, London: UCL Press.

Fothergill, S. (2005) 'A new regional policy for Britain', *Regional Studies* 39(5): 659–667.

Fothergill, S. and Gudgin, G. (1979) *The job generation process in Britain*, Research Series 32, London: Centre for Environmental Studies.

—— (1985) 'Ideology and methods in industrial location research', in D. Massey and R. Meegan (eds) *Politics and Method*, London: Methuen.

Fothergill, S. and Guy, N. (1990) *Retreat from the Regions*, London: Jessica Kingsley/Regional Studies Association.

Fothergill, S., Kitson, M. and Monk, S. (1985) *Urban Industrial Decline: The Causes of Urban Rural Contrasts in Manufacturing Employment Change*, London: HMSO.

Fothergill, S., Monk, S. and Perry, M. (1987) *Property and Industrial Change*, London: Hutchinson.

Franklin, S., Wright, M. and Lockett, A. (2001) 'Academic and surrogate entrepreneurs in university spin-out companies', *Journal of Technology Transfer* 26(1–2): 127–141.

Freel, M. and Robson, P. (2004) 'Small firm innovation, growth and performance', *International Small Business Journal* 22(6): 561–575.

Freeman, C. (1982) *The Economics of Innovation*, 2nd edition, London: Pinter.

—— (1987) *Technology, Policy and Economic Performance*, London: Pinter.

Freeman, R. (1984) *Strategic Management; A Stakeholder Approach*, Boston, MA: Pitman.

Freiberger, P. and Swaine, M. (1984) *Fire in the Valley: The Making of the Personal Computer*, New York: McGraw-Hill.

Friedmann, H. (1994) 'Food politics: new dangers, new possibilities', in M.Philip (ed.) *Food and Agrarian Orders in the World Economy*, Wesport, CT: Praeger.

Frosch, R. and Gallopoulos, N. (1989) 'Strategies for manufacturing', *Scientific American* 261(3): 94–102.

Fuchs, M. (2005) 'Internal networking in the globalising firm: the case of R&D allocation in German automobile component supply companies', in C. Alvstam and E. Schamp

230 References

(eds) *Linking Industries Across the World – Processes of Global Networking*, Aldershot: Ashgate.

Fuchs, M. and Winter, J. (2008) 'Competencies in subsidiaries of multinational companies: the case of the automotive supply industry in Poland', *Zeitschrift für Wirtschaftsgeographie* 52(4): 193–202.

Fujita, M. and Thisse, J.-F. (2000) 'The formation of economic agglomerations: old problems and new perspectives', in J.-M. Huriot and J.-F. Thisse (eds) *Economics of Cities*, Cambridge: Cambridge University Press.

Fukuyama, F. (1995) *Trust: The Social Virtues and the Creation of Prosperity*, London: Hamish Hamilton.

Fuller, C., Bennett, R. and Ramsden, M. (2003) 'Organised for inward investment? Development agencies, local government, and firms in the inward investment process', *Environment and Planning A* 35: 2025–2051.

Gardiner, B., Martin, R. and Tyler, P. (2004) 'Competitiveness, productivity and economic growth across the European regions', *Regional Studies* 38(9): 1045–1067.

Gertler, M. (1995) 'Being there: proximity, organization and culture in the development and adoption of advanced manufacturing technologies', *Economic Geography* 71(1): 1–26.

—— (2003) 'Tacit knowledge and the economic geography of context, or the undefinable tacitnesss of being (there)', *Journal of Economic Geography* 3: 75–99.

Gibbons M. and Johnston, R. (1975) 'The roles of science in technological innovation', *Research Policy* 19: 220–242.

Gibbs, D. (2000) 'Ecological modernisation, regional economic development and regional development agencies', *Geoforum* 31: 9–19.

—— (2002) *Local Economic Development and the Environment*, London: Routledge.

Gibbs, D. and Deutz, P. (2005) 'Implementing industrial ecology? Planning for eco-industrial parks in the USA', *Geoforum* 36: 452–464.

Gibbs, D., Deutz, P. and Proctor, A. (2005) 'Industrial ecology and eco-industrial development: a potential paradigm for local and regional development?', *Regional Studies* 39(2): 171–183.

Glaeser, E. (1994) 'Cities, information, and economic growth', *Cityscape* 1(1): 9–47.

—— (1998) 'Are cities dying?', *Journal of Economic Perspective* 12: 139–160.

—— (2000) 'The new economics of urban and regional growth', in G. Clark, M. Feldman and M. Gertler (eds) *The Oxford Handbook of Economic Geography*, Oxford: Oxford University Press.

—— (2004) Review of Richard Florida's 'The Rise of the Creative Class', available online at http://post.economics.harvard.edu/faculty/glaeser/papers/Review_Florida.pdf (last accessed 12 November 2009).

—— (2005) *Smart growth: Education, Skilled Workers and the Future of Cold Weather Cities*, Policy Brief PB-2005-1, Cambridge, MA: Kennedy School, Harvard University.

Glaeser, E., Kolko, J. and Saiz, A. (2001) 'Consumer city', *Journal of Economic Geography* 1: 27–50.

Glaeser, E., Kallal, H., Scheinkman, J. and Schleifer, A. (1992) 'Growth in cities', *Journal of Political Economy* 100(6): 1126–1152.

Glasmeier, A. (2000) 'Local economic development policy', in G. Clark, M. Feldman and M. Gertler (eds) *The Oxford Handbook of Economic Geography*, Oxford: Oxford University Press.

Glassman, U. and Voelzkow, H. (2001) 'The governance of local economies in Germany', in C. Crouch, P. Le Galés, C. Trogilia and H. Voelzkow (eds) *Local Production Systems in Europe: Rise or Demise?*, Oxford: Oxford University Press.

Goldstein, H. (2009) 'Theory and practice of technology-based economic development', in J. Rowe (ed.) *Theories of Local Economic Development – Linking Theory to Practice*, Aldershot: Ashgate.

Goodman, D. (2004) 'Rural Europe Redux? Reflections on alternative agro-food networks and paradigm change', *Sociologia Ruralis* 44(1): 3–16.

Gordon, I. (2000) 'Targeting a leaky bucket – the case against localised employment creation', *New Economy* 6(4): 199–203.

Gottlieb, P. (2004) 'Labor supply pressures and the "brain drain": signs from Census 2000', *The Living Cities Census Series*, Washington, DC: Brookings Institute Press.

Gouldson, A. and Murphy, J. (1996) 'Ecological modernization and the European Union', *Geoforum*, 27: 11–21.

—— (1998) *Regulatory Realities: The Implementation and Impact of Industrial Environmental Policy*, London: Earthscan.

Grabher, G. (1993) 'The weakness of strong ties: the lock-in of regional development in the Ruhr area', in G. Grabher (ed.) *The Embedded Firm: On the Socioeconomics of Industrial Networks*, London: Routledge.

—— (2002) 'Cool projects, boring institutions: temporary collaboration in social context', *Environment and Planning A* 33: 351–374.

Graedel, T. And Allenby, B. (1995) *Industrial Ecology*, Eaglewood Cliffs, NJ: Prentice-hall.

Granovetter, M. (1973) 'The strength of weak ties', *American Journal of Sociology* 78: 1360–1380.

—— (1983) 'The strength of weak ties: a network theory revisited', *Sociology Theory* 1: 201–233.

—— (1985) 'Economic action and social structure: the problem of embeddedness', *American Journal of Sociology* 91(3): 481–510.

—— (1992) 'Problems of explanation in economic sociology', in N. Nohria and R. Eccles (eds) *Networks and Organizations: Structure, Form and Action*, Boston, MA: Harvard Business School Press.

Gray, M. (2002) 'The micro level matters: evidence from the bio-pharmaceutical industry', *Zeitschrift für Wirtschftsgeogrraphie* 46: 124–136.

Gray, M., Golob, E. and Markusen, A. (1996) 'Big firms, long arms, wide shoulders: The "hub and spoke" industrial district in the Seattle region', *Regional Studies* 30(7): 651–666.

Green, A. (1997) 'Exclusion, unemployment and non-employment', *Regional Studies* 31(5): 505–520.

Greene, F. (2009) 'Spinning the wheel', *Enterprising Matters* Summer09, available online www.isbe.org.uk/spinning (last accessed 8 February 2010).

Greene, F., Mole, K. and Storey, D. (2004) 'Does more mean worse? Three decades of enterprise policy in the Tees Valley', *Urban Studies* 41(7): 1207–1228.

Greene, F., Tracey, P. and Cowling, M. (2007) 'Recasting the city into city-regions: place promotion, competitiveness benchmarking and the quest for urban supremacy', *Growth and Change* 38: 1–22.

Greening, D. (1995) 'Conservation strategies, firm performance, and corporate reputation in the US electric utility industry', in D. Collins and M. Starik (eds) *Research in Corporate Social Performance and Policy, Sustaining the Natural Environment: Empirical Studies on the Interface Between Nature and Orgernizations*, London: JAI Press.

Gunder, M. (2004) 'Shaping the planner's ego-ideal: a Lacanian interpretation of planning education', *Journal of Planning Education and Research* 23(3): 299–311.

Guthrie, J., Guthrie, A., Lawton, R. and Cameron, A. (2006) 'Farmers' markets: the small business counter-revolution in food production and retailing', *British Food Journal* 108(7): 560–573.

Hackett, S. and Dilts, D. (2004) 'A systematic review of business incubation research', *Journal of technology Transfer* 29(1): 55–82.

Hadjimichalis, C. (2006) 'The end of the Third Italy as we knew it?', *Antipode* 38(1): 82–106.

Hajer, M. (1993) 'Discourse coalitions and the institutionalisation of practice: the case of acid rain in Great Britain', in F. Fischer and J. Forester (eds) *The Argumentative Turn in Policy Analysis and Planning*, Durham, NC: Duke University Press.

Hall, P. (1981) 'Enterprise zones: British origins, American adaptations', *Built Environment* 7: 5–12.

Hamel, G. and Prahalad, C. (1994) *Competing for the Future*, Boston, MA: Harvard Business School Press.

Hamilton, C. (2005) *Affluenza*, Sydney: Allen & Unwin.

Hamilton, I. (1998) 'The UK experience with technology incubators', in *Technology Incubators: Nurturing Small Firms*, Paris: OECD.

Hannigan, J. (1995) *Environmental Sociology: A Social Constructionist Perspective*, London: Routledge.

Hansen, H. and Niedomysl (2009) 'Migration of the creative class: evidence from Sweden', *Journal of Economic Geography* 9(2): 191–206.

Hansen, M., Chesbrough, H., Nohira, N. and Sull, D. (2000) 'Networked incubators: hothouses of the new economy', *Harvard Business Review* September/October: 74–84.

Harris, R. (1993) 'Retreat from policy: the rationale and effectiveness of automatic investment grants', in R. Harrison and M. Hart (eds) *Spatial Policy in a Divided Nation*, London: Jessica Kingsley/Regional Studies Association.

Hart, M. and Scott, R. (1994) 'Measuring the effectiveness of small firm policy: some lessons from Northern Ireland', *Regional Studies* 28(9): 849–858.

Hauser, C., Tappeiner and Walde, J. (2007) 'The learning region: the impact of social capital and weak ties on innovation', *Regional Studies* 41(1): 75–88.

Hawkes, S. (2008) 'Tesco cashes in on taste for local food and drink', *The Times* 26 August.

Hayter, R. (1982) 'Truncation, the international firm and regional policy', *Area* 14: 277–282.

Healey, M. (1991) 'Obtaining information from business', in M. Healey (ed.) *Economic Activity and Land Use*, Harlow: Longman.

HEBCI (2007) *Higher Education Business Interaction Survey*, London: Higher Education Funding Council for England (HEFCE).

Henderson, R., Jaffe, A. and Trajtenberg, M. (1998) 'Universities as a source of commercial technology: a detailed analysis of university patenting', *Review of Economics and Statistics* 80: 119–127.

Henderson, V. (1974) 'The sizes and types of cities', *American Economic Review* 64(4): 640–656.

—— (1988) *Urban Development: Theory, Fact and Illusion*, Oxford: Oxford University Press.

Hendrickson, M. and Heffernan, W. (2002) 'Opening spaces through relocalization: locating potential resistance in the weaknesses of the global food system', *Sociologia Ruralis* 42(4): 347–369.

Hendry, C., Brown, J. and Defillip, R. (2000) 'Regional clustering of high technology-based firms: opto-electronics in three countries', *Regional Studies* 34(2): 129–144.

Hendry, C., Brown, J., Defillip, R. and Hassink, R. (1999) 'Industry clusters as commercial, knowledge and institutional networks: opto-electronics in six regions in the UK, USA and Germany', in A. Grandori (ed.) *Interform Networks: Organization and Industrial Competitiveness*, London: Routledge.

Henriksen, L. B. (1995) 'Formal cooperation among firms in networks: the case of Danish joint ventures and strategic alliances', *European Planning Studies* 3(2): 254–260.

Henry, N., Pollard, J. and Sidaway, J. (2001) 'Beyond the margins of economics: geographers, economists and policy relevance', *Antipode* 33: 200–207.

Heyes, J. and Smith, A. (2008) 'Could food miles become a non-tariff barrier?', *Acta Horticulturae* (International Society for Horticultural Science) 768: 431–436.

Hines, C. (2000) *Localization – A Global Manifesto*, London: Earthscan.

Hinrichs, C., Gillespie, G. and Feenstra, G. (2004) 'Social learning and innovation at retail farmers' markets', *Rural Sociology* 69(1): 31–58.

HM Treasury (2001) *Productivity in the UK, 3 The Regional Dimension*, London: HMSO.

HM Treasury, Department of Trade and Industry and Office of the Deputy Prime Minister (2003) *A Modern Regional Policy for the United Kingdom*, London: HM Treasury.

Hochtberger, K., White, M. and Grimes, S. (2004) *The Evolution of Multinational Computer Services Affiliates in Ireland*, Working paper 13, Galway: Centre for innovation and Structural Change, University of Galway.

Hoffman, A. (2005) 'Climate change strategy: the business logic behind voluntary greenhouse gas reductions', *California Management Review* 47(3): 21–46.

Holloway, L. and Kneafsey, M. (2004) 'Reading the space of the farmers' market: case study from the United Kingdom', *Sociologia Ruralis* 40(3): 285–299.

Holman, D. and Wood, S. (2003) 'The new workplace: an introduction', in D. Holman, T. Wall, C. Clegg, P. Sparrow and A. Howard (eds) *The New Workplace: A Guide to the Human Impact of Modern Working Practices*, Chichester: John Wiley & Sons.

Honore, C. (2004) *In Praise of Slow*, London: Orion.

Hoover, E. (1937) *Location Theory and the Shoe and Leather Industry*, Cambridge, MA: Harvard University Press.

—— (1948) *The Location of Economic Activity*, New York: McGraw Hill.

Hospers, G.-J. (2006) 'Silicon somewhere? Assessing the usefulness of best practices in regional policy', *Policy Studies* 27(1): 1–15.

Howell, J. (1999) 'Regional systems of innovation?', in D. Archibugi, J. Howells and J. Michie (eds) *Innovation Policy in a Global Economy*, Cambridge: Cambridge University Press.

Huber, J. (1982) *The Lost Innocence of Ecology: New Technologies and Super-industrialized Development*, Frankfurt: Fisher.

—— (1985) *The Rainbow Society: Ecology and Social Politics*, Frankfurt am Main: Fisher Verlag.

Hubert, F. and Pain, N. (2002) *Fiscal Incentives, European Integration, and the Location of Foreign Direct Investment*, Working Paper 195, London: National Institute of Economic and Social Research.

Hudson, R. (1999) 'The learning economy, the learning firm and the learning region. a sympathetic critique of the limits to learning', *European Urban and Regional Studies* 6: 59–72.

Huggins, R. (1996) 'Technology policy, networks and small firms in Denmark', *Regional Studies* 30(5): 523–552.

—— (2000) 'The success and failure of policy-implanted inter-firm network initiatives: motivations, processes and structure', *Entrepreneurship & Regional Development* 12: 111–135.

234 References

—— (2003) 'Creating a UK competitiveness index: regional and local benchmarking', *Regional Studies* 37: 89–96.

—— (2009) 'Regional competitive intelligence: benchmarking and policy making', *Regional Studies* 43(1): 1–20.

Hughes, H. (1993) 'An external view', in L. Low, M. H. Toh, T. W. Soon, K. Y. Tan and H. Hughes (eds) *Challenge and Response, Thirty Years of the Economic Development Board: Sharing Singapore's Experiences and Future Challenges*, Singapore: The Institute of Policy Studies/Times Academic Press.

Humphrey, J. and Schmitz, H. (2002) 'How does insertion in global value chains affect upgrading in industrial clusters?', *Regional Studies* 36(9): 1017–1027.

Imrie, R. and Thomas, H. (1999) *British Urban Policy and the Urban Development Corporations*, London: Sage.

Inglehart, R. and Norris, P. (2003) *Rising Tide*, New York: Cambridge University Press.

Inglehart, R. and Welzel, C. (2005) *Modernization, Cultural Change and Democracy*, New York: Cambridge University Press.

Isserman, A. (1994) 'State economic development policy and practice in the United States, a survey article', *International Regional Science Review* 16(1&2): 49–100.

Jacobs, J. (1961) *The Death and Life of Great American Cities*, New York: Random House.

—— (1969) *The Economy of Cities*, New York: Random House.

Jacobsen, N. B. (2003) 'The industrial symbiosis in Kalundborg, Denmark', in E. Cohen-Rosenthal (ed.) *Eco-industrial Strategies*, Sheffield: Greenleaf.

Jaffe, A. (1989) 'Real effects of academic research', *American Economic Review* 79: 957–970.

Jaffe, A., Peterson, S., Portney, P. and Stavins, R. (1995) 'Environmental regulation and the competitiveness of U.S. manufacturing: what does the evidence tell us?', *Journal of Economic Literature* 33: 132–163.

James, A. (2005) 'Demystifying the role of culture in innovative regional economies', *Regional Studies* 39(9): 1197–1216.

Jänicke, M. (1985) *Preventive Environmental Policy as Ecological Modernization and Structural Policy*, Discussion Paper IIUG dp85-2, Internationales Institut Für Umwelt und Gesellschaft, Wissenschaftszentrum Berlin Für Sozialforschung.

—— (2008) 'Ecological modernization: new perspectives', *Journal of Cleaner Production* 16: 557–565.

Jänicke, M., Mönch, H. and Binder, M. (2000) 'Structural change and environmental policy', in S. Young (ed.) *The Emergence of Ecological Modernization: Integrating the Environment and the Economy?*, London: Routledge.

Jensen, R. and Thursby, M. (2001) 'Proofs and prototypes for sale: the licensing of university inventions', *American Economic Review* 91(1): 240–259.

John Lewis Partnership (2009) *Corporate Social Responsibility Report 2009*, London: John Lewis Partnership.

Jones, J. and Wren, C. (2004) 'Do foreign inward investors achieve their job targets?', *Oxford Bulletin of Economics and Statistics* 66(4): 483–513.

Kay, J. (2004) 'Driving through the spin on Honda', *The Financial Times* 15 November.

Kemp, R. (1993) 'An economic analysis of cleaner technology: theory and evidence', in K. Fischer and J. Schot (eds) *Environmental Strategies for Industry: International Perspectives on Research Needs and Policy Implications*, Washington, DC: Island Press.

Kenney, M. (1986) *Biotechnology: The University-Industrial Complex*, New Haven, CT: Yale University Press.

Kenney, M. and Florida, R. (2000) 'Introduction', in M. Kenney (ed.) *Understanding Silicon Valley: The Anatomy of an Entrepreneurial Region*, Stanford, CA: Stanford University Press.

Kenny, C. and Williams, D. (2001) 'What do we know about economic growth? Or, why don't we know very much?', *World Development* 29(1): 1–22.

Kim, S. (1995) 'Expansion of markets and the geographic distribution of economic activities: the trends in US regional manufacturing structure, 1860–1987', *The Quarterly Journal of Economics* 110: 881–908.

Kim, S. and Margo, R. (2004) 'Historical perspectives on U.S. economic geography', in J. Henderson and J. Thisse (eds) *Handbook of Regional and Urban Economics, Volume 4 Cities and Geography*, Amsterdam: Elsevier.

King, J. (1990) *Regional Selective Assistance, 1980–84: An Evaluation by DTI, IDS and WOID*, London: HMSO.

Kirkham, J. and Watts, H. (1998) 'Multinational manufacturing organisations and plant closures in urban areas', *Urban Studies* 35(9): 1559–1575.

Kitch, E. (1977) 'The nature and function of the patent system', *Journal of Law and Economics* 20(2): 265–290.

Kitson, M., Martin, R. and Tyler, P. (2004) 'Regional competitiveness: an elusive yet key concept?', *Regional Studies* 38(9): 991–999.

Klepper, S. (2006) 'Disagreements, spinoffs, and the evolution of Detroit as the capital of the U.S. automobile industry', *Management Science* 53(4): 616–631.

—— (2009) 'Silicon Valley – a chip off the old Detroit block', in D. Audretsch, R. Strom and Z. Acs (eds) *Entrepreneurship, Growth, and Public Policy*, Cambridge: Cambridge University Press.

Kloosterman, R. (2008) 'Walls and bridges: knowledge spillover between "superdutch" architectural firms', *Journal of Economic Geography* 8: 545–563.

Knudsen, B., Florida, R., Stolarick, K. and Gates, G. (2008) 'Density and creativity in U.S. regions', *Annals of the Association of American Geographers* 98(2): 461–478.

Korhonen, J. (2002) 'Two paths to industrial ecology: applying the product-based and geographical approaches', *Journal of Environmental Planning and Management* 45(1): 39–57.

Koser, K. and Salt, J. (1998) 'The geography of highly skilled international migration', *International Journal of Population Geography* 3(4): 285–303.

Kotler, P., Haider, D. and Rein, I. (1993) *Marketing Places: Attracting Investment, Industry and Tourism to Cities, States and Nations*, New York: Free Press.

Kotval, Z. and Mullin, J. (1998) 'The potential for planning an industrial cluster in Barre, Vermont: a case of "hard rock" resistance in the granite industry', *Planning Practice & Research* 13(3): 311–18.

Kruger, J. (2005) *From SO2 to Greenhouse Gases: Trends and Events Shaping Future Emissions Trading Programs in the United States*, Resources for the Future Discussion Paper 05-20, Washington DC: Resources for the Future.

Krugman, P. (1993) 'Lessons of Massachusetts for EMU', in F. Torres and F. Giavazzi (eds) *Adjustment and Growth in the European Monetary Union*, Cambridge: Cambridge University Press.

—— (1994) 'Competitiveness: a dangerous obsession', *Foreign Affairs* 73: 28–44.

—— (1996) *Pop Internationalism*, Cambridge, MA: MIT Press.

—— (2005) 'Second winds for industrial regions', in D. Coyle, W. Alexander and B. Ashcroft (eds) *New Wealth for Old Nations*, Princeton, NJ: Princeton University Press.

Labatt, S., and Maclaren, V. (1998) 'Voluntary corporate environmental initiatives: a typology and preliminary investigation', *Environment and Planning C* 16: 191–209.

Lagendijk, A. (1999). 'Learning in non-core regions: towards intelligent clusters addressing business and regional needs', in R. Rutten, S. Bakkers, K. Morgan and F. Boekem (eds) *Learning Regions: Theory, Policy and Practice*, Cheltenham: Edward Elgar.

Lambert, R. (2003) *Lambert Review of Business–University Collaboration*, London: HM Treasury.

Lankoski, L. (2000) 'Determinants of environment profit. An analysis of the firm-level relationship between environmental performance and economic performance', Doctoral dissertation, Department of Industrial Engineering and Management, Helsinki University of Technology, Helsinki.

Lawson, C. and Lorenz, E. (1999) 'Collective learning, tacit knowledge and regional innovation capacity', *Regional Studies* 33: 305–317.

Leamer, E. and Storper, M. (2001) 'The Economic Geography of the Internet Age', *Journal of International Business Studies* 32(4): 641–665.

Lehmann, C. (2003) 'Class acts', *Raritan* 22: 147–167.

Leitner, H. and Garner, M. (1993) 'The limits of local initiatives: a reassessment of urban entrepreneurialism for urban development', *Urban Geography* 14: 57–77.

Lever-Tracy, C. (1992) 'Interpersonal trust in ethnic business – traditional, modern or postmodern?', *Policy Organisation and Society* 5 Winter: 50–63.

Levine, M. (1987) 'Downtown redevelopment as an urban growth strategy: a critical appraisal of the Baltimore renaissance', *Journal of Urban Affairs* 9: 103–124.

Levy, S. (2001) *Hackers: Heroes of the Computer Revolution*, London: Penguin.

Lewicki, R., McAllister, D. and Bies, R. (1998) 'Trust and distrust: new relationships and realities' *Academy of Management Review* 22(3): 438–458.

Liberatoire, A. (1995) 'The social construction of environmental problems', in P. Gasbergen and A. Blowers (eds) *Environmental Policy in an International Context*, London: Arnold.

Linder, S. (2003) *State of the Business Incubation Industry*, Athens, OH: National Business Incubation Association.

Link, A. and Scott, J. (2007) 'The economics of university research parks', *Oxford Review of Economic Policy* 23(4): 661–674.

Longhi, C. (1999). 'Networks, collective learning and technology development in innovative high technology regions: the case of Sophia-Antipolis', *Regional Studies* 33(4): 333–342.

Lovering, J. (1999) 'Theory led by policy: the inadequacies of the "new regionalism" (illustrated from the case of Wales)', *International Journal of Urban and Regional Research* 23: 379–395.

—— (2001) 'The coming regional crisis (and how to avoid it)', *Regional Studies* 35(4): 349–354.

—— (2003) 'MNCs and wannabes – inward investment, discourses of regional development, and the regional service class', in N. Phelps and P. Raines (eds) *The New Competition for Inward Investment*, Cheltenham: Edward Elgar.

Lowe, E. (1997) 'Creating by-product resource exchanges: strategies for eco-industrial parks', *Journal of Cleaner Production* 5(1–2): 57–65.

Lucas, R. (1988) 'On the mechanics of economic development', *Journal of Monetary Economics* 22: 3–42.

Luger, M. (2009) 'Configuring to be globally competitive', in J. Rowe (ed.) *Theories of Local Economic Development – Linking Theory to Practice*, Aldershot: Ashgate.

Lumpkin, J. and Ireland, R. (1988) 'Screening practices of new business incubators: the evaluation of critical success factors', *American Journal of Small Business* 12(4): 59–81.

Lundvall, B.-Å. (1992) *National Systems of Innovation*, London: Pinter.
—— (1999) 'Technology policy in the learning economy,' in D. Archibugi, J. Howells and J. Michie (eds) *Innovation Policy in a Global Economy*, Cambridge: Cambridge University Press.
Lundvall, B-Å. and Johnson, B. (1994) 'The learning economy', *Journal of Industry Studies* 1: 23–42.
McAdam, M. and McAdam, R. (2006) 'The role and operation of entrepreneurial networking with the university science park incubator (USI)', *Entrepreneurship and Innovation* 7(2): 87–97.
McCann, P. (1997) 'How deeply embedded is Silicon Glen? A cautionary note', *Regional Studies* 31(7): 695–703.
—— (2001) *Urban and Regional Economics*, Oxford: Oxford University Press.
—— (2007) 'Observational equivalence? Regional studies and regional science', *Regional Studies* 41(9): 1209–1221.
McCrone, G. (1969) *Regional Policy in Britain*, London: George Allen & Unwin.
Macdonald, S. (1987) 'British science parks: reflections on the politics of high technology', *R&D Management* 17(1): 25–37.
McDonough, W. and Braungart, M. (2002) *Cradle to Cradle: Remaking the Way We Make Things*, New York: North Point Press.
McGranahan, D. and Wojan, T. (2007) 'Recasting the creative class to examine growth processes in rural and urban counties', *Regional Studies* 41(2): 197–216.
Mackie, J. (1980) *The Cement of the Universe: A Study of Causation*, Oxford: Oxford University Press.
MacKinnon, D., Cumbers, A. and Chapman, K. (2002) 'Learning, innovation and regional development: a critical appraisal of recent debates', *Progress in Human Geography* 26: 293–311.
McVittie, E. and Swales, K. (2007) 'Constrained discretion in UK monetary and regional policy', *Regional Studies* 38(9): 1101–1120.
McWilliams, A. and Siegel, D. (2000) 'Corporate social responsibility and financial performance: correlation or misspecification?', *Strategic Management Journal* 21(5): 603–609.
Mair, A. (1999) 'Learning from Honda', *Journal of Management Studies* 36(1): 25–44.
Malanga, S. (2004) 'The curse of the creative class', *City Journal* Winter: 36–45.
Malecki, E. (1991) *Technology and Economic Development*, Harlow: Longman Scientific and Technical.
—— (2004) 'Jockeying for position: what it means and why it matters to regional development policy when places compete', *Regional Studies* 38(9): 1101–1120.
—— (2007) 'Cities and regions competing in the global economy: knowledge and local development policies', *Environment and Planning C: Government and Policy* 25: 638–654.
Malecki, E. and Oinas, P. (1999) *Making Connections: Technological Learning and Regional Economic Change*, Aldershot: Ashgate.
Malecki, E. and Tootle, D. (1996) 'The role of networks in small firm competitiveness', *International Journal of Technology Management* 11(1/2): 43–57.
Malmberg, A. and Maskell, P. (2002) 'The elusive concept of localization economies: towards a knowledge-based theory of spatial clustering', *Environment and Planning A* 34: 429–449.
Malmberg, A., Malmberg, B. and Lundequist, P. (2000) 'Agglomeration and firm performance: economies of scale, localisation, and urbanisation among Swedish export firms', *Environment and Planning A* 32: 305–321.

Marcuse, P. (2003) Review of Richard Florida's 'The Rise of the Creative Class', *Urban Land* 62: 40–41.
Margolis, J. and Walsh, J. (2003) 'Misery loves companies: rethinking social initiatives by Business', *Administrative Science Quarterly* 48(2): 268–305.
Markides, C. (1998) 'Strategic innovation in established companies', *Sloan Management Review* 39(3):31–42.
Markusen, A. (1999) 'Fuzzy concepts, scanty evidence, policy distance: the case for rigour and policy relevance in critical regional studies', *Regional Studies* 33: 869–884.
—— (2004) 'Targeting occupations in regional and community economic development', *Journal of American Planning Association* 70(3):253–269.
—— (2006) 'Urban development and the politics of a creative class: evidence from the study of artists', *Environment and Planning A* 38: 1921–1940.
Markusen, A. and Schrock, G. (2006) 'The artistic dividend: urban artistic specialisation and economic development implications', *Urban Studies* 43(10): 1661–1686.
Marlet, G. and van Woerkens, C. (2004) *Skills and creativity in a cross section of Dutch cities*, Tjalling C. Koopmans Research Institute Discussion Paper 04-29, Utrecht: Utrecht School of Economics, Universiteit Utrecht, Netherlands.
Marsden, T. (1999) 'Rural futures? The consumption countryside and its regulation', *Sociologia Ruralis* 39(6): 501–520.
Marsden, T. and Smith, E. (2005) 'Ecological entrepreneurship: sustainable development in local communities through quality food production and local branding', *Geoforum* 36: 440–451.
Marsden, T., Murdoch, J. and Morgan, K. (1999) 'Sustaianble agriculture, food supply chains and regional development', *International Planning Studies* 4(3): 295–301.
Marshall, A. (1890) *Principles of Economics*, London: MacMillan.
—— (1923) *Industry and Trade*, 4th edition, London: MacMillan.
—— (1927) *Principles of Economics*, 8th edition, London: MacMillan.
Martin, R. and Sunley, P. (1998) 'Slow convergence? The new endogenous growth theory and regional development', *Economic Geography* 74(3): 201–227.
—— (2003) 'Deconstructing clusters: chaotic concept or policy panacea?', *Journal of Economic Geography* 3: 5–35.
Maskell, P. (1998) 'Learning in the village economy of Denmark: the role of institutions and policy in sustaining competitiveness', in H-J. Braczyk, P. Cooke and M. Heidenreich (eds) *Regional Innovation Systems*, London: UCL Press.
—— (2001) 'Towards a knowledge-based theory of the geographical cluster', *Industrial and Corporate Change* 10(4): 921–943.
Maskell, P. and Malmberg, A. (1999) 'Localized learning and industrial competitiveness', *Cambridge Journal of Economics* 23: 167–186.
Maskell, P., Eskelin, H., Hannibalsson, I., Malmberg, A. and Vatne, E. (1998) *Competitiveness, Localised Learning and Regional Development*, London: Routledge.
Massey, D. (1984) *Spatial Divisions of Labour*, London: MacMillan.
—— (2004) 'The responsibilities of place', *Local Economy* 19: 97–101.
Massey, D., Quintas, P. and Weild, D. (1992) *High Tech Fantasies: Science Parks in Society*, London: Routledge.
May, W., Mason, C. and Pinch, S. (2001) 'Explaining industrial agglomeration: the case of the British high-fidelity industry', *Geoforum* 32(3): 363–376.
Mellander, C. and Florida, R. (2006) *Human capital or the creative class – explaining regional development in Sweden*, KTH/CESIS Working Paper Series in Economics and Institutions of Innovation.

Merges, R. and Nelson, R. (1990) 'On the complex economics of patent scope', *Columbia Law Review* 90(4): 839–916.

Metcalfe, J. (1995) 'Technology systems and technology policy in an evolutionary framework', *Cambridge Journal of Economics* 19(1): 25–46.

Meyer, P. (2003) *Episodes of Collective Invention*, Bureau of Labor Statistics Working Paper 368, Washington DC: US Department of Labor, Office of productivity and technology.

Mian, S. (1996) 'Assessing value-added contributions of university technology business incubators to tenant firms', *Research Policy* 25: 325–335.

—— (1997) 'Assessing and managing the university technology business incubator: an integrative framework', *Journal of Business Venturing* 12: 251–285.

Midmore, P. and Thomas, D. (2006) 'Regional self reliance and economic development: the Pembrokeshire case', *Local Economy* 21(4): 391–408.

Miles, R. and Snow, C. (1992) 'Causes of failure in network organizations', *California Management Review* 34(4):53–72.

Mintzberg, H. (1987) 'Crafting strategy', *Harvard Business Review* July–August: 66–75.

Mol, A. (1997) 'Ecological modernization: industrial transformations and environmental reform', in M. Redclift and M. Woodgate (eds) *The International Handbook of Environmental Sociology*, Cheltenham: Edward Elgar.

Monck, C., Porter, R., Quintas, P., Storey, D. and Wynarczyk, P. (1988) *Science Parks and the Growth of High Technology Firms*, London: Croom Helm.

Moore, B. and Begg, I. (2004) ' Urban growth and competitiveness in Britain: a long run perspective', in M. Boddy and M. Parkinson (eds) *City Matters: Competitiveness, Cohesion and Urban Governance*', Bristol: Policy Press.

Moore, G. (2001) 'Corporate social and financial performance: an investigation into the UK supermarket industry', *Journal of Business Ethics* 34: 299–315.

Morad, M. (2007) 'An exploratory review of the role of ecological modernisation in supporting local economies' green drive', *Local Economy* 22(1): 27–39.

Moreno, A. and Casillas, J. (2007) 'High growth SMEs versus non high growth SMEs: a discriminant analysis', *Entrepreneurship & Regional Development* 19(1): 69–88.

Morgan, K. (1997) 'The learning region: institutions, innovation and regional renewal', *Regional Studies* 31: 491–503.

Murdoch, J. and Miele, M. (1999) '"Back to nature": changing worlds of production in the food sector', *Sociologia Ruralis* 39(4): 312–338.

—— (2002) 'The practical aesthetics of traditional cuisines: slow food in Tuscany', *Sociologia Ruralis* 42(4): 312–328.

Murdoch, J., Marsden, T. and Banks, J. (2000) 'Quality, nature and embeddedness: some theoretical considerations in the context of the food sector', *Economic Geography* 76(2): 107–125.

Murphy, J. and Gouldson, A. (2000) 'Environmental policy and industrial innovation: integrating environment and economy through ecological modernization', *Geoforum* 31: 33–44.

Myrdal, G. (1957) *Economic Theory and Underdeveloped Regions*, London: Duckworth.

National Audit Office (2003) *Success in the Regions*, Report by the Comptroller and Auditor-General HC 1268, London: TSO.

Nelson, A. (2009) 'Measuring knowledge spillovers: what patents, licenses and publications reveal about innovation diffusion', *Research Policy* 38: 994–1005.

Nelson, R. (2001) 'Observations on the Post-Bayh-Dole rise of patenting at American universities', *Journal of Technology Transfer* 26(1–2): 13–19.

Nelson, R. and Rosenberg, N. (1993) 'Technical innovation and national systems', in R. Nelson (ed.) *National Systems of Innovation: A Comparative Analysis*, Oxford: Oxford University Press.

Nelson, R. and Winter, S. (1982) *An Evolutionary View of Economic Change*, Cambridge, MA: Harvard University Press.

Nerkat, A. and Shane, S. (2003) 'When do start-ups that exploit academic knowledge survive?', *International Journal of Industrial Organization* 21(9): 1391–1410.

Nonaka, I. (1994) 'A dynamic theory of organizational knowledge creation', *Organization Science* 5(1): 14–37.

Nuti, F. and G. Cainelli (1996) 'Changing directions in Italy's manufacturing industrial districts: the case of the Emilian footwear districts of Fusignano and San Mauro Pascoli', *Journal of Industry Studies* 3(2): 105–118.

Oakey, R. (1995) *High Technology Small Firms: Innovation and Regional Development in Britain and the United States*, London: Pinter.

Oakey, R., Kipling, M. and Wildgust, S. (2001) 'Clustering among firms in the non-broadcast visual communications (NBVC) sector', *Regional Studies* 35(5): 401–414.

Oakey, R., Faulkner, W., Cooper, S. and Walsh, V. (1990) *New Firms in the Biotechnology Industry: Their Contribution to Innovation and Growth*, London: Pinter.

OECD (1995) *Boosting Business Advisory Services*, Paris: Organization for Economic Cooperation and Development.

Ohlin, B. (1933) *Interregional and Internal Trade*, Cambridge, MA: Harvard University Press.

Oke, A., Burke, G. and Myers, A. (2007) 'Innovation types and performance in growing UK SMEs', *International Journal of Operations and Production Management* 27(7): 735–753.

Oldenburg, K. and Geiser, K. (1997) 'Pollution prevention and … or industrial ecology?', *Journal of Cleaner Production* 5(1–2): 103–108.

Opoku, H. (2004) 'Policy implications of industrial ecology conceptions', *Business Strategy and the Environment* 13(5): 320–333.

O'Rourke, D., Connelly, L. and Koshland, C. (1996) 'Industrial ecology: a critical review', *International Journal of Environment and Pollution* 6(2–3): 89–112.

Oswald, A (1997) 'Happiness and economic performance', *Economic Journal* 107(445): 1815–1831.

OTA (Office of Technology Assessment) (1984) *Commercial Biotechnology: An International Analysis*, Washington DC: Government Printing Office.

Ottaviano, G. and Peri, G. (2005) 'Cities and culture', *Journal of Urban Economics* 58: 304–337.

Overman, H. (2004) 'Can we learn from economic geography proper?', *Journal of Economic Geography* 4: 501–516.

PA Cambridge Economic Consultants (1993) *Regional Selective Assistance 1985–88*, London: Department of Trade and Industry.

—— (1995) *Final Evaluation of Enterprise Zones*, London: Department of the Environment.

Page, S. (2007) *The Difference: How the Power of Diversity Creates Better Groups, Firms, Schools, and Societies*, Princeton, NJ: Princeton University Press.

Paija, L. (2001) 'The ICT cluster: the engine of knowledge-driven growth in Finland', in P. den Hertog, E. Bergman and D. Charles (eds) *Innovative Clusters: Drivers of National Innovation Systems*, Paris: Organization for Economic Cooperation and Development.

Pakes, A. and Griliches, Z. (1984) 'Patents and R&D at the firm level: a first look', in Z. Griliches (ed.) *R&D, Patents and Productivity*, Chicago, IL: Chicago University Press.

Paniccia, I. (2002) *Industrial Districts Evolution and Competitiveness in Italian Firms*, Cheltenham: Edward Elgar.
Parker, S., Storey, D. and van Witteloostuijn, A. (2006) 'What happens to gazelles? The importance of dynamic management theory', paper presented the Fourth Symposium of the New Zealand Centre for SME Research, Wellington: Massey University.
Parliamentary Commissioner for the Environment (PCE) (2004) *Growing For Good: Intensive Farming, Sustainability and New Zealand's Environment*, Wellington: PCE.
Parr, J. (2002) 'Agglomeration economies: ambiguities and confusions', *Environment and Planning A* 34: 717–731.
Pascale, R. (1984) 'Perspectives on strategy: the real story behind Honda's success', *California Management Review* 26(3): 47–72.
Pawson, R. (2006) *Evidence-based policy: a realist perspective*, London: Sage.
Pawson, R. and Tilley, N. (1997) *Realistic Evaluation*, Sage, London.
Paxton, A. (1994) *The Food Miles Report: The Dangers of Long Distance Food Transport*, London: Safe Alliance.
Peach, C. (2005) 'The ghetto and the ethnic enclave', in D. Varady (ed.) *Desegregating the City*, Albany: State University of New York Press.
Pearce, R. (1999) 'The evolution of technology in multinational enterprises: the role of creative subsidiaries', *International Business Review* 8: 125–148.
Peck J (1999) 'Grey geography', *Transactions of the Institute of British Geographers. New Series* 24: 131–136.
—— (2005) 'Struggling with the Creative Class', *International Journal of Urban and Regional Research* 29(4): 740–770.
Penrose, E. (1959) *The Theory of Growth of the Firm*, Oxford: Blackwell.
Perry, M. (1985) 'Searching for jobs in Workington', *Northern Economic Review* 9(1): 28–36.
—— (1999) *Small Firms and Network Economies*, London: Routledge.
—— (2001) *Shared Trust Strategies for Small Industrial Countries*, Wellington: Institute of Policy Studies, Victoria University of Wellington.
—— (2003) 'Job transfers and regional labour migrants in New Zealand', *Australasian Journal of Regional Studies* 8(2): 165–182.
—— (2004) 'Business cluster promotion in New Zealand and the limits of exemplar clusters', *Policy and Society* 23(4): 82–103.
—— (2005) *Business Clusters: An International Perspective*, London: Routledge.
—— (2007a) 'From networks to clusters and back again: a decade of unsatisfied policy aspiration in New Zealand', in R. MacGregor and A. Hodgkinson (eds) *Small Business Clustering Technologies*, Hershey, PA: Idea Group.
—— (2007b) 'Business environments and cluster attractiveness to managers'. *Entrepreneurship & Regional Development* 19(1): 1–24.
Perry, M. and Tan B. H. (1998) 'Global manufacturing and local linkage in Singapore', *Environment and Planning A* 30:1603–1624.
Peters, E. and Hood, N. (2000) 'Implementing the cluster approach', *International Studies of Management & Organization* 30(2): 68–92.
Pettus, M. (2001) 'The resource-based view as a development growth process: evidence from the deregulated trucking industry', *Academy of Management Journal* 44: 878–896.
Phan, P., Siegel, D. and Wright, M. (2005) 'Science parks and incubators: observations, synthesis and future research', *Journal of Business Venturing* 20: 165–182.
Phelps, N. (1993) 'Contemporary industrial restructuring and linkage change in an older industrial region: examples from the northeast of England', *Environment and Planning A* 25: 863–882.

Phelps, N. and Tewdwr-Jones, M. (2001) 'Globalisation, regions and the state: exploring the limitations of economic modernisation through inward investment', *Urban Studies* 38(8): 1253–1272.

Phelps, N., MacKinnon, D., Stone, I. and Braidford, P. (2003) 'Embedding the multinationals? Institutions and the development of overseas manufacturing affiliates in Wales and North East England', *Regional Studies* 37(1): 27–40.

Pike, A. (1998) 'Making performance plants from branch plants? *In-situ* restructuring in the automotive industry in UK Region', *Environment and Planning A* 30: 881–900.

Pike, A., Rodríguez-Pose, A. and Tomaney, J. (2006) *Local and Regional Development*, London: Routledge.

Pinch, S. and Henry, N. (1999) 'Paul Krugman's geographical economics, industrial clustering and the British motor sport industry', *Regional Studies* 33(9): 815–827.

Pinch, S., Henry, N., Jenkins, M. and Tallman, S. (2003) 'From "industrial districts" to "knowledge clusters": a model of knowledge dissemination and competitive advantage in industrial agglomerations', *Journal of Economic Geography* 3: 373–388.

Piore, M. and Sabel, C. (1984) *The Second Industrial Divide*, New York: Basic Books.

Plambeck, E. and Denend, L. (2008) 'The greening of WalMart', *Stanford Social Innovation Review* Spring: 53–59.

Porter, M. (1990) *The Competitive Advantage of Nations*, New York: Free Press.

—— (1991) 'America's green strategy', *Scientific American* 264(4): 96–103.

—— (2000) 'Locations, clusters and company strategy', in G. Clark, M. Feldman and M. Gertler (eds) *The Oxford Handbook of Economic Geography*, Oxford: Oxford University Press.

—— (2003) 'The economic performance of regions', *Regional Studies* 37(6–7): 549–578.

Porter, M. and Ketels, C. (2003) *UK Competitiveness: Moving to the Next Stage*, DTI Economics Paper 3, London: Department of Trade and Industry.

Porter, M. and Van der Linde, C. (1995) 'Toward a new conception of the environment–competitiveness relationship', *Journal of Economic Perspectives* 9(4): 97–118.

Preston, L. and O'Bannon, D. (1997) 'The corporate social–financial performance relationship: a typology and analysis', *Business and Society* 36(4): 419–428.

Prevezer (1998). 'Clustering in biotechnology in the USA', in G. Swann, M. Prevezer and D. Stout (eds) *The Dynamics of Industrial Clustering: International Comparisons in Computing and Biotechnology*, Oxford: Oxford University Press.

Qadeer, M. (2005) 'Ethnic segregation in a multicultural city', in D. Varady (ed.) *Desegregating the City*, Albany: State University of New York Press.

Quintas, P., Wield, D. and Massey, D. (1992) 'Academic-industry links and innovation: questioning the science park model', *Technovation* 12: 161–175.

Rabellotti, R. and Schmitz, H. (1999) 'The internal heterogeneity of industrial districts in Italy, Brazil and Mexico', *Regional Studies* 33: 97–108.

Radosevich, R. (1995) 'A model for entrepreneurial spin-offs from public technology sources', *International Journal of Technology Management* 10(7/8): 879–893.

Raines, P. (2000) 'Regions in competition: inward investment and regional variation in the use of incentives', *Regional Studies* 34(3): 291–296.

—— (2002) *Cluster Development and Policy*, Aldershot: Ashgate.

Rainey, D. (2005) *Sustainable Business Development*, Cambridge: Cambridge University Press.

Rallet, A. and Torre, A. (1999) 'Is geographical proximity necessary in the innovation networks in the era of the global economy?', *GeoJournal* 49: 373–380.

Rao, H. and Drazin, R. (2002) 'Overcoming resource constraints on product innovation by recruiting talent from rivals: a study of the mutual fund industry, 1986–1994', *Academy of Management Journal* 45: 215–240.

Rauch, J. (1993) 'Productivity gains from geographic concentration of human capital: evidence from the cities', *Journal of Urban Economics* 34: 380–400.

Renting, H., Marsden, T. and Banks, J. (2003) 'Understanding alternative food networks: exploring the role of short food supply chains in rural development', *Environment and Planning A* 35(3): 393–411.

Roberts, E. and Berry, C. (1985) 'Entering new businesses: selecting strategies for success', *Sloan Management Review* Spring: 3–17.

Roberts, E. and Malone, D. (1996) 'Policies and structures for spinning off new companies from research and development organizations', *R&D Management* 26: 17–48.

Robson, C. (2002) *Real World Research* 2nd edition, London: Routledge.

Robson, P. and Bennet, R. (2001) 'SME growth: the relationship with business advice and external collaboration', *Small Business Economics* 15: 193–208.

Roest, K. and Menghi, A. (2000) 'Reconsidering "traditional" food: the case of Parmigiano Reggiano cheese', *Sociologia Ruralis* 40(4): 439–451.

Romanelli, E. (1989) 'Environments and strategies of organization start-up: effects on early survival', *Administrative Science Quarterly* 34: 369–387.

Romer, P. (1986) 'Increasing returns and long run growth', *Journal of Political Economy* 90: 1002–1037.

—— (1987) 'Crazy explanations of the productivity slowdown', *NBER Macroeconomics Annual* 2: 163–202.

—— (1990) 'Endogenous technical change', *Journal of Political Economy* 98(5): 1257–1278.

Roper, S. and Hewitt-Dundas, N. (2001) 'Grant assistance and small firm development in Northern Ireland and the Republic of Ireland', *Scottish Journal of Political Economy* 48: 99–117.

Rose, R. (1993) *Lesson-Drawing in Public Policy: A Guide to Learning Across Time and Space*, Chatham, NJ: Chatham House Publishers.

Rosenberg, N. (1982) *Inside the Black Box: Technology and Economics*, Cambridge: Cambridge University Press.

Rosenfeld, S. (2003) 'Expanding opportunities: cluster strategies that reach more people and more places', *European Planning Studies* 11(4): 359–377.

—— (2005) 'Industry clusters: business choice, policy outcome, or branding strategy?', *Journal of New Business Ideas and Trends* 3(2): 4–13.

Rothaermel, F. and Thursby, M. (2005) 'Incubator firm failure or graduation? The role of university linkages', *Research Policy* 34: 1076–1090.

Rowe, J. (2005) 'Lessons learned and future directions', in J. Rowe (ed.) *Economic Development in New Zealand*, Aldershot: Ashgate.

—— (2009a) 'The importance of theory: linking theory to practice', in J. Rowe (ed.) *Theories of Local Economic Development – Linking Theory to Practice*, Aldershot: Ashgate.

—— (2009b) 'Towards an alternative theoretical framework for understanding local economic development', in J. Rowe (ed.) *Theories of Local Economic Development – Linking Theory to Practice*, Aldershot: Ashgate.

Rubin, H. (1988) 'Shoot anything that flies, claim anything that falls: conversations with economic development practitioners', *Economic Development Quarterly* 2(3): 236–251.

Ryans, J. and Shanklin, W. (1986) *Guide to Marketing for Economic Development: Competing in America's Second Civil War*, Columbus, OH: Publishing Horizons.

Sabel, C. (1992) 'Studied trust: building new forms of co-operation in a volatile economy', in F. Pyke and W. Sengenberger (eds) *Industrial Districts and Local Economic Regeneration*, Geneva: International Institute for Labour Studies.
Saiz, A. (2003a) 'The impact of immigration on American cities: an introduction to the issues', *Federal Reserve Bank of Philadelphia Review* 4: 11–23.
—— (2003b) 'Room in the kitchen for the melting pot: Immigration and rental prices', *Review of Economics and Statistics* 85(3): 502–521.
Sako, M. (1992) *Prices, Quality and Trust: Inter-firm Relations in Britain and Japan*, Cambridge: Cambridge University Press.
Salzmann, O., Ionescu-Somers, A. and Steger, U. (2005) 'The business case for corporate sustainability: literature review and research options', *European Management Journal* 23(1): 27–36.
Samson, K. and Gurdon, M. (1993) 'University scientists as entrepreneurs: a special case of technology transfer and high technology venturing', *Technovation* 13(2): 63–71.
Saunders, C., Barber, A. and Taylor, G. (2006) *Food miles – comparative energy/emissions performance of New Zealand's agriculture industry*, AERU Research Report 285, Lincoln University, New Zealand.
Saunders, C., Cagatay, S. and Moxey, A. (2004) *Trade and the Environment: Economic and Environmental Impacts of Global Dairy Trade Liberalisation*, Research Report 267, Lincoln, Canterbury: Agribusiness and Economics Research Unit, Lincoln University.
Saxenian, A. (1994) *Regional Advantage: Culture and Competition in Silicon Valley and Route 128*, Cambridge, MA: Harvard University Press.
—— (2002) 'Silicon Valley's new immigrant high-growth entrepreneurs', *Economic Development Quarterly* 16(1): 20–31.
Sayers, J., Low, W. and Davenport, E. (2008) 'Te Warewhare: the impact of the Warehouse on Māori', *University of Auckland Business Review* 10(2): 36–53.
Schlarb, M. (2001) *Eco-industrial Development: A Strategy for Building Sustainable Communities*, Washington DC: United States Economic Development Administration, Cornell University.
Schlich, E. and Fleisssner, U. (2003) 'A comparison of regional energy turnover with global food', *The International Journal of Life Cycle Assessment* 8(4): 252.
Schmitz, H. (1995) 'Collective efficiency: growth path for small-scale industry', *Journal of Development Studies* 31: 529–566.
—— (1999) 'Global competition and local cooperation: success and failure in the Sinos Valley, Brazil', *World Development* 27: 1627–1650.
—— (2004) *Local Enterprises in the Global Economy: Issues of Governance and Upgrading*, Cheltenham: Edward Elgar.
—— (2007) 'Regional systems and global chains', in A. Scott and G. Garofoldi (eds) *Development on the Ground: Clusters, Networks and Regions in Emerging Economies*, Routledge: London.
Schmitz, H. and Nadvi, K. (1999) 'Clustering and industrialization: introduction', *World Development* 27: 1503–1514.
Schrader, S. (1991) 'Informal technology transfer between firms: co-operation through information trading', *Research Policy* 20: 153–170.
Schutjens, V. and Stam, E. (2000) 'The evolution and nature of young firms networks: a longitudinal study', paper presented at the Uddevalla Seminar, Lund-Jonkoping, Sweden.
Scott, A. (1988) *New Industrial Spaces: Flexible Production, Organization and Regional Development in North America and Western Europe*, London: Pion.

—— (2006a) 'Entrepreneurship, innovation and industrial development: geography and the creative field revisited', *Small Business Economics* 26(1), 1–24.
—— (2006b) 'Creative cities: conceptual issues and policy questions', *Journal of Urban Affairs* 28(1): 1–17.
Scott, A. and Storper, M. (1987) 'High technology industry and regional development: a theoretical critique and reconstruction', *International Social Science Journal* 112: 215–232.
—— (1992) 'Industrialization and regional development', in M. Storper and A. Scott (eds) *Pathways to Industrialization and Regional Development*, London: Routledge.
Segal, N. (1979) 'The limits and means of self-reliant regional economic growth', in D. Maclennan and J. Parr (eds) *Regional Policy: Past Experiences and New Directions*, Oxford: Martin Robinson.
Sforzi, F. (1990) 'The quantitative importance of Marshallian industrial districts in the Italian economy', in F. Pyke, G. Becattini and W. Sengenberger (eds) *Industrial Districts and Inter-Firm Co-operation in Italy*, Geneva: International Institute for Labour Studies.
Shane, S. (2001) 'Technology regimes and new firm formation', *Management Science* 47(9): 1173–1190.
Sharp, M. (1990) 'European countries in science-based competition: the case of biotechnology', in D. Hague (ed.) *The Management of Science*, Basingstoke: Macmillan.
—— (1999) 'The science of nations: European multinationals and American biotechnology', *Biotechnology* 1(1): 132–162.
Sheller, M. and Urry, J. (2006) 'The new mobilities paradigm', *Environment and Planning A* 38: 207–226.
Sherman, H. and Chappell, D. (1998) 'Methodological challenges in evaluating business incubator outcomes', *Economic Development Quarterly* 12(4): 313–321.
Shipman, M. (1997) *The Limitations of Social Research* 4th edition, London: Longman.
Siegel, D. and Wright, M. (2007) 'Intellectual property: the assessment', *Oxford Review of Economic Policy* 23(4): 529–540.
Siegel, D., Westhead, P. and Wright, M. (2003) 'Assessing the impact of science parks on the research productivity of firms: exploratory evidence from the United Kingdom', *International Journal of Industrial Organization* 21(9): 1357–1369.
Simon, C. (1998) 'Human capital and metropolitan employment growth', *Journal of Urban Economics* 43: 223–243.
Simpson, G. and Kohers, T. (2002) 'The link between corporate social and financial performance: evidence from the banking industry', *Journal of Business Ethics* 37: 97–109.
Sirsly, C-A. and Lamertz, K. (2008) 'When does a corporate social responsibility initiative provide a first-mover advantage?', *Business & Society* 47(3): 343–369.
Slowe, P. (1981) *The Advance Factory in Regional Development*, Aldershot: Gower.
Smallbone, D., Baldock, R. and Burgess, S. (2002) 'Targeted support for high growth start-ups: some policy issues', *Environment and Planning C: Government and Policy* 20: 195–209.
Smilor, R. (1987) 'Commercialising technology through new business incubators', *Research Management* 30(5): 36–41.
Smilor, R. and Gill, M. (1986) *The New Business Incubator: Linking Talent, Technology, Capital and Know How*, Lexington, MA: Lexington Books.
Smith, A. and Fox, T. (2007) 'From event-led to event-themed regeneration: the 2002 Commonwealth Games legacy programme', *Urban Studies* 44: 1125–1143.
Smith, M. (2005) 'Transnational urbanism revisited', *Journal of Ethnic and Migration Studies* 31: 235–244.

Smith, N. (2003) 'Corporate social responsibility: whether or how?', *California Management Review* 45(14): 52–76.

Solow, R. (1956) 'A contribution to the theory of economic growth', *Quarterly Journal of Economics* 70: 65–94.

Sölvell, Ö., Lindquist, G. and Ketels, C. (2003) *The Cluster Initiative Greenbook*, Stockholm: Ivory Tower AB.

Sorenson, O. and Audia, P. (2000) 'The social structure of entrepreneurial activity: geographic concentration of footwear production in the United States, 1940–1989', *American Journal of Sociology* 106(2): 424–462.

Soyez, D. (2002) 'Environmental knowledge, the power of framing and industrial change', in R. Hayter and R. Le Heron (eds) *Knowledge, Industry and Environment*, Aldershot: Ashgate.

Spaargaren, G. and Mol, A. (1992) 'Sociology, environment and modernity: ecological modernization as a theory of social change', *Society and Natural Resources* 5: 323–344.

Squires, G. And Kubrin, C. (2005) 'Privileged places: race, uneven development and the geography of opportunity in urban America', *Urban Studies* 42(1): 47–68.

Stavins, R. (2003) *Market-Based Environmental Policies: What Can We Learn From US Experience (and Related Research)?*, Resources for the Future Discussion Paper 03-43, Washington DC: Resources for the Future.

Steger, U. (2004) *The Business of Sustainability: Building Industry Cases for Corporate Sustainability*, Basingstoke: Palgrave Macmillan.

Stelder, D. (2002) 'Geographical grids in "new economic geography" models', in P. McCann (ed.) *Industrial Location Economics*, Cheltenham: Edward Elgar.

Sternberg, R. (1990) 'The impact of innovation centers on small technology-based firms; the example of the Federal Republic of Germany', *Small Business Economics* 2: 105–118.

Sterner, T. (2003) *Policy Instruments for Environmental and Natural Resource Management*, Washington DC: Resources for the Future.

Stolarick, K. and Florida, R. (2006) 'Creativity, connections and innovation: a study of linkages in the Montréal region', *Environment and Planning A* 38: 1799–1817.

Stone, I. and Peck, F. (1996) 'The foreign-owned manufacturing sector in UK peripheral regions, 1978–1993: restructuring and comparative performance', *Regional Studies* 30(1): 55–68.

Storey, D. (1982) *Entrepreneurship and the New Firm*, London: Croom Helm.

—— (1985) 'Manufacturing employment change in northern England 1965–78: the role of small businesses', in D. Storey (ed.) *Small Firms in Regional Economic Development*, Cambridge: Cambridge University Press.

—— (1994) *Understanding the Small Business Sector*, London: Routledge.

—— (1999) 'Six steps to heaven: evaluating the impact of public policies to support small businesses in developed economies', in D Sexton and H. Landstrom (eds) *Handbook of Entrepreneurship*, Oxford: Blackwell.

—— (2006) 'Evaluating SME policies and programmes: technical and political dimensions', in M. Casson, B. Yeung, A. Basu and N. Wadeson (eds) *The Oxford Handbook of Entrepreneurship*, Oxford: Oxford University Press.

Storper, M. (1995a)'Competitiveness policy options: the technology-regions connection', *Growth and Change* Spring: 285–308.

—— (1995b) 'The resurgence of regional economies, ten years later: the region as a nexus of untraded interdependencies', *European Urban and Regional Studies* 2: 191–222.

—— (1997) *The Regional World: Territorial Development in a Global Economy*, New York: Cambridge University Press.

Storper, M. and Scott, A. (1995) 'The wealth of regions: market forces and policy imperatives in local and global context', *Futures* 27: 505–526.

—— (2009) 'Rethinking human capital, creativity and urban growth', *Journal of Economic Geography* 9: 147–167.

Storper, M. and Venables, A. (2004) 'Buzz: face-to-face contact and the urban economy', *Journal of Economic Geography* 4(4): 351–370.

Strom, E. (2002) 'Converting pork into porcelain: cultural institutions and downtown development', *Urban Affairs Review* 38: 3–21.

Stuart, T. and Sorenson, O. (2003) 'The geography of opportunity: spatial heterogeneity in founding rates and the performance of biotechnology firms', *Research Policy* 32: 229–253.

Stuart, T., Hoand, H. and Hybels, R. (1999) 'Interorganizational endorsements and the performance of entrepreneurial ventures', *Administrative Science Quarterly* 44: 315–349.

Sturdivant, F. and Ginter, J. (1977) 'Corporate social responsiveness, management attitudes and economic performance', *California Management Review* 19(3): 30–39.

Suchman, M. (2000) 'Dealmakers and counselors: law firms as intermediaries in the development of Silicon Valley', in M. Kenney (ed.) *Understanding Silicon Valley: The Anatomy of an Entrepreneurial Region*, Stanford, CA: Stanford University Press.

Sunley, P. (2000) 'Urban and regional growth', in T. Barnes and E. Sheppard (eds) *A Companion to Economic Geography*, Oxford: Blackwell.

Suzuki, D. and Dressel, H. (2002) *Good News For a Change: Hope For a Troubled Planet*, Sydney: Allen & Unwin.

Swales, J. (1997) 'A cost-benefit approach to the evaluation of Regional Selective Assistance', *Fiscal Studies* 18(1): 73–85.

Székely, F. and Knirsch, M. (2005) 'Responsible leadership and corporate social responsibility: metrics for sustainable performance', *European Management Journal* 23(6): 628–647.

Szmigin, I., Maddock, S. and Carrigan, M. (2003) 'Conceptualising community consumption: farmers' markets and the older consumer', *British Food Journal* 105(8): 542–550.

Tambunan, T. T. H. (2005) 'Promoting small and medium enterprises with a clustering approach: a policy experience from Indonesia', *Journal of Small Business Management* 43(2), 138–154.

Taylor, J. and Wren, C. (1997) 'UK regional policy: an evaluation', *Regional Studies* 37(9): 835–848.

Taylor, M. and Plummer, P. (2003) 'Reclaiming the past: lessons for "cluster" policy, *Environment and Planning A* 35: 2091–2093.

Teece, D. (1986) 'Profiting from technological innovation: implications for integration, collaboration, licensing and public policy', *Research Policy* 15(6): 285–306.

Thomas, A. (2003) *Controversies in Management – Issues, Debates, Answers*, London: Routledge.

Thomas, J. and Darnton, J. (2006) 'Social diversity and economic development in the metropolis', *Journal of Planning Literature* 21(2): 153–168.

Thomas, K. (2003) 'Geographic scales and the competition for economic growth', *American Behavioural Scientist* 46: 987–1001.

Thorngate, W. (1976) 'Possible limits on a social science of social behaviour', in L. Strickland, F. Aboud and K. Gergen (eds) *Social Psychology in Transition*, New York: Plenum Press.

Thursby, J. and Thursby, M. (2003) 'University licensing and the Bayh-Dole act', *Science* 301: 1052.

—— (2004) 'Are faculty critical? Their role in university-industry licensing', *Contemporary Economic Policy* 22: 162–178.
—— (2007) 'University licensing', *Oxford Review of Economic Policy* 23(4): 620–639.
Thursby, J., Jensen, R. and Thursby, M. (2001) 'Objectives, characteristics and outcomes of university licensing: a survey of major U.S. universities', *Journal of Technology Transfer* 26(1): 59–72.
Tibbs, H. (1992) *Industrial Ecology: An Environmental Agenda for Industry*, Washington, DC: Center of Excellence for Sustainable Development, United States Department of Energy.
Townroe, P. (1975) 'Branch plants and regional development', *Town Planning Review* 46: 47–62.
Turok, I. (1993) 'Inward investment and local linkages: how deeply embedded is Silicon Glen?', *Regional Studies* 27(7): 401–417.
—— (2004) 'Cities, regions and competitiveness', *Regional Studies* 38(9): 1069–1083.
—— (2009) 'The distinctive city: pitfalls in the pursuit of differential advantage', *Environment and Planning A* 41(1): 13–30.
Turok, I. and Bailey, N. (2004) 'Twin track cities: competitiveness and cohesion in Glasgow and Edinburgh', *Progress in Planning* 62: 135–204.
Tushman, M. and Anderson, P. (1986) 'Technological discontinuities and organizational environments', *Administrative Science Quarterly* 31: 439–465.
Tversky, A. and Kahneman, D. (1973) 'Availability: a heuristic for judging frequency and probability', *Cognitive Psychology* 5: 207–232.
—— (1974) 'Judgement under uncertainty: heuristics and biases', *Science* 185(4157): 1124–1131.
Twomey, J. and Taylor, J. (1985) 'Regional policy and the interregional movement of manufacturing industry in great Britain', *Scottish Journal of Political Economy* 32(3): 257–277.
Uzzi, B. (1997) 'Social structures and competition in interfirm networks: the paradox of embeddedness', *Administrative Science Quarterly* 42: 35–67.
van der Ploeg, J. and Renting, H. (2000) 'Impact and potential: a comparative review of European development practices', *Sociologia Ruralis* 40(4): 391–408.
van Stel, A. and Storey, D. (2004) 'The link between firm births and job creation: is there an Upas Tree effect?', *Regional Studies* 38(8): 893–909.
Venkataraman, S., MacMillan, I. and McGrath, R. (1992) 'Progress in research on corporate venturing', in D. Sexton and J. Kasarda (eds) *The State of the Art of Entrepreneurship*, Boston, MA: PWS-Kent.
Vernon, R. and Hoover, E. (1959) *Anatomy of a Metropolis*, Cambridge, MA: Harvard University Press.
Vogel, D. (2005) *The Market for Virtue: the Potential and Limits of Corporate Social Responsibility*, Washington, DC: Brookings Institute Press.
Walley, N. and Whitehead, B. (1996) 'It's not easy being green', in R. Welford and R. Starkey (eds) *The Earthscan Reader in Business and the Environment*, London: Earthscan.
Walsh, J. and Bayma, T (1996) 'Computer networks and scientific work', *Social Studies of Science* 26: 661–703.
Watts, H. (1981) *The Branch Plant Economy: A Study of External Control*, Harlow: Longman.
—— (2003) 'Cross-border plant closures in the EU: UK perspectives', in N. Phelps and P. Raines (eds) *The New Competition for Inward Investment*, Cheltenham: Edward Elgar.

Watts, H., Wood, A. and Wardle, P. (2003) '"Making friends or making things?": interfirm transactions in the Sheffield metal-working cluster', *Urban Studies* 40(3): 615–630.

Weiss, G. (2008) 'The influence of the local level on innovations in environmental technology. The case of the German kraft pulp industry', *Geoforum* 39: 20–31.

Wellman, B., Salaff, J., Dimitrova, D., Garton, L., Guilia, M. and Haythornthwaite, C. (1996) 'Computer networks as social networks: collaborative work, telework and virtual community', *Annual Review of Sociology* 22: 213–238.

Wells, P. and Nieuwenhuis, P. (2004) 'Decentralisation and small-scale manufacturing: the basis of sustainable regions?', *Journal of Environmental Policy and Planning* 6(3–4): 191–205.

Westhead, P. (1997) 'R&D "inputs" and "outputs" of technology-based firms located on and off Science Parks', *R&D Management* 27: 45–62.

Westhead, P. and Storey, D. (1994) *An Assessment of Firms Located On and Off Science Parks in the UK*, London: HMSO.

Whitley, R (1999) *Divergent Capitalisms: The Social Structuring and Change of Business Systems*, Oxford: Oxford University Press.

Wilkinson, S. (1992) 'Towards a new city? A case study of image-improvement initiatives in Newcaste upon Tyne', in P. Healey, M. O'Toole and D. Usher (eds) *Rebuilding the City: Property-led Urban Regeneration*, London: E&FN Spon.

Williams, A. (2006) *Comparative study of cut roses for the British Market produced in Kenya and the Netherlands*, Précis report prepared for World Flowers, Cranfield University: Natural Resources Management Institute.

Williamson, O. E. (1991) 'Comparative economic organization: the analysis of discrete structural alternatives', *Administrative Science Quarterly* 36: 269–296.

—— (1994) 'Transaction cost economics and organization theory', in N. Smelser and R. Swedberg (eds) *The Handbook of Economic Sociology*, Princeton, NJ: Princeton University Press.

Wilson, J. and Singleton, J. (2003) 'The Manchester industrial district, 1750–1939: clustering, networking and performance', in J. Wilson and A. Popp (eds) *Industrial Clusters and Regional Business Networks in England, 1750–1970*, Aldershot: Ashgate.

Winter, M. (2003) 'Embeddedness, the new food economy and defensive localism', *Journal of Rural Studies* 19: 23–32.

Wojan, T., Lambert, D. and McGranahan, D. (2007) 'Emoting with their feet: Bohemian attraction to creative milieu', *Journal of Economic Geography* 7: 711–736.

Wood, A. (1996) 'Analysing the politics of local economic development: making sense of cross national convergence', *Urban Studies* 33: 1281–1295.

WPSMEE (2007) *High growth SMEs, innovation, intellectual assets and value creation: literature review*, Working Party on SMEs and entrepreneurship (WPSMEE) CFE/SME(2007)16, Paris: OECD.

Wren, C. (1994) 'The build up and duration of subsidy-induced employment: evidence from UK regional policy', *Journal of Regional Science* 34(3): 387–410.

—— (1996) *Industrial Subsidies: the UK Experience*, London: MacMillan.

—— (2001) 'The industrial policy of competitiveness: a review of recent developments in the UK', *Regional Studies* 35(9): 847–860.

—— (2005) 'Regional grants: are they worth it?', *Fiscal Studies* 26(2): 245–275.

Wren, C. and Storey, D. (2002) 'Evaluating the effect of soft business support upon small firm performance', *Oxford Economic Papers* 54: 334–365.

Wren, C. and Waterson, M. (1991) 'The direct employment effects of financial assistance to industry', *Oxford Economic Papers* 43: 116–138.

Wright, M., Binks, M., Vohora, A. and Lockett, A. (2003) *UK University Commercialisation Survey: Financial Year 2002*, Nottingham: NUBS/UNICO/AURIL

Wyen, E. and Vanzetti, D. (2008) *No through road: the limitations of food miles*, Asian Development Bank Institute Working Paper 116, Japan.

Wynarczyk, P. and Raine, A. (2005) 'The performance of business incubators and their potential development in the north east region of England', *Local Economy* 20(2): 205–220.

Wynne, B. (1992) 'Misunderstood misunderstanding: social identities and public uptake of science', *Public Understanding of Science* 1: 281–304.

Yetton P., Craig, J., Davis, J. and Hilmer, F. (1992) 'Are diamonds a country's best friend? A critique of Porter's theory of national competition as applied to Canada, New Zealand and Australia', *Australian Journal of Management* 17(1): 1–32.

Zeitlin, J. and Herrigel, G. (eds) (2000) *Americanization and its Limits – Reworking US Technology and Management in Post-war Europe and Japan*, Oxford: Oxford University Press.

Zucker, L., Darby, M. and Armstrong, J. (2002) 'Commercializing knowledge: university science, knowledge capture and firm performance in biotechnology', *Management Science* 48(1): 138–153.

Zucker, L., Darby, M. and Brewer, M. (1998) 'Intellectual human capital and the birth of the US biotechnology enterprises', *American Economic Review* 88: 290–306.

Index

absolute advantage 24, 25, 30–2
academic entrepreneurs 167, 178–80
academic publishing 6–7
activity-complex economies 116
administration 163
administrative simplification 73
advisory assistance 72
agency rivalry 54–8
agglomeration 109, 124–7
agglomeration economies 115–24, 142, 148; benefits of 115–16
amenities 48
anti-globalization 91
appellation d'origine controllee (AOC) 200
arborescent thinking 9
architectural knowledge 128
arm's length exchange 90
artistic activities 151–3
Asnæs Power Station 206
Association of University Technology Managers 168–9
asymmetric evaluation 52

Baden Württemberg 3
Barre, New England 131
Bayh-Dole Act 169–70
BBC, relocation of 146–7
benchmarking 24, 25, 36–9; tests for 38–9
best practice 72, 89, 216; rapid improvement 109
biotechnology industry 118, 119; links and information flows 127; start-up companies 166
Bohemian index 138
Bohemian populations 140; Montréal 150
Boston Consulting Group 1, 2
branch plant economy syndrome 63–7
branch plants: closures 66; new economy 66
built environment 43

business clusters *see* enterprise clusters
business competitiveness 24, 25; factors shaping 32–3
business culture 19
business pull 174
business structures 129

Cambridge Science Park 168
carbon emissions 85
catalytic converters 194
causality 48
causation 11–12; circular 13
choice of location 12
circular causation 13
clean air legislation 194
clean technologies 185
climate change 193
cluster brands 6
cluster idealism 122–3
cluster realism 115
cluster templates 35, 113–14
Co-operative Bank, sustainability downside 190
collective invention 100–2
collective learning 100
collective marketing 130
collective resources 130
common property goods 10
comparative advantage 19
competition 49, 109; destructive 10; focus on 163
competition exclusion principle 132
competitive advantage 5, 71
competitiveness: as productivity 21; regional 18–50
complex firms 125
components 15
conscious consumption 199
consultancy services 176

controversies: of facts 8; of frameworks 8–9; of values 8
cooperative partnerships 110, 130
core competencies 111
core markets, focus on 162
corporate reputation index scores 191
Corporation for Enterprise Development 55
creative class 135, 146; Bohemian populations 138, 140, 150; critical reflections 140–7; curse of 135; finding space for 147–55; gay populations 139, 140; human capital theories of urban economic growth 136–40; occupations 138; super creatives 138, 149
creative professionals 138
creativity 137, 143
credit costs 23
culture: regional 104–5; as shift parameter 88
cumulative causation 80
cumulative causation economies 142
customer base diversity 61

dairy farms, environmental demands 188
Dalarna Crystal Valley 45
Danish Technological Institute 37
decentralization 56; advantages of 57
Dell, Michael 137
demand 47
demand conditions 34
demand side 52
destructive competition 10
Development Areas 68
Development Report Card 55–6
devolution 57, 58
diamond model 33, 34, 35, 46–7
direct sales 74
discretionary assistance 61, 63
dissemination mode 106
distinctiveness 44
distribution 74; of production 119
distrust 89
diversification 75
documentation mode 106
dominant enterprises 121
Dow Chemicals 189
DSP Valley 45

eco-effective development 197–208; eco-localism 198–203; industrial ecology as environmental strategy 206–8; localization 203–6
eco-effectiveness 186, 212
eco-efficiency 186, 212

eco-industrial parks 204–6; Kalundborg, Denmark 205–6
eco-localism 198–9; staying home to eat 199–203
ecological modernization 193, 210
ecological switchover 210
economic development 88; application of philosophical frameworks to 9; processes of 4–5
economic development agencies 42–3
economic geography 11
education 137
Electricité de France 105
embedded economic activity 87
embeddedness theory 88
embodied transactions 103
emissions trading 195
employment 162
employment rate 21
endogenous growth theory 80–1
Enright, Michael 33
enterprise churning 71, 78
enterprise clusters 5–6, 33, 35, 47, 108–33; advantages of 108–9; bottom up evaluation 114; employment in 36; and environmental performance 196; hub and spoke 121–2, 125; impact on business performance 109; numbers of 112–14; Schmitz two-stage model 119–20, 121; spinoffs 125, 126–7; spinouts 127, 132, 166; top down evaluation 112–14; *see also individual industries*
enterprise formation *see* start-up companies; technology incubators
enterprise zones 73
enthusiastic borrowing 3
entrepreneurs 74, 137; academic 167, 178–80; firms' reliance on 163; surrogate 179; technology incubators 159
environment-friendly policy: business case for 189–97; competitive advantage 189; cost of 188; downside of 190; eco-effective development 197–208; evaluation frameworks 209; financial advantage 189; and financial performance 191; first-mover advantage 192; popular causes 194
environmental leadership 187
environmental management systems 211
environmental offsetting 195
epistemic communities 97

Index 253

ethnic enclaves 154–5
Europe, technology incubators 159
European Report on Science and Technology Indicators 185
evolutionary economics 27, 29
excessive investment 191
exchange rates 23
experience 137
export capacity 21
extended enclaves 65
extended producer responsibility 208
externalities 10, 31; pecuniary 94

face-to-face contact 97, 103
factor conditions 34
facts, controversies surrounding 8
factual evidence 9
farmers' markets 199–200
fast policy circulation 147
Fiat 105
financial incentives 68; concerns regarding 52; environmental improvement 191; innovation 52
Finland, telecommunications industry 34
firm learning 105–6
first-mover advantage 192
fiscal federalism 57
Flanders Multimedia Valley 45
flexible accumulation 216
flexible specialization 110–12
Florida, Richard 6, 134–5, 215; human capital theory 136–40; melting pot index 153; performance indicators 144
Florida talent (creative class) index 144
food: local production 198–203; transport costs 202; transport modes 202–3
food miles 199, 202
footwear industry 118; Italy 122–3; Sinos Valley 120
Fordism 216
foreign investors: grants for 63; regional assistance 75–6
fragmented industries, entry points 165
framework controversies 8–9
France: *appellation d'origine controllee* (AOC) 200; *terroir* 200
Fujisawa, Takeo 2
fuzzy concepts 7, 215

Gates, Bill 137
Gause's law 132
gay index 139, 149
gay populations 140

gay/lesbian-based enterprise 149
'gazelles' 161, 163, 164
GDP 26
Georgia Institute of Technology, Advanced Technology Development Centre 179–80
Germany 114; kraft pulp industry 197
good environmental practice 185
governance 163
granite industry 131
Grant Thornton index 55
greenfield operations 66
GREMI research group 31–2
gross domestic product *see* GDP
gurus 3, 4, 44; academic 6; application of ideas 5
Gyproc 206

hard network programmes 37
Harvard cluster-mapping project 35–6
heterogeneity 121
hierarchical norms 90
high growth enterprises 160–4; attributes of 162–3; and new technology 166–7; theory of learning 161
high growth, selection for 72
high technology industries 41
home-base activities 33
Homebrew Computer Club 101–2
homosexual enterprises *see* gay/lesbian enterprises
Honda 1–3; supercar 2; supercub motorcycle 1
Honda, Soichiro 2
hub and spoke clusters 121–2, 125
human capital theory 136–40, 143
human resource management 163
Hyundai 56

image building 43–4
immigrant/minority enterprise 153–5, 157
immigration 153–5
imperfect information 10
increasing returns 80
industrial ecology: as environmental strategy 206–8; extended producer responsibility 208; and localization 203–6
industrial location 109–12
industrial movement, cost barriers 59
industry conditions 34
information sharing 100–1
information spillover 116

infrastructure 43; organizational 90–1
inner city incubators 117
innovation 83, 143, 163; inadequate incentives 52; incremental 91; process 162; product 162; technology incubators 160–4
innovative production 88
integration 7
intellectual property 143, 169
intelligence 137
intermediaries 74
internal labour market 125
internal scale economies 115–16
intra-industry differences 84
investment: excessive 191; incentives for 217
Investment Funds Group 105
investor bargaining 54–8
Ireland 65; economic boom 135
Italy 28–9; footwear industry 122–3; industrial districts 114, 121, 133; *Istituto Nazionale di Statistica* 114

Jacobs, Jane 136
Japan 13–15
job competition 68
job creation 61–2, 70
job hoppers 92

know-how 89
know-who 89
knowledge: codification of 97; forms of 82; new 80; scientific 177; sharing 102; tacit 81, 82, 85, 90, 97; technical 177; trading 101; transmission of 94–6, 98–9; types of 96–7
knowledge economies 79
knowledge flows 20
knowledge pool 95
knowledge source 106
knowledge spillover 80, 94, 99, 102, 110, 148; evidence for 96
knowledge theories 3–5; scientists vs economic development professionals 5
knowledge transfer 95
Kyoto Protocol 85

labour costs: and competitiveness 22; and locality 3
labour market 23; flexibility 62; pooling 99
labour mobility 142, 156; and knowledge dispersion 98
Lambert Review 169

Las Vegas critique 141
learning: collective 100; and economic success 87; incremental low tech 91; region as focus of 87
learning economies 47, 79, 84, 90
learning focus 106
learning processes 27–8, 31
learning regions 79–107; evaluation of 94–9; infrastructure 87, 90–1; macro context 84–5; micro context 85–7; types of 87–93
learning through interacting 83
learning-by-doing 89
learning-by-searching 89
LG 56
liability of newness 161
licensing agreements 169, 170
light bulbs, energy-efficient 189, 192
LINUX 101
local economic controversy 1–17; participants 3–7; resolution of 7–15
local economic development 51, 185–213; 3Ts of 147, 156
local economic policy 52, 69–75
local economies as leaky buckets 68
Local Employment Act (1960) 67
local governance 31
local service provision 130
localization economies 116, 118
location 143; choice of 12; and labour costs 3
location assets 20
lock-in 92
low selective incubators 175

manufacturing, distribution of structural materials 110
market deregulation 111
market diversification 125
market dominance 22
market failures 52; and cluster intervention 131; welfare economics 10
market research 74
marketing, collective 130
marketing strategy 163
Marshall, Alfred 79; cluster realism 115
mass production 112, 216
matched pairs analysis 172–4
Materials Valley 45
Mechanic Valley 45
Medicon Valley 45
melting pot index 153
mentoring 72

migration: graduates 142, 145; improved living environment 145; organizational 146; significance of 145; workers 59
Milken score 149
Mintzberg, Henry 1
Monitor Consultancy 5
Montréal, Canada 149–52
Mormon enterprises 104–5
Motor Sport Valley 3, 45, 97, 128–9
Motorola 126
multi-site organizations 69

N curve dilemma 186
National Business Incubation Association 158
national templates 113
natural ecosystems 203–4
natural monopoly 10
natural trajectories 27
network building tools 181–2
network incubators 181–3
new economic geography 6, 108
new economy 91
new enterprises: formation 133; survival 164–6; *see also* start-up companies; technology incubators
New Industry: red sheds 201–2; timber industry 123–4
new knowledge 80
new regionalism 19, 26, 29, 70
New Zealand: hard networks programme 37; timber industry 123–4
niche opportunities 109
niche species 203
Nokia 34
non-broadcast visual communications 124
non-traded local inputs 116
Nordic region 86; people climate score 144–5
North of England, small to medium size enterprises 162
north–south divide 22
Northern Ireland 75
Novo Nordisk 206

obligational contracting 13–14
observational data 11–12
off-the-peg sourcing 111
off-the-shelf theories, customization of 5
on-the-job knowledge 137
one-size-fits-all approach 3
ontological universalism 12
open access 120

open science 170, 171
opportunity: social structure of 119; windows of 142
Öresund medical cluster 128
organizational infrastructure 90–1
organizational memory 27
organizational migration 146
outsourcing 110
owner managers 74

Paris Optics Valley 45
Parmesan cheese cluster 200
partnerships 72
patenting activities 142–3; universities 170
pecuniary externalities 94
people climate score 144–6
performance 24, 25, 26–30; benchmarking 24, 25, 36–9; effect of local environment 46
performance indicators 144
personal mobility 134
personal relationships 103
photonics industry 124–5
plant closures 60; reasons for 66–7
Plastics Valley 45
policy analysis: deep 11; shallow 11
policy-maker friendliness 148
political choices 194
pollution control 187, 194, 195–6, 207
popular causes 194
Porter, Michael 32, 44, 215; business clusters 5–6; diamond model 33, 34, 35, 46–7
post-new regionalism 20
principal agents 58
privileged locations 128
process innovation 162
product cycles 15
product development 3
product innovation 162
product labelling 200–1
product-process focus 106
production: distribution of 119; innovative 88; knowledge intensity 61
productivity 21, 162
public sector employment 76
pure incubators 176

quasi experiments 173, 174
quest for consensus 90

recycling 204, 207
regeneration 52

regional competitiveness 18–50; absolute advantage 24, 25, 30–2; benchmarking 24, 25, 36–9; components of 26–7; economic framework 22; enterprise-related 32–6; exploration of 24–5; nature of 20–6; performance 24, 25, 26–30; regional strategies 24, 25, 39–45
regional culture 104–5
regional development agencies 58
regional development strategy 88
regional economic development 51
regional employment premium 68
regional growth, unbalanced 53
regional incentives 57–8
regional policy 51–78; discriminatory 76; revival of 75–6
regional science 11–12
regional selective assistance 58–63
regional service class 20, 44
regional strategies 24, 25, 39–45; intangible and amenable to change 40; intangible and slow to change 40; tangible and amenable to change 40; tangible and slow to change 40; transfer between countries 45
regional studies 11–12
regulation theory 215
related industries 34
reputation 43
research: commercialization of 160; market 74; presentation of 6–7
resources, availability of 110
responsibility, devolution of 57
restraint of trade 126
revealed preferences 12
rhizomial thinking 9
risk minimisation 207
Route 128 3, 87
routines 27

sales strategy 163
sales turnover 162
Samsung 56
Schmitz two-stage model 119–20, 121
scientific knowledge 177
Scotland 64–5; plant closure 66–7; return of workers to 153; small to medium size enterprises 162
self-containment 212
semiconductor manufacture 129–30
services, local provision 130
shared information 100–1
shared location 182

shared trust 86
shift parameters 88
Shockley Laboratories 126
Silicon Glen 64
Silicon Valley 3, 33, 45, 48, 81, 87, 92–3, 126, 142; comparison with second-wave clusters 128; effect of localization economies 125–6; high turnover rates 99; spinout enterprises 127, 132
Sinos Valley 120
skill development focus 106
skilled labour pools 116
small enterprises: characteristics of 74; and churning 78; promotion of 70
small to medium size enterprises 73–4; technology incubators 161–2
social inclusion 52
social networks 148; web-based 153
social science theory 3–4
socioeconomic relations 31
Sophia-Antipolis 128
spaces of flows 23
spatial agglomeration 110–11
spatial division of labour 69
specialist suppliers 116
specialization 19–20
spill-acrosses 149–50
spinoff enterprises 125, 126–7
spinout enterprises 127, 132, 166; university-related 168
standardization 111
start-up companies: biotechnology industry 166; chances of survival 164; interaction with established firms 167; need for capital investment 165; role of academic entrepreneurs 178–80; rules for success 165–6; stage models 174–5; *see also* technology incubators
Statoil Refinery 206
Strängäs Biotech Valley 45
structured relationships 16
studied trust 30
subnational institutional capacity 57
successionist logic 11–12
sulphur dioxide emissions, control of 195–6
Sunrise Valley 45
super creatives 138, 149
super performers 162
super-industrialization 198
supply side 52
supportive incubators 175–6
surrogate entrepreneurs 179

survival 164–6
survival of the fittest 71
sustainable buildings 211
Sweden, pulp and paper industry 196–7
Sweet Valley 45
symbiosis 204

tacit knowledge 81, 82, 85, 90, 97; localized 82
talent 147, 156
tax rates 23
tech pole index 144
technical knowledge 177
technology 147, 156
technology forecasting 102
technology incubators 158–84; efficient outcomes 159; entrepreneurs 159; Europe 159; evaluation of 172–6; implications for 166–8; inefficient outcomes 159; innovation and high growth enterprises 160–4; inside 176–83; low selective 175; as network builders 181–3; new enterprise survival 164–6; pure 176; sector characteristics 164–6; selection of enterprises for 159–60; small to medium size enterprises 161–2; sponsors of 158, 160; supportive 175–6; university-linked 171; USA 158–9
technology transfer 168–9; to established enterprises 167
technology-based enterprises 158
telecommunications 34
territorial learning 82
terroir 200
Tesco 200
Texas Instruments 126
theory informed practice 127–32
theory of learning 161
theory, over-reliance on 215
thinking: arborescent 9; rhizomial 9
Third Italy 3, 28
timber industry 123–4
tolerance 140, 144–5, 147, 156
trade 21
trade barriers 111
trade secrets 126

transferable quotas 195
truncated miniature replica plant 65
trust 86, 89; shared 86

ubiquitification 91
underperformers 162
unemployment 19, 68; effects of reduction 53; high 54; spatial disparities 53
Unilever 189
United Kingdom 27
universities: commercialization of research 160; connections with technology-based enterprise 168; intellectual property rights 169; inventions 172; licensing agreements 169, 170; patenting activities 170; spinout enterprises 168; and technology incubators 171; technology transfer 168–9
untraded interdependencies 20, 79
urban economic growth, human capital theory 136–40
urban renewal 146
urbanization economies 116; 3Ts of 147, 156; artistic activities 151–3; Bohemian index 138; employment growth in 117; gay index 139; measurement of success 139–40; specialized vs diversified cities 118; success of 134–57
USA, technology incubators 158–9

value-adding functions 19
value-chain focus 106
values, differences in 8

Waitrose 200
Wal-Mart 189
waste control 187; recycling 204, 207
welfare economics 9–10; market failures 10
West Midlands cluster 112
white/non-white economic divide 155
win-win strategies 185, 186, 194, 197, 212; incremental 187–9
win-win-win outcomes 185
windows of opportunity 142
winner's competitive cycle 2
workers as knowledge bearers 98–9

eBooks – at www.eBookstore.tandf.co.uk

A library at your fingertips!

eBooks are electronic versions of printed books. You can store them on your PC/laptop or browse them online.

They have advantages for anyone needing rapid access to a wide variety of published, copyright information.

eBooks can help your research by enabling you to bookmark chapters, annotate text and use instant searches to find specific words or phrases. Several eBook files would fit on even a small laptop or PDA.

NEW: Save money by eSubscribing: cheap, online access to any eBook for as long as you need it.

Annual subscription packages

We now offer special low-cost bulk subscriptions to packages of eBooks in certain subject areas. These are available to libraries or to individuals.

For more information please contact webmaster.ebooks@tandf.co.uk

We're continually developing the eBook concept, so keep up to date by visiting the website.

www.eBookstore.tandf.co.uk